Model Context Protocol for LLMs

Build secure, scalable, and context-aware AI agents using a standardized protocol

Naveen Krishnan

<packt>

Model Context Protocol for LLMs

This book was written by Naveen Krishnan. Generative AI tools were used only to assist with ideation, phrasing, and diagram drafts, and all technical content and code were created, verified, and tested by the author and Packt's editorial team. Packt does not accept AI-generated content that replaces expert authorship.

Portfolio Director: Gebin George
Relationship Lead: Vignesh Raju
Project Manager: Prajakta Naik
Content Engineer: Mark D'Souza
Technical Editor: Aditya Bharadwaj
Copy Editor: Safis Editing
Indexer: Pratik Shirodkar
Proofreader: Mark D'Souza
Production Designer: Deepak Chavan
Growth Lead: Nimisha Dua

First published: February 2026

Production reference: 1250226

Published by Packt Publishing Ltd.
Grosvenor House
11 St Paul's Square
Birmingham
B3 1RB, UK.

ISBN 978-1-80666-227-2
www.packtpub.com

I would like to dedicate this book to my wife, Abi, and my lovely daughter, Laya, whose patience and support made this book possible.

– Naveen Krishnan

Contributors

About the author

Naveen Krishnan is a data and AI solutions engineer with over 17 years of experience in delivering enterprise-grade systems across retail, banking, healthcare, and manufacturing. As an AI lead at Microsoft, Fellow of BCS, and senior IEEE member, he has designed and deployed large-scale RAG and multi-agent systems using LangChain, AutoGen, and MCP. A judge at global NASA Space Apps and Microsoft hackathons and author of 35+ technical publications, he specializes in secure, scalable AI architectures and responsible AI practices for real-world deployment.

About the reviewers

Nishant Arora is a solutions architect at **Amazon Web Services** (**AWS**) with deep expertise in cloud computing, generative AI, and agentic AI. He works closely with customers in the automotive and manufacturing industries to design and scale intelligent, cloud-native systems that deliver measurable business outcomes. Nishant is a co-author of *Gen AI Atlas*, published by AWS, and actively contributes to the AI community through technical reviews, judging global hackathons, and thought leadership. His interests include large language models, multi-agent systems, responsible AI, and applying AI at scale in real-world industrial environments.

Sankara Reddy Thamma is a seasoned solutions architect, technical delivery specialist, and AI innovator with over 15 years of experience driving large-scale enterprise modernization, cloud migration, and AI-powered automation initiatives across industries, including banking, healthcare, utilities, and manufacturing. His technical expertise spans legacy mainframes, IBM DataStage, big data ecosystems, Snowflake, Databricks, Agentic AI, and multi-cloud platforms (AWS, Azure, and GCP). Coupled with deep proficiency in cloud modernization and legacy modernization, he is a trusted leader in transforming complex enterprise landscapes.

At the core of his contributions is a transformative vision for agentic AI.

Beyond enterprise outcomes, Thamma plays an active role in advancing the AI and technology community. He is a senior member of IEEE, contributing as a peer reviewer across domains including AI, machine learning, generative AI, and data engineering. His contributions also extend to technical publishing, where he serves as a technical book reviewer for Packt and Manning and supports leading AI journals and editorial boards. His expertise is globally recognized, with patents granted in the UK and India for intelligent code transformation using agent-based accelerators.

As a published researcher, he has authored works in IEEE, Springer, and Scopus-indexed journals, covering themes such as secure prompt engineering, neurovisualization, and applied AI in healthcare. His ability to bridge cutting-edge research with applied enterprise solutions positions him uniquely at the intersection of theory and practice.

Join our Discord and Reddit space

You're not the only one navigating fragmented tools, constant updates, and unclear best practices. Join a growing community of professionals exchanging insights that don't make it into documentation.

Stay informed with updates, discussions, and behind-the-scenes insights from our authors. Join our Discord space at `https://packt.link/z8ivB` or scan the QR code below:	Connect with peers, share ideas, and discuss real-world GenAI challenges. Follow us on Reddit at `https://packt.link/0rExL` or scan the QR code below:

Table of Contents

Preface

Large language models (**LLMs**) have reshaped what is possible in software engineering, from automated code generation and intelligent assistants to autonomous decision-making agents. Yet as organizations move beyond prototypes and into production, a critical gap has emerged: LLMs operate in isolation, disconnected from the tools, data sources, and contextual signals that they need to deliver reliable, grounded responses. Every team ends up building custom integrations from scratch, resulting in brittle architectures that are difficult to secure, scale, or maintain.

The **Model Context Protocol** (**MCP**) was created to solve this problem. Introduced as an open standard for connecting AI models to external context, MCP provides a unified, modular framework for resource discovery, tool invocation, prompt management, and multi-agent coordination. Rather than reinventing integrations for every application, MCP gives engineers a standardized way to build interoperable, context-aware AI systems that can be composed, extended, and governed with confidence.

This book is a comprehensive, hands-on guide to designing, building, and deploying MCP-based systems. It begins with the foundational concepts and architecture, walks you through server-side and client-side implementation in Python, and then progressively tackles security, performance optimization, multi-agent orchestration, and framework integration with LangChain and AutoGen. The later chapters apply MCP to real-world domains, including retrieval-augmented generation, enterprise knowledge management, personalization, and multimodal applications, before addressing evaluation methodologies, benchmarking, and performance tuning. The book closes with a forward-looking discussion of emerging trends and the future of the protocol.

Whether you are building your first MCP server or designing enterprise-scale multi-agent architectures, this book provides the architectural patterns, production-ready code examples, and design principles you need to move from concept to deployment.

Who this book is for

This book is for AI/ML engineers, software engineers, and solution architects who are building LLM-powered applications and want a standardized, modular approach to managing context across agents and tools. Cloud architects and platform engineers designing AI infrastructure will also find the architectural patterns and deployment strategies directly applicable. Intermediate Python proficiency, working knowledge of LLM concepts and REST APIs, and familiarity with system design patterns are expected.

What this book covers

Chapter 1, Introduction to the Model Context Protocol, introduces the evolution of AI systems, explains the disconnected model problem that plagues modern LLM deployments, and presents MCP as the solution. You will set up your development environment and understand the historical context behind the protocol.

Chapter 2, Theoretical Foundations of Multi-Agent Systems, explores the concept of agency in AI, traces the evolution from single-agent to multi-agent architectures, and examines the coordination challenges that MCP is designed to address.

Chapter 3, The MCP for Non-Technical Readers, provides an accessible, jargon-free overview of what MCP is and why it matters. It uses everyday scenarios to explain the protocol and prepare you for the technical depth that follows.

Chapter 4, MCP Components and Interfaces, examines the building blocks of MCP, including resource providers, tool providers, prompt providers, and the standardized interfaces that connect them.

Chapter 5, MCP Architecture Overview, covers the client-server architecture, core component relationships, standardized primitives, communication mechanisms, message formats, and the security and authentication framework.

Chapter 6, Server-Side Implementation, walks you through building MCP servers in Python, including implementing resource providers, tool providers, and prompt providers, with attention to authentication, authorization, and scalability.

Chapter 7, Client-Side Integration, focuses on the client layer, covering context retrieval, tool execution orchestration, security handling, session management, and integration with AI models and frameworks.

Chapter 8, MCP Security Model, provides a thorough treatment of authentication mechanisms, authorization and access control, transport layer security, data privacy, auditing, and advanced security topics for MCP deployments.

Chapter 9, MCP Performance Optimization, addresses performance profiling, server-side and client-side optimization strategies, protocol-level optimizations, and monitoring for continuous improvement. It includes a case study on scaling an MCP deployment.

Chapter 10, MCP and Multi-Agent Systems, demonstrates how MCP facilitates multi-agent coordination, collaborative task execution, and integration with agent frameworks. It covers security and trust patterns for multi-agent environments.

Chapter 11, MCP for Retrieval-Augmented Generation, shows how MCP standardizes and simplifies RAG architectures. You will build a basic RAG system with MCP, implement advanced RAG techniques, and learn about evaluation and best practices.

Chapter 12, Integrating MCP with LangChain, covers how to use MCP as a document store, tool provider, and memory backend for LangChain applications. You will build a complete LangChain application powered by MCP.

Chapter 13, Integrating MCP with AutoGen, explains how to connect MCP with Microsoft AutoGen to build sophisticated multi-agent collaboration workflows with shared context and coordinated task execution.

Chapter 14, MCP for Enterprise Knowledge Management, applies MCP to enterprise knowledge management challenges, including knowledge silos, search and discovery, and compliance. It presents architectural patterns such as federated search and knowledge graphs.

Chapter 15, MCP for Personalization and Recommendation Systems, demonstrates how MCP solves data integration, real-time adaptation, and cross-platform consistency challenges in personalization engines. It covers privacy and ethical considerations.

Chapter 16, MCP for Multimodal Applications, shows how MCP enables coordinated processing across text, image, audio, and video modalities using an orchestrated pipeline, collaborative processing, and adaptive routing patterns.

Chapter 17, MCP Evaluation Methodologies, introduces a structured evaluation framework covering functional evaluation, performance evaluation, and continuous monitoring for MCP-based systems.

Chapter 18, Performance Benchmarks and Testing, teaches you how to design effective benchmarks, define core performance metrics, implement a comprehensive benchmarking suite, and perform comparative analysis across MCP configurations.

Chapter 19, Optimization Strategies and Performance Tuning, provides server-side, client-side, and protocol-level optimization strategies, along with a performance optimization framework and continuous monitoring approach.

Chapter 20, *Future Directions and Emerging Trends*, explores the evolution of MCP standards, integration with emerging AI technologies, advanced multi-agent coordination, enterprise adoption challenges, and the societal and ethical implications of the protocol.

To get the most out of this book

To follow the examples in this book, you will need intermediate proficiency in Python and a working understanding of LLM concepts such as prompts, tokens, and embeddings. Familiarity with REST APIs and basic system design patterns will help you absorb the architectural discussions more quickly.

For chapters that include code examples, you will need the following:

- Python 3.10 or later installed on your machine
- A code editor such as Visual Studio Code
- Access to an LLM API (OpenAI, Azure OpenAI, or equivalent)
- Git for cloning the example code repository
- Basic familiarity with virtual environments and pip
- Optional: Docker for containerized deployment examples

All code examples in this book are written in Python and have been tested on Windows, macOS, and Linux.

Download the example code files

This book includes a complete downloadable code bundle containing all the example projects and files used throughout the chapters. We recommend downloading the bundle so you can follow along smoothly and experiment with the examples.

Use the bundle as a practical starting point. Modify it, extend it, and apply what you learn by creating your own variations as you progress through the chapters.

Get the code bundle

If you bought the book directly from Packt:

1. Go to `packtpub.com`
2. Click your **profile picture** and select **Your Orders**
3. Find this book and click **Download Code**

If you bought this book from Amazon or any other channel partner:

1. Go to `packtpub.com/unlock` or scan the following QR code:
2. Search for this book
3. Sign up or log in to your free Packt account
4. Upload your proof of purchase and download the code bundle locally

Usage note: You're free to use and modify this code for personal learning and non-commercial projects.

Conventions used

There are a number of text conventions used throughout this book.

`CodeInText`: Indicates code words in text, database table names, folder names, filenames, file extensions, pathnames, dummy URLs, user input, and Twitter handles. For example: "Create an `MCPServer` instance and register your resource providers."

A block of code is set as follows:

```
server = MCPServer(config=server_config)
server.register_resource_provider(DocumentProvider())
server.start()
```

Any command-line input or output is written as follows:

```
pip install mcp-sdk langchain autogen
```

Bold: Indicates a new term, an important word, or words that you see on the screen. For instance, words in menus or dialog boxes appear in the text like this. For example: "It's worth noting that the official MCP specification defines three core **server features** (resources, prompts, and tools) and three **client features** (sampling, roots, and elicitation)."

Note

Warnings or important notes appear like this.

Tip

Tips and tricks appear like this.

Get in touch

Feedback from our readers is always welcome.

General feedback: If you have questions about any aspect of this book or have any general feedback, please email us at `customercare@packt.com` and mention the book's title in the subject of your message.

Errata: Although we have taken every care to ensure the accuracy of our content, mistakes do happen. If you have found a mistake in this book, we would be grateful if you reported this to us. Please visit `http://www.packt.com/submit-errata`, click **Submit Errata**, and fill in the form.

Piracy: If you come across any illegal copies of our works in any form on the internet, we would be grateful if you would provide us with the location address or website name. Please contact us at `copyright@packt.com` with a link to the material.

If you are interested in becoming an author: If there is a topic that you have expertise in and you are interested in either writing or contributing to a book, please visit `http://authors.packt.com/`.

Free benefits with your book

This book includes free benefits designed to support your learning and help you apply what you learn effectively. Activate them now for instant access (see the *How to unlock* section for instructions).

Here's a quick overview of what you can instantly unlock with your purchase:

Complete Code Bundle

Download the full source code for this book's examples and projects.

DRM-Free PDF Version

Download DRM-free PDF and ePub copies of this book.

7-Day Packt Library Access

Get 7-day unlimited access to 8,000+ books and videos. No credit card required.

Available for first-time Packt+ trial users only.

Next-Gen Reader Access

Read this book on Packt Reader with progress sync, dark mode and note-taking.

How to unlock

Scan the QR code (or go to `packtpub.com/unlock`). Search for this book by name, confirm the edition, and then follow the steps on the page.

UNLOCK NOW

Note: Have your invoice handy. Purchases made directly from the Packt website don't require an invoice.

Part 1

Foundations and Concepts

In this first part of the book, you will develop a solid understanding of the Model Context Protocol and the problems it was designed to solve. We begin by exploring the evolution of AI systems and the disconnected model problem that has created integration headaches across the industry. You will then examine the theoretical foundations of multi-agent systems, understanding how agency, coordination, and communication work at a conceptual level. The final chapter in this part offers an accessible, jargon-free overview of MCP for readers who want to build intuition before diving into implementation. By the end of this part, you will have the conceptual grounding needed to understand why MCP exists and how it fits into the broader AI landscape.

This part of the book includes the following chapters:

- *Chapter 1, Introduction to the Model Context Protocol*
- *Chapter 2, Theoretical Foundations of Multi-Agent Systems*
- *Chapter 3, The MCP for Non-Technical Readers*

1

Introduction to the Model Context Protocol

> *The best way to predict the future is to invent it.*
>
> *- Alan Kay*

You know that feeling when you're trying to explain something complex to a friend, and you realize halfway through that you're missing half the context? That's exactly where we've been with AI systems for the past few years. We've built these incredibly sophisticated language models that can write poetry, debug code, and even help plan your vacation, but they're like brilliant scholars locked in separate rooms, unable to share their knowledge or work together effectively.

Naturally, that frustration pushed people (me included) to think that if a single model was this limited in isolation, maybe the next step was to get them working together. That's how the whole idea of **multi-agent systems** started creeping in.

My first attempt at building a multi-agent system, in 2023, demonstrated how challenging coordination can be. Picture this: I had one agent that was great at analyzing financial data, another that excelled at generating reports, and a third that could send emails. Sounds perfect, right? Wrong. Getting them to talk to each other was like trying to organize a conference call between people who speak different languages, use different phones, and live in different time zones. The amount of custom glue code I had to write just to pass a simple piece of data between agents was... well, let's just say it wasn't pretty.

That's where the **Model Context Protocol** (**MCP**) comes in. Think of MCP as the universal translator for AI systems, but it's so much more than that.

Before we jump in, here's what this chapter will do for you. You'll learn what MCP is, how it came out of the chaos of disconnected AI systems, and why it matters. The goal is simple: to show you the "why" behind MCP so the rest of the book clicks into place.

And the value? If you've ever wrestled with AI tools that don't talk to each other, you'll see how MCP can save time, reduce headaches, and open new possibilities. Think of this chapter as the foundation of the context you'll need before we start building the bigger ideas.

In this chapter, we'll be covering the following topics:

- The evolution of AI systems
- The disconnected model problem
- What is the Model Context Protocol (MCP)?
- Historical development and timeline
- Code example: Setting up a development environment

Note

Your purchase includes a free PDF copy + code bundle

Your purchase includes a DRM-free PDF copy of this book, the code bundle, and additional exclusive extras. See the *Free benefits with your book* section in the *Preface* to unlock them instantly and maximize your learning.

Technical requirements

Before we start, make sure you have the following:

- A dual-core CPU of 2 GHz or higher
- At least 2 GB RAM (8 GB recommended for AI/ML work), and 10 GB of free disk space
- Python 3.11 or later installed
- A text editor or IDE of your choice

You can download the code for this book by following the instructions in the ***Download the example code files*** section in the *Preface* of this book. This chapter's code files are included in the downloadable code bundle.

The evolution of AI systems

Let's take a step back and look at how we got here. The journey of AI systems has been fascinating, and honestly, a bit chaotic.

In the early days of AI, and I'm talking about the 1950s and 60s here, researchers were building these monolithic systems that tried to do everything; notable early successes included **ELIZA** (1966), a chatbot that mimicked conversation, the **DENDRAL** expert system (late 1960s) that inferred chemical structures, and **MYCIN** (1970s) for medical diagnosis. They were like Swiss Army knives: theoretically capable of many tasks, but not particularly good at any of them. These systems were self-contained, isolated, and about as social as a hermit crab. Think of ELIZA, the early chatbot from the 1960s. It could mimic a psychotherapist in conversation, but only within its narrow script. Step outside that script, and the illusion collapsed instantly.

Fast-forward to the 1980s and 90s, and we started seeing the emergence of expert systems. These were more specialized. Think of them as the first real attempt at creating AI "specialists." You'd have one system that was good at medical diagnosis, another for financial planning, and so on. But here's the thing: they still couldn't talk to each other. It was like having a hospital full of brilliant doctors who refused to consult with their colleagues.

Then came the internet age, and everything changed. Suddenly, we got distributed systems, web services, APIs, and the whole digital ecosystem started becoming interconnected. But AI systems? They were still living in their own little bubbles.

The real breakthrough came with **large language models (LLMs)**. GPT-3, GPT-4, then GPT-5, Claude, and others showed us what's possible when you have truly powerful AI systems. But even these marvels have a fundamental limitation: they were designed to work in isolation. Sure, you could build applications on top of them, but getting them to work together? That requires custom solutions, proprietary APIs, and a lot of prayer.

Here's where it gets interesting. As these models became more powerful, developers started realizing that the future wasn't about building one super-intelligent AI tool that could do everything. Instead, it was about building ecosystems of specialized AI agents that could collaborate, share context, and work together toward common goals.

But there was a big problem: how do you get AI systems from different vendors, built with different technologies, running on different platforms, to communicate effectively? How do you ensure that when Agent A discovers something important, Agent B can understand and act on that information?

This is what I like to call the *Tower of Babel* problem in AI. We had all these powerful systems, but they couldn't understand each other.

The disconnected model problem

Let me paint you a picture of what the AI landscape looked like before MCP, the standard for enabling agents to share context and coordinate effectively, which is the core topic of this book and will be defined more clearly later in the chapter. Imagine you're running a modern business, and you've invested in several AI tools:

- A customer service chatbot that handles support tickets
- An AI assistant that helps with document analysis
- A recommendation engine for your e-commerce platform
- A financial forecasting model
- A content generation tool for marketing

Each of these tools is excellent at what it does. But here's the frustrating part: they exist in complete isolation from each other. Your customer service bot might learn that a particular product is causing issues, but your recommendation engine has no idea and keeps suggesting it to customers. Your financial model might predict a cash flow problem, but your content generation tool is still creating expensive marketing campaigns.

It's like having a team of experts who never attend the same meetings. This situation is often referred to as the "disconnected model problem," a term used to describe how powerful AI tools end up working in silos, unable to share context or coordinate effectively.

I experienced this firsthand when I was consulting for a mid-sized e-commerce company. They had implemented five different AI solutions across their organization. Each one was working beautifully in its own domain, but the lack of coordination was costing the company money and frustrating its customers.

The customer service team would get the same questions over again because the knowledge base AI couldn't share insights with the chatbot. The marketing AI would generate campaigns for products that the inventory AI knew were about to be discontinued. The pricing AI would make adjustments that the recommendation AI wouldn't know about for hours or even days.

Such disconnection can result in the following:

- **Context loss**: When information moves between systems, crucial context gets lost in translation. It's like playing telephone (Chinese whispers), but with million-dollar business decisions.
- **Redundant processing**: Multiple AI systems end up doing similar work because they can't share results. I've seen companies where three different AI tools were all analyzing the same customer data, each coming to slightly different conclusions.

- **Inconsistent experience**: Customers interact with different AI systems that have different knowledge bases and capabilities. One minute, they're talking to a chatbot that knows their entire purchase history, the next, they're dealing with a recommendation engine that acts like they're a brand-new customer.
- **Integration nightmares**: Developers spend more time building custom integrations than improving the AI capabilities. I once worked on a project where 70% of the code base was just glue code to make different AI services talk to each other.
- **Security vulnerabilities**: When every integration is custom, security becomes a nightmare. Each connection point is a potential vulnerability, and maintaining consistent security policies across all these custom integrations is nearly impossible.

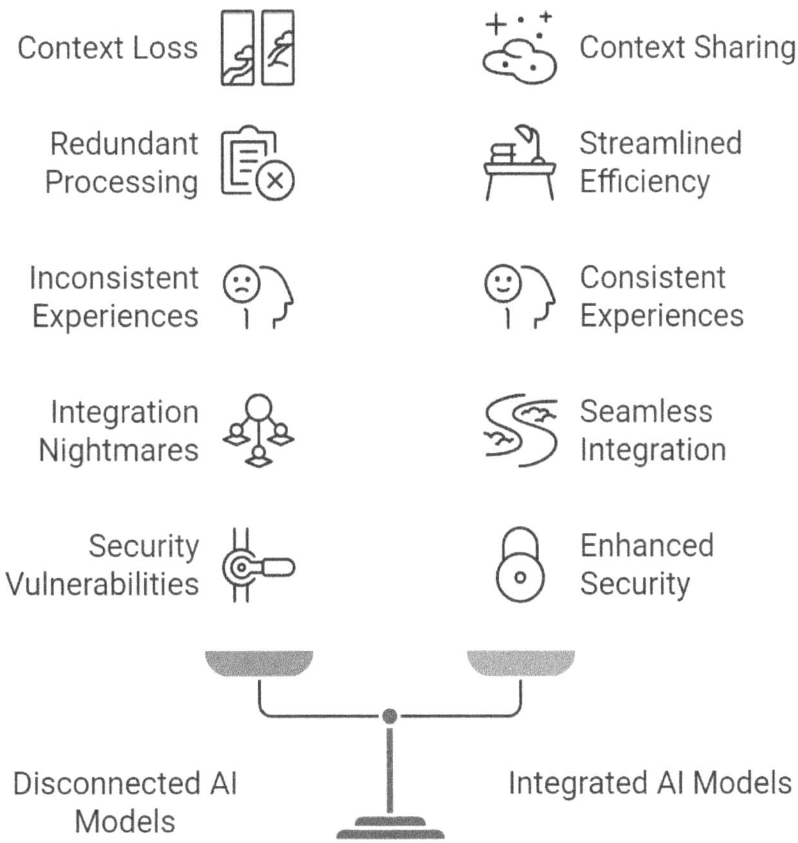

Figure 1.1 – Transitioning from disconnected to integrated models: this diagram illustrates how MCP connects isolated AI systems into a cohesive context-sharing network, eliminating redundant integrations and preserving context

The real kicker? As AI systems become more sophisticated, these problems get worse, not better. More capable AI means more complex interactions, which means more opportunities for things to go wrong.

This brings us to the heart of the matter: MCP, the missing piece we've been waiting for.

What is the Model Context Protocol (MCP)?

So, what exactly is MCP? At its core, MCP is an open standard that defines how AI applications can provide context to LLMs. But that's the technical definition, and honestly, it doesn't capture the full picture.

Think of MCP as the USB-C of the AI world. Just as USB-C standardized how we connect devices, allowing your laptop, phone, tablet, and external monitor to all use the same cable, MCP standardizes how AI systems connect and share information.

But here's where the analogy breaks down: MCP isn't just about physical connections. It's about semantic connections. It's about ensuring that when one AI system says "customer satisfaction is down 15%," every other AI system in your ecosystem understands exactly what that means and can act on it appropriately.

Let me break down what MCP does:

- **Standardized communication**: MCP defines a common language for AI systems. Instead of each vendor creating its own proprietary way of sharing data, everyone speaks the same language.
- **Context preservation**: When information moves between systems, the context travels with it. It's like having a good translator who doesn't just translate words but also explains cultural nuances and background information.
- **Secure information sharing**: MCP includes built-in security mechanisms that ensure sensitive information is protected as it moves between systems.
- **Dynamic discovery**: AI systems can discover what capabilities other systems offer and adapt their behavior accordingly. It's like having a universal directory of AI services.
- **Bidirectional communication**: Unlike traditional APIs, where one system requests information from another, MCP enables true collaboration where systems can proactively share relevant information.

Here's a simple example to illustrate the difference between the old, brittle way of integrating AI systems and the streamlined approach enabled by MCP. In the old world, if you wanted your customer service AI to access your inventory system, you'd need to do the following:

1. Build a custom API integration.

2. Handle authentication and security.
3. Map data formats between systems.
4. Write error handling code.
5. Maintain the integration as both systems evolve.

With MCP, your customer service AI can simply say, "I need current inventory levels for product X," and the inventory system responds with not just the numbers, but also context about why those levels might be significant, recent trends, and any relevant alerts.

The beauty of MCP is that it's designed to be both simple enough for small teams to implement and robust enough for enterprise-scale deployments. You don't need a PhD in computer science to use it, but it's sophisticated enough to handle the most complex AI workflows.

Here are the concrete benefits you get when you implement it in your AI systems:

- **Reduced development time**: This is probably the most immediate benefit. Instead of spending weeks or months building custom integrations, you can connect to AI systems in hours or days. I worked on a proof of concept with a start-up recently that was able to integrate five different AI services in a single afternoon using MCP. Without it, that same integration would have taken its small team several months.
- **Improved AI performance**: When AI systems can share context effectively, they make better decisions. It's like the difference between making decisions with partial information versus having the full picture. I've seen recommendation systems improve their accuracy by 30% or more simply by having access to real-time inventory and customer service data through MCP.
- **Enhanced security**: Instead of having dozens of custom integration points, each with its own security considerations, MCP provides a standardized security model. This makes it much easier to audit, monitor, and secure your AI ecosystem.
- **Better user experiences**: When AI systems can coordinate, users get more consistent and intelligent interactions. No more explaining your problem to three different AI systems; they all have access to the same context.
- **Scalability**: As your AI ecosystem grows, MCP makes it much easier to add new systems and capabilities. Instead of an exponential increase in integration complexity, you get linear growth.

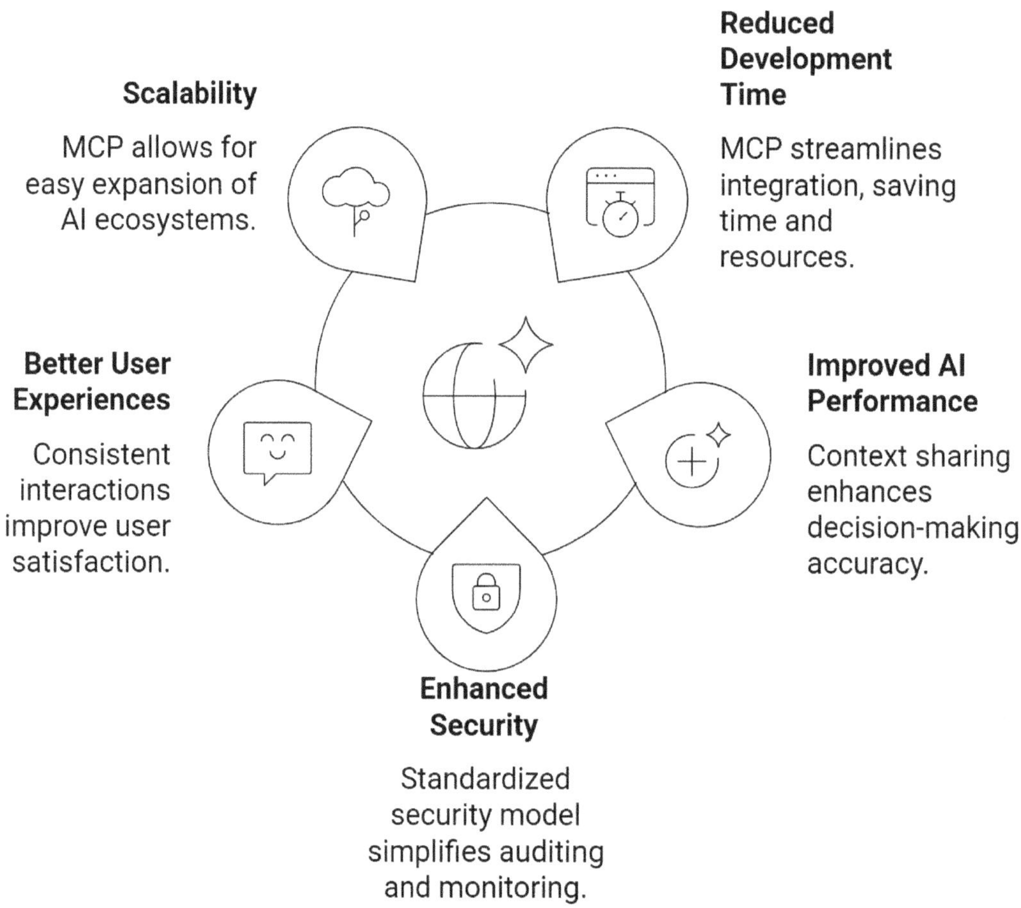

Figure 1.2 – Benefits of MCP

Here are some concrete examples of MCP in action:

- **E-commerce platform**: An online retailer uses MCP to connect its recommendation engine, inventory management system, customer service chatbot, and fraud detection AI. When a customer asks the chatbot about a product, it can provide real-time availability, personalized recommendations based on their history, and even flag potential fraud concerns, all in a single interaction.
- **Healthcare system**: A hospital network uses MCP to coordinate between diagnostic AI, treatment recommendation systems, and patient management tools. When a radiologist's AI spots something concerning on a scan, it can immediately alert the treatment planning AI and update the patient's care coordination system.

- **Financial services**: A bank uses MCP to connect its fraud detection, customer service, loan processing, and investment advisory AI systems. When the fraud system detects suspicious activity, it can immediately inform customer service and temporarily adjust the customer's risk profile across all systems.
- **Content creation**: A media company uses MCP to coordinate between its content generation AI, fact-checking systems, SEO optimization tools, and publication workflow. Writers can get real-time feedback on accuracy, optimization suggestions, and publication scheduling, all integrated into their writing environment.

The applications are limitless. Anywhere you have multiple AI systems that could benefit from coordination, MCP can help. Now that you've seen what MCP does in practice, let's rewind a bit and look at how it all came to be.

Historical development and timeline

In this section, we'll look at how MCP evolved from early ideas to a widely adopted standard. The timeline matters because it shows not just when things happened, but why the community moved so quickly and how collaboration shaped the protocol we have today.

The seeds of MCP were planted around 2023, when several major AI labs and open source contributors started running into the same problems I described earlier. They were all building increasingly sophisticated AI systems, but they were also developing custom solutions to make these systems work together.

The Model Context Protocol was first introduced by Anthropic in November 2024. In December 2025, Anthropic donated MCP to the **Agentic AI Foundation** (**AAIF**), a directed fund under the Linux Foundation, co-founded by Anthropic, Block, and OpenAI. Within months, major providers such as OpenAI and Google DeepMind adopted the standard.

Here's how the timeline unfolded:

- **Early 2023**: The first informal discussions about standardization began. I remember reading some early blog posts from researchers who were frustrated with the amount of time they were spending on integration work instead of AI research.
- **Mid-2023**: Several companies started experimenting with common protocols. There were at least three different competing standards being developed simultaneously. It was a bit like the early days of video formats, Betamax versus VHS, but for AI protocols.
- **Late 2023**: The AI community started coalescing around the idea that we needed an open standard, not a proprietary solution. This was crucial because it meant that MCP would be developed in the open, with input from the entire community.

- **Early 2024**: The first draft of MCP specification was released. I remember downloading it and being impressed by how thoughtfully it was designed. The authors had clearly learned from the mistakes of earlier attempts.
- **Mid-2024**: Major AI platforms started implementing MCP support. This was the tipping point – once you had a critical mass of platforms supporting the standard, adoption accelerated rapidly.
- **Late 2024**: Early enterprise pilots and proofs of concept went live. Companies started reporting significant improvements in AI system coordination and efficiency.
- **2025**: MCP is rapidly becoming a standard for AI system integration.
- **2026**: Today, it's increasingly common to see new AI platforms that support MCP. We hear or talk about MCP daily, and there are both existing and new products I see that for sure come with MCP support.

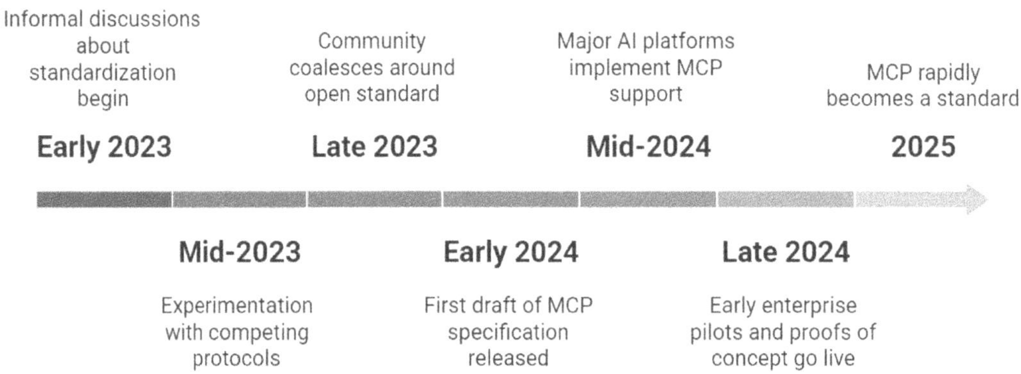

Figure 1.3 – The evolution of MCP

What's interesting about this timeline is how quickly things moved once the community agreed on the need for standardization. In the tech world, standards battles can drag on for years (anyone remember the browser wars?), but the AI community seemed to recognize that fragmentation would hurt everyone.

The development process itself was also noteworthy. Instead of being developed behind closed doors by a single company, MCP was developed through an open process with input from researchers, developers, and users. This collaborative approach is part of why it's been so successful.

With that history in mind, let's roll up our sleeves and look at how to set it up with some actual code.

Code example: Setting up a development environment

Now that we've covered the theory, let's dive into a practical example and build a simple MCP server. I'm a firm believer that the best way to understand technology is to start using it, even if you don't understand all the details yet.

We're going to set up a basic MCP development environment and create a simple "Hello World" MCP server. The point of this exercise isn't just to get code running; it's to give you a hands-on feel for how MCP works. By the end, you'll understand the basic setup, see how servers and tools are defined, and build confidence before tackling more complex scenarios. Think of it as your warm-up lap before the main race.

Don't worry if some of the concepts seem unclear right now; we'll cover everything in detail in later chapters.

Setting up the environment

First, let's create a new directory for our MCP experiments and set up a virtual environment:

```
mkdir mcp_experiments
cd mcp_experiments
python -m venv venv
source venv/bin/activate  # On Windows: venv\Scripts\activate
```

Now, let's install MCP Python SDK:

```
pip install mcp==0.3.1
```

Creating your first MCP server

Let's create a simple MCP server that provides a basic greeting tool. Create a file called `hello_server.py`:

```
import asyncio
import json
from mcp.server import Server
from mcp.server.stdio import stdio_server
from mcp.types import Tool, TextContent

# Create a server instance
server = Server("hello-world-server")
```

```
# Expose available tools to clients
@server.list_tools()
async def list_tools():
    """List available tools."""
    return [
        Tool(
            name="greet",
            description="Generate a personalized greeting",
            inputSchema={
                "type": "object",
                "properties": {
                    "name": {
                        "type": "string",
                        "description": "The name of the person to greet"
                    },
                    "style": {
                        "type": "string",
                        "enum": ["formal", "casual", "enthusiastic"],
                        "description": "The style of greeting"
                    }
                },
                "required": ["name"]
            }
        )
    ]

@server.call_tool()
async def call_tool(name: str, arguments: dict):
    """Handle tool calls."""
    if name == "greet":
        person_name = arguments.get("name", "World")
        style = arguments.get("style", "casual")

        greetings = {
            "formal": f"Good day, {person_name}. I hope this message finds you
well.",
            "casual": f"Hey {person_name}! How's it going?",
            "enthusiastic": f"Hello there, {person_name}! Great to meet you! "
        }
```

```
        greeting = greetings.get(style, greetings["casual"])

        return [TextContent(
            type="text",
            text=greeting
        )]
    else:
        raise ValueError(f"Unknown tool: {name}")

# entry point to start the server using STDIO transport
async def main():
    """Main server function."""
    options = server.create_initialization_options()
    async with stdio_server() as (read_stream, write_stream):
        await server.run(read_stream, write_stream, options)

if __name__ == "__main__":
    asyncio.run(main())
```

Before we jump into testing, let's see what happens in the preceding code. We're spinning up a simple MCP server that exposes one tool called `greet`. That tool takes a name (and optionally a style) as input and returns a personalized greeting. The `@server.list_tools()` function tells clients what's available, and the `@server.call_tool()` function actually runs the greeting logic when invoked. Finally, the `main()` function ties everything together and launches the server so it can talk to clients. Under the hood, MCP uses a **client–server architecture** that separates the data layer from the transport layer. The data layer defines JSON-RPC 2.0 message structures for lifecycle management, tool discovery, tool execution, resources, prompts, and notifications. The transport layer supports both STDIO (for local servers) and Streamable HTTP transports with secure authentication and optional server-sent events. Understanding these layers will help you extend the examples in later chapters. We will be discussing all of these in the upcoming chapters.

Testing the server

Now let's create a simple client to test our server. Create a file called `test_client.py`:

```
import asyncio
import json
import subprocess
import sys
from mcp.client import ClientSession
```

```
from mcp.client.stdio import stdio_client

async def test_hello_server():
    """Test our hello world server."""

    # Start the server as a subprocess
    server_process = subprocess.Popen(
        [sys.executable, "hello_server.py"],
        stdin=subprocess.PIPE,
        stdout=subprocess.PIPE,
        stderr=subprocess.PIPE,
        text=True
    )

    try:
        # Connect to the server
        async with stdio_client(server_process) as (read, write):
            async with ClientSession(read, write) as session:
                # Initialize the session
                await session.initialize()

                # List available tools
                tools = await session.list_tools()
                print("Available tools:")
                for tool in tools.tools:
                    print(f"  - {tool.name}: {tool.description}")

                # Test the greet tool with different styles
                test_cases = [
                    {"name": "Alice", "style": "formal"},
                    {"name": "Bob", "style": "casual"},
                    {"name": "Charlie", "style": "enthusiastic"},
                    {"name": "Diana"}  # No style specified
                ]

                for args in test_cases:
                    print(f"\nCalling greet with args: {args}")
                    result = await session.call_tool("greet", args)
                    for content in result.content:
                        print(f"Response: {content.text}")
```

```
    finally:
        # Clean up the server process
        server_process.terminate()
        server_process.wait()

if __name__ == "__main__":
    asyncio.run(test_hello_server())
```

This client script spins up the server in the background, connects to it, and then interacts with the `greet` tool. First, it asks the server to list all available tools (in this case, just one). Then it runs a few test cases with different names and greeting styles to show how the server responds. Finally, it cleans up by shutting the server down. In short, this is your first end-to-end test of MCP: a client discovering a tool, calling it, and getting back a result.

Now let's run our test:

```
python test_client.py
```

You should see output like this:

```
Available tools:
  - greet: Generate a personalized greeting

Calling greet with args: {'name': 'Alice', 'style': 'formal'}
Response: Good day, Alice. I hope this message finds you well.

Calling greet with args: {'name': 'Bob', 'style': 'casual'}
Response: Hey Bob! How's it going?

Calling greet with args: {'name': 'Charlie', 'style': 'enthusiastic'}
Response: Hello there, Charlie! Great to meet you!

Calling greet with args: {'name': 'Diana'}
Response: Hey Diana! How's it going?
```

Congratulations! You just created and tested your first MCP server. Let's break down what happened:

1. **Server creation**: We created an MCP server that exposes a single tool called `greet`.
2. **Tool definition**: We defined the tool's schema, including its parameters and types.
3. **Tool implementation**: We implemented the actual greeting logic.

4. **Client communication**: We created a client that can discover and call the server's tools.
5. **Testing**: We tested different parameter combinations to see how the tool responds.

This might seem like a lot of code for a simple greeting, but notice what we got for free:

- Automatic tool discovery
- Parameter validation
- Standardized communication protocol
- Error handling
- Type safety

In a traditional API, you'd need to implement all of this yourself. With MCP, it's built into the protocol.

This is just the beginning. In the upcoming chapters, we'll explore the following:

- How to build more sophisticated tools
- How to handle resources and prompts
- How to implement security and authentication
- How to integrate with popular AI frameworks
- How to build multi-agent systems

But for now, take a moment to appreciate what you've accomplished. You've just taken your first step into the world of standardized AI system communication. The greeting server might be simple, but the principles you've learned here scale up to enterprise-level AI systems.

Summary

In this chapter, we laid the groundwork for understanding MCP. We started by looking at the problem of disconnected AI systems and how powerful tools such as chatbots, recommendation engines, and forecasting models often work in isolation, leading to inefficiency, redundancy, and confusion. We then introduced MCP as the "missing piece" that standardizes communication between AI systems, preserving context and enabling true collaboration.

The chapter also traced the history of AI system design, from early monolithic programs to expert systems, large language models, and finally to the need for multi-agent coordination. We walked through MCP's own development timeline from its first informal discussions in 2023 to its rapid adoption across major AI platforms by 2025. Along the way, we saw the benefits of MCP: faster development, better performance, stronger security, improved user experiences, and scalable system design.

Finally, the chapter moved from theory into practice. Through real-world use cases (in e-commerce, healthcare, finance, and media) and a hands-on "Hello World" code example, you saw how MCP works in action.

You should now have a clear sense of both why MCP exists and how it changes the way we build AI systems.

In the next chapter, we'll go deeper into the theoretical foundations that make MCP possible. We'll explore the concept of agency in AI systems and understand why multi-agent coordination is such a challenging problem. But don't worry, we'll keep it practical and grounded in real-world examples.

Get this book's PDF copy, code bundle, and more

2

Theoretical Foundations of Multi-Agent Systems

The whole is greater than the sum of its parts.

– Aristotle

I once spent months building single AI systems, thinking I was pretty clever. But at the end, I faced a common problem, where one system attempted to perform many tasks, but none excelled at specialized functions. Then, one day, I was watching a soccer team practice, and it hit me. The best players weren't necessarily the most skilled individually; they were the ones who could work together, anticipate each other's moves, and create something greater than what any of them could achieve alone.

That's when I really understood what **multi-agent systems** were all about. It's not just about having multiple AI systems; it's about having them work together in ways that amplify their individual capabilities.

But here's the thing: getting AI systems to collaborate effectively is way harder than getting soccer players to work together. At least soccer players can see each other, understand the same rules, and communicate in a common language. AI systems? Well, that's where things get interesting.

Why do multi-agent systems matter for MCP? Multi-agent systems lie at the heart of MCP, which was designed to solve the communication and coordination problems that arise when multiple autonomous agents must work together. Without a standard protocol, agents speak different "languages," lose context between interactions, and require ad hoc integrations for every pair of agents. By defining common message formats, context sharing, and task-discovery semantics, MCP enables multi-agent systems to cooperate seamlessly and eliminates the N^2 explosion of custom interfaces. Understanding multi-agent systems, therefore, sets the stage for appreciating why MCP is necessary.

In this chapter, you'll understand what *agency* means in AI, why and how multiple agents work together, the historical roots of multi-agent systems, and the challenges of coordinating them. This context makes the value of MCP much clearer. Since the rest of the book builds on these ideas, this chapter serves as an essential foundation.

In this chapter, we'll be covering the following topics:

- Historical development of multi-agent systems
- Understanding agency in AI
- From single agents to multi-agent systems
- Historical development of multi-agent systems
- Challenges in multi-agent coordination

Historical development of multi-agent systems

The journey of multi-agent systems is fascinating because it mirrors our evolving understanding of intelligence itself. Let me take you through the key milestones that led us to where we are today:

- **1950s–1960s (the birth of AI)**: The earliest AI systems were monolithic single programs trying to solve complex problems. Think of programs such as the Logic Theorist (1956) or the General Problem Solver (1957). These were impressive for their time, but they were essentially very sophisticated calculators.
- **1970s–1980s (the expert systems era)**: This is when we first started thinking about specialized intelligence. Expert systems such as MYCIN (medical diagnosis) and DENDRAL (chemical analysis) showed that AI could be incredibly effective when focused on specific domains. But they were still isolated systems.
- **1980s–1990s (the distributed AI revolution)**: This is where things get interesting. Researchers started realizing that complex problems might be better solved by multiple specialized systems working together. The **Distributed Vehicle Monitoring Testbed** (**DVMT**) was one of the first real multi-agent systems, designed to track vehicles using multiple sensors and reasoning systems.

I find this period fascinating because it's when researchers started grappling with the same problems we face today: How do you coordinate multiple intelligent systems? How do you handle conflicts? How do you ensure consistent behavior?

- **1990s–2000s (agent-oriented programming)**: This era saw the development of formal frameworks for building multi-agent systems. Languages such as AgentSpeak and platforms such as JADE emerged. The focus shifted from just building multiple AI systems to building systems that were designed from the ground up to work together.
- **2000s–2010s (web services and service-oriented architecture (SOA))**: The rise of the internet brought new possibilities for distributed AI. Suddenly, agents didn't need to be on the same machine or even in the same building. Web services and SOA provided the infrastructure for truly distributed multi-agent systems.
- **2010s–present (the LLM revolution)**: The emergence of **large language models (LLMs)** has significantly impacted AI by enabling general-purpose models. Suddenly, we had AI systems that could perform a wide range of tasks while remaining broadly applicable. This introduced new challenges: coordinating these broad models with more specialized agents.

This trend underscored the need for robust coordination frameworks. Protocols such as MCP aim to address the long-standing problem researchers identified in the 1980s: How do you get disparate intelligent systems to work together effectively?

Understanding agency in AI

Before we dive into multi-agent systems, we need to understand what we mean by *agency* in the context of AI. This isn't just academic jargon; it's fundamental to understanding why MCP matters.

When I talk about an AI agent, I'm referring to a system that exhibits four key properties: **autonomy**, **social ability**, **reactivity**, and **proactivity**.

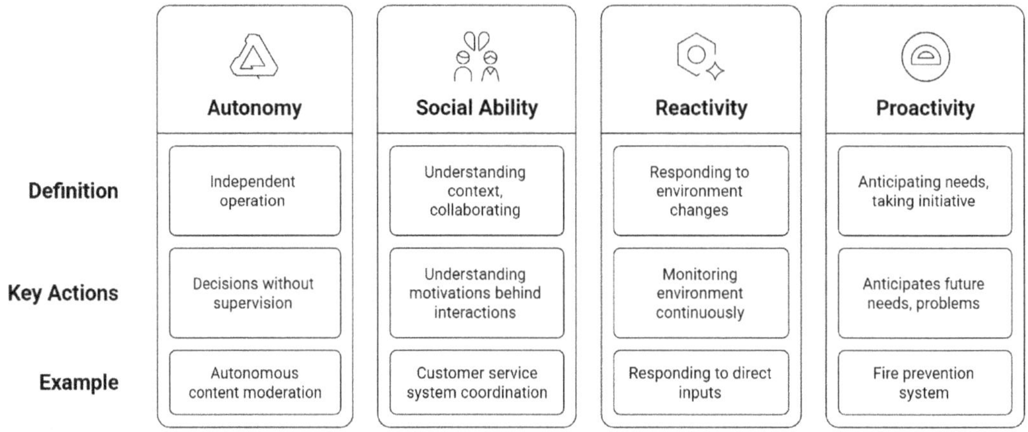

Figure 2.1 – Key properties in agency

Autonomy: the foundation of independent operation

Autonomy is perhaps the most fundamental property of an AI agent. It's what separates a true agent from a simple tool or script. An autonomous agent can make decisions and take actions without constant human supervision. Think about your email spam filter. Once you set it up, it makes decisions about what's spam and what isn't without asking you every time. It has its own decision-making process based on patterns it has learned.

But autonomy isn't just about independence; it's about intelligent independence. A truly autonomous agent must do the following:

- Make decisions based on its goals and current situation
- Adapt its behavior when circumstances change
- Manage its own resources and priorities
- Learn from experience to improve future decisions

I remember working on an autonomous content moderation system for a social media platform. The challenge wasn't just identifying inappropriate content; any rule-based system could do that. The challenge was handling the gray areas, the context-dependent situations, and the constantly evolving nature of online communication.

The system had to be autonomous enough to make thousands of decisions per minute, but smart enough to escalate edge cases to human moderators. It had to balance speed with accuracy, and consistency with adaptability. That's real autonomy in action.

Social ability: the art of AI communication

Social ability in AI agents is about more than just exchanging data; it's about understanding context, negotiating, collaborating, and building relationships with other agents and humans.

A socially capable agent must understand the following:

- When to communicate (not just responding to requests, but proactively sharing relevant information)
- How to communicate (choosing the right format, tone, and level of detail)
- What to communicate (filtering information based on the recipient's needs and capabilities)
- Why to communicate (understanding the goals and motivations behind interactions)

I once worked on a customer service system where the AI agents had to coordinate with each other to provide seamless support. A customer would start a conversation with a general support agent, get transferred to a technical specialist, and then need to involve a billing agent. Each handoff required not just transferring the conversation, but also the context, the customer's emotional state, and the progress made so far.

The breakthrough came when we realized that social ability isn't just about protocols, it's about empathy and understanding. The agents needed to understand not just what was being said, but what was meant, what was needed, and how to best help.

Reactivity: responding to a dynamic world

Reactivity is the ability to perceive environmental changes and respond appropriately. But it's not just about speed; it's also about intelligent response. A reactive agent doesn't just follow a script; it adapts its behavior based on what's happening around it.

A reactive agent must do the following:

- Monitor its environment continuously
- Recognize significant changes in its environment
- Evaluate the implications of changes
- Respond appropriately and proportionally

The key insight about reactivity is that it's not just about reacting to direct inputs. A truly reactive agent monitors multiple information sources, recognizes patterns, and can respond to subtle environmental changes that might not be immediately obvious.

Proactivity: anticipating and acting

Proactivity is perhaps the most sophisticated property of intelligent agents. It's the ability to take initiative, anticipate needs, and work toward goals without being explicitly instructed.

A proactive agent would do the following:

- Anticipate future needs and problems
- Take the initiative to prevent issues
- Seek opportunities to improve outcomes
- Plan and execute long-term strategies

This shift from monolithic AI to coordinated multi-agent systems wasn't immediate; it was the result of decades of research and evolving paradigms. In general, a proactive agent doesn't wait for something to happen; it anticipates needs and acts accordingly.

Now that we understand what makes an AI system an "agent," let's talk about what happens when you have multiple agents working together. This is where things get interesting and really complicated.

From single agents to multi-agent systems

A multi-agent system is essentially a collection of autonomous agents that interact with each other to achieve individual or collective goals. Think of it like a jazz ensemble: each musician is skilled individually, but the magic happens when they improvise together, responding to each other's cues and creating something none of them could produce alone.

When I was building a trading system for a hedge fund, I started with one monolithic AI doing everything: market analysis, risk assessment, trade execution, and portfolio management. This monolithic approach proved far from optimal, whereas dividing the system into specialized agents markedly improved performance. The lesson was clear: complex systems are far more effective when broken into specialized agents that collaborate, rather than relying on a single system to do it all.

The breakthrough came when I split the system into specialized agents:

- A **Market Analyst** agent that focused solely on identifying trends and opportunities
- A **Risk Assessment** agent that evaluated the potential downside of each trade
- An **Execution** agent that handled the actual buying and selling
- A **Portfolio Manager** agent that maintained the overall strategy and balance

Each agent was excellent at its specific task, but the real power came from their interactions. The Market Analyst agent would identify opportunities, the Risk Assessment agent would evaluate them, and if both agreed, the Execution agent would act while the Portfolio Manager agent ensured that everything aligned with the overall strategy.

But here's where it gets tricky: how do these agents actually communicate and coordinate? In my early implementation, I had to build custom interfaces between each pair of agents. It was like creating a different language for every possible conversation. The Market Analyst agent spoke "market-speak" to the Risk agent, "risk-speak" to the Execution agent, and so on. It was a nightmare to maintain.

This is exactly the problem that MCP solves, but I'm getting ahead of myself. Let's first understand the different types of interactions that can happen in multi-agent systems:

- **Cooperative interactions**: Agents work together toward a common goal. In our trading example, all agents are ultimately trying to maximize returns while minimizing risk. They share information freely and coordinate their actions.
- **Competitive interactions**: Agents have conflicting goals and compete for limited resources. Think about multiple AI bidding agents in an online auction; each wants to win, but only one can.
- **Neutral interactions**: Agents operate independently but may occasionally interact when their paths cross. An example is different AI systems in a smart city that usually work independently but might need to coordinate during emergencies.

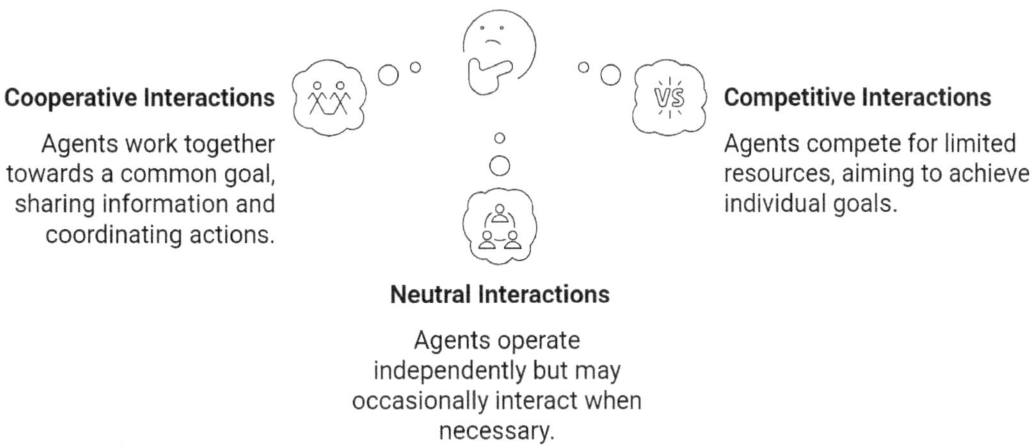

Figure 2.2 – What type of interaction should be implemented in the multi-agent system?

Here are some key parameters that must be followed when designing a multi-agent system:

- **Specialization**: Each agent must have specific skills and can only handle certain types of tasks

- **Coordination**: The coordinator, if it exists, will only assign tasks based on agent availability and capabilities
- **Load balancing**: Tasks must be distributed among agents to optimize overall performance
- **Communication**: Agents can send messages to each other only via the standard protocol
- **Fault tolerance**: Failed tasks must be re-queued with adjusted priority

Dividing work among specialized agents and coordinating them always makes the agents more powerful. Specialization, communication, load balancing, and fault tolerance all come together to create a system greater than the sum of its parts.

When we design a multi-agent system, it comes with its own challenges. Let's take a closer look at the challenges that you face frequently, which are very common.

Challenges in multi-agent coordination

Let me be honest with you: coordinating multiple AI agents is hard. Really hard. I've been working in this field for over a decade, and I still encounter new challenges regularly. But understanding these challenges is crucial for appreciating why MCP is such a significant development:

- **The communication challenge**: This is the big one. How do agents communicate with each other? It's not just about the technical protocol, though that's important; it's about semantics. When Agent A tells Agent B that "customer satisfaction is down 15%," what exactly does that mean? Down from what baseline? What time period? What methodology was used to measure satisfaction?
- **The coordination challenge**: Even when agents can communicate, coordinating their actions is complex. Who decides what? How do you handle conflicts? What happens when agents have different goals or priorities?

Consider a smart city scenario where you have traffic management agents, emergency response agents, and environmental monitoring agents. During a fire emergency, traffic agents want to optimize evacuation routes, the emergency agents want clear paths for fire trucks, and the environmental agents want to minimize air pollution. How do you coordinate these potentially conflicting goals?

- **The trust challenge**: In a multi-agent system, agents need to trust each other to some degree. But how do you establish and maintain trust between AI systems? How do you handle situations where one agent provides incorrect information or behaves unexpectedly?

- **The scalability challenge**: As you add more agents to a system, the complexity grows exponentially. With two agents, you have one potential communication channel. With 10 agents, you have 45 potential channels. With 100 agents, you have 4,950 potential channels. How do you manage this complexity? One way to manage this scalability issue is to adopt structured communication patterns. In a hub-and-spoke pattern, a central controller agent delegates tasks to sub-agents, which reduces peer-to-peer connections. A mesh collaboration pattern uses message brokers such as Kafka or Redis Streams so that agents publish and subscribe rather than communicate directly. Finally, hierarchical clusters organize agents into pods managed by director agents, allowing specialized teams to scale independently. These patterns, combined with message brokers, shrink the number of direct connections and mitigate the N^2 communication problem.
- **The consistency challenge**: How do you ensure that all agents have a consistent view of the world? What happens when information changes? How do you propagate updates? How do you handle situations where different agents have conflicting information?

These challenges aren't just theoretical; every multi-agent system must grapple with them in practice. Frameworks such as MCP provide standardized mechanisms to address these fundamental issues, simplifying communication and coordination among agents.

To see these challenges in action and understand why a standardized protocol such as MCP is so valuable, let's walk through a concrete example.

Let me show you a practical example that demonstrates some of these challenges and how they might be addressed. We'll build a simple multi-agent system for managing a smart home, and you'll see firsthand why standardized communication protocols are so important:

1. First, we import the necessary modules and build the smart home messaging framework:

```
import asyncio
import json
import random
from datetime import datetime, timedelta
from dataclasses import dataclass, asdict
from typing import Dict, List, Optional, Any from enum import Enum

class MessageType(Enum):
    STATUS_UPDATE = "status_update"
    REQUEST = "request"
```

```
    RESPONSE = "response"
    ALERT = "alert"
    COORDINATION = "coordination"

@dataclass
class Message:
    sender: str
     recipient: str
     message_type: MessageType
    content: Dict[str, Any]
    timestamp: datetime
    message_id: str

class SmartHomeAgent:
    """Base class for smart home agents."""
     def __init__(self, name: str, agent_type: str):
        self.name = name
        self.agent_type = agent_type
        self.message_queue: List[Message] = []
        self.other_agents: Dict[str, 'SmartHomeAgent'] = {}
        self.status: Dict[str, Any] = {}
        self.running = False

     def register_agent(self, agent: 'SmartHomeAgent'):
        self.other_agents[agent.name] = agent

    async def send_message(
        self, recipient: str, message_type: MessageType,
        content: Dict[str, Any]
    ):
        if recipient not in self.other_agents:
            print(f" {self.name}: Unknown recipient {recipient}")
            return          message = Message(
            sender=self.name,
            recipient=recipient,
            message_type=message_type,
            content=content,
            timestamp=datetime.now(),
            message_id=f"{self.name}_{datetime.now().timestamp()}"
         )
        self.other_agents[recipient].message_queue.append(message)
```

```
            print(f" {self.name} → {recipient}: {message_type.value}")

    async def broadcast_message(
            self, message_type: MessageType, content: Dict[str, Any]
    ):
        for agent name in self.other_agents:
            await self.send_message(
                agent_name, message_type, content)

    async def process_messages(self):
        while self.message_queue:
            message = self.message_queue.pop(0)
            await self.handle_message(message)

    async def handle_message(self, message: Message):
        print(f" {self.name}: Received {message.message_type.value} from
{message.sender}")
    async def run(self):
        self.running = True
        while self.running:
            await self.process_messages()
            await self.update_status()
            await asyncio.sleep(1)
    async def update_status(self):
        pass      def stop(self):
        self.running = False
```

The smart home example begins with a flexible messaging system. An enumeration defines different message types (status updates, requests, responses, alerts, and coordination messages). The `SmartHomeAgent` base class stores the agent's name, type, message queue, and knowledge of its peers. Methods for sending and broadcasting messages lay the foundation for **communication complexity** – each agent has to understand and act upon messages from others.

2. Implement the Thermostat agent to manage climate control:

```
class ThermostatAgent(SmartHomeAgent):
    def __init__(self):
        super().__init__("Thermostat", "climate_control")
        self.current_temp = 72.0
        self.target_temp = 72.0
```

```
        self.heating = False
        self.cooling = False
        self.energy_efficiency_mode = False

    async def update_status(self):
        # Simulate temperature changes
        if self.heating:
            self.current_temp += random.uniform(0.1, 0.3)
        elif self.cooling:
            self.current_temp -= random.uniform(0.1, 0.3)
        else:
            self.current_temp += random.uniform(-0.1, 0.1)
        temp_diff = self.target_temp - self.current_temp
        if temp_diff > 1.0 and not self.heating:
            self.heating = True
            self.cooling = False             await
            self.broadcast_message(MessageType.STATUS_UPDATE, {
                "heating_started": True,
                "current_temp": self.current_temp,
                "target_temp": self.target_temp
            })
        elif temp_diff < -1.0 and not self.cooling:
            self.cooling = True                self.heating = False
            await self.broadcast_message(MessageType.STATUS_UPDATE,{
                "cooling_started": True,
                "current_temp": self.current_temp,
                "target_temp": self.target_temp
            })
        elif abs(temp_diff) < 0.5:
            if self.heating or self.cooling:
                self.heating = False
                self.cooling = False
                await  self.broadcast_message(
                MessageType.STATUS_UPDATE, {
                    "climate_control_off": True,
                    "current_temp": self.current_temp
                })
               self.status = {
                    "current_temp": round(self.current_temp, 1),
                    "target_temp": self.target_temp,
                    "heating": self.heating,
```

```
                    "cooling": self.cooling,
                "energy_efficiency_mode": self.energy_efficiency_mode
                }

    async def handle_message(self, message: Message):
        await super().handle_message(message)
        if message.message_type == MessageType.REQUEST:
            if "set_temperature" in message.content:
                new_temp = message.content["set_temperature"]
                self.target_temp = new_temp
                print(f"  {self.name}: Temperature set to
                      {new_temp}°F")
                await self.send_message(message.sender,
                MessageType.RESPONSE, {
                    "temperature_set": True,
                    "new_target": new_temp
                })
             elif "energy_efficiency_mode" in message.content:
                self.energy_efficiency_mode = message.content[
                    "energy_efficiency_mode"]
                if self.energy_efficiency_mode:
                    if self.heating:
                        self.target_temp -= 2
                  elif self.cooling:
                        self.target_temp += 2
                 print(f" {self.name}: Energy efficiency mode {'enabled'
if self.energy_efficiency_mode else 'disabled'}")
```

`ThermostatAgent` monitors and adjusts the home's temperature. Its `update_status` method simulates temperature changes and broadcasts events when heating or cooling starts or stops. Handling messages lets other agents request a new set-point or enable energy-efficiency mode. This agent illustrates **reactivity** (responding to temperature differences) and **social ability** (cooperating with energy and controller agents).

3. Design Security and Energy agents with specific responsibilities:

```
class SecurityAgent(SmartHomeAgent):
    def __init__(self):
        super().__init__("Security", "security")
        self.armed = False
        self.motion_detected = False
```

```
        self.doors_locked = True
        self.windows_locked = True
        self.last_motion_time = None

    async def update_status(self):
        if random.random() < 0.05:
            self.motion_detected = True
            self.last_motion_time = datetime.now()
            if self.armed:
                await self.broadcast_message(MessageType.ALERT, {
                    "motion_detected": True,
                    "location": random.choice(
                        ["living_room", "kitchen", "hallway"]),
                    "timestamp": self.last_motion_time.isoformat()
                })
        else:
            self.motion_detected = False
            self.status = {
                "armed": self.armed,
                "motion_detected": self.motion_detected,
                "doors_locked": self.doors_locked,
                "windows_locked": self.windows_locked,
                "last_motion": self.last_motion_time.isoformat()
        if self.last_motion_time else None         }

    async def handle_message(self, message: Message):
        await super().handle_message(message)
        if message.message_type == MessageType.REQUEST:
            if "arm_system" in message.content:
                self.armed = message.content["arm_system"]
                print(f" {self.name}: System {'armed' if self.armed else
'disarmed'}")
                await self.send_message(
                    message.sender, MessageType.RESPONSE,
                    {"system_armed": self.armed})
        elif message.message_type == MessageType.STATUS_UPDATE:
            if "heating_started" in message.content or "cooling_started"
in message.content:
                print(f" {self.name}: Adjusting motion sensitivity due to
HVAC activity")
```

```
class EnergyAgent(SmartHomeAgent):
    def __init__(self):
        super().__init__("Energy", "energy_management")
        self.total_consumption = 0.0
        self.peak_hours = False
        self.energy_saving_mode = False
        self.appliance_usage: Dict[str, float] = {}

    async def update_status(self):
        current_hour = datetime.now().hour
        self.peak_hours = 16 <= current_hour <= 20
        consumption = 5.0
        thermostat = self.other_agents.get("Thermostat")
        if thermostat:
            if thermostat.status.get("heating"):
                consumption += 15.0
            elif thermostat.status.get("cooling"):
                consumption += 12.0
        security = self.other_agents.get("Security")
        if security and security.status.get("armed"):
                 consumption += 2.0
                 self.total_consumption += consumption / 60
                 self.appliance_usage["hvac"] = consumption - 5.0
            if self.peak_hours and consumption > 20.0 and not
self.energy_saving_mode:
            await self.broadcast_message(MessageType.COORDINATION, {
                "energy_saving_request": True,
                "reason": "peak_hours_high_consumption",
                "current_consumption": consumption
            })
            self.energy_saving_mode = True
        self.status = {
            "total_consumption": round(self.total_consumption, 2),
            "current_consumption": round(consumption, 2),
            "peak_hours": self.peak_hours,
            "energy_saving_mode": self.energy_saving_mode,
            "appliance_usage": self.appliance_usage
        }

    async def handle_message(self, message: Message):
        await super().handle_message(message)
```

```
        if message.message_type == MessageType.COORDINATION:
            if "energy_saving_request" in message.content:
                await self.send_message(
                    "Thermostat", MessageType.REQUEST,
                    {"energy_efficiency_mode": True})
```

SecurityAgent watches for motion and sends alerts when the system is armed; it also responds to requests to arm or disarm the system. EnergyAgent monitors total consumption, identifies peak hours, and requests efficiency measures from other agents when necessary. These agents illustrate how different parts of a smart home have distinct responsibilities yet must communicate and coordinate – a good example of coordination challenges and communication complexity.

4. Build the home controller and run the smart home simulation:

```
class HomeControllerAgent(SmartHomeAgent):
    def __init__(self):
        super().__init__("Controller", "central_control")
        self.user_preferences = {
            "preferred_temp": 72,
            "auto_arm_security": True,
            "energy_saving": True          }
        self.home_occupied = True
        self.last_activity_time = datetime.now()

    async def update_status(self):
        if random.random() < 0.1:
            self.last_activity_time = datetime.now()
            self.home_occupied = True
            time_since_activity =
                 datetime.now() - self.last_activity_time
        if time_since_activity > timedelta(minutes=30):
            if self.home_occupied:
                self.home_occupied = False
                await self._handle_home_empty()
        self.status = {
            "home_occupied": self.home_occupied,
            "last_activity": self.last_activity_time.isoformat(),
            "user_preferences": self.user_preferences
        }
```

```
    async def _handle_home_empty(self):
        print(f" {self.name}: Home appears to be empty, activating energy
saving mode")
        await self.send_message(
            "Thermostat", MessageType.REQUEST,
            {
                "set_temperature": self.user_preferences[
                    "preferred_temp"] - 3
            }
        )
        if self.user_preferences["auto_arm_security"]:
            await self.send_message(
                "Security", MessageType.REQUEST,
                {"arm_system": True})

    async def handle_message(self, message: Message):
        await super().handle_message(message)
        if message.message_type == MessageType.ALERT:
            if "motion_detected" in message.content:
                print(f" {self.name}: Motion alert received, checking if
home should be occupied")
                self.home_occupied = True
                self.last_activity_time = datetime.now()
                await self.send_message(
                    "Security", MessageType.REQUEST,
                    {"arm_system": False})
                await self.send_message(
                    "Thermostat", MessageType.REQUEST,
                    {"set_temperature": self.user_preferences[
                        "preferred_temp"]
                    }
                )

async def demo_smart_home_system():
    thermostat = ThermostatAgent()
    security = SecurityAgent()
    energy = EnergyAgent()
    controller = HomeControllerAgent()
    agents = [thermostat, security, energy, controller]
    for agent in agents:
        for other_agent in agents:
```

```
                if agent != other_agent:
                    agent.register_agent(other_agent)
        print(" Starting Smart Home Multi-Agent System...\n")
        agent_tasks = [asyncio.create_task(agent.run()) for agent in agents]
        try:
            await asyncio.sleep(30)
            for agent in agents:
                agent.stop()
            await asyncio.gather(*agent_tasks, return_exceptions=True)
            print("\n Final System Status:")
            for agent in agents:
                print(f"   {agent.name}: {agent.status}")
        except KeyboardInterrupt:
            print("\n System stopped by user")
            for agent in agents:
                agent.stop()
```

The central controller maintains user preferences, detects occupancy, and coordinates temperature and security accordingly. If the home is empty, it reduces the temperature and arms the security system; if motion is detected, it does the opposite. The `demo_smart_home_system` function instantiates all agents, registers them with each other, and runs the system for 30 seconds before printing the final statuses. Together, these components highlight the coordination challenges inherent in multi-agent systems and the need for clear protocols.

When you run this example, you'll see output similar to the following:

```
Starting Smart Home Multi-Agent System...
Thermostat → Security: status_update
Thermostat → Energy: status_update
Thermostat → Controller: status_update
Security: Received status_update from Thermostat
Energy: Received status_update from Thermostat
Controller: Received status_update from Thermostat
Security: Adjusting motion sensitivity due to HVAC activity
 Thermostat: Temperature set to 72 °F
Energy → Thermostat: coordination
Energy → Security: coordination
Energy → Controller: coordination
Thermostat: Energy efficiency mode enabled
Controller: Home appears to be empty, activating energy saving mode
```

```
Security: System armed
Controller: Motion alert received, checking if home should be occupied
Security: System disarmed
Final System Status:
  Thermostat: {...}
  Security: {...}
  Energy: {...}
  Controller: {...}
```

The printed output for the smart home system is rich with inter-agent messages: status updates from the thermostat, coordination requests from the energy manager, alerts from the security system, and decisions from the controller. This stream of messages makes the communication complexity described earlier tangible and shows how agents collaborate to keep the home comfortable, secure, and energy-efficient. The final status objects summarize the state of each agent after the simulation.

This example demonstrates several key challenges in multi-agent coordination:

- **Communication complexity**: Each agent needs to understand messages from every other agent
- **Coordination challenges**: Agents need to coordinate their actions (energy saving, security, and temperature)
- **Semantic understanding**: Agents need to understand what different status updates mean
- **Conflict resolution**: When the energy agent requests efficiency mode, it conflicts with user comfort preferences

Notice how much custom code we needed just to handle basic communication and coordination. Each agent has its own message handling logic, its own understanding of what different messages mean, and its own way of coordinating with others.

This is exactly the problem that MCP solves. Instead of each agent implementing its own communication protocol, they can all use a standardized protocol that handles the following:

- Message formatting and routing
- Semantic understanding of different message types
- Coordination patterns
- Error handling and recovery

In the next chapter, we'll explore how MCP makes this kind of multi-agent coordination much simpler and more reliable.

Summary

In this chapter, we learned what defines an AI "agent" (autonomy, social ability, reactivity, proactivity) and why those properties matter. We saw how single agents scale into multi-agent systems, why specialization and coordination are powerful, and the historical milestones that led to today's multi-agent systems. We also examined the core challenges of communication, coordination, trust, scalability, and consistency, and built a smart home multi-agent system to illustrate them. With these foundations, you're ready to understand why MCP is a breakthrough for multi-agent coordination.

In *Chapter 3*, we'll take a step back from the technical details and explore what MCP means for non-technical readers. We'll look at how this technology will impact everyday life and why everyone, not just developers should understand its implications.

3

The MCP for Non-Technical Readers

The best way to find out if you can trust somebody is to trust them.

- Ernest Hemingway

Let me tell you a story. Last week, I was at my local coffee shop, and I watched something fascinating happen. A customer ordered a complex drink: half-caf, oat milk, extra hot, with a shot of vanilla, and a sprinkle of cinnamon. The barista took the order, called it out to the person making drinks, who then coordinated with someone else to get the oat milk from the back, while another person handled the register for the next customer.

It was like watching a perfectly choreographed dance. Each person had their role, they communicated clearly, and they all worked toward the same goal: getting customers their coffee quickly and correctly. No one person could have handled the entire rush alone, but together, they were incredibly efficient.

That's essentially what the **Model Context Protocol** (**MCP**) does for AI systems. It's the communication system that lets different AI "specialists" work together as smoothly as that coffee shop team.

But here's the thing: most people don't need to understand the technical details of how the MCP works any more than you need to understand the mechanics of how your smartphone connects to cell towers. What matters is understanding what it means for your daily life and why it's going to change how you interact with technology.

By the end of this chapter, you'll understand why MCP matters to non-technical readers, see how it's already simplifying everyday tasks, and discover where it's headed next. We'll cover the basics of the MCP, how it differs from existing AI tools, and why collaboration between systems is so powerful. Knowing this context will make the later technical chapters easier to follow.

In this chapter, we'll be covering the following topics:

- Understanding MCP without the technical jargon
- Why MCP matters for everyone
- MCP in everyday scenarios
- The future with MCP
- Common questions about MCP
- Preparing for an MCP-enabled future

Understanding MCP without the technical jargon

Imagine you're planning a vacation. In the old days, you would have called a travel agent who would handle everything: flights, hotels, car rentals, and restaurant recommendations. That travel agent was like the old-style AI systems: one person (or system) trying to do everything.

Instead of relying on a single AI system to handle every aspect of your trip, MCP coordinates specialized assistants: one for flights, one for hotels, one for local recommendations, and so on. Each task is handled by an expert system: a flight expert who knows all the airlines and routes, a hotel specialist who understands accommodation in every city, a local guide who knows the best restaurants and attractions, and a budget expert who can optimize your spending. Each specialist is incredibly good at their specific area, and they all work together to plan your perfect trip.

That's what MCP enables for AI systems. Instead of one AI system trying to do everything (and being mediocre at most things), you get a team of AI specialists that excel in their areas and coordinate seamlessly.

Let me give you some concrete examples of what this looks like in practice:

- **Your smart home gets smarter**: Right now, you might have a smart thermostat, a security system, and some smart lights, but they don't really talk to each other. With MCP, they become a coordinated team. When your security system detects that you've left for work, it can tell your thermostat to save energy, your lights to turn off, and your entertainment system to go into standby mode. When you're coming home, your phone's location can trigger the whole house to prepare for your arrival: lights on, temperature adjusted, and maybe even your favorite music queued up.
- **Healthcare that actually connects**: Today, your fitness tracker knows your heart rate, your doctor has your medical history, your pharmacy has your prescriptions, and your

insurance company has your claims data. But they're all isolated islands of information. With MCP, these systems can work together (with your permission, of course). Your fitness tracker notices an irregular pattern, shares it with your health monitoring AI, which cross-references it with your medical history and automatically schedules a check-up with your doctor if needed.

- **Shopping that anticipates your needs**: Instead of getting random product recommendations, imagine AI systems that truly understand your preferences, budget, and needs. Your calendar AI knows you have a business trip coming up, your weather AI knows it's going to be cold at your destination, your wardrobe AI knows what you already own, and your budget AI knows how much you can spend. Together, they suggest exactly the right coat, find the best price, and even coordinate the delivery timing.
- **Work that actually works**: Picture this: You're working on a presentation for next week. Your research AI gathers relevant data, your writing AI helps structure your thoughts, your design AI creates compelling visuals, and your scheduling AI finds the best time for your presentation based on everyone's calendars and energy levels. Instead of juggling multiple tools and manually transferring information between them, everything flows seamlessly.

The key insight is that MCP isn't about making AI more complicated; it's about making it more helpful by letting different AI systems specialize and collaborate.

Why MCP matters for everyone

You might be thinking, "This sounds nice, but why should I care? I'm not a programmer or a tech person." Here's why MCP matters for everyone, regardless of your technical background:

- **It's about your time**: How much time do you spend each day switching between apps, copying information from one place to another, or explaining the same context to different systems? I bet it's more than you realize. MCP eliminates much of this friction. When AI systems can share context and coordinate, you spend less time being a human copy-paste machine and more time on things that matter to you.
  Let's think about a teacher's daily routine: checking email, updating lesson plans, entering grades, communicating with parents, ordering supplies, and coordinating with other teachers. Each task requires a different system, and they constantly must re-enter information or explain context. With MCP-enabled systems, their grading AI could automatically update their lesson planning AI about which concepts students are struggling with, which could then suggest modifications to upcoming lessons and automatically generate targeted practice materials.

- **It's about better decisions**: Right now, you make decisions with incomplete information because your various AI tools and apps don't share what they know. Your navigation app doesn't know about your calendar, your budget app doesn't know about your shopping habits, and your health app doesn't know about your stress levels from work.
  With MCP, you get AI assistance that has the full picture. Planning a weekend trip? Your AI team considers your budget, your calendar, your health goals, your social preferences, and even your past travel experiences to suggest options that truly fit your life.
- **It's about reducing frustration**: Have you ever felt like you're constantly training different AI systems? You tell Siri your preferences, then you must tell Alexa the same things, then you set up your smart home app, then your car's AI system. It's exhausting. MCP enables AI systems to learn from each other (with your permission). When you teach one AI system that you prefer morning meetings, that preference can be shared with other systems that need to know about your scheduling preferences. You train once, benefit everywhere.
- **It's about privacy and control**: You might assume that letting more systems talk to each other reduces your privacy; however, MCP was designed to put users in control. The core specification requires explicit user consent before any data is accessed, and hosts must not transmit resource data without permission. The protocol encourages implementers to provide clear UIs so you can decide what information is shared, with whom, and under what circumstances.
  In practice, this means MCP acts like a trusted personal assistant who understands your preferences and coordinates with services on your behalf, but who always asks before sharing sensitive information and gives you the ability to revoke access at any time. When implemented properly, MCP reduces the need to duplicate data across apps and lets you set fine-grained permissions, rather than surrendering your information to siloed systems.

> **Note**
>
> While MCP defines mechanisms for requesting user consent and managing permissions, it does not enforce security or authorization itself. The official specification focuses on connecting tools, not on deciding who can access them. Implementers are therefore responsible for adding identity checks, permission policies, and access controls. Your privacy ultimately depends on how each service implements these controls, so choose providers that take data protection seriously.

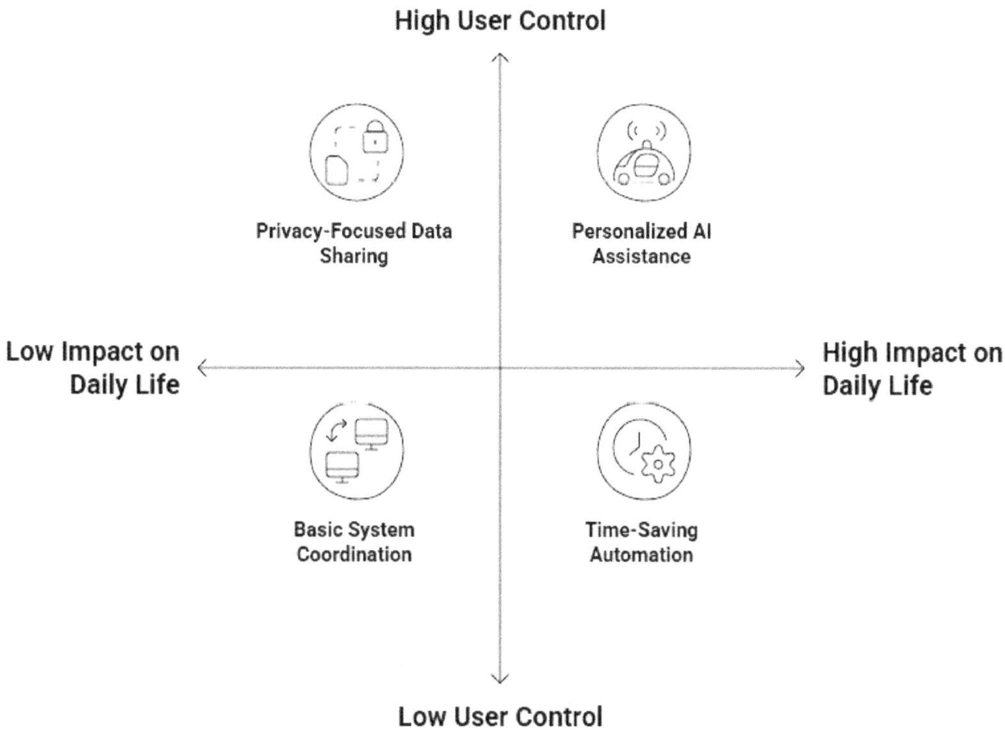

Figure 3.1 – Benefits of MCP

We've seen how fragmented systems frustrate users; now it's time to explore how MCP solves those issues in practice.

MCP in everyday scenarios

Let me walk you through some realistic scenarios to show how MCP might change your daily experience.

- **Morning routine revolution**: Currently, your morning might involve checking multiple apps: weather, calendar, news, traffic, and maybe a fitness app. Each one gives you a piece of the puzzle, but you must mentally combine all the information. With MCP, your morning briefing AI coordinates with all these systems to give you a personalized morning report: "Good morning! It's going to rain this afternoon, so I've moved your outdoor meeting to the conference room and reminded you to bring an umbrella. Your 9 A.M. meeting was moved to 9:30, which gives you time for that workout you've been trying to fit in. Traffic is light, but there's construction on your usual route, so I've found an alternative that's 5 minutes faster."

- **The intelligent shopping experience**: Today's shopping experience is fragmented. You might use one app to compare prices, another to read reviews, a third to check if something's in stock locally, and a fourth to see if you have coupons. Then you must remember what you already own to avoid buying duplicates. With MCP, your shopping AI team works together: "I noticed you're looking at winter coats. Based on your wardrobe inventory, you have a black wool coat but nothing waterproof. This jacket has great reviews for your climate, it's 20% off today, and it's available for pickup at the store you're driving past this afternoon. Should I reserve it for you?"
- **Healthcare that helps**: Right now, healthcare is incredibly fragmented. Your doctor doesn't know about your daily stress levels, your fitness tracker doesn't know about your medications, and your mental health app doesn't know about your physical symptoms. Imagine instead, your sleep tracker notices you've been restless, your calendar AI sees you have a stressful week ahead, your nutrition AI notices you've been stress-eating, and your health monitoring AI puts it all together to suggest some specific stress-management techniques and maybe recommend a check-in with your healthcare provider.
- **Travel planning that works**: Current travel planning involves juggling multiple websites and apps: flights, hotels, car rentals, restaurant recommendations, weather forecasts, currency converters, and more. You end up with a dozen confirmation emails and must manually coordinate everything. With MCP, instead of juggling flights, hotels, and reservations across multiple sites, your AI assistant can plan an entire trip in one go: it books a hotel, schedules a cooking class, makes dinner reservations, checks your work calendar for conflicts, and even configures your phone for local transport without you having to coordinate anything.
- **The smart home that thinks**: Today's smart homes are more like "connected homes." You can control things remotely, but they don't really think or coordinate. With MCP, your home becomes truly intelligent: It knows your family's schedules, preferences, and habits. When your teenager comes home from school, the house knows they usually have a snack and do homework, so it adjusts the lighting in the kitchen and study area, maybe plays some focus music, and ensures the Wi-Fi is optimized for their devices. When you're working late, it coordinates with your calendar to keep dinner warm and lets your family know your updated arrival time.
- **Financial management that makes sense**: Right now, your financial life is probably spread across multiple apps and accounts. Your banking app shows transactions, your investment app shows portfolio performance, your budget app tries to categorize spending, and your credit monitoring app watches for fraud. But none of them talk to each other. With MCP, your financial AI team provides holistic guidance: "I noticed

you're spending more on dining out this month, which is pushing you over your entertainment budget. However, you're under budget on groceries and transportation, so overall you're still on track. Also, that subscription you forgot about is renewing next week. Should I cancel it? And based on your spending patterns, you might want to consider the rewards credit card I found that would save you about $200 a year."

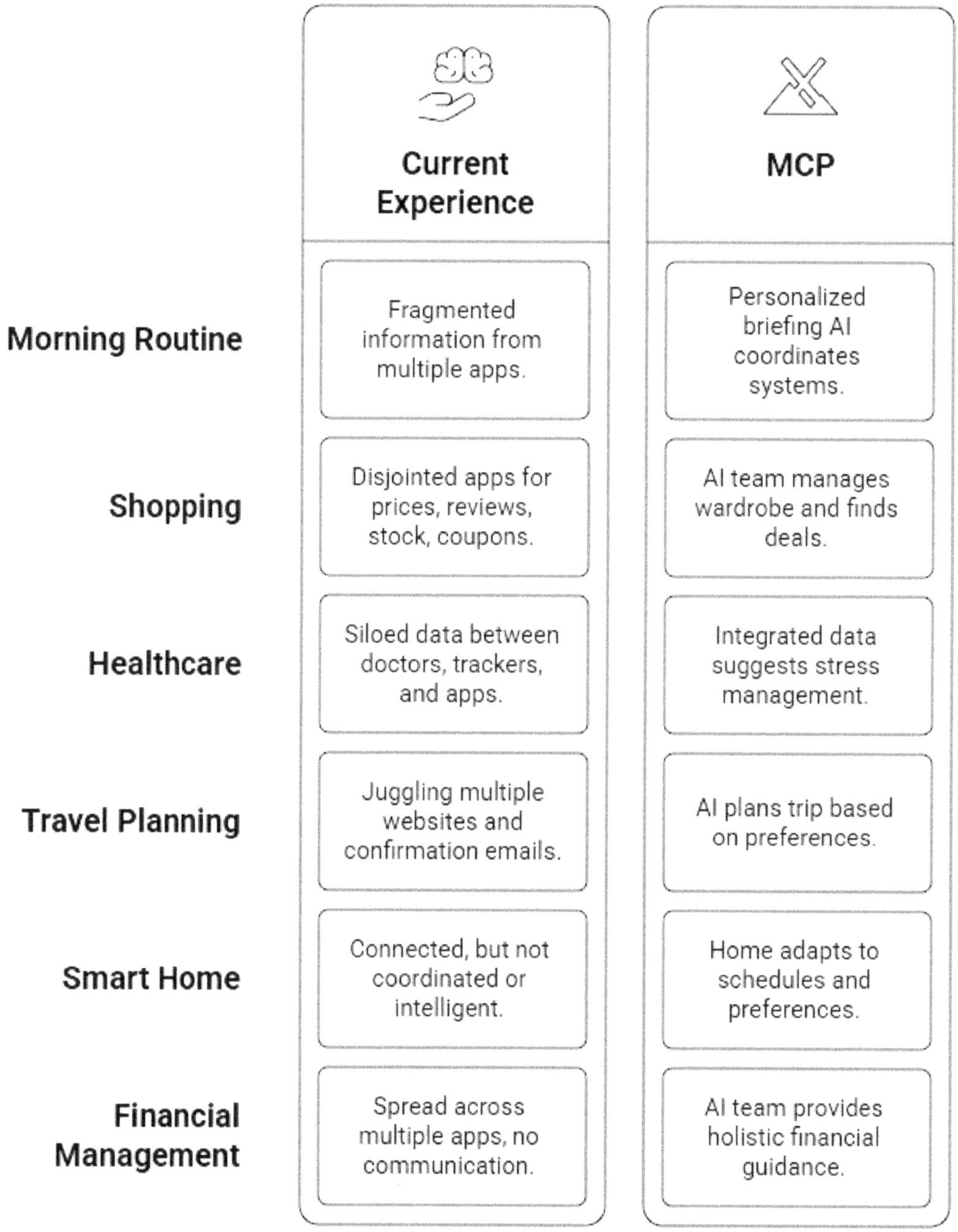

Figure 3.2 – MCP versus current experience

So far, we've looked at how MCP improves today's AI experiences. But MCP isn't just about the present; its real promise lies in what it unlocks next.

The future with MCP

Looking ahead, MCP isn't just about making current AI systems work better together; it's about enabling entirely new kinds of AI experiences that aren't possible today.

To see what's on the horizon, here are a few scenarios MCP could make possible:

- **Truly personalized AI assistants**: Imagine an AI assistant that truly knows you; not just your calendar and contacts, but your communication style, your decision-making patterns, your stress triggers, and your goals. This assistant could represent you in various digital interactions, making decisions you would make and communicating in your voice. For example, when you're in a meeting, your AI could be handling your email, scheduling follow-up meetings, ordering lunch, and even doing preliminary research for your next project. It's not just automation; it's delegation to a digital version of yourself.
- **Predictive life management**: With MCP enabling AI systems to share context and coordinate, we're moving toward AI that doesn't just respond to your requests but anticipates your needs. Your AI team might notice patterns you don't even see and proactively address issues before they become problems. Maybe your AI notices that you always get stressed during quarterly reports, so it starts preparing earlier, blocks out focused work time, and even suggests stress-management activities. Or, it notices that you tend to overspend when you're busy, so it automatically implements stricter budget controls during hectic periods.
- **Collaborative intelligence**: MCP enables not just your AI systems to work together, but your AI systems to collaborate with other people's AI systems. Imagine planning a group vacation where everyone's AI assistants coordinate to find dates that work for everyone, destinations that match everyone's preferences and budgets, and activities that the group will enjoy. Or, consider collaborative work projects where team members' AI assistants coordinate to optimize meeting schedules, share relevant research, and even identify potential conflicts or synergies before they become issues.
- **Adaptive environments**: As MCP enables better coordination between AI systems, our physical and digital environments will become more adaptive. Your car will coordinate with your home, your office, and your calendar to optimize your entire day. Your workspace will adapt to your energy levels, your current projects, and your collaboration needs.

While it may sound futuristic, the building blocks for these experiences are already in development. MCP provides a common standard to coordinate them, though the ecosystem is still maturing and real-world use cases are only beginning to emerge.

Before we wrap up, let's tackle some of the most common questions people ask me about MCP.

Common questions about MCP

Whenever I talk to non-technical people about MCP, I get similar questions. Let me address the most common ones.

- **"Is MCP going to make AI take over everything?"**
  This is probably the most common concern, and it's understandable. Rather than handing over control, MCP is designed to put you in charge. Instead of having AI systems that work in isolation and make decisions without full context, MCP enables AI systems to coordinate and provide better recommendations based on the information you decide to share.

  Think of it this way: would you rather have a financial advisor who only knows about your checking account, or one who understands your complete financial picture? An advisor with complete information can give you better advice, but you're still the one making the decisions.

- **"What about my privacy?"**
  This is a crucial question. MCP was designed with privacy as a core principle, meaning you explicitly decide what is shared and with whom. Because the protocol reduces the need to duplicate your personal information across multiple systems and encourages sharing insights without exposing raw data, it can strengthen privacy when implemented responsibly.

  For example, your health AI might communicate to your fitness AI that you should focus on stress reduction this week without disclosing the underlying medical details, thanks to fine-grained controls on what data flows where.

- **"Will this make everything more complicated?"**
  The opposite. MCP makes your experience simpler by handling the complexity behind the scenes. Instead of you having to coordinate between multiple AI systems and apps, they coordinate with each other. You interact with fewer interfaces but get more comprehensive and intelligent assistance.

- **"What if I don't want all this AI assistance?"**
  That's completely fine! MCP is about enabling better AI coordination for those who want it, not forcing AI on everyone. You can choose which AI systems to use, how much

they coordinate, and what level of assistance you want. It's like having the option of a personal assistant. Some people love it, while others prefer to handle things themselves.

- **"When will this actually happen?"**
  The technology is available now, and early implementations are rolling out. Several major tech companies, including Google, Microsoft, OpenAI, Replit, and Zapier, have announced support for MCP, and adoption is growing across the AI ecosystem. While it's still early, you can expect to see MCP-enabled features gradually appear in your tools and services over the next few years as the ecosystem matures.
- **"Do I need to learn anything new?"**
  You don't need to learn programming or master new interfaces to benefit from MCP. However, it does help to understand how to grant and manage permissions, how your data may be shared between services, and how to troubleshoot multi-agent interactions. Knowing about these concepts will allow you to maintain control and privacy as you adopt MCP-enabled systems.

While you don't need to become a technical expert, there are some things you can do to prepare for and benefit from MCP-enabled future.

Preparing for an MCP-enabled future

As AI tools and apps start working together more smoothly through systems such as MCP, here are the key benefits you can expect in real-world situations:

Here are the main advantages MCP delivers:

- **Start thinking about your digital ecosystem**: Take inventory of the AI-powered tools and services you use: your smartphone assistant, smart home devices, navigation apps, shopping apps, financial apps, health and fitness trackers, and work tools. Think about how these could work better together and what kinds of coordination would be most valuable to you.
- **Consider your privacy preferences**: Start thinking about what information you're comfortable sharing between systems and what you want to keep separate. MCP will give you more granular control over data sharing, but it's helpful to think through your preferences in advance.
- **Experiment with current AI tools**: The more comfortable you become with current AI assistants and tools, the easier it will be to benefit from MCP-enabled coordination. Try using voice assistants, smart home controls, or AI-powered apps in your daily routine.

- **Stay informed about your options**: As MCP-enabled services become available, take time to understand what they offer and how they protect your privacy. Look for services that give you clear control over data sharing and coordination.
- **Think about your goals**: Consider what you want to achieve with AI assistance. Do you want to save time? Make better decisions? Reduce stress? Having clear goals will help you choose which MCP-enabled services will be most valuable to you.

Summary

MCP represents a fundamental shift in how AI systems work together. For non-technical users, this means moving from a world of isolated AI tools that require constant human coordination to a world of collaborative AI systems that work together seamlessly.

This isn't about replacing human intelligence or decision-making; it's about giving you AI assistance that's more helpful, more efficient, and more aligned with your actual needs and preferences.

The coffee shop analogy I started with is apt: MCP enables AI systems to work together like a well-coordinated team, each contributing its expertise toward your goals. The result is AI assistance that's greater than the sum of its parts.

As we move into this MCP-enabled future, the key is to stay informed about your options, think carefully about your preferences, and choose AI services that give you the level of assistance and control you want.

The future of AI isn't about one super-intelligent system that does everything; it's about teams of specialized AI systems that work together to help you live better, work smarter, and achieve your goals more effectively. MCP is the technology that makes this vision possible.

In the next chapter, we'll get into the technical components and interfaces that make MCP possible by examining how resource providers, tool providers, and security interfaces work together to create seamless AI coordination. Don't worry, you don't need to understand every detail to benefit from MCP, but this overview will give you a sense of the machinery behind the magic.

Get this book's PDF copy, code bundle, and more

Scan the QR code (or go to `packtpub.com/unlock`). Search for this book by name, confirm the edition, and then follow the steps on the page.

UNLOCK NOW

Note: Have your invoice handy. Purchases made directly from the Packt website don't require an invoice.

Part 2

Architecture and Core Implementation

With the foundational concepts in place, this part takes you into the technical heart of MCP. You will examine MCP components and interfaces in detail, understand the client-server architecture and its standardized primitives, and then build working MCP systems from both the server and client perspectives. These four chapters provide the core engineering knowledge needed to implement MCP in real projects. By the end of this part, you will be able to design, build, and connect MCP servers and clients using Python, with a clear understanding of resource providers, tool providers, communication mechanisms, and session management.

This part of the book includes the following chapters:

- *Chapter 4, MCP Components and Interfaces*
- *Chapter 5, MCP Architecture Overview*
- *Chapter 6, Server-Side Implementation*
- *Chapter 7, Client-Side Integration*

4

MCP Components and Interfaces

> *Coming together is a beginning, staying together is progress, and working together is success.*
>
> *– Henry Ford*

Alright, let's roll up our sleeves and get into the meat of how MCP works. If the previous chapters were about the "why" of MCP, this chapter is about the "how." We're going to explore the core components that make MCP tick, and I'll show you exactly how to implement each one with working code examples.

I must admit, when I first started working with MCP, I was a bit overwhelmed by all the different interfaces and components. It felt like learning a new language. But here's what I discovered: MCP is elegantly simple once you understand the core concepts. It's like learning to drive; there are a lot of controls and rules, but once you get the hang of it, it becomes second nature.

The beauty of MCP lies in its modular design. Instead of one monolithic protocol that tries to handle everything, MCP is built from several focused interfaces that each handle specific aspects of AI system communication. Think of it like a well-designed toolkit; each tool has a specific purpose, but they all work together seamlessly.

In this chapter, we'll be covering the following topics:

- Overview of MCP architecture components
- Client features

Overview of MCP architecture components

Before we dive into the specifics, let me give you the big picture. MCP consists of several key components, each with a specific role:

- **Servers and clients**: These are the fundamental building blocks. Servers provide capabilities (tools, resources, and prompts), while clients consume these capabilities. It's a classic client-server architecture but designed specifically for AI systems. We'll explore server and client roles more deeply in *Chapter 5*, including how they discover and negotiate with each other.
- **Resource providers**: These expose data and information that AI systems can access. Think of them as the "knowledge base" components; they provide context, documents, databases, APIs, and other information sources.
- **Tool providers**: These expose actions that AI systems can perform. They're the "hands" of the AI system; they can execute code, make API calls, manipulate files, send emails, and perform other actions in the real world.
- **Prompt providers**: These expose reusable prompt templates and patterns. They're like the "conversation starters" that help AI systems communicate more effectively.
- **Security interfaces**: These handle authentication, authorization, and secure communication between components. They ensure that AI systems can trust each other and that sensitive information is protected.
- **Discovery interfaces**: These help AI systems find and connect to each other. They're like the "yellow pages" of the MCP ecosystem.
- **Registry**: This serves as a central catalog service for MCP server implementations.
- **Sampling**: This controls how the client generates or selects model outputs.
- **Roots**: These define starting contexts for conversations.
- **Elicitation**: This governs how results are gathered from a model.

It's worth noting that the official MCP specification defines three core **server features** (resources, prompts, and tools) and three **client features** (sampling, roots, and elicitation). Discovery and registry services are an active area of discussion within the MCP community, but are not yet part of the formal standard. Dynamic discovery is being explored as a future enhancement to allow AI agents to automatically detect and connect to new services.

Let's see the core server-side components at a high level here and have a dedicated chapter focusing on all these in much more detail.

Resource provider interface

Resource providers are the knowledge base of your MCP system. They expose data, documents, databases, and other information sources that AI systems can access. Think of them as read-only data sources that provide context and information.

The official MCP specification lists resources as one of the three features that servers can offer, alongside prompts and tools. Resource providers deliver structured context and data that can be consumed by AI clients.

Earlier, we built a simple task manager, where tasks are stored via a resource provider and manipulated via a tool provider. In that example, we implemented several resource providers:

- `tasks://all`: Provides access to all tasks in the system
- `tasks://active`: Provides access to only active tasks
- `users://all`: Provides team member information
- `analytics://task_metrics`: Provides calculated metrics and analytics

The key insight about resource providers is that they're not just static data dumps. They can provide computed information, filtered views, and context-specific data. Notice how our `analytics://task_metrics` resource calculates metrics on demand rather than storing pre-computed values.

The following example shows how to build a resource provider capable of serving multiple document types and formats. It demonstrates dynamic retrieval and metadata handling within MCP:

1. Define a document provider and initial document store:

```
class DocumentResourceProvider:
    """A resource provider that exposes various document types and
formats."""

    def __init__(self):
        self.documents = {
            "project_charter": {
                "title": "Project Charter",
                "content": "This project aims to...",
                "format": "markdown",
                "last_modified": datetime.now() - timedelta(days=5)
            },
            "api_spec": {
```

```
                "title": "API Specification",
                "content": "# REST API Documentation\n\n## Endpoints\n...",
                "format": "markdown",
                "last_modified": datetime.now() - timedelta(days=2)
            }
        }
```

Note

The documents dictionary in this example stores content in memory for simplicity. In-memory storage is fast, but it is volatile and non-persistent; data is lost when the process stops. It is also expensive to scale and can lead to data loss if the machine crashes. For production systems, implement the resource provider against a persistent datastore (e.g., a relational database, object storage, or a distributed document store) to ensure durability and scalability.

This class demonstrates how to implement a custom resource provider. The documents dictionary holds several example documents with titles, contents, formats, and modification dates. Resource providers play the role of the knowledge base in MCP, exposing structured data that clients can query. By encapsulating documents within an object, the provider can control access, perform searches, and compute additional views.

2. List available documents and computed resources:

```
@server.list_resources()
async def list_resources():
    resources = []
    # Individual documents
    for doc_id, doc in self.documents.items():
        resources.append(Resource(
            uri=f"doc://{doc_id}",
            name=doc["title"],
            description=f"{doc['format']} document, last modified
{doc['last_modified'].strftime('%Y-%m-%d')}",
            mimeType="text/markdown" if doc["format"] == "markdown" else
"text/plain"
        ))
    # Computed resources
    resources.extend([
```

```
        Resource(uri="docs://recent", name="Recent Documents",
description="Documents modified in the last week", mimeType="application/
json"),
        Resource(uri="docs://search", name="Document Search",
description="Search across all documents (use query parameter)",
mimeType="application/json")
    ])
    return resources
```

The `list_resources` function advertises individual document URIs and two computed collections: `docs://recent` for recently modified documents and `docs://search` for performing searches. This pattern echoes the earlier example's `_register_resources` method, showing how resource providers can offer both direct and derived views over their data. Clients can discover what information is available by calling `list_resources`, and then they can choose the specific resource they need.

3. Read documents and filter by recency or query:

```
@server.read_resource()
async def read_resource(uri: str):
    if uri.startswith("doc://"):
        doc_id = uri[6:]  # remove "doc://" prefix
        if doc_id in self.documents:
            doc = self.documents[doc_id]
            return [TextContent(type="text", text=doc["content"])]
        else:
            raise ValueError(f"Document {doc_id} not found")
    elif uri == "docs://recent":
        cutoff = datetime.now() - timedelta(days=7)
        recent_docs = {
            doc_id: doc for doc_id, doc in self.documents.items()
            if doc["last_modified"] > cutoff}
        return [TextContent(type="text", text=json.dumps(recent_docs,
indent=2))]
    elif uri.startswith("docs://search"):
        query = "api"
# In a real implementation, this would come from URI parameters
        matching_docs = {doc_id: doc for doc_id, doc in
self.documents.items() if query.lower() in doc["content"].lower() or
query.lower() in doc["title"].lower()}
        return [TextContent(type="text", text=json.dumps(matching_docs,
```

```
indent=2))]
    else:
        raise ValueError(f"Unknown resource: {uri}")
```

The `read_resource` handler returns the full content for a specific document, a JSON listing of documents modified in the last week, or search results. It shows how resource providers can offer filtered or computed datasets instead of static files. By supporting both exact identifiers and pattern-based URIs, the provider becomes a versatile source of context for AI agents.

Resource providers are incredibly powerful because they can do the following:

- Provide real-time data
- Filter and transform information based on context
- Aggregate data from multiple sources
- Implement access control and permissions
- Cache expensive computations

Tool provider interface

Tool providers are the hands of your MCP system. They expose actions that AI systems can perform in the real world. Unlike resources (which are read-only), tools can modify state, interact with external systems, and perform complex operations. The official MCP specification designates tools as one of the core server features available to clients.

The key to designing good tools is to think about the level of abstraction. You don't want tools that are too low-level (such as "write byte to memory address") or too high-level (such as "solve all my problems"). You want tools that represent meaningful actions that an AI system might need to perform.

The following `EmailToolProvider` exposes three separate email operations, which are sending a message immediately, scheduling a message for later, and creating reusable templates illustrating how a single provider can register multiple tools:

1. Define email tools and their input schemas:

```
class EmailToolProvider:
    """Tool provider for email operations."""

    def __init__(self, email_service):
        self.email_service = email_service

    @server.list_tools()
```

```
    async def list_tools():
        return [
            Tool(
                name="send_email",
                description="Send an email to one or more recipients",
                inputSchema={...}
            ),
            Tool(
                name="schedule_email",
                description="Schedule an email to be sent at a specific
time",
                inputSchema={...}
            ),
            Tool(
                name="create_email_template",
                description="Create a reusable email template",
                inputSchema={...}
            )
        ]
```

This provider exposes three email-related tools: immediate sending, scheduling, and template creation. Each tool is described with a name, a human-friendly description, and a JSON schema specifying the expected arguments. This aligns with the idea that tool providers are the hands of an AI system performing actions such as sending emails or scheduling them while still offering clear interfaces for clients to follow.

2. Handle email tool calls and send messages:

```
@server.call_tool()
async def call_tool(name: str, arguments: dict):
    if name == "send_email":
        return await self._send_email(arguments)
    elif name == "schedule_email":
        return await self._schedule_email(arguments)
    elif name == "create_email_template":
        return await self._create_template(arguments)
    else:
        raise ValueError(f"Unknown tool: {name}")

async def _send_email(self, args):
    """Send an email immediately."""
```

```
        try:
            # Validate email addresses
            for email in args["to"]:
                if "@" not in email:
                    raise ValueError(f"Invalid email address: {email}")
            # Send the email using the underlying service
            message_id = await self.email_service.send(
                to=args["to"],
                subject=args["subject"],
                body=args["body"],
                cc=args.get("cc", []),
                priority=args.get("priority", "normal")
            )
            result = {"success": True, "message_id": message_id, "sent_to":
args["to"], "sent_at": datetime.now().isoformat()}
            return [
                TextContent(
                    type="text", text=json.dumps(result, indent=2)
                )
            ]
        except Exception as e:
            result = {"success": False, "error": str(e)}
            return [
                TextContent(
                    type="text", text=json.dumps(result, indent=2)
                )
            ]
```

The `call_tool` function dispatches each tool invocation to a corresponding coroutine. `_send_email` validates addresses, sends the message using an injected service, and returns a success payload; any exceptions are caught and reported. Similar coroutines (not shown) handle scheduling and template creation. This design emphasizes clear error handling and idempotent operations, echoing the guidelines for good tool design principles, as mentioned next.

Good tool design follows several principles:

- **Atomic operations**: Each tool should do one thing well
- **Clear interfaces**: The input schema should be unambiguous
- **Error handling**: Tools should handle errors gracefully and provide useful feedback

- **Idempotency**: When possible, tools should be safe to call multiple times
- **Validation**: Always validate inputs before performing actions

Prompt providers interfaces

Prompts supply precomposed messages that guide the model's behavior. They can encode system instructions (e.g., the policy for interacting with a travel booking API) or user-facing text (e.g., a stand-up meeting template). Prompts enable the reuse of tested instructions and ensure consistent interactions across sessions.

Servers implement two operations for prompts:

- `listPrompts()`: Returns a catalog of prompt identifiers and metadata. Each entry includes a prompt ID, a human-readable name, and a description. Servers may also return a `help` field describing how the prompt should be used.
- `getPrompt(promptId, [args])`: Returns the content of the specified prompt. Some prompts accept optional arguments (e.g., `date` or `userName`) that customize the returned messages.

Prompts are returned as an array of prompt messages. Each message contains a role (e.g., `system`, `user`, or `assistant`) and a `content` field. The `content` field is typically text but may include embedded resources or links; the `contentType` annotation specifies the MIME type.

The following pseudocode illustrates a minimal prompt provider that generates two prompts: a daily summary and a stand-up report. Both prompts read data from the `tasks` and `users` dictionaries:

```
"""Task Prompt Provider for MCP servers."""

from typing import Any, Optional

class TaskPromptProvider:
    """Provides prompt templates for task-related operations."""

    def __init__(self, tasks: dict, users: dict) -> None:
        """
        Initialize the prompt provider.

        Args:
            tasks: Dictionary of tasks keyed by task ID
            users: Dictionary of users keyed by user ID
        """
```

```
        self.tasks = tasks
        self.users = users

    def list_prompts(self) -> list[dict[str, str]]:
        """
        List all available prompt templates.

        Returns:
            List of prompt metadata dictionaries
        """
        return [
            {
                "id": "dailySummary",
                "displayName": "Daily Summary",
                "description": "Summarise open tasks",
            },
            {
                "id": "standupReport",
                "displayName": "Stand up Report",
                "description": "Report tasks per user",
            },
        ]

    def get_prompt(
        self, prompt_id: str, args: Optional[dict] = None
) -> list[dict[str, str]]:
        """
        Get a specific prompt template with context.

        Args:
            prompt_id: The ID of the prompt to retrieve
            args: Optional arguments for the prompt

        Returns:
            List of message dictionaries with role and content

        Raises:
            KeyError: If the prompt ID is not found
        """
        if prompt_id == "dailySummary":
            return self._build_daily_summary()
```

```
        elif prompt_id == "standupReport":
            return self._build_standup_report()
        else:
            raise KeyError(f"Prompt not found: {prompt_id}")

    def _build_daily_summary(self) -> list[dict[str, str]]:
        """Build a summary of open tasks."""
        lines = [
            f"• {task['title']} ({task['status']})"
            for task in self.tasks.values()
        ]
        content = "Here is today's task summary:\n" + "\n".join(lines)
        return [{"role": "system", "content": content}]

    def _build_standup_report(self) -> list[dict[str, str]]:
        """Build a standup report grouped by user."""
        report_lines = []

        for uid, user in self.users.items():
            user_tasks = [
                task["title"]
                for task in self.tasks.values()
                if task.get("assignedTo") == uid
            ]
            task_summary = ", ".join(user_tasks) if user_tasks else "no tasks"
            report_lines.append(f"{user['name']}: {task_summary}")

        content = "Stand up report:\n" + "\n".join(report_lines)
        return [{"role": "user", "content": content}]
```

In practice, prompts often embed domain-specific instructions such as system prompts that direct the model to act within defined boundaries. These should be authored carefully: keep instructions concise, avoid ambiguous language, and emphasize that the model should invoke tools rather than hallucinate answers.

When defining prompts, consider the following guidelines:

- **Modularity**: Break complex instructions into multiple prompt messages. Use the `system` role for high-level guidelines and the `user` role for specific tasks.
- **Parameterization**: Allow clients to supply arguments to customize prompts (e.g., user names, dates, or time zones). Define default values where appropriate.

- **Clarity**: Use clear, concise language and explicitly state when the model should call a tool rather than answer directly. For example, a travel booking prompt might instruct, "If the user asks about flight availability, call the `searchFlights` tool rather than guessing schedules."
- **Versioning**: Provide version identifiers in prompt metadata so clients can select appropriate prompts. If a prompt changes semantics, update its version and, optionally, keep the old version available for backward compatibility.

Security interfaces

Security is crucial in MCP systems because you're enabling AI systems to access data and perform actions. The security model needs to be both robust and flexible. The MCP specification explicitly calls out security principles such as user consent and control, data privacy, tool safety, and sampling controls, and implementers are encouraged to build robust consent and authorization flows.

MCP security operates on several levels:

- **Authentication**: Verifying the identity of clients and servers
- **Authorization**: Determining what actions a client is allowed to perform
- **Encryption**: Protecting data in transit
- **Audit logging**: Tracking what actions were performed by whom

Here's an example of how to implement security in an MCP server:

1. Initialize `SecureMCPServer` and its security middleware:

```
class SecureMCPServer:
    """An MCP server with comprehensive security features."""

    def __init__(self, name: str, api_key: str):
        self.server = Server(name)
        self.api_key = api_key
        self.authorized_clients = {}
        self.audit_log = []
        self.rate_limits = {}
        # Register security middleware
        self._setup_security()

    def _setup_security(self):
        """Set up security middleware and handlers."""
        original_handle_request = self.server._handle_request
```

```
        async def secure_handle_request(request):
            # Authenticate the request
            if not await self._authenticate_request(request):
                raise ValueError("Authentication failed")
            # Check rate limits
            if not await self._check_rate_limit(request):
                raise ValueError("Rate limit exceeded")
            # Log the request
            await self._log_request(request)
            # Process the request
            response = await original_handle_request(request)
            # Log the response
            await self._log_response(request, response)
            return response

        self.server._handle_request = secure_handle_request
```

Security interfaces ensure that only authorized clients can invoke tools and resources and that requests are logged for auditing. In the `SecureMCPServer` constructor, the server stores an API key, sets up dictionaries for authorized clients, an audit log, and rate-limit tracking, then calls `_setup_security`. The `setup_security` method wraps the server's internal request handler with a `secure_handle_request` coroutine that authenticates the request, enforces rate limits, logs the request and response, and then delegates to the original handler.

2. Perform authentication, rate limiting, and audit logging:

```
    async def _authenticate_request(self, request) -> bool:
        """Authenticate incoming requests."""
        auth_header = request.get("auth")
        if not auth_header:
            return False
        # Simple API key check
        return auth_header == self.api_key

    async def _check_rate_limit(self, request) -> bool:
        """Check if the request exceeds rate limits."""
        client_id = request.get("client_id", "unknown")
        current_time = time.time()
        if client_id not in self.rate_limits:
```

```
            self.rate_limits[client_id] = []
        # Remove old requests (older than 1 minute)
        self.rate_limits[client_id] = [
            req_time for req_time in self.rate_limits[client_id]
            if current_time - req_time < 60
        ]
        # Check if under limit (max 100 requests per minute)
        if len(self.rate_limits[client_id]) >= 100:
            return False
        # Add current request timestamp
        self.rate_limits[client_id].append(current_time)
        return True

    async def _log_request(self, request):
        """Log incoming requests for audit purposes."""
        log_entry = {
            "timestamp": datetime.now().isoformat(),
            "type": "request",
            "method": request.get("method"),
            "client_id": request.get("client_id", "unknown"),
            "request_id": request.get("id")
        }
        self.audit_log.append(log_entry)

    async def _log_response(self, request, response):
        """Log responses for audit purposes."""
        log_entry = {
            "timestamp": datetime.now().isoformat(),
            "type": "response",
            "request_id": request.get("id"),
            "success": not response.get("error"),
            "response_size": len(str(response))
        }
        self.audit_log.append(log_entry)

    def get_audit_log(self) -> List[Dict]:
        """Get the audit log for security monitoring."""
        return self.audit_log.copy()
```

These methods implement the core of the security layer. `_authenticate_request` checks the provided API key, `_check_rate_limit` ensures that no client can exceed a defined request rate, and the logging functions record both requests and responses for later review. Collectively, they enforce the security principles of authentication, authorization, audit logging, and rate limiting that are essential in real-world MCP deployments.

Security in MCP systems should also consider the following:

- **Principle of least privilege**: Give clients only the minimum permissions they need
- **Defense in depth**: Use multiple layers of security
- **Regular security audits**: Monitor and review access patterns
- **Secure defaults**: Make the secure option the default option

Discovery interfaces

Discovery interfaces help AI systems find and connect to each other. This is crucial in large MCP ecosystems where you might have dozens or hundreds of different servers providing various capabilities.

The following example implements a simple discovery service that allows clients to query available MCP servers. It illustrates how discovery might work even though it's not yet part of the spec:

1. Set up a discovery service and its tools:

```
class MCPDiscoveryService:
    """A service for discovering available MCP servers and their 
capabilities."""

    def __init__(self):
        self.registered_servers = {}
        self.server = Server("mcp-discovery")
        self._setup_discovery_interface()

    def _setup_discovery_interface(self):
        """Set up the discovery interface."""
        @self.server.list_tools()
        async def list_tools():
            return [
                Tool(
                    name="register_server",
                    description="Register an MCP server with the discovery 
service",
                    inputSchema={...}
```

```
                ),
                Tool(
                    name="discover_servers",
                    description="Discover servers based on capabilities or
tags",
                    inputSchema={...}
                ),
                Tool(
                    name="get_server_info",
                    description="Get detailed information about a specific
server",
                    inputSchema={...}
                )
            ]

        @self.server.call_tool()
        async def call_tool(name: str, arguments: dict):
            if name == "register_server":
                return await self._register_server(arguments)
            elif name == "discover_servers":
                return await self._discover_servers(arguments)
            elif name == "get_server_info":
                return await self._get_server_info(arguments)
            else:
                raise ValueError(f"Unknown tool: {name}")
```

Discovery interfaces help AI systems find and connect to each other. This class maintains a registry of servers and exposes three tools: one to register a server, another to search for servers based on capabilities or tags, and a third to fetch detailed information about a specific server. The `call_tool` handler routes incoming requests to private methods, mirroring the pattern seen in earlier examples.

2. Register servers and discover them by capabilities or tags:

```
async def _register_server(self, args):
    """Register a new server."""
    server_info = {
        "name": args["name"],
        "description": args["description"],
        "endpoint": args["endpoint"],
        "capabilities": args["capabilities"],
```

```
            "tags": args.get("tags", []),
            "registered_at": datetime.now().isoformat(),
            "last_seen": datetime.now().isoformat()
        }
        self.registered_servers[args["name"]] = server_info
        result = {"success": True, "message": f"Server '{args['name']}'
    registered successfully"}
        return [TextContent(type="text", text=json.dumps(result, indent=2))]

    async def _discover_servers(self, args):
        """Discover servers based on criteria."""
        required_capabilities = args.get("capabilities", [])
        required_tags = args.get("tags", [])
        matching_servers = []
        for server_name, server_info in self.registered_servers.items():
            # Check capabilities
            if required_capabilities and not all(cap in
    server_info["capabilities"] for cap in required_capabilities):
                continue
            # Check tags
            if required_tags and not any(
                tag in server_info["tags"] for tag in required_tags
            ):
                continue
            matching_servers.append(server_info)
        result = {
            "query": args, "matches": len(matching_servers),
            "servers": matching_servers}
        return [
            TextContent(
                type="text", text=json.dumps(result, indent=2)
            )
        ]
```

The `_register_server` method stores metadata about a new MCP server and returns a confirmation. `_discover_servers` filters the registry based on required capabilities or tags, allowing clients to find servers that meet their needs. This dynamic discovery capability reflects the future-looking aspect of MCP highlighted in the chapter:

although standardized discovery is still an active discussion, such registries could let agents automatically detect and integrate new services.

3. Retrieve detailed information about a specific server:

```
async def _get_server_info(self, args):
    """Get detailed information about a server."""
    server_name = args["server_name"]
    if server_name not in self.registered_servers:
        raise ValueError(f"Server '{server_name}' not found")
    server_info = self.registered_servers[server_name]
    return [
        TextContent(
            type="text", text=json.dumps(server_info, indent=2)
        )
    ]
```

Finally, `_get_server_info` looks up a server by name and returns its stored metadata or raises an error if the server is unknown. Together, these discovery functions provide a simple but powerful registry that complements the server and client features defined in the MCP specification. They illustrate how discovery interfaces could serve as a "yellow pages" for AI services.

Discovery services enable the following:

- **Dynamic service discovery**: Find services at runtime
- **Load balancing**: Distribute requests across multiple servers
- **Health monitoring**: Track which services are available
- **Capability matching**: Find services that provide specific capabilities

While this section describes a discovery interface for illustration, as mentioned earlier, such functionality is not yet part of the official MCP specification. The community is actively discussing the creation of a standardized registry to support dynamic discovery of MCP servers. Articles exploring MCP's future suggest that a registry could let AI agents automatically detect and integrate new services at runtime.

While dynamic discovery isn't yet standardized, MCP already defines other providers (prompt providers, tool providers, and resource providers) and security interfaces that work together to orchestrate AI systems. These components and their interactions are covered in subsequent chapters.

Let's see the few client-side components at a high level here. We have covered the client side integration in detail in *Chapter 7*.

Client features

While servers provide resources, tools, and prompts, clients control how model outputs are generated and persisted. MCP defines three client-side features, which we will see at a very high level.

Sampling

Sampling controls how text is generated from the model. Parameters include temperature, top-p (nucleus) sampling, and stop sequences. Clients may set a global sampling policy or adjust settings for specific turns. For example, a client might generate a creative draft with a high temperature and then reduce the temperature when calling a tool to ensure deterministic arguments.

For example, suppose the user asks the model to brainstorm product names. The client could set `temperature=0.9` and `top_p=0.95` to encourage diverse outputs. Once the model chooses a name and prepares to call the `createProduct` tool, the client reduces `temperature` to `0` to ensure that the arguments match the schema.

Roots

Roots provide a persistent filesystem-like storage accessible to the model across calls. Roots contain files or directories that the model can read and write, enabling tasks such as saving code snippets or storing intermediate results. The client controls which files are exposed by specifying a set of allowed directories when creating a root. Roots are sandboxed: they cannot access arbitrary system files, and each root belongs to a specific session. When the session ends, the root can be persisted or discarded according to client policy.

Elicitation

Elicitation allows the server to request information directly from the end user when the model cannot proceed autonomously. For instance, a travel booking agent may need explicit approval before charging a credit card. During a tool call, the server returns an elicitation request specifying what information is needed. The client then pauses the model, displays a prompt to the user, and captures the response. Once the user responds, the client resumes the tool call with additional data. Elicitation keeps humans in the loop and ensures compliance with policies such as payment authorization.

Summary

In this chapter, we explored MCP's architecture from a systems perspective, examining server and client roles, the core features they expose, and how resource, tool, and prompt providers fit together. We built a working task manager example and outlined discovery services that may become part of future MCP standards.

This concludes *Part I* of our journey into MCP. We've covered the foundational concepts, theoretical background, practical implications, and technical components that make MCP possible. In *Part II*, we'll dive deeper into the architecture and implementation details, exploring how to build robust MCP systems in production environments.

In *Chapter 5*, we'll take a deeper look into MCP's server and client interactions, client-server architecture, core components, communication mechanisms, message formats and protocols, and, finally, security and authentication framework.

5

MCP Architecture Overview

Architecture is about the important stuff. Whatever that is.

– Ralph Johnson

You know what's funny? I've been building distributed systems for over a decade, and I still get that little thrill when I see a well-designed architecture. It's like looking at a perfectly organized toolbox: everything has its place, everything serves a purpose, and somehow, the whole thing just... works.

MCP's architecture gave me that feeling the first time I really dug into it. Not because it's revolutionary, though it is clever, but because it's so refreshingly *sensible*. After years of wrestling with proprietary APIs, custom protocols, and the inevitable spaghetti code that comes from trying to make incompatible systems talk to each other, MCP feels like someone finally said, "*You know what? Let's just do this right.*"

But here's the thing about good architecture: it looks simple from the outside, but there's usually a lot of careful thinking underneath. MCP is no exception. What appears to be a straightforward client-server setup embodies years of lessons learned from distributed systems, web protocols, and, perhaps most importantly, the specific challenges of AI system integration.

In this chapter, you'll see how MCP is put together: we'll review its core components (resources, tools, and prompts), examine the simple primitives that let clients list and use them, explore MCP's use of JSON-RPC and message structure, discuss security considerations, and build a minimal MCP server. Understanding these pieces up front will make the technical details that follow easier to digest and will show you why MCP's architecture is both flexible and practical.

In this chapter, we'll be covering the following topics:

- Client-server architecture
- Core components and their relationships
- Standardized primitives
- Communication mechanisms
- Message formats and protocols
- Security and authentication framework

Client-server architecture

Let's start with the basics, because honestly, this is where a lot of people get confused. When we say MCP uses a "client-server architecture," we're not talking about your typical web application setup. This isn't like a browser talking to a web server, though there are some similarities.

In MCP, the relationship is more nuanced. In MCP, the server acts as a specialized interface that knows how to locate specific information and execute certain tasks. The client, who is usually an AI application or agent, is like a researcher who needs access to that information and those capabilities.

But here's where it gets interesting. Unlike a traditional web server that just serves up static content or processes simple requests, an MCP server is designed to be *contextually aware*. It understands not just what you're asking for, but why you might be asking for it and how it relates to other information in the system.

I remember the first time I tried to explain this to my team. One of the developers asked, "*So it's just an API server?*" And I found myself struggling to articulate the difference. Yes, it's technically an API server, but it's an API server that's been designed specifically for the needs of AI systems. It's like the difference between a regular hammer and a specialized tool designed for a specific craft – they might look similar, but one is purpose-built for the job. Unlike a traditional API server, where the client must know in advance which endpoints exist and how to call them, an MCP server is built specifically for LLMs. It provides dynamic discovery and standardized interactions: the client can ask the server what tools and resources are available and receive a machine-readable list of functions, input/output formats, and usage examples. Because all MCP servers speak the same protocol, an AI agent can connect to a new server at runtime without prior integration work.

The client-server model in MCP serves several crucial purposes.

First, it provides a clear separation of concerns. The server handles the complexities of data access, tool execution, and resource management, while the client focuses on the AI-specific logic, reasoning, planning, and decision-making. This separation isn't just good software engineering; it's essential for building systems that can scale and evolve.

Second, the client-server architecture enables what I like to call *capability distribution*. Instead of trying to cram every possible capability into a single monolithic AI system, you can distribute different capabilities across multiple specialized servers. Need access to a company's internal documents? There's an MCP server for that. Need to execute code in a sandboxed environment? Different server. Need to access real-time market data? Yet another server.

This distribution has profound implications for how we think about AI system design. Instead of building increasingly complex monoliths, we can compose systems from smaller, focused components. It's like the microservices revolution, but specifically tailored for AI workloads. The architecture also supports what the MCP specification calls *capability negotiation*. When a client connects to a server, they don't just establish a connection; they have a conversation about what the server can do and what the client needs. This negotiation process ensures that both sides understand the available capabilities and can work together effectively.

But perhaps most importantly, the client-server architecture provides a natural boundary for security and trust. The server can implement its own authentication and authorization mechanisms, controlling exactly what each client can access and do. This is crucial when you're dealing with sensitive data or powerful tools that could cause damage if misused.

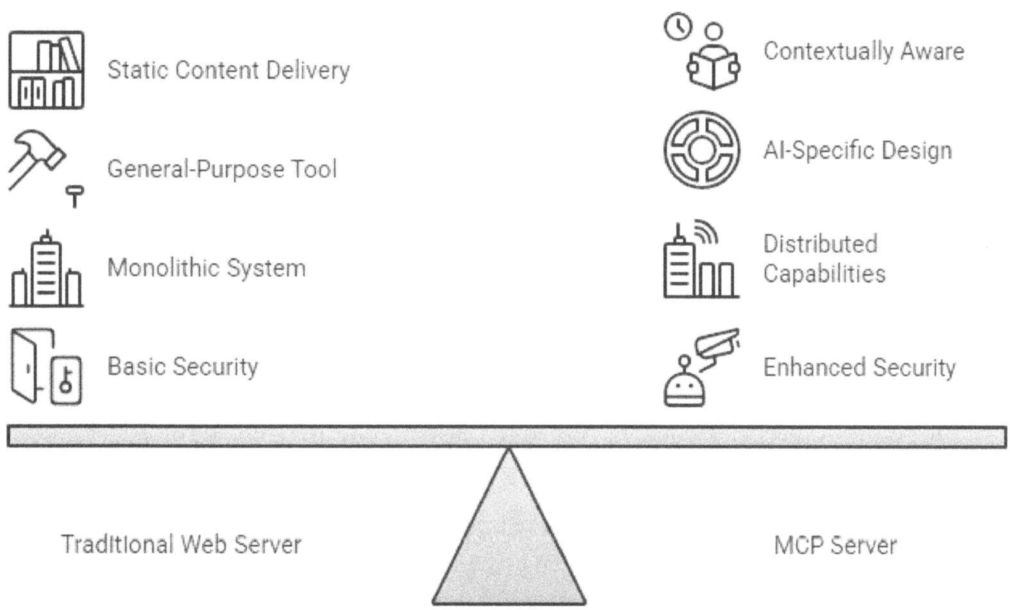

Figure 5.1 –Traditional web server architecture vs. MCP server architecture

With the high-level architecture in mind, let's look more closely at MCP's building blocks (resources, tools, and prompts) and how they fit together.

Core components and their relationships

Now, let's talk about the pieces that make up an MCP system. I've found that the best way to understand these components is to think about them in terms of their relationships rather than as isolated entities. It's like understanding a jazz ensemble; you can't really appreciate what the drummer is doing without understanding how they're interacting with the bass player and the pianist.

As discussed in the previous chapter, MCP is organized around three core component types: resources, tools, and prompts. We won't repeat all the details here; instead, we'll briefly recap and then focus on the primitives and message formats that let clients interact with them:

- **Resources** are essentially sources of information. They're like the reference materials in our librarian analogy (books, databases, documents, and APIs) that provide data. But here's what makes MCP resources special: they're not just static data stores. They can be dynamic, contextual, and intelligent about what information they provide.
  I worked on a project recently where we had an MCP resource that provided access to a company's customer database. But it wasn't just a dumb SQL interface. The resource interpreted the intent behind each query using natural language processing and semantic embeddings, rewrote vague requests using synonyms or related terms, and then used a retriever-ranker pipeline to fetch and rank the most relevant records. LLMs provided summarized responses, making the interface feel intelligent rather than like a dumb SQL gateway.
- **Tools** are where things get really interesting. Tools are capabilities that perform actions or computations. Beyond simple retrieval, they can examine, summarize, translate, or transform information, or use it to accomplish a specific task.
  The beauty of MCP tools is their composability. You can chain them together, use the output of one as the input to another, and build complex workflows from simple building blocks. I've seen systems where dozens of different tools work together to accomplish tasks that would have required custom code in traditional architectures.
- **Prompts** are perhaps the most AI-specific component. These are templates or patterns that help AI systems understand how to interact with resources and tools effectively. They're like conversation starters that help the AI client communicate more effectively with the server.

What's clever about the MCP approach is how these components relate to each other. Resources provide raw material, tools provide the processing capabilities, and prompts provide the communication patterns. But the relationships aren't rigid; a single MCP server might provide all three types of components, or it might specialize in just one.

The relationships between components can evolve over time. For instance, a resource might hint at which tools are best suited to process its data, and a tool might expose information about the data types it expects. In MCP, self-describing resources embed metadata that defines their own structure, similar to self-describing JSON schemas that include a `self` object specifying the vendor, name, format, and version of the schema. This metadata allows clients to discover and use resources without external documentation.

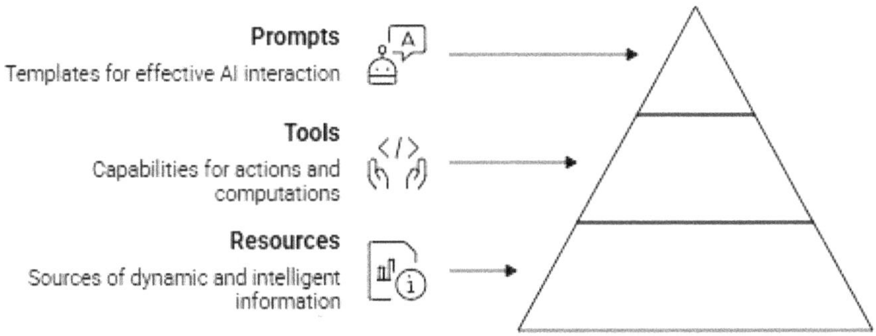

Figure 5.2 – MCP component relationship

There's also a meta-level relationship that I find fascinating: components can provide information about other components. A resource might include metadata about which tools are best suited for processing its data, or a tool might provide information about what types of resources it works best with. This self-describing nature makes MCP systems more discoverable and easier to compose.

Now that we know the parts and how they relate, let's examine the primitives that let clients discover and use resources, tools, and prompts.

Standardized primitives

Here's where MCP really shows its thoughtful design. Instead of trying to accommodate every possible use case with a complex, feature-rich protocol, the designers chose to focus on a small set of standardized primitives that can be combined in powerful ways.

This decision reminds me of the Unix philosophy: do one thing and do it well, and make it easy to combine simple tools into complex workflows. MCP's primitives are like the basic commands in a Unix shell: simple individually, but incredibly powerful when combined.

The core primitives in MCP are straightforward. There are primitives for listing available resources, for listing available tools, and for listing available prompts. Additional primitives let you read resource content, call tools, and retrieve prompt templates, and still others handle session management and error reporting.

Examples include `list_resources`, `list_tools`, `list_prompts`, `read_resource`, `call_tool`, `get_prompt`, `begin_session`, `resume_session`, and `handle_error`. We'll use some of these in the code examples later in this chapter.

What makes these primitives powerful isn't their individual complexity, but their consistency and composability. Every MCP server implements the same basic set of operations, which means that clients can interact with any server using the same patterns. It's like having a universal remote control that works with any device.

I've seen this standardization pay dividends in real projects. We built an AI system that needed to integrate with five different data sources, each provided by a different team. In the old world, this would have meant learning five different APIs, handling five different authentication schemes, and writing five different sets of integration code. With MCP, we wrote one client that could talk to all five servers using the same primitives.

The primitives also provide a natural extension point. If you need capabilities that aren't covered by the standard primitives, you can implement custom tools that provide those capabilities. The beauty is that these custom tools still use the standard tool execution primitive, so clients don't need to know anything special about them.

But here's what I find most elegant about MCP's primitives: they're designed to be *discoverable*. A client doesn't need to know in advance what resources, tools, or prompts a server provides. It can ask the server to list its capabilities and then decide how to use them. This discoverability is crucial for building adaptive AI systems that can work with new servers without requiring code changes.

The standardization also extends to error handling and status reporting. Every MCP operation returns results in a consistent format, with standardized error codes and status information. This consistency makes it much easier to build robust clients that can handle unexpected situations gracefully.

Communication mechanisms

Now we get to the nuts and bolts of how MCP systems actually talk to each other. And honestly, this is where I think the MCP designers made some really smart choices that aren't immediately obvious.

The primary communication mechanism in MCP is JSON-RPC over various transport layers. If you're not familiar with JSON-RPC, think of it as a way to call functions on a remote system using JSON messages (see the official spec at `https://www.jsonrpc.org/specification`). It's simpler than REST in some ways, more structured than raw HTTP, and well-suited for the kind of request-response patterns that AI systems typically use.

The choice of JSON-RPC as the message format is thoughtful. JSON is ubiquitous, human-readable, and well-supported across programming languages. **RPC** (which stands for **remote procedure call**) provides a natural abstraction for the kind of operations that AI systems typically perform: calling functions, passing parameters, and receiving results.

But here's the thing: MCP doesn't mandate a single way of sending bits across the wire. The core protocol is deliberately transport-agnostic: it defines JSON-RPC messages and a connection life cycle, but leaves the choice of carrier up to the implementation. The specification defines two standard transports, **stdio** and **Streamable HTTP**, and notes that clients and servers may implement custom transports as long as they preserve the JSON-RPC message format and life cycle. In other words, it's perfectly acceptable to talk to an MCP server over a pipe in your terminal or via an HTTP endpoint. Some communities have experimented with other transports, such as WebSocket or message queues, but these are custom extensions rather than part of the core spec.

In development environments, **stdio** transport is incredibly convenient: you can run an MCP server as a subprocess and communicate with it through standard input and output streams – no network configuration, port management, or firewall issues, just simple process communication.

For production deployments, **Streamable HTTP** transport leverages familiar web infrastructure load balancing, TLS termination, caching, and monitoring. An MCP endpoint is exposed over HTTP, and JSON-RPC requests and responses are exchanged via `POST`/`GET`; servers may stream responses to clients via **server-sent events** (**SSE**). Because the protocol is transport-agnostic, implementations can use other mechanisms (such as WebSockets) where appropriate, but those are considered custom transports rather than part of the official standard.

But what I really appreciate about MCP's communication design is how it handles the inherent challenges of AI system integration. AI operations can be long-running; they often involve large amounts of data, and they frequently need to handle partial results or streaming responses.

MCP addresses the challenges of long-running operations through **optional progress tracking**: a client can attach a progress token when making a request, and the server can send `notifications/progress` messages to report intermediate progress values. Clients can choose how often to send these updates, and progress notifications stop once the operation completes.

There is also a mechanism for cancelling in-progress requests: either side may send a `notification(s)/canceled` message specifying the request ID, signaling that work should be stopped. Implementations are expected to establish request timeouts and issue cancellation notifications when a response is not received within the configured time. When using the HTTP transport, servers may stream partial results via SSE, but this is optional and transport-specific.

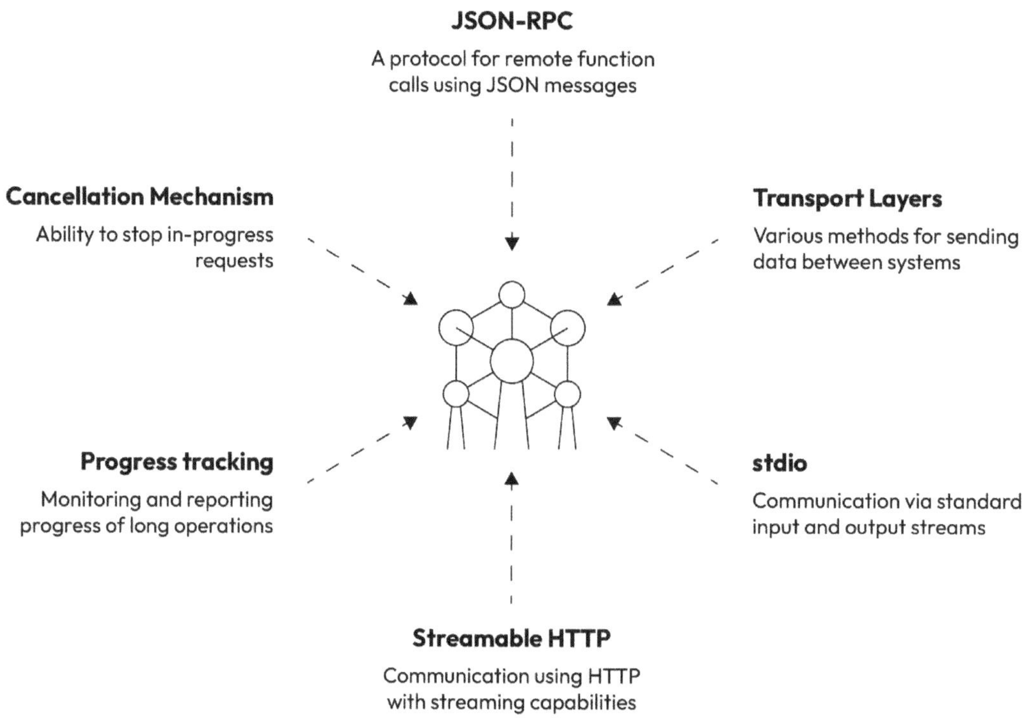

Figure 5.3 – MCP communication design

Next, let's dive into the actual structure of MCP messages, because this is where the rubber meets the road. The message format might seem like a dry technical detail, but it actually reveals a lot about how MCP is designed to support AI workflows.

Message formats and protocols

Every MCP message follows the JSON-RPC 2.0 specification, which provides a consistent structure for requests, responses, and notifications. But MCP extends this basic structure with AI-specific conventions and patterns.

A typical MCP request looks something like this:

```
{
  "jsonrpc": "2.0",
  "id": "request-123",
  "method": "tools/call",
  "params": {
    "name": "search_documents",
    "arguments": {
      "query": "quarterly financial results",
      "limit": 10
    }
  }
}
```

What I find elegant about this structure is its simplicity and extensibility. The basic JSON-RPC framework provides the plumbing: request identification, method naming, and parameter passing. The MCP-specific parts are in the method names and parameter structures.

The method naming convention is particularly thoughtful. Methods are organized into namespaces such as `resources/`, `tools/`, and `prompts/`, which makes it easy to understand what type of operation you're performing. Within each namespace, the method names are descriptive and consistent.

Response messages follow a similar pattern:

```
{
  "jsonrpc": "2.0",
  "id": "request-123",
  "result": {
    "content": [
      {
        "type": "text",
        "text": "Found 3 documents matching your query..."
      }
    ]
  }
}
```

What's interesting here is how MCP handles different types of content. Instead of just returning raw data, responses include type information that helps clients understand how to process the results. This is crucial for AI systems that might need to handle text, images, structured data, or other content types differently.

Error handling follows JSON-RPC conventions but includes MCP-specific error codes and messages:

```
{
  "jsonrpc": "2.0",
  "id": "request-123",
  "error": {
    "code": -32000,
    "message": "Tool execution failed",
    "data": {
      "details": "Authentication required for this operation"
    }
  }
}
```

The protocol also supports notification messages that don't expect a response. This is useful for scenarios where servers need to push updates to clients, or where clients need to send fire-and-forget messages.

One aspect of the message format that I particularly appreciate is how it handles metadata. MCP reserves a `_meta` property on requests, responses, and notifications for attaching additional information about an interaction. The specification deliberately leaves this field flexible so that implementers can attach context-specific annotations such as progress tokens, correlation IDs, or application-defined hints without breaking compatibility. While a server *could* choose to include metrics such as execution time or resource usage here, the protocol itself does not prescribe any particular set of metadata keys; these details are left to the application layer.

With the message structure explained, it's time to address another critical aspect: how MCP secures these interactions through transport encryption, authentication, and authorization.

Security and authentication framework

Security in MCP is complicated. Not because the framework is overly complex, but because security in AI systems involves challenges that traditional web applications don't face.

Think about it: when an AI agent uses MCP to access resources and execute tools, it's not just making API calls; it's potentially accessing sensitive data, performing actions with real-world consequences, and making decisions that affect users and systems. The security implications are significant.

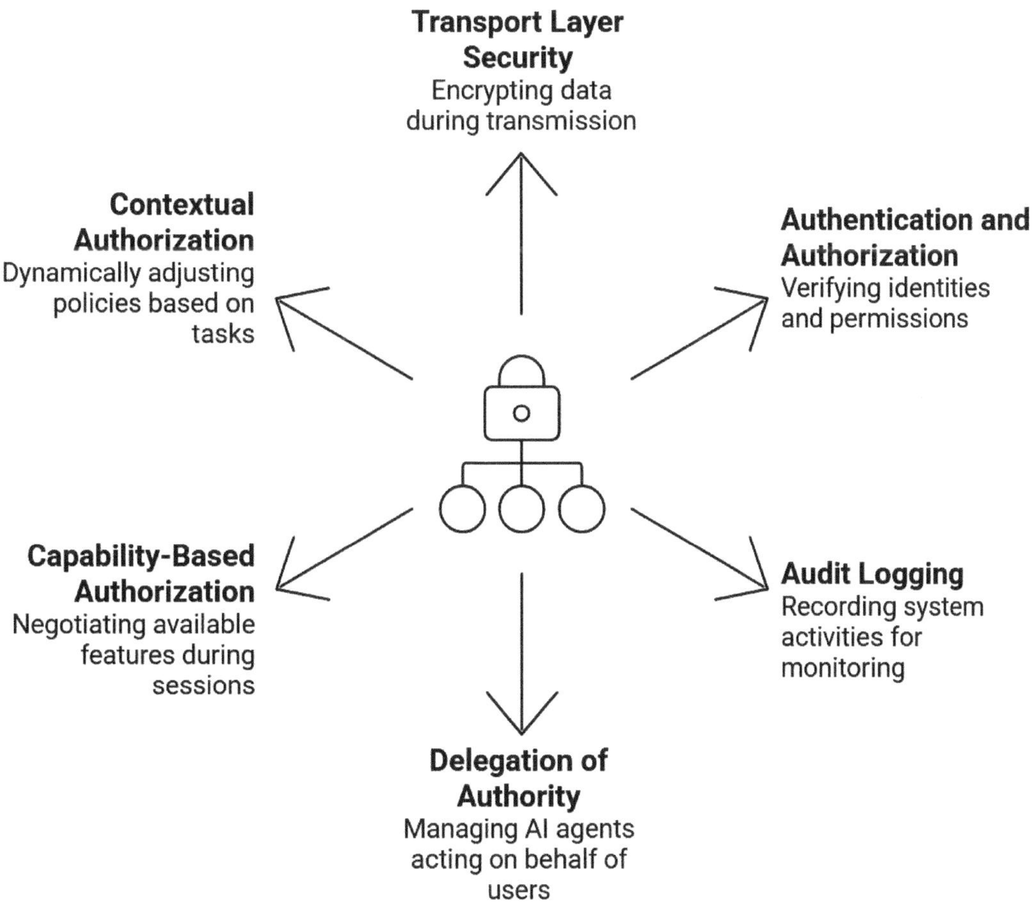

Figure 5.4 – MCP security approaches

MCP approaches security through multiple layers, which I think is the right approach. At a minimum, implementations should secure the transport layer (e.g., TLS for encrypted HTTP) and implement robust authentication, authorization, and audit logging. Authentication and authorization are deliberately left up to implementers: for HTTP-based transports, the official authorization specification builds on OAuth 2.1 and related standards to enable secure token-based access. stdio transports typically rely on environment variables or operating-system-level isolation for credentials. Custom transports must follow appropriate security best practices for the chosen protocol. Beyond the core specification, developers may choose to layer additional mechanisms such as API keys or mutual TLS on top of their deployments, but these are implementation choices rather than features defined by MCP itself.

What I find interesting is how MCP handles the delegation of authority. When an AI agent acts on behalf of a user, it needs to prove not just its own identity, but also that it has permission to act for that user. This is more complex than traditional API authentication because there are multiple parties involved (the user, the AI agent, and the MCP server).

The authorization model for MCP sessions is *capability-based*: clients and servers negotiate which features (roots, sampling, prompts, resources, tools, logging, etc.) are available during the session. Once established, both parties must respect the negotiated capabilities. This model is more flexible than static role-based access control and better suited to the dynamic nature of AI workflows.

Finally, it's worth mentioning that some practitioners are exploring more advanced **contextual authorization** models for AI agents, where policies are generated at runtime based on the specific task and context. These approaches can provide fine-grained control over which tool calls are allowed during a given task, but they are an emerging pattern outside the current MCP specification. In other words, MCP doesn't natively enforce contextual authorization; instead, developers may build such enforcement layers on top of the protocol to guard sensitive data and actions.

To see how these concepts come together, let's build a tiny MCP server and walk through its key components.

Code example

Alright, let's get our hands dirty with some actual code. I'm going to show you a simple but complete example of MCP architecture in action. This isn't production-ready code; it's designed to illustrate the concepts we've been discussing.

This example illustrates how a client and server cooperate using standardized JSON-RPC primitives, how resources and tools are registered on the server, and how a client discovers and uses those capabilities. Each part of the code is broken down with concise explanations that connect back to the architectural concepts described earlier in the chapter:

1. First, set up asynchronous and JSON messaging imports:

   ```
   import asyncio
   import json
   from typing import Dict, Any, List
   ```

   This snippet imports Python's `asyncio` library for asynchronous execution and typing definitions used throughout the example. The MCP specification relies on asynchronous operations because clients and servers may handle many requests concurrently. JSON is used as the wire format for messages, aligning with the chapter's emphasis on standardized, language-agnostic communication.

2. Define the `SimpleMCPServer` class with resource and tool registries:

```
class SimpleMCPServer:
    """A minimal MCP server demonstrating core architecture concepts."""

    def __init__(self):
        self.resources = {
            "company_docs": {
                "description": "Company documentation and policies",
                "uri": "internal://docs"
            }
        }

        self.tools = {
            "search": {
                "description": "Search through available resources",
                "parameters": {
                    "query": {"type": "string", "description": "Search
query"}
                }
            }
        }
```

The `server` class encapsulates the core functions of an MCP server. Its constructor registers a **resource** (company documentation) and a **tool** (a simple search capability). In this chapter, resources are described as dynamic, contextual sources of information, while tools provide computational capabilities. This minimal registry demonstrates how a server organizes these components internally.

3. Process incoming JSON-RPC requests in the server:

```
    async def handle_request(
        self, message: Dict[str, Any]
    ) -> Dict[str, Any]:
        """Handle incoming MCP requests."""
        method = message.get("method")
        params = message.get("params", {})
        request_id = message.get("id")
```

```
        try:
            if method == "resources/list":
                result = await self.list_resources()
            elif method == "tools/list":
                result = await self.list_tools()
            elif method == "tools/call":
                result = await self.call_tool(params)
            else:
                raise ValueError(f"Unknown method: {method}")
            return {
                "jsonrpc": "2.0", "id": request_id,
                "result": result}
        except Exception as e:
            return {
                "jsonrpc": "2.0",
                "id": request_id,
                "error": {"code": -32000, "message": str(e)}
            }
```

This method reads the `method` field of an incoming JSON-RPC message and dispatches the request to the appropriate handler. Supported operations include listing resources, listing tools, and calling a tool. If an unknown method is requested, the server raises an error and returns a JSON-RPC error response. This pattern exemplifies standardized primitives: small, composable operations valued for their simplicity and consistency.

4. List registered resources and tools:

```
    async def list_resources(self) -> Dict[str, Any]:
        """Return available resources."""
        return {"resources": list(self.resources.values())}

    async def list_tools(self) -> Dict[str, Any]:
        """Return available tools."""
        return {"tools": list(self.tools.values())}
```

These helper methods return the server's resource and tool metadata. They illustrate the capability discovery process highlighted in the chapter: clients can ask servers what they offer without prior knowledge. Each response is wrapped in a dictionary that follows JSON-RPC conventions, setting the stage for clients to parse the information easily.

5. Implement a simple search tool via `call_tool`:

```
    async def call_tool(
        self, params: Dict[str, Any]
    ) -> Dict[str, Any]:
        """Execute a tool with given parameters."""
        tool_name = params.get("name")
        arguments = params.get("arguments", {})
        if tool_name == "search":
            query = arguments.get("query", "")
            # Simulate search operation
            results = f"Found documents matching '{query}'"
            return {"content": [{"type": "text", "text": results}]}
        raise ValueError(f"Unknown tool: {tool_name}")
```

When clients call `tools/call`, this method locates the requested tool and runs it with the provided arguments. In this simplified example, only the search tool is implemented. It simulates a document search by returning a textual result; unknown tool names trigger an error. The design underscores the chapter's point that tools are independent building blocks that can be composed and extended.

6. Build a minimal MCP client to interact with the server:

```
class SimpleMCPClient:
    """A minimal MCP client demonstrating core architecture concepts."""

    def __init__(self, server):
        self.server = server
        self.request_id = 0
```

The client class encapsulates logic for communicating with the server. It maintains a request counter and holds a reference to the server. According to the narrative, the client is responsible for orchestrating operations and delegating data retrieval and computation to the server. Separating these roles promotes scalability and maintainability.

7. Send JSON-RPC requests from the client:

```
    async def send_request(
        self, method: str, params: Dict[str, Any] = None
    ) -> Dict[str, Any]:
```

```
        """Send a request to the MCP server."""
        self.request_id += 1
        message = {
            "jsonrpc": "2.0",
            "id": self.request_id,
            "method": method,
            "params": params or {}
        }
        response = await self.server.handle_request(message)
        return response
```

This function constructs a JSON-RPC message containing the method name and parameters, assigns a unique ID, and then forwards the request to the server. By reusing the same `handle_request` method on the server, the client benefits from the standardized communication pattern emphasized in the narrative, ensuring consistency across different servers and clients.

8. Discover server capabilities via the client:

```
    async def discover_capabilities(self):
        """Discover what the server can do."""
        resources_response = await self.send_request(
            "resources/list")
        tools_response = await self.send_request("tools/list")
        print("Available resources:")
        for resource in resources_response["result"]["resources"]:
            print(f"  - {resource['description']}")
        print("\nAvailable tools:")
        for tool in tools_response["result"]["tools"]:
            print(f"  - {tool['description']}")
```

Here, the client queries the server for its registered resources and tools, then prints their descriptions. This method embodies the concept of capability discovery, where the client learns what the server offers without hardcoding that knowledge. In larger systems, this discovery process would allow an AI agent to dynamically choose appropriate resources and tools based on context.

9. Use the search tool to retrieve documents:

```
    async def search_documents(self, query: str):
        """Use the search tool to find documents."""
```

```
        response = await self.send_request("tools/call", {
            "name": "search",
            "arguments": {"query": query}
        })
        if "result" in response:
            content = response["result"]["content"][0]["text"]
            print(f"Search results: {content}")
        else:
            print(f"Search failed: {response['error']['message']}")
```

The client wraps the `tools/call` primitive with a convenience method that passes a search query and prints the result. It demonstrates how tool calls return structured responses, either containing a result or an error. This method ties back to the earlier discussion on tool composability and error handling, which allows tools to be combined in sequences while providing consistent feedback.

10. Here's the end-to-end MCP workflow:

```
async def demonstrate_mcp_architecture():
    """Demonstrate MCP architecture concepts."""
    print(" MCP Architecture Demonstration")
    print("=" * 40)
    server = SimpleMCPServer()
    client = SimpleMCPClient(server)
    print("\n Discovering server capabilities:")
    await client.discover_capabilities()
    print("\n Using the search tool:")
    await client.search_documents("financial reports")
    print("\n Architecture demonstration complete!")

if __name__ == "__main__":
    asyncio.run(demonstrate_mcp_architecture())
```

This final segment brings all the pieces together. It constructs the server and client, demonstrates capability discovery, invokes the search tool with a sample query, and signals completion.

When you run this example, you'll see output similar to the following:

```
 MCP Architecture Demonstration
========================================
```

```
 Discovering server capabilities:
Available resources:
  - Company documentation and policies

Available tools:
  - Search through available resources

 Using the search tool:
Search results: Found documents matching 'financial reports'

 Architecture demonstration complete!
```

The output shown highlights the step-by-step results: listing available resources and tools, performing a search, and concluding with a success message. The demonstration underscores the separation of concerns (server vs. client responsibilities) and the extensibility of MCP systems, as new resources and tools could be added without altering the client logic.

This example illustrates several key architectural concepts and sets the stage for more advanced scenarios in later chapters:

- **Separation of concerns**: The server handles resource and tool management, while the client focuses on orchestrating operations
- **Standardized communication**: All communication follows the JSON-RPC pattern with consistent message formats
- **Capability discovery**: The client can discover what the server offers without prior knowledge
- **Extensibility**: New resources and tools can be added without changing the core protocol

What this simple example doesn't show is the full complexity of real MCP deployments: authentication, error handling, streaming responses, and complex tool chains. But it gives you a feel for how the pieces fit together.

The architecture we've explored in this chapter provides the foundation for everything else we'll discuss in this book. Understanding these core concepts (the client-server model, the component relationships, and the communication patterns) is essential for building effective MCP systems.

In the next chapter, we'll dive deeper into server-side implementation, exploring how to build robust, scalable MCP servers that can handle real-world workloads. But before we move on, take a moment to appreciate the elegance of what we've covered. MCP's architecture might look simple on the surface, but it embodies years of hard-won lessons about building distributed systems that work.

Summary

The beauty of good architecture isn't in its complexity; it's in how it makes complex things simple. MCP's architecture does exactly that, providing a clean, consistent foundation for building the next generation of AI systems. In this chapter, we explored MCP's architecture in detail. We reviewed its core components (resources, tools, and prompts), examined the simple primitives that let clients discover and use them, learned why MCP chooses JSON-RPC and how its messages are structured, discussed security layers and transport mechanisms, and worked through a minimal server implementation. Understanding these elements sets the stage for more advanced topics.

In the next chapter, we'll dive into MCP's server-side implementation, its design principles, authentication, authorization, scalability, and performance, along with some code examples.

6

Server-Side Implementation

> *I like to think of the best servers as good butlers: they anticipate your needs, handle complexity gracefully, and never make you think about how they do what they do.*

I've built a lot of servers in my career: web servers, API servers, database servers, message brokers... You name it. I've probably cursed at servers during a 3 A.M. debugging session. But MCP servers? They're different. They're not just about serving data or processing requests; they're about understanding intent, managing context, and enabling intelligent collaboration between AI systems.

An **MCP server** is a service that implements the Model Context Protocol. It exposes standardized **resources**, **tools,** and **prompts** via JSON-RPC endpoints so that AI clients can discover capabilities dynamically, request context, and invoke operations without prior knowledge of specific APIs. In other words, it acts as a translator between the AI's high-level goals and the underlying computational functions.

The first MCP server I built was for a client who wanted their AI assistant to access internal company documents. Sounds straightforward, right? Just expose some files through an API. But as I dug deeper, I realized this wasn't about file serving; it was about understanding what the AI was trying to accomplish, providing the right information at the right level of detail, and doing it all securely and efficiently. In reality, it was anything but straightforward. I had to design a custom resource provider from scratch, wrestle with messy access-control rules, and debug context-handling logic that kept breaking in subtle ways. Those early pains motivated much of the guidance you'll read in this chapter.

That project taught me that MCP servers aren't just technical infrastructure; they're intelligent intermediaries that need to understand both the capabilities they provide and the needs of the AI systems that use them. AI systems often reason at the level of goals rather than specific function calls. For example, a model may be tasked with *summarizing the contents of a contract* or *retrieving the latest invoices*. The MCP server must interpret those high-level requests, decide which tools or resources are needed (such as a document reader or search tool), and then orchestrate the appropriate calls. Bridging goal-oriented reasoning with low-level operations is what makes MCP servers so powerful.

In this chapter, we'll move from theory to practice. First, we'll explore how to build MCP servers by implementing resource, tool, and prompt providers. Then we'll cover critical security concepts such as user consent, context, and authentication. Finally, we'll look at scalability, performance, and a working example. Knowing this roadmap will help you connect each topic to the bigger picture.

In this chapter, we'll be covering the following topics:

- Design principles for MCP servers
- Implementing resource providers
- Implementing tool providers
- Implementing prompt providers
- Handing authentication and authorization
- Scalability and performance considerations

Design principles for MCP servers

Before we dive into the technical details, let's talk about the principles that should guide MCP server design.

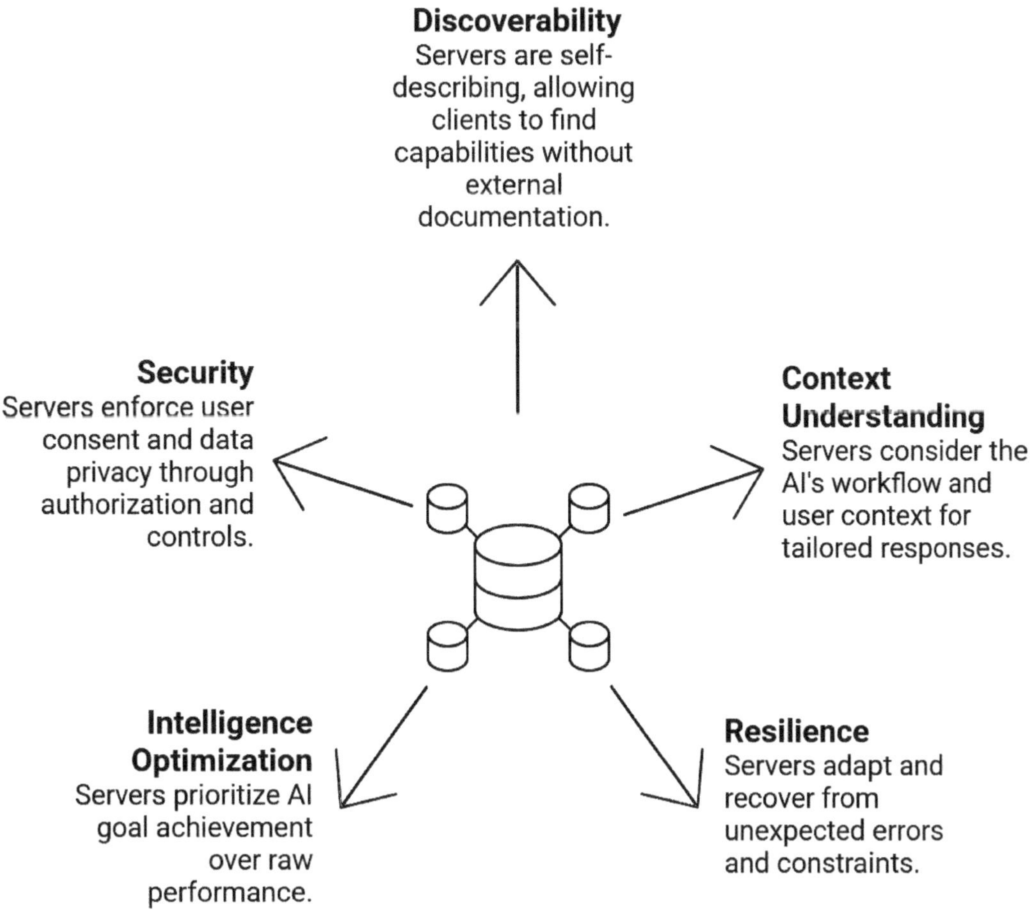

Figure 6.1 – MCP server design principles

These aren't just abstract concepts; they're practical guidelines that I've learned through building servers that work (and a few that spectacularly didn't).

Be discoverable, not just documented

One of the MCP's core strengths is that servers are self-describing. The protocol defines discovery methods such as `tools/list`, `resources/list`, and `prompts/list` that allow a client to enumerate all available capabilities without relying on external documentation. Each capability is accompanied by a JSON schema that describes its inputs and outputs, making it possible for an AI system to understand how to call a tool or consume a resource. Good server design builds on these primitives by supplying clear names, descriptions, and examples, and by attaching additional information in the optional `_meta` field. Embedding this metadata in the protocol means the client can ask "What can you help me with?" and receive a structured, machine-readable answer. In practice, this reduces misuse and eliminates the need to consult a separate wiki or manual. The schemas attached to each capability are not just hints; they are formal contracts. Servers must ensure that structured results conform to the declared `outputSchema`, and clients should validate responses against that schema. When a schema omits a `$schema` field, it defaults to **JSON Schema 2020-12**, and implementations must support that dialect; they may support additional dialects, but should document which ones they accept. Clients and servers must validate schemas according to their declared or default dialect and handle unsupported dialects gracefully

I learned this lesson the hard way on a project where we built an MCP server for financial data analysis. The server had dozens of tools for different types of analysis, but the AI clients kept using them incorrectly because they didn't understand the nuances of each tool. We ended up spending more time debugging misused tools than we did building new features. The problem wasn't the tools themselves; it was that we hadn't made them sufficiently self-explanatory through the discovery APIs.

Understand context, don't just process requests

Unlike traditional APIs that treat each call in isolation, MCP servers often need to consider why an AI tool is making a request and how it fits into an ongoing workflow. While the protocol itself doesn't enforce any particular context model, servers can use client-provided information (such as user role or previous actions) to tailor responses. For example, a search tool might return different results based on the requester's permissions, or a document processing tool might adjust its output format for downstream consumption. Thinking about context means going beyond individual operations to consider broader goals and constraints of the AI system you're serving.

Be resilient, not just robust

AI systems will inevitably ask for things you didn't anticipate. They may send malformed inputs, request long-running computations, or repeatedly try operations when resources are constrained. Robust error handling is therefore essential, but resilience goes further: design your server so it can adapt and recover. The MCP specification includes optional progress and cancellation notifications for long-running operations; implementing these allows the client to monitor work and cancel if necessary. When errors occur, return clear messages with actionable guidance. Where possible, infer what the client intended and offer suggestions. Finally, degrade gracefully by slowing down or returning partial results instead of failing catastrophically so AI workflows remain productive even under stress. Here are a few error responses that are returned when requests fail: MCP servers return JSON-RPC error objects that include a numeric code and message. Standard codes include **32700 (Parse error)** for invalid JSON, **32600 (Invalid request)** when the message structure is wrong, **32601 (Method not found)** when a requested method is unavailable, **32602 (Invalid params)** for parameter validation failures, and **32603 (Internal error)** for unexpected server problems. Codes in the range **32000 to –32099** are reserved for server-specific errors such as rate limiting or authentication failures. Using the correct code helps clients distinguish between protocol errors and tool-execution errors and recover gracefully.

Optimize for intelligence, not just performance

While throughput and latency matter, MCP servers also benefit from optimizations that make AI interactions more effective. Intelligent caching can account for why data was requested and precompute related results. Batching related operations can preserve semantic relationships. HTTP transports support streaming responses via **server-sent events** (**SSEs**), and the progress API allows partial updates, so AI systems can start processing before a response is complete. The goal isn't only to be fast; it's to help AI achieve its goals efficiently.

Security: user consent and context

The MCP places strong emphasis on user consent and data privacy. Tools are model-controlled and require explicit user approval before execution, and servers should expose only the data and operations that have been authorized for the current user. For HTTP transports, the protocol defines an OAuth 2.1-based authorization flow and recommends robust authentication and authorization practices. Implementers should also follow the security best-practice guidelines of the specification: provide clear audit trails, enforce tool safety and LLM sampling controls, and limit data exposure to the minimum necessary. Applications may choose to implement more nuanced, context-aware, or risk-based policies (e.g., adjusting permissions based on time of day or workflow stage), but these are design choices layered on top of the base protocol rather than requirements of the MCP.

With these design principles in mind, let's shift from theory to practice and learn how to implement the core components of an MCP server.

Chapter 4 introduced **resource providers**, **tool providers,** and **prompt providers** conceptually. In this chapter, we'll build on that foundation by walking through how to implement each provider type and by discussing design considerations that arise in production servers.

Implementing resource providers

A resource provider is a component of an MCP server that exposes data or context via URI-based identifiers. For example, a document provider might serve files such as `document://policy/HR-001`, a CRM provider could expose customer records such as `customer://12345`, and a search provider might allow parameterized queries such as `search/{query}`. Each resource is described with a name, description, MIME type, and optional template variables so that clients can understand how to use it. Resource providers aren't just passive data access layers; they're the ones that understand how their data will be used and optimize accordingly.

The key insight is that AI systems don't just want data; they want the right data in the right format at the right level of detail for their specific use case. A good resource provider doesn't just serve raw information as is; it provides contextually appropriate views of that information.

Let me give you an example from a recent project. We built an MCP server that provided access to a company's customer database. The naive approach would have been to expose the database tables directly and let the AI query whatever it wants. But that would have been both inefficient and potentially dangerous.

Instead, we built resource providers that understood different use cases. The customer support resource provider returned customer information formatted for support interactions, such as recent tickets, account status, contact preferences, and escalation history. The sales resource provider returned the same underlying customer data but formatted for sales activities, such as purchase history, preferences, potential upsell opportunities, and relationship timeline.

The same data, different perspectives, optimized for different contexts and use cases. When designing these different views, remember that switching execution contexts (for example, between threads handling different requests) has a real cost on modern Linux systems: a thread context switch typically takes in the order of 1–3 microseconds. Therefore, minimizing unnecessary context switches and prefetching related data can improve latency.

Resource providers should also be intelligent about access patterns.

Resource providers can learn from how they're being used and optimize accordingly.

If certain types of queries are common, cache the results. If certain data combinations are frequently requested together, pre-compute them. If certain access patterns indicate specific use cases, provide shortcuts or suggestions.

The goal is to make resource providers feel less like databases and more like knowledgeable colleagues who understand what you're trying to accomplish and help you get there efficiently.

A well-designed resource provider learns from access patterns, progressively discloses complexity, and adapts its behavior to the user's needs. We'll explore why metadata is also important as data and progressive disclosure of complexity in the following subsections.

Metadata is as important as data

AI systems need to understand not just what information is available, but how reliable or current it is and how it relates to other data. The MCP reserves a `_meta` field where servers and clients can attach additional metadata to messages. Implementers may use `_meta` to provide data quality indicators, freshness timestamps, confidence scores, or usage hints, but the protocol doesn't prescribe specific keys or values. Whatever metadata you include should help AI systems make better decisions about how to use the information they receive. When in doubt, keep the core data format simple and add richer context through `_meta` so clients can choose how to interpret it.

Progressive disclosure of complexity

Resource providers should follow a progressive disclosure pattern: start simple, but provide access to complexity when needed. The basic interface should handle common cases automatically, but more sophisticated clients should be able to access detailed control when necessary. For instance, a document provider might first present a list of titles and summaries, but also let clients request the full content, metadata, or related documents when needed. This approach keeps the interface simple for common use cases while still offering depth for advanced workflows.

This might mean providing both high-level summary views and detailed drill-down capabilities. It might mean offering both automated data processing and manual override options. The key is to make the simple cases simple while keeping the complex cases possible. A log provider might deliver aggregated error counts for a quick dashboard but also allow you to drill down into individual log entries for troubleshooting. An analytics provider could automatically generate trend reports while still giving you the option to adjust parameters or run a custom query. These examples show how to balance convenience with control.

Now that you know how to expose data, let's look at how to expose actions. The next section covers tool providers, components that wrap callable functions for your AI agents.

Implementing tool providers

Tool providers are where MCP servers really shine, but they're also where the design challenges are most complex. In the MCP, each tool is a schema-defined function that specifies its inputs and outputs. Clients can discover available tools by calling `tools/list` and invoking them via `tools/call`, and tool executions require explicit user approval. You're bridging the gap between AI reasoning (which thinks in terms of goals and intentions) and computational execution (which operates on specific inputs and parameters).

The challenge is that AI systems are fundamentally different from traditional API clients. They don't just want to execute predefined operations; they want to explore possibilities, experiment with approaches, and adapt their strategies based on results. Your tool providers need to support this kind of exploratory, adaptive behavior.

Tool providers present unique challenges. We'll begin by designing tools that compose cleanly with others, so AI systems can build sophisticated workflows from simple parts.

Design for composability

The best MCP tools are designed to work well with other tools. They accept standard input formats, produce standard output formats, and handle chaining gracefully. This composability is what enables AI systems to build complex workflows from simple building blocks.

But composability isn't just about data formats; it's about semantic compatibility. Tools should be designed so that the output of one tool naturally fits as input to related tools. They should provide metadata that helps AI systems understand how to chain operations effectively.

I've seen AI systems create incredibly sophisticated workflows by chaining together simple tools in creative ways. The key is designing tools that are both powerful individually and synergistic when combined.

Provide multiple levels of abstraction

Good tool providers offer multiple levels of abstraction for the same underlying capability. There should be high-level tools that handle common cases automatically, and lower-level tools that provide detailed control for sophisticated use cases.

For example, a document analysis tool might have a simple interface such as `analyze_document(document, purpose)` that handles the most common cases automatically. But it might also provide detailed parameters for users who need fine-grained control over the analysis process, specific algorithms, custom thresholds, output formats, and so on.

This layered approach makes tools accessible to AI systems with different levels of sophistication while still providing the flexibility needed for complex use cases.

Handle uncertainty gracefully

AI systems often work with incomplete or uncertain information, and your tools need to handle this gracefully. This might mean accepting partial inputs and doing the best job possible with available information. It might mean providing confidence scores or uncertainty estimates with results. It might mean offering multiple alternative approaches when the optimal approach isn't clear.

The goal is to make tools that are helpful even when the inputs aren't perfect or the requirements aren't fully specified.

With resources and tools in place, we can now focus on how to generate the instructions that drive them. Prompt providers supply reusable templates that help your models interact effectively with the server.

Implementing prompt providers

Prompt providers are perhaps the most AI-specific component of MCP servers, and honestly, they're the ones that took me the longest to fully appreciate. In the MCP, prompts are structured templates defined by the server and exposed via `prompts/list` and `prompts/get` operations. They require explicit user invocation and can include parameter definitions with completion hints. Prompt providers supply templates and patterns that help AI systems interact more effectively with your server's capabilities.

If you're coming from traditional API development, this might seem like a strange concept. Why would a server provide templates for how clients should talk to it? But in the AI world, this makes perfect sense. AI systems are essentially sophisticated pattern-matching and generation engines. Providing them with good patterns to work from dramatically improves their effectiveness.

Think of prompt providers as conversation starters that help AI systems understand not just what your server can do, but how to ask for it effectively. They bridge the gap between the natural language reasoning that AI systems excel at and the structured parameter passing that computational tools require.

Provide context, not just templates

Good prompts don't just provide template text; they provide context about when and how to use different approaches. They explain the reasoning behind different parameter choices, suggest alternative formulations for different use cases, and help AI systems understand the trade-offs between different options.

This contextual information is crucial for helping AI systems make good decisions about how to interact with your server. It's the difference between providing a script to follow and providing the understanding needed to improvise effectively.

Make prompts adaptive

The best prompt providers don't just return static templates; they adapt their suggestions based on context, user history, and current system state. A prompt for searching documents might be different if the user has been working on financial analysis versus technical documentation. A prompt for data analysis might suggest different approaches based on the type and size of the dataset.

This adaptability helps AI systems learn more effective interaction patterns over time and makes the overall system more intelligent and responsive.

Once you have providers exposing data, tools, and prompts, the next critical step is to control who can access them. Let's explore how to authenticate users and authorize requests.

Having walked through the implementation of resource providers, tool providers, and prompt providers, the next concern is who can access them and under what conditions. The following sections examine authentication and authorization in MCP servers.

Handling authentication and authorization

Security in MCP servers is fundamentally different from traditional web application security because you're dealing with AI systems that might be acting on behalf of users, accessing sensitive data, and performing actions with real-world consequences.

The authentication challenge is that you often have multiple parties involved: the user who initiated the request, the AI system that's making the request, and potentially other systems or agents in the chain. You need to verify the identity of all these parties and ensure that the request is legitimate.

But authentication is just the beginning. Authorization is where things get really complex because AI systems don't just access data; they reason about it, combine it with other information, and use it to make decisions. Traditional role-based access control isn't sufficient; you need more nuanced policies that consider context, purpose, and risk.

In the following subsections, we will take a look at how authorization can be handled efficiently and flawlessly with context-aware and risk-based conditions.

Context-aware authorization

While traditional role-based access control may be insufficient for AI workflows, the core MCP authorization mechanism uses OAuth 2.1 for HTTP transports and encourages explicit user consent. Implementers can layer additional policies that consider not just who is making a request, but also what they're trying to accomplish and how the request fits into a broader workflow. For example, you might allow certain operations during business hours but not after hours, permit read access for analysis but restrict data export, or grant temporary elevated permissions for a specific task. The key is to move beyond simple yes/no decisions and to design policies that reflect the purpose and risk of each request.

Risk-based security

AI systems often need to make rapid decisions based on incomplete information, which creates unique security challenges. While the MCP specification doesn't define "risk-based" security, developers can build adaptive policies on top of the standard authorization framework. For example, you might implement dynamic rate limiting based on request patterns, require additional authentication for particularly sensitive operations, or adjust permitted scopes based on the confidence of user authentication. The goal is to balance security with usability, ensuring that legitimate AI operations can proceed efficiently while protecting against potential threats.

With security accounted for, let's turn to designing for performance and scalability. Building a production-ready MCP server means addressing performance and scalability. In the remainder of this chapter, we'll dig into concurrency and caching strategies and load-balancing techniques that allow MCP servers to maintain low latency and high throughput under real-world workloads.

Scalability and performance considerations

Building MCP servers that can handle real-world AI workloads requires thinking carefully about scalability and performance from the beginning. AI workloads have some unique characteristics that affect how you design for scale. These include bursty request patterns, large context sizes, and unpredictable model latencies. To handle these, we'll look at concurrency strategies, caching, and streaming responses in the subsections that follow.

AI operations are computationally intensive

A single MCP request might trigger complex analysis, large data retrievals, or expensive model inference. To avoid blocking other requests, you should embrace asynchronous processing patterns, design for concurrent execution, and make use of the protocol's optional progress and cancellation notifications for long-running operations. These allow clients to track progress and cancel work when appropriate.

But it's not just about raw computational power; it's about intelligent resource management. Some operations can be cached, some can be precomputed, and some can be approximated when exact results aren't necessary.

Request patterns are unpredictable

AI systems often make many requests in rapid succession as they explore different approaches to solving a problem. They might suddenly discover a particularly useful capability and start using it heavily. They might chain operations together in unexpected ways.

Your server needs to handle these unpredictable patterns gracefully. This might mean implementing intelligent load balancing, adaptive caching strategies, and graceful degradation when resources are constrained.

Context matters for performance

Traditional performance optimization focuses on making individual operations faster. For MCP servers, you also need to consider the performance of entire workflows and interaction patterns.

This might mean optimizing common operation sequences, pre-loading related data when certain patterns are detected, or providing bulk operations that handle multiple related requests efficiently.

- **Concurrency strategies**: MCP servers can adopt different concurrency models depending on workload. A thread-per-request model is simple but may waste resources under bursty AI workloads; event-driven frameworks such as Python's asyncio or Node.js can scale to tens of thousands of concurrent connections by sharing threads. For CPU-bound tasks such as model inference, spawning worker processes or using a task queue prevents the event loop from blocking. Choosing the right model helps the server remain responsive.
- **Caching strategies**: Caching can dramatically reduce latency for repeated or expensive operations. Common techniques include in-memory caches for frequently accessed documents, request–response caches keyed by query and user context, and memorization of tool outputs that depend only on their inputs. For distributed

deployments, external caches such as Redis or Memcached allow multiple server instances to share cached data. Remember to include expiration policies and invalidation hooks when underlying data changes.

- **Load balancing**: To scale horizontally, run multiple instances of your MCP server behind a load balancer that distributes requests based on connection count or observed latency. For long-running operations, ensure that progress tokens and session state are either stateless or stored in a shared data store so that any instance can resume work.

Now that we've covered the theory, let's build a concrete MCP server. The following example shows a document server that lists resources based on user role and performs context-aware searches. We'll break it down step by step to highlight the important concepts.

Code example: Building an MCP server

Now that we understand what makes a good server – anticipating needs, handling complexity gracefully, and remaining invisible to the user – let's see those principles in action. The following code implements a basic MCP server that lists resources and calls tools based on context. Notice how it filters resources by user role and adapts search results to the user's context, illustrating the ideas of discoverable capabilities and contextual awareness we discussed earlier.

Here's a minimal example that illustrates the key concepts we've discussed:

This example demonstrates contextual awareness (filtering documents based on user role), discoverability (listing available resources), and adaptivity (modifying search results using the user's context).

1. Define the `DocumentMCPServer` class:

```
class DocumentMCPServer:
    """A simple MCP server demonstrating core concepts."""

    async def handle_request(self, message, context):
        method = message.get("method")
        if method == "resources/list":
            return await self.list_resources(context)
        elif method == "tools/call":
            return await self.call_tool(message["params"], context)
```

This server class forms the backbone of the example. Its `handle_request` method inspects the incoming JSON-RPC message and dispatches it to either `list_resources` or `call_tool` based on the method name. By delegating work through standardized primitives, the server remains self-describing and easy for clients to explore. The additional `context` argument allows the server to tailor responses based on user role or session information, reflecting the principle that MCP servers should understand the "why" behind each request.

2. List resources based on user role:

```
async def list_resources(self, context):
    # Return resources appropriate for the requesting context
    user_role = context.get("user_role", "guest")
    resources = []
    for doc in self.get_accessible_documents(user_role):
        resources.append({
            "uri": f"document://{doc.id}",
            "name": doc.title,
            "description": doc.summary
        })
    return {"resources": resources}
```

The `list_resources` method queries available documents according to the requester's role and returns a list of resource descriptors. This illustrates two key ideas: *discoverability*, providing structured metadata that clients can enumerate, and *context awareness* – the server filters data based on user permissions. It also hints at the importance of intelligent resource providers that understand how their data will be used.

3. Route tool calls via `call_tool`:

```
async def call_tool(self, params, context):
    tool_name = params["name"]
    arguments = params["arguments"]
    if tool_name == "search":
        return await self.search_documents(arguments, context)
```

Tool invocation is handled by `call_tool`, which examines the requested tool name and delegates to the appropriate method. In this minimal example, only a `search` tool is implemented, but the `handle_request`/`call_tool` pattern will support additional tools in the future. By centralizing tool routing, the server upholds the design principle of exposing capabilities clearly and avoiding misuse, a lesson emphasized in the narrative's discussion of self-explanatory discovery APIs.

4. Implement a context-aware search tool:

```
async def search_documents(self, args, context):
    # Implement contextually aware search
    query = args["query"]
    user_context = context.get("user_context", {})
    # Adapt search based on context
    results = self.perform_search(query, user_context)
    return {
        "content": [{"type": "text", "text": f"Found {len(results)} 
documents"}],
        "results": results
    }
```

The `search_documents` method performs a search using the provided query and additional context (such as user preferences or prior actions). It returns a summary text and a list of detailed results. This design embodies the chapter's advice to understand context and adjust output accordingly. By adapting its behavior to the user's role or workflow, the server moves beyond simple request processing towards intelligent collaboration.

This sample highlights how this server demonstrates key principles: contextual awareness, discoverable capabilities, and adaptive behavior.

Building effective MCP servers requires balancing many concerns: security, performance, usability, and maintainability. But when done well, they provide a powerful foundation for AI systems that can access and manipulate information in intelligent, contextual ways.

The server-side implementation is where the theoretical elegance of MCP meets the practical challenges of real-world deployment. It's where you learn that building systems for AI isn't just about handling requests; it's about enabling intelligence.

Summary

The best MCP servers don't just serve data; they serve understanding. They bridge the gap between what AI systems need and what computational systems can provide, making both sides more effective in the process.

MCP servers are more than just data pipelines; they act as intelligent intermediaries that understand AI intent, manage context, and enable collaboration. In this chapter, we covered practical design principles: servers must be discoverable (self-describing via `tools/list` and `resources/list`), context-aware (tailoring responses to a requester's role), resilient (providing progress updates and implementing graceful degradation), and optimized for intelligence via smart caching and streaming. Resource providers should return context-appropriate views of data rather than raw tables, include metadata, and offer progressively richer access patterns. Tool providers are schema-defined functions that support exploratory use, compose with other tools, and offer both high-level and low-level abstractions. Prompt providers supply structured templates and adaptive guidance to bridge natural language requests with structured API calls. The chapter also stressed robust security via user consent and OAuth-based authorization and noted that AI workloads demand careful attention to concurrency and caching.

We implemented a simple `DocumentMCPServer` example to illustrate contextual search and adaptive responses. Altogether, the chapter showed how well-designed servers "serve understanding," translating AI goals into meaningful actions.

Upcoming chapters will build on this foundation by focusing on MCP clients, the components that discover server capabilities, maintain context, and orchestrate tool execution. They will explore integrating clients with frameworks such as LangChain and AutoGen, discuss security and state management from the client's perspective, and show how to plan and execute multi-step workflows across multiple servers, demonstrating how servers and clients work together to enable coherent reasoning and action. This will prepare you to implement end-to-end agent workflows across multiple servers.

Subscribe for a free eBook

7

Client-Side Integration

The client is where the magic happens, where abstract capabilities become concrete actions, where distributed resources become unified intelligence.

If servers are the heart of MCP systems, then clients are the brain. They're where all the distributed capabilities come together, where context gets managed, where decisions get made about which tools to use and how to use them. An MCP client is the orchestration layer that discovers, manages, and invokes server capabilities on behalf of an AI system. It manages context, decides which tools to use, and coordinates their execution, bridging the gap between AI reasoning and computational actions. Building effective MCP clients is less about technical implementation and more about orchestrating intelligence.

I've built a lot of integration layers over the years: API clients, service meshes, message brokers, you name it. But MCP clients are different. They're not just about moving data around or calling remote functions. They're about understanding intent, managing context, and coordinating complex workflows across multiple intelligent systems.

The first MCP client I built was for an AI assistant that needed to help users with research tasks. On the surface, it seemed straightforward to have the client connect to a few MCP servers, expose their capabilities to the AI, and let it figure out how to use them. But as I dug deeper, I realized the client wasn't just a conduit between the AI and the servers. It was the conductor of an orchestra, coordinating multiple capabilities to create something greater than the sum of its parts.

That project taught me that MCP clients aren't just technical infrastructure; they're the intelligence layer that makes distributed AI systems actually work together effectively.

In this chapter, you'll learn how MCP clients discover and manage server capabilities, maintain context across interactions, orchestrate tool execution, integrate with frameworks such as LangChain and AutoGen, and handle security and state management, and we'll tie everything together with a practical code example. Understanding these roles is crucial because the client is what makes distributed capabilities work together seamlessly.

In this chapter, we'll be covering the following topics:

- The role of the MCP client
- Integrating with AI models and frameworks
- Managing context retrieval
- Orchestrating tool execution
- Handling security on the client side

The role of the MCP client

Let's start by understanding what an MCP client actually does, because it's more nuanced than you might think. On one level, yes, it's just making requests to MCP servers and handling responses. But on a deeper level, it involves managing the complexity of distributed intelligence.

Think of an MCP client as a personal assistant who knows how to work with a team of specialists. The assistant doesn't need to be an expert in every domain, but they need to understand what each specialist can do, how to communicate with them effectively, and how to coordinate their efforts to accomplish complex goals.

The MCP architecture enforces isolation at the client level: each client instance establishes a single stateful session with one server and maintains its own context. Servers never receive the full conversation history, but only the contextual snippets they need, and they cannot inspect data intended for other servers. This design keeps sampling and context exchange strictly separated, preventing information from leaking across servers.

To build such a "personal assistant," we'll explore the core client features of capability discovery, context management, and tool orchestration here.

Discovery and capability management

One of the first things an MCP client does when it connects to a server is discover what that server can do. This isn't just a one-time setup process; it's an ongoing conversation. Servers can add new capabilities, modify existing ones, or temporarily disable features based on load or maintenance requirements.

The client needs to maintain an up-to-date understanding of the available capabilities across all connected servers. But more than that, it needs to understand how these capabilities relate to each other and how they can be combined to accomplish larger goals.

In addition to basic capability discovery, MCP clients must negotiate and manage three built-in client features defined by the MCP specification:

- **Sampling** allows a server to ask the client to run a model on its behalf, but such requests always require explicit user consent, and the model operates in an isolated context
- **Roots** define filesystem boundaries for file URIs; a client can specify which directories are accessible to the server and can update these boundaries dynamically
- **Elicitation** enables a server to request structured input from the user via schemas, then users can confirm, decline, or cancel these requests, preserving privacy and control.

An effective MCP client manages these features transparently alongside other server capabilities.

Recent MCP specification updates (June 2025 `https://modelcontextprotocol.io/specification/2025-06-18/changelog`) also strengthen client–server security. MCP servers are now formally defined as OAuth resource servers, and clients must include a resource indicator (RFC 8707) when requesting access tokens. Resource indicators bind a token to a specific server, preventing cross-server token misuse. Servers may advertise the location of their authorization server, and implementers are encouraged to follow the updated security guidance when implementing clients. In practice this means an MCP client must handle token acquisition and renewal on a per-server basis and respect each server's advertised authorization endpoint.

> **Note**
>
> An OAuth 2.1 resource server is the service that hosts protected resources (such as MCP tools and data). An OAuth client is the application (agent or client library) that requests access tokens to call those resources on behalf of a user.

Suppose a client needs a token for the MCP server at `https://mcp.example.com`. When requesting the token, the client must include a resource parameter identifying the server, for example:

```
POST /token
grant_type=client_credentials&client_id=client123&client_secret=secret&resource=ht
tps://mcp.example.com
```

The authorization server returns a token whose audience (`aud`) claim is set to `https://mcp.example.com`, making it unusable on other servers. This binding of tokens to a specific resource ensures that an access token issued for one MCP server cannot be redeemed against another. Clients should always include the canonical URI of the server when requesting tokens.

Context management and state coordination

Perhaps the most critical role of an MCP client is managing context across multiple servers and operations. AI workflows often involve long chains of related operations, and maintaining context throughout these chains is essential for effective collaboration.

This goes beyond just passing data from one operation to the next. It's about maintaining semantic context, that is, understanding what the user is trying to accomplish, what constraints and preferences apply, and what the current state of the investigation or task is.

The client becomes the memory of the distributed system, keeping track of what's been done, what's been learned, and what still needs to be accomplished.

Intelligent orchestration

MCP clients don't just execute predefined workflows; they make intelligent decisions about how to accomplish goals using available capabilities. This might mean choosing between different approaches based on current conditions, adapting workflows when certain capabilities are unavailable, or discovering new ways to combine capabilities.

The best MCP clients exhibit emergent intelligence. They become more effective over time as they learn from experience, discover new capability combinations, and adapt to changing requirements.

We'll discuss client-side security and credential management in the *Handling security on the client side* section later in this chapter.

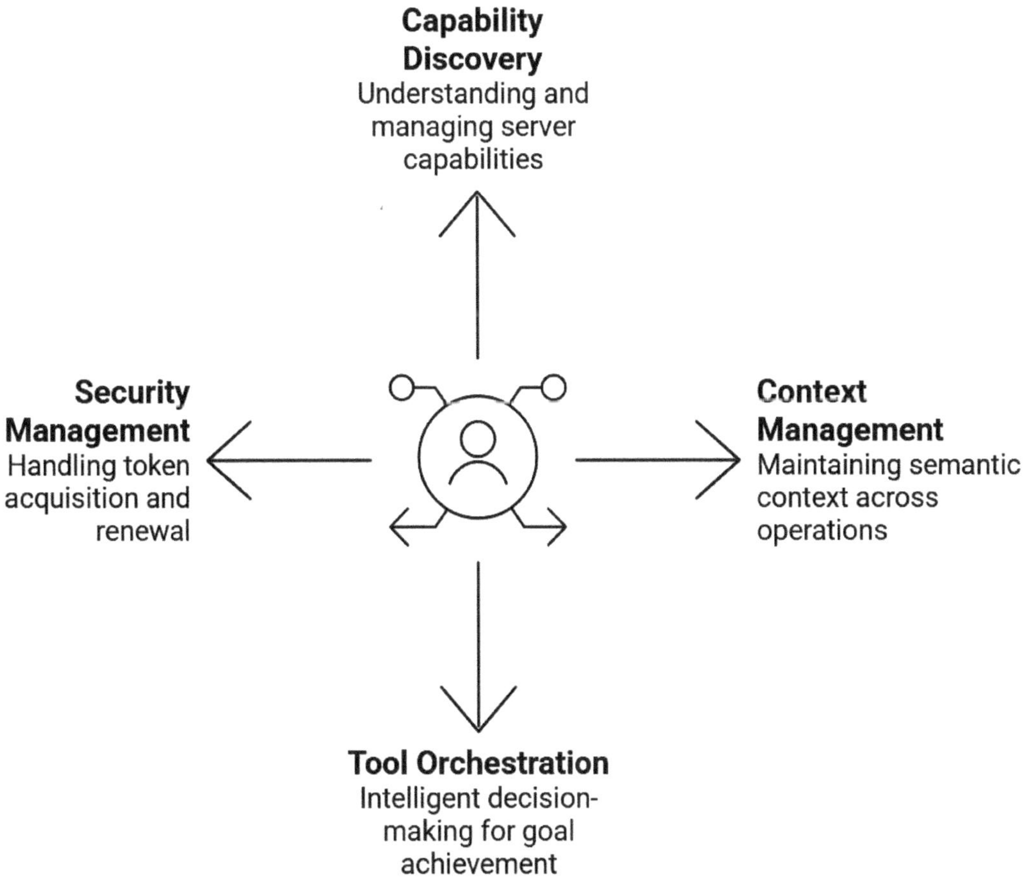

Figure 7.1 – MCP client roles and responsibilities

We've covered the client's foundational role; next, let's examine the built-in features clients must manage, namely, integrating with AI frameworks, retrieving and caching context, orchestrating tool execution, maintaining sessions and state, and managing security and credentials.

Integrating with AI models and frameworks

This is where things get really interesting, and where I've seen the most innovation in recent MCP implementations. The challenge is bridging the gap between how AI models think (in terms of natural language, goals, and intentions) and how MCP servers operate (in terms of structured requests, parameters, and responses). This is very important because closing the gap determines whether your AI agents behave intelligently or get stuck at the API boundary. The upcoming sections break down how clients discover capabilities, manage context, and orchestrate tools to achieve this.

We will focus on LangChain and AutoGen because they were among the earliest open source frameworks to ship official MCP adapters, and their integration patterns illustrate how to wrap MCP tools into agent frameworks. The same concepts apply to other frameworks, such as Semantic Kernel, or bespoke tool-calling systems, so you can adapt the examples here to your preferred stack.

LangChain integration patterns

LangChain has become one of the most popular frameworks for building AI applications, and integrating MCP with LangChain opens up powerful possibilities. The key insight is that MCP servers can provide both tools and memory for LangChain applications.

MCP tools can be exposed as LangChain tools, allowing AI agents to discover and use capabilities dynamically. But more interestingly, MCP resources can serve as external memory for LangChain applications, providing access to vast amounts of contextual information that would be impossible to fit into a model's context window.

I've seen LangChain applications that use MCP to access dozens of different information sources and capabilities, creating AI systems that are far more capable than what you could build with a single model or a fixed set of tools.

A notable development in 2025 is the release of the `langchain-mcp-adapters` package for LangGraph and LangChain. This library makes it straightforward to connect a LangChain agent to one or more MCP servers and expose their tools to the agent. `MultiServerMCPClient` accepts a configuration that maps server identifiers to transport definitions and provides a `get_tools()` method that returns tool specifications. You can then pass these tools to LangChain's `create_react_agent` or bind them directly to a chat model. The official documentation shows how to configure a math server using the stdio transport mechanism and a weather server using the Streamable HTTP transport, retrieve the MCP tools, and invoke them through a LangGraph agent. LangGraph also includes a `ToolNode` abstraction and a `StateGraph` builder that simplify orchestrating tool calls in workflows. These adapters eliminate much of the boilerplate required in early MCP integrations and allow LangChain agents to dynamically discover and use MCP tools.

LangChain's documentation also provides sample MCP server implementations using the `mcp.server.fastmcp` library. A developer can create tools simply by decorating Python functions and running them over different transports (stdio or Streamable HTTP). This makes it easy to spin up custom MCP servers for testing and to integrate them into LangChain workflows.

AutoGen integration strategies

AutoGen is an open source Python framework for building multi-agent systems. AutoGen's multi-agent approach is particularly well-suited to MCP integration. Each AutoGen agent can be connected to different MCP servers, creating a distributed system where different agents have access to different capabilities.

This enables sophisticated collaboration patterns where agents can specialize in different domains while still working together on complex tasks. An agent focused on data analysis might have access to statistical MCP servers, while an agent focused on communication might have access to document generation and formatting servers.

The key is designing the integration so that agents can discover and share capabilities dynamically, rather than having fixed, predetermined roles.

Direct model integration

For applications that connect directly to language models (without frameworks such as LangChain or AutoGen), integrating MCP requires careful prompt engineering as well as robust response parsing.

The client needs to help the model understand what capabilities are available and how to use them effectively. This often involves generating dynamic prompts that include information about available tools and resources, and parsing model responses to extract structured requests for MCP operations.

Figure 7.2 – Integrating AI models with MCP servers

With framework integrations covered, we now turn to another critical client capability, called retrieving context. Within the next section, we will see intelligent context selection, progressive context loading, and caching and optimization.

Managing context retrieval

Context retrieval is one of the hardest parts of building MCP clients; it's where the biggest differences between effective and ineffective systems emerge. The challenge is that AI systems often need access to large amounts of contextual information, but they also have limited attention spans and processing capacity.

To tackle this challenge, the following subsections explore strategies for context retrieval and optimization, intelligent selection, progressive loading, and caching to handle limited context windows and large knowledge bases.

Intelligent context selection

The naive approach to context retrieval is to just grab everything that might be relevant and dump it into the AI's context window. This doesn't work for several reasons: context windows are limited, too much information can be overwhelming, and irrelevant information can actually hurt performance and may not be cost effective.

Effective MCP clients implement intelligent context selection strategies. They understand what information is most relevant for the current task, what the AI's current focus is, and how to prioritize and filter information accordingly.

For example, many retrieval systems set a cosine similarity threshold around 0.8 to filter candidate documents with a similarity score of 0.8 or higher. Thresholds are not one-size-fits-all; developers should experiment with values (e.g., 0.3–0.8) based on the embedding model and domain.

This might involve using embedding-based similarity search to find the most relevant documents, implementing attention mechanisms to focus on the most important parts of large datasets, or using summarization techniques to distill large amounts of information into key insights.

Progressive context loading

Rather than trying to load all relevant context upfront, sophisticated MCP clients implement progressive context loading strategies. They start with the most essential information and then load additional context as needed based on the AI's requests and the evolution of the task.

This approach is more efficient and often more effective because it allows the AI to focus on the most important information first and then drill down into details as needed.

Context caching and optimization

Context retrieval can be expensive, especially when dealing with large datasets or complex analysis operations. Effective MCP clients implement intelligent caching strategies that consider not just what information was requested, but why it was requested and how it might be used in the future.

This might involve caching not just raw data, but processed insights, relationship information, and contextual summaries that can be reused across similar tasks.

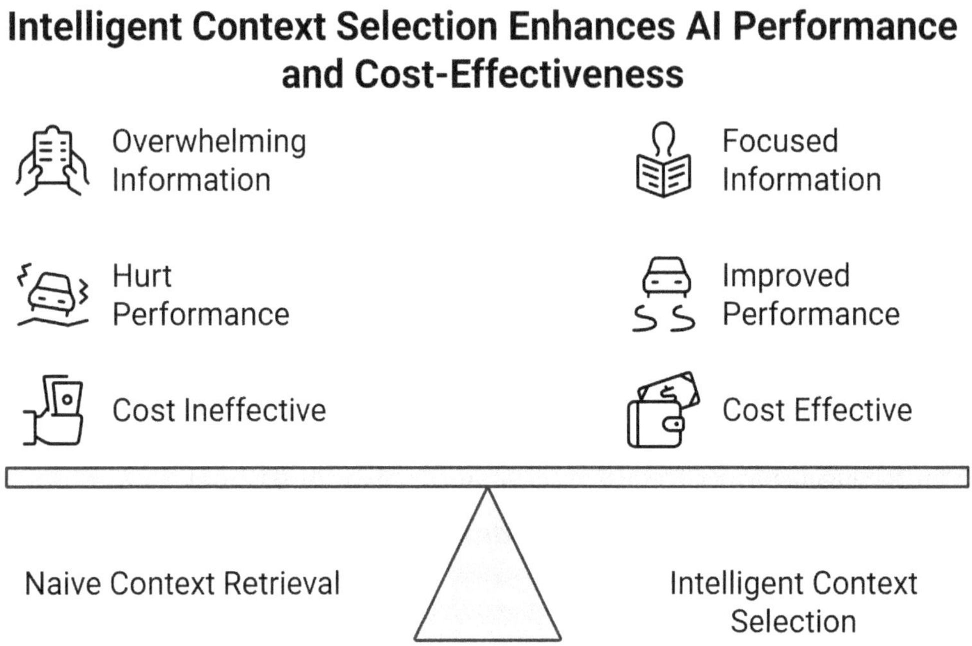

Figure 7.3 – Optimizing AI context retrieval for efficiency

We've addressed context retrieval. Next, we'll explore tool orchestration, error handling, and client-side security. Session and state management will be covered in its own section later in the chapter.

Orchestrating tool execution

Tool orchestration is where MCP clients really show their intelligence. It's not just about calling tools in sequence; it's about understanding how tools relate to each other, how to handle dependencies and failures, and how to adapt workflows based on intermediate results.

Before we get into security, it's important to understand how MCP clients orchestrate multiple tools. The upcoming subsections describe how clients plan and execute sequences of tool calls, handle dependencies and failures, and adapt workflows based on intermediate results.

Dependency management

Many AI workflows involve complex dependencies between operations. The output of one tool might be required as input to another, or certain operations might need to be completed before others can begin.

Effective MCP clients understand these dependencies and can automatically orchestrate tool execution to respect them. This might involve parallel execution of independent operations, automatic retry logic for failed operations, and intelligent fallback strategies when preferred tools are unavailable.

Adaptive workflow management

The best MCP clients don't just execute predefined workflows; they adapt workflows based on intermediate results and changing conditions. If a particular approach isn't working, they can try alternative strategies. If new information becomes available, they can adjust their approach accordingly.

This adaptive behavior is what makes MCP-based AI systems feel more intelligent and flexible than traditional scripted approaches.

Error handling and recovery

AI workflows are inherently uncertain, and tool execution can fail for many reasons (e.g., network issues, server overload, invalid parameters, or simply because the requested operation isn't possible with the available data).

Effective MCP clients implement sophisticated error handling and recovery strategies. They can distinguish between temporary failures (that should be retried) and permanent failures (that require alternative approaches). They can gracefully degrade functionality when certain tools are unavailable. And they can provide meaningful feedback to the AI about what went wrong and what alternatives might be available.

With context and orchestration covered, we will now get into the most important and long-awaited topic – yes, it's security. Client-side security is equally as important as server-side security. Let's take a look at it in detail.

Handling security on the client side

Client-side security in MCP systems involves challenges that go beyond traditional application security. You're dealing with AI systems that might be making autonomous decisions about what data to access and what operations to perform, often on behalf of users who might not fully understand the implications.

The following subsections cover credential management, permission delegation, and data protection. In *Chapter 8*, we explore security topics in greater depth, including authentication mechanisms, authorization and access control, transport layer security, and auditing.

Credential management

MCP clients often need to manage credentials for multiple servers, each with potentially different authentication requirements. This needs to be done securely while still allowing for the dynamic, exploratory behavior that makes AI systems effective.

The challenge is balancing security with usability. You want to make it easy for AI systems to access the capabilities they need, but you also want to ensure that credentials are protected and that access is properly controlled.

Permission delegation

When an AI system acts on behalf of a user, the client needs to ensure that it only performs operations that the user has authorized. This is more complex than traditional access control because AI systems might discover new capabilities or approaches that weren't anticipated when permissions were originally granted.

Effective MCP clients implement permission delegation strategies that allow for flexible, adaptive behavior while still maintaining appropriate controls and audit trails.

Data protection

AI systems often handle sensitive data, so MCP clients must ensure that this data is protected throughout the processing pipeline. This means encrypting data in transit and at rest, and also preventing sensitive information from leaking through logs, error messages, or intermediate results.

The challenge is implementing these protections without interfering with the AI's ability to reason about and process the data effectively.

As we have seen on the server side, the same requirements apply on the client as well. The 2025 MCP specification introduces new security requirements: servers are treated as OAuth resource servers, and clients using HTTP transports must obtain tokens with resource indicators (RFC 8707), binding each token to a specific server. Implementers should build per-server credential routines and follow the updated best practices.

With security considerations addressed, it's time to see how all these pieces work together in practice. Let's get into the last topic of this chapter.

Session and state management

Managing sessions and state across multiple MCP servers and long-running AI workflows is one of the more complex aspects of client implementation. AI tasks often involve extended interactions that span multiple servers and can take a significant amount of time to complete.

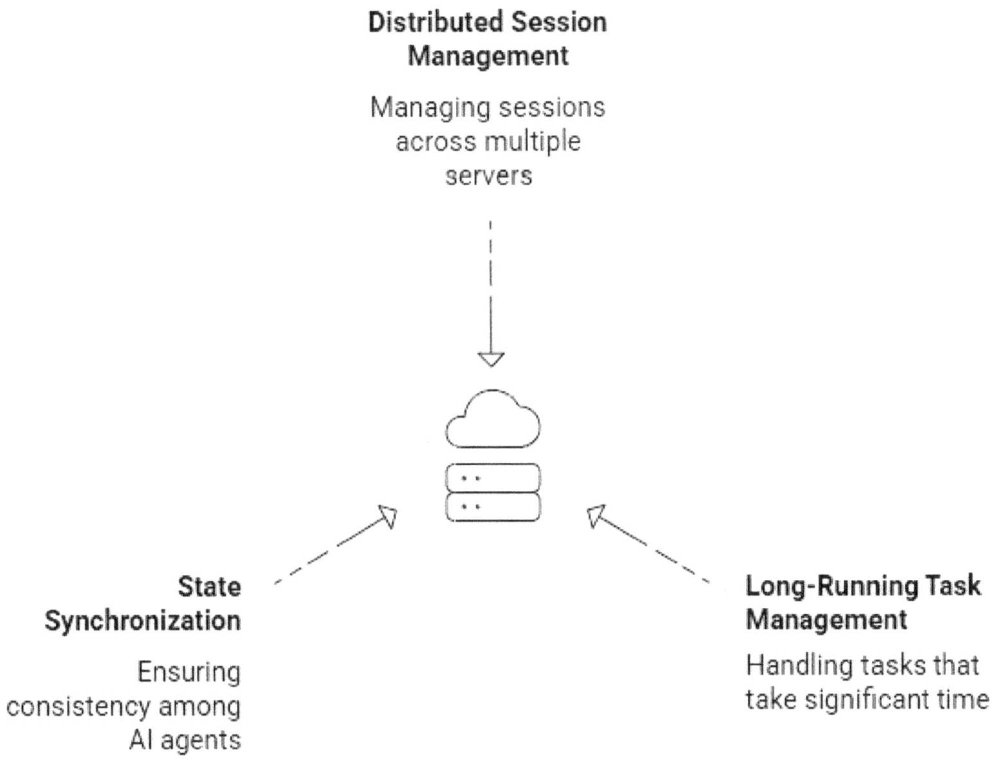

Figure 7.4 – Challenges in MCP client implementation

We will now see how session is managed, especially when distributed for long-running tasks, and how state synchronization works.

Distributed session management

Unlike traditional web applications where sessions are typically managed by a single server, MCP clients need to coordinate sessions across multiple servers. Each server might have its own session requirements and state management needs.

The client becomes responsible for maintaining consistency across these distributed sessions, ensuring that authentication tokens remain valid, and coordinating cleanup when sessions end.

Long-running task management

AI workflows can involve operations that take minutes, hours, or even days to complete. MCP clients need to manage these long-running tasks effectively, providing status updates, handling interruptions, and coordinating recovery if systems restart or connections are lost.

This often involves implementing persistent state storage, checkpoint mechanisms, and resumption strategies that allow complex workflows to survive system restarts and network interruptions.

State synchronization

When multiple AI agents or processes are working with the same MCP servers, the client needs to coordinate state synchronization to ensure consistency and avoid conflicts.

This might involve implementing distributed locking mechanisms, conflict resolution strategies, or event-driven synchronization patterns that keep all participants aware of relevant state changes.

To see these concepts in action, we'll now build a minimal MCP client. The following example shows how to connect to servers, plan workflows, execute tool calls, and maintain context. We break the code into parts to highlight each responsibility.

Code example: Building MCP client integrations

To make these ideas more concrete, the following example implements a minimal but working MCP client. In this example, we will explore the client side of the MCP ecosystem, where AI applications orchestrate and coordinate distributed capabilities. Here, we'll implement a minimal yet functional MCP client that connects to a dummy server, plans a simple workflow based on a goal description, executes it, and maintains context. The example is deliberately small to illustrate context management and orchestration without relying on external libraries.

1. Import `asyncio` and declare the dummy server:

```
import asyncio

# A simple server implementation exposing math tools.
class DummyServer:
    def __init__(self, tools: dict[str, callable]):
        self.tools = tools
    async def discover_capabilities(self) -> list[str]:

# In a real MCP server this would return tool schemas; here we just list
tool names.
        return list(self.tools.keys())
    async def call_tool(self, tool_name: str, *args):
        # Dispatch to the appropriate tool function.
        func = self.tools[tool_name]
        return func(*args)
```

The example begins by importing `asyncio` for asynchronous operations, then defines a dummy server that exposes two mathematical tools. The `discover_capabilities` method returns the list of available tool names, illustrating the capability discovery process described earlier. The `call_tool` method dispatches calls to the corresponding function. In a real MCP server, these methods would return structured schemas and handle error cases, but the simplified interface keeps the focus on client orchestration.

2. Represent workflow steps and workflows:

```
# Data structure representing a step in a workflow.
class WorkflowStep:
    def __init__(self, server_id: str, tool_name: str, args: tuple):
        self.server_id = server_id
        self.tool_name = tool_name
        self.args = args
        self.id = f"{server_id}_{tool_name}"

class Workflow:
    def __init__(self, steps: list[WorkflowStep]):
        self.steps = steps
```

These lightweight classes define a workflow plan as an ordered list of `WorkflowStep` objects, each specifying which server to call, which tool to invoke, and the arguments to pass. `Workflow` encapsulates these steps. The concept of breaking a user goal into discrete steps echoes the chapter's notion of context management, where the client tracks what needs to be done and in what order.

3. Plan and execute workflows with `WorkflowOrchestrator`:

```
# Minimal orchestrator for planning and executing workflows.
class WorkflowOrchestrator:
    async def plan_workflow(self,
                            goal: str,
                            context: dict) -> Workflow:
        """Parse a goal description and generate workflow steps."""
        steps: list[WorkflowStep] = []
        goal_lower = goal.lower()
        # Decide which operations are needed based on keywords in the goal.
        if 'sum' in goal_lower or 'add' in goal_lower:
            steps.append(WorkflowStep('math', 'add', (2, 3)))
        if 'multiply' in goal_lower or 'product' in goal_lower:
```

```
            steps.append(WorkflowStep('math', 'multiply', (4, 5)))
        return Workflow(steps)

    async def execute_workflow(self,
                               workflow: Workflow,
                               servers: dict[str, DummyServer],
                               context: dict) -> list:
        """Execute each step in sequence and update the context."""
        results: list = []
        for step in workflow.steps:
            server = servers[step.server_id]
            result = await server.call_tool(
                        step.tool_name,
                        *step.args
                        )
            # Store result in context for potential downstream use.
            context[f"{step.tool_name}_result"] = result
            results.append(result)
        return results
```

`WorkflowOrchestrator` parses a natural-language goal and produces a sequence of workflow steps based on keyword detection. This demonstrates the intelligent orchestration role of an MCP client, choosing which operations to perform based on the user's intent. The `execute_workflow` method iterates through the steps, calling the appropriate server and storing results in a shared context. Updating the context after each step aligns with the chapter's emphasis on state coordination across operations.

4. Maintain context with a simple context manager:

```
# Simple context manager storing key-value pairs.
class ContextManager:
    def __init__(self):
        self.store: dict[str, any] = {}
    def update(self, key: str, value: any):
        self.store[key] = value
    def get_current(self) -> dict:
        return dict(self.store)
```

The `ContextManager` class encapsulates a dictionary used to store intermediate results and other state information. In real MCP clients, context can include user preferences, prior outputs, and metadata from multiple servers. By isolating context handling in its own component, the example mirrors the context management responsibilities described in the chapter.

5. Bring it together in `MCPClient`:

```
# The MCP client ties everything together.
class MCPClient:
    def __init__(self):
        self.servers: dict[str, DummyServer] = {}
        self.context = ContextManager()
        self.orchestrator = WorkflowOrchestrator()

    async def connect_server(self,
                             server_id: str,
                             server: DummyServer) -> None:
        # Discover and potentially register capabilities (omitted for
brevity).
        await server.discover_capabilities()
        self.servers[server_id] = server

    async def execute_goal(self, goal_description: str) -> list:
        # Plan and execute a workflow based on the goal.
        workflow = await self.orchestrator.plan_workflow(
            goal_description,
            self.context.get_current()
        )


    results = await self.orchestrator.execute_workflow(
        workflow,
        self.servers,
        self.context.store
    )
        return results
```

`MCPClient` combines server connections, the context manager, and the orchestrator. When connecting to a server, it calls `discover_capabilities`, reflecting the ongoing discovery conversation between clients and servers. The `execute_goal` method delegates planning and execution to the orchestrator and returns the results. By encapsulating these responsibilities, `MCPClient` exemplifies how a client becomes the conductor of distributed capabilities.

6. Here, we'll demonstrate client usage:

```
# Demo function illustrating client usage.
async def demo():
    # Create a dummy math server with two tools.
    math_server = DummyServer({'add': lambda a, b: a + b,
                               'multiply': lambda a, b: a * b})
    client = MCPClient()
    await client.connect_server('math', math_server)
    # Execute goals using the MCP client.
    result_sum = await client.execute_goal('Compute the sum of two
numbers')
    result_both = await client.execute_goal('Find sum and multiply
numbers')
    print('Results for sum:', result_sum)
    print('Results for both operations:', result_both)
    print('Context state:', client.context.get_current())

if __name__ == '__main__':
    asyncio.run(demo())
```

This script defines a minimal dummy server that exposes two simple tools (`add` and `multiply`), a basic context manager, a workflow orchestrator that maps goal descriptions to workflow steps, and an MCP client that manages server connections and context. This demonstration illustrates how an MCP client can orchestrate operations without knowing the details of each tool, just as the chapter describes a client acting as a personal assistant that coordinates multiple specialists.

When you run it, the client discovers the server, plans a workflow based on the goal and prints the results. For example, running the script produces output similar to the following:

```
Results for sum: [5]
Results for both operations: [5, 20]
Context state: {'add_result': 5, 'multiply_result': 20}
```

This working example is intentionally simple as it does not implement error recovery, dynamic capability discovery, or the advanced features described earlier. However, it demonstrates how a client can connect to an MCP-style server, plan a workflow, and update its context based on the results. Real clients will build upon these foundations to handle authentication, permission delegation, long-running operations, and intelligent orchestration.

Building effective MCP clients requires thinking beyond traditional API integration patterns. You're not just connecting to services; you're orchestrating intelligence across distributed systems. The client becomes the conductor of an orchestra of AI capabilities, coordinating their efforts to accomplish complex goals.

Client-side integration is where the theoretical elegance of MCP meets the practical challenges of real-world AI applications. It's where distributed capabilities become unified intelligence, where abstract possibilities become concrete actions.

Summary

The best MCP clients are invisible to their users; they make complex distributed systems feel like unified, intelligent assistants. They handle the complexity so the AI can focus on reasoning, and they coordinate the capabilities so the user can focus on their goals.

In this chapter, you learned that MCP clients are the brains of distributed AI systems. You discovered how clients discover and manage server capabilities, maintain context across requests, orchestrate tool execution, integrate with popular frameworks, handle security and state, and ensure fault tolerance and performance. A working example showed these responsibilities in code. Now that you understand how to build intelligent clients, the next chapter emphasizes robust security: per-server authorization, context-aware policies, and careful handling of sensitive data.

Get this book's PDF copy, code bundle, and more

Scan the QR code (or go to `packtpub.com/unlock`). Search for this book by name, confirm the edition, and then follow the steps on the page.

UNLOCK NOW

Note: Have your invoice handy. Purchases made directly from the Packt website don't require an invoice.

Part 3

Security and Performance

Building an MCP system is only the first step; making it secure and performant is what separates prototypes from production-ready deployments. This part provides a comprehensive treatment of the MCP security model, covering authentication, authorization, transport layer security, data privacy, and auditing. It then addresses performance optimization, including profiling, caching strategies, asynchronous execution, and scaling patterns. By the end of this part, you will have the knowledge to strengthen and tune your MCP deployments for enterprise-grade reliability.

This part of the book includes the following chapters:

- *Chapter 8, MCP Security Model*
- *Chapter 9, MCP Performance Optimization*

8

MCP Security Model

> *I've always believed that security in AI systems isn't just about keeping the bad guys out; it's about ensuring that the intelligence itself can be trusted.*

I've been thinking about security for most of my career, but AI security? That's a whole different beast. Traditional security models were designed for predictable systems with well-defined boundaries and clear chains of responsibility. AI systems, especially distributed ones such as those built with MCP, challenge every assumption we've made about how security should work.

The first time I had to secure an MCP deployment, I started with the usual playbook: authentication, authorization, encryption, and audit logs. Standard stuff. But as I dug deeper, I realized that AI systems create security challenges that traditional approaches simply weren't designed to handle. When an AI agent makes autonomous decisions about what data to access and what actions to take, how do you ensure that those decisions are appropriate? When multiple AI systems collaborate through MCP, how do you maintain accountability and prevent malicious behavior?

That project taught me that security for AI systems isn't just about protecting against external threats; it's about ensuring that the intelligence itself can be trusted, that autonomous decisions are appropriate, and that collaboration between AI systems doesn't create new vulnerabilities.

In this chapter, we'll explore why each of the following matters for MCP: authentication, authorization, transport security, data protection, auditing, and client-side safeguards. Understanding the "why" behind each layer of defense will help you build systems that are both trustworthy and effective.

In this chapter, we'll be covering the following topics:

- Importance of security in MCP

- Authentication mechanisms
- Authorization and access control
- Transport layer security (TLS)
- Data security and privacy
- Auditing and logging
- Security considerations for clients
- Advanced security topics

Importance of security in MCP

MCP systems create new kinds of risk. AI agents make autonomous decisions about what data to access, multiple agents collaborate through shared resources, and operations depend heavily on context. Unexpected behaviors can emerge when such capabilities are combined. These factors mean security isn't just about preventing data leaks, but about ensuring that intelligent agents behave appropriately and cooperatively.

In the remainder of this section, we examine four key security challenges that set MCP systems apart from traditional applications: the autonomous decision problem, the collaboration complexity, the context sensitivity challenge, and the emergent risk. Each of these areas addresses a different dimension of the risks introduced by autonomous agents and shared context.

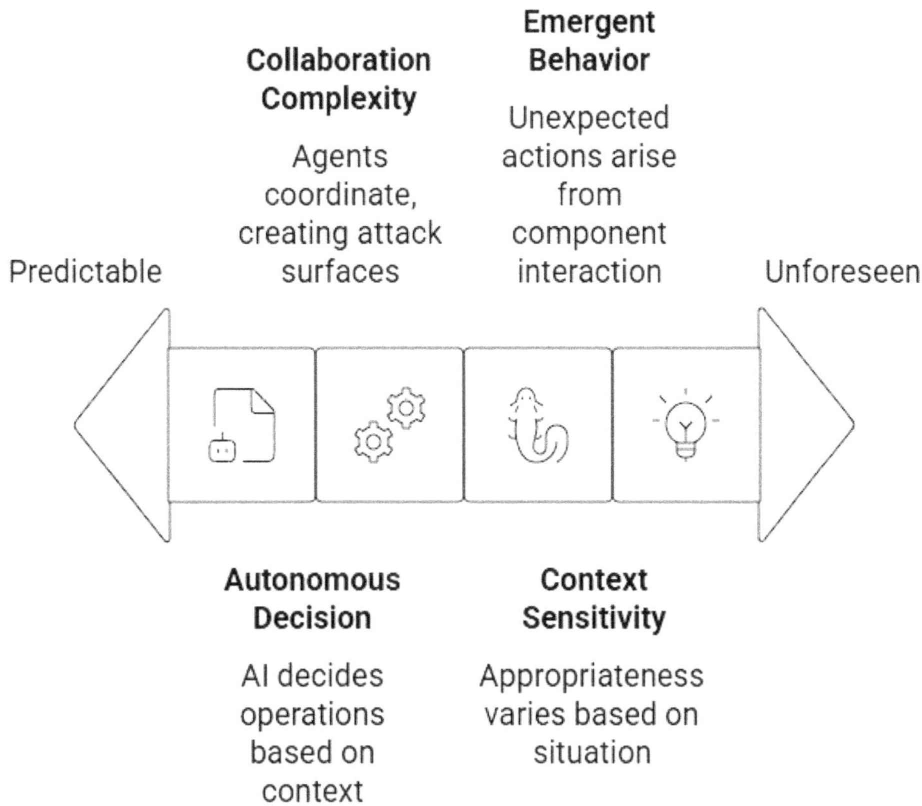

Figure 8.1 – Range of MCP security challenges

The autonomous decision problem

Traditional systems execute predefined operations based on explicit user requests, whereas AI systems make autonomous decisions about what operations to perform based on their understanding of goals and context. This autonomy is what makes AI systems powerful, but it also creates security challenges that didn't exist before.

When an AI agent decides to access sensitive data or execute a powerful tool, how do we ensure that the decision is appropriate? Traditional access control mechanisms can tell us whether the agent has permission to perform the operation, but they can't tell us whether the agent should perform the operation in this specific context.

I worked on a project where an AI assistant had access to customer data for support purposes. The traditional security model would have just checked whether the assistant was authorized to access customer records. But what we really needed to know was whether accessing this specific customer's data was appropriate for this specific support request. The difference is subtle but crucial.

The collaboration complexity

MCP systems often involve multiple AI agents collaborating through shared resources and tools. This collaboration creates new attack surfaces and new opportunities for malicious behavior. An agent that appears benign in isolation might become dangerous when it can coordinate with other agents or access capabilities through MCP servers.

The challenge is maintaining security boundaries while still enabling the flexible, dynamic collaboration that makes MCP systems effective. You need to prevent malicious coordination without breaking legitimate collaboration patterns.

The context sensitivity challenge

AI systems are highly context-sensitive; the same operation might be appropriate in one context and inappropriate in another. Traditional security models struggle with this context sensitivity because they're designed around static rules and permissions rather than dynamic, contextual decision-making.

MCP security needs to be context-aware, considering not just what operation is being requested, but also why it's being requested, how it fits into the larger workflow, and what the potential risks and benefits are.

The emergent behavior risk

Perhaps the most challenging aspect of AI security is dealing with emergent behaviors such as capabilities or actions that arise from the interaction of multiple components in ways that weren't explicitly programmed or anticipated.

When AI agents use MCP to access multiple tools and resources, they might discover new ways to combine capabilities that create unexpected behaviors. Some of these emergent behaviors might be beneficial, but some could be harmful or dangerous.

The MCP specification underlines that any access to user data or invocation of a tool must occur only with explicit user consent and that servers must not transmit resource data without user permission. Tools represent arbitrary code execution and should be treated cautiously; hosts must obtain explicit user approval before invoking them. External analyses note that MCP creates direct pathways between AI systems and enterprise resources, effectively eliminating some traditional isolation boundaries. As a result, real-time policy enforcement has become essential, and so each request should be evaluated based on identity, environment, and the specific action being attempted. These principles reinforce why security and trust considerations are foundational to MCP.

Now that we've established why security matters, let's look at how MCP systems establish trust through authentication.

Authentication mechanisms

Authentication in MCP systems is more complex than traditional web application authentication because you often have multiple parties involved in each interaction, such as the user who initiated the request, the AI agent making the request, and, potentially, other systems or agents in the chain.

We'll begin with multi-party authentication – that is, building a chain of nested credentials that covers every actor in an MCP interaction – before we discuss agent identity and attestation.

Multi-party authentication

The fundamental challenge is establishing a chain of trust that covers all parties involved in an MCP interaction. You need to verify not just that the immediate requester is who they claim to be, but that they have legitimate authority to act on behalf of the ultimate user or system.

This often involves nested authentication schemes where each party in the chain provides credentials that establish both their identity and their authority to act for the previous party in the chain. It's like a diplomatic chain of credentials, where each ambassador carries not just their own credentials but also proof of their authority to represent their government.

Agent identity and attestation

AI agents present unique authentication challenges because they're not human users with traditional identity attributes. An agent's identity might be tied to its training data, its operational parameters, its deployment context, or its intended purpose.

Effective MCP authentication systems need to support agent attestation, a mechanism for agents to prove not just who they are, but also what they're designed to do, how they've been trained, and what constraints govern their behavior.

I've seen systems where agent authentication includes cryptographic proofs of training provenance, behavioral constraints, and operational limits. This goes beyond traditional identity verification to include verification of the agent's intended behavior and capabilities.

Dynamic trust assessment

Unlike traditional authentication systems that make binary decisions (authenticated or not), MCP systems often need to make nuanced trust assessments that consider the full context of the interaction.

This might involve assessing the trustworthiness of the requesting agent based on its past behavior, the sensitivity of the requested operation, the current risk environment, and the potential consequences of the operation.

Dynamic trust assessment allows for more flexible and context-appropriate security decisions, but it also requires sophisticated risk modeling and behavioral analysis capabilities. As discussed in *Chapter 5*, HTTP-based MCP transports use OAuth 2.1: the server acts as an OAuth resource server and the client as an OAuth client. Revisiting this here shows how the protocol's security model fits into MCP's broader framework. These requirements provide a formal framework for multi-party authentication in MCP. Concepts such as agent attestation and dynamic trust assessment are active research areas rather than protocol requirements, but they illustrate how MCP systems may evolve.

With the importance of security and authentication mechanisms in place, we now turn to authorization and access control, covering how to grant agents specific capabilities, evaluate policies in context, and manage identities across multiple parties.

Authorization and access control

Authorization in MCP systems goes far beyond traditional role-based access control. You need to make decisions not just about what an agent can do, but about what it should do in specific contexts.

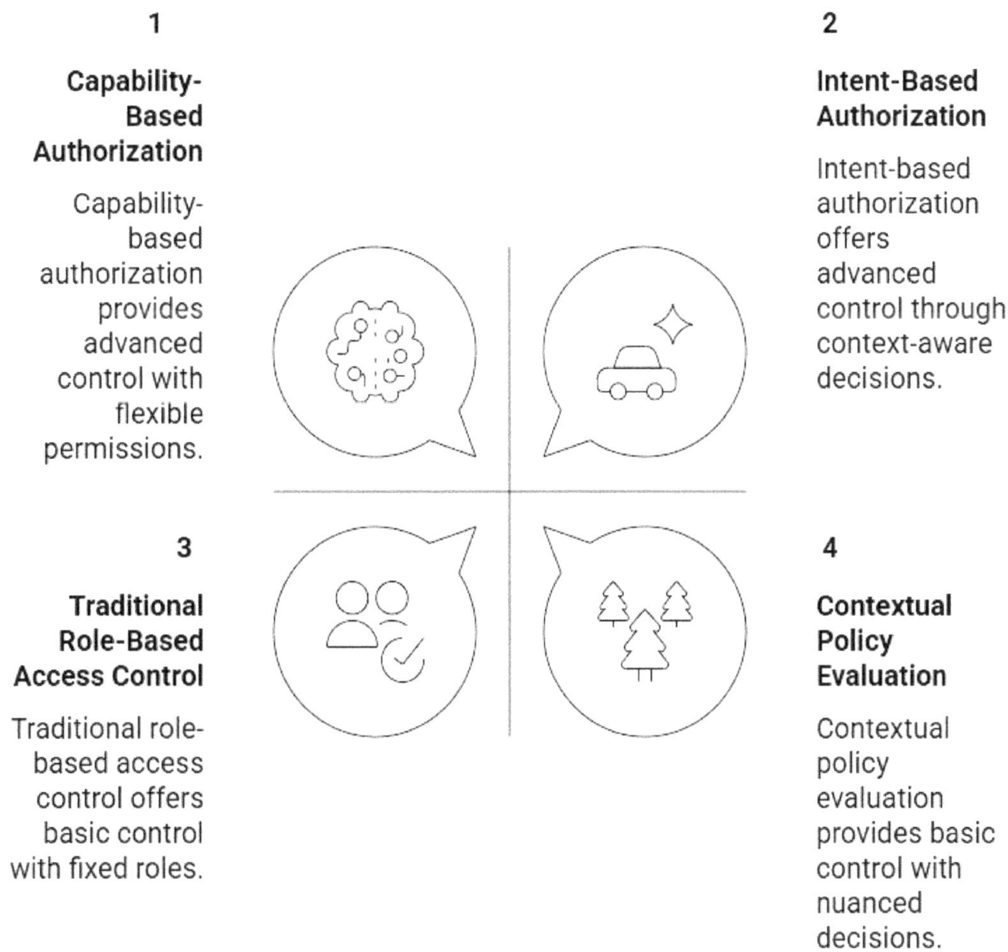

Figure 8.2 – MCP authorization approaches

In this section, we'll go deep into authorization and access control and see how MCP regulates which tools and resources can be used, and under what circumstances.

Capability-based authorization

In *Chapter 6*, we mentioned that **role-based access control** (**RBAC**) simplifies access management by assigning permissions based on predefined roles and hierarchies. This works well for stable organizations, but can lead to role explosion and lacks the context awareness needed for dynamic AI systems. In contrast, capability-based or attribute-based authorization grants rights based on combinations of attributes such as the user's identity, the resource being accessed, the action, and environmental conditions, which then enables fine-grained, context-dependent control. MCP adopts capability-based authorization because agents must make context-aware decisions that RBAC cannot express. If you need a primer on RBAC, then you can refer back to the access control discussion in *Chapter 6*.

Rather than organizing permissions around fixed roles, MCP systems often use capability-based authorization where agents are granted specific capabilities that they can exercise under certain conditions.

This approach is more flexible than role-based systems because it allows for fine-grained control over what operations can be performed, under what circumstances, and with what constraints. An agent might have the capability to access customer data, but only for support purposes, only during business hours, and only with appropriate audit logging.

Contextual policy evaluation

The most sophisticated MCP authorization systems evaluate policies based on the full context of the request: who is making the request, what they're trying to accomplish, what other operations have been performed recently, what the current risk level is, and what the potential consequences are.

This contextual evaluation allows for much more nuanced and appropriate authorization decisions. The same operation might be authorized in one context and denied in another, based on factors that go beyond simple identity and role checks.

Intent-based authorization

One of the most interesting developments in MCP authorization is the emergence of intent-based systems that make authorization decisions based on the declared or inferred intent of the requesting agent.

Rather than just checking whether an agent has permission to perform a specific operation, these systems evaluate whether the operation is consistent with the agent's stated goals and whether those goals are appropriate given the current context.

This approach requires sophisticated intent inference and goal reasoning capabilities, but it enables much more intelligent and context-appropriate authorization decisions.

Current MCP security principles emphasize that users must explicitly consent to operations and maintain control over data sharing, and that hosts should build robust consent and authorization flows into their applications. Capability-based and contextual policy evaluation are natural extensions of these principles, but they are not formally defined in the specification. Industry practitioners recommend implementing policy-as-code frameworks and centralized policy engines to evaluate each request in real time, which aligns with the intent-based authorization described here. Such approaches remain implementation choices rather than standard requirements.

Once we've defined who can do what, it's time to secure the channel itself. Let's look at transport layer security for MCP systems.

Transport layer security (TLS)

In MCP, the transport layer is the underlying protocol (which is HTTP, WebSocket, or gRPC) that carries serialized requests and responses between clients and servers. Securing this channel ensures the confidentiality and integrity of data in transit. Transport layer security in MCP systems follows many of the same principles as traditional web security, but with some important considerations specific to AI workloads and distributed intelligence systems.

In this section, we'll cover end-to-end encryption, certificate management for autonomous agents, and the performance trade-offs of TLS in AI workloads.

End-to-end encryption

MCP communications often involve sensitive data and powerful capabilities, so end-to-end encryption is essential. But the challenge is implementing encryption in a way that doesn't interfere with the dynamic, exploratory behavior that makes AI systems effective.

This might involve using forward secrecy to ensure that past communications remain secure even if current keys are compromised, or implementing key rotation strategies that can adapt to changing security requirements without disrupting ongoing operations.

Certificate management for AI systems

AI agents and MCP servers need digital certificates for secure communication, but managing certificates for dynamic, autonomous systems presents unique challenges.

Traditional certificate management assumes human administrators who can manually renew certificates and handle exceptions. AI systems need automated certificate management that can handle renewal, revocation, and exception handling without human intervention.

Performance considerations

AI workloads often involve large data transfers and computationally intensive operations. The encryption and decryption overhead of TLS can become significant, especially for systems that need to process large amounts of data in real time.

Effective MCP security implementations need to balance security requirements with performance needs, potentially using hardware acceleration, optimized cipher suites, or selective encryption strategies that protect the most sensitive data without creating unnecessary overhead.

With transport security addressed, we turn to protecting the data itself and preserving privacy.

Data security and privacy

Data security in MCP systems involves challenges that go beyond traditional data protection because AI systems often need to process, combine, and reason about data in ways that create new privacy and security risks.

In the upcoming subsections, we will explore specific techniques for safeguarding data in MCP systems: data minimization and purpose limitation, differential privacy and anonymization, and data lineage and provenance. Each practice addresses a different aspect of confidentiality, compliance, and accountability.

Data minimization and purpose limitation

AI systems have a tendency to collect and process as much data as possible, on the theory that more data leads to better results. But from a security and privacy perspective, this creates unnecessary risks.

Effective MCP data security implementations include data minimization strategies that ensure AI systems only access the data they actually need for their specific purposes. This might involve implementing purpose-based access controls, automatic data expiration policies, or privacy-preserving analysis techniques.

Differential privacy and anonymization

Differential privacy is a mathematical framework that protects individuals by ensuring that the inclusion or exclusion of a single person's data does not significantly affect the result of an analysis. It achieves this by adding calibrated randomness so adversaries cannot infer any single participant's involvement. Anonymization, by contrast, means transforming data so completely that no one, not you, a data broker, or even a nation-state, could reasonably re-identify an individual, even with all available auxiliary data. Once data is truly anonymized, it ceases to be considered personal data under regulations such as the GDPR.

When AI systems need to work with sensitive data, differential privacy and anonymization techniques can provide protection while still enabling useful analysis.

MCP systems can implement these techniques at various levels, such as at the data sources themselves, in the transport layer, or in the processing tools. The key is choosing the right approach based on the specific use case and privacy requirements.

Data lineage and provenance

AI systems often combine data from multiple sources and transform it in complex ways. Maintaining data lineage and provenance information is crucial for understanding how sensitive data is being used and ensuring compliance with privacy regulations.

MCP systems should track not just what data is accessed, but how it's processed, combined with other data, and used to make decisions. This lineage information is essential for audit purposes and for ensuring that data usage remains within appropriate bounds.

The MCP specification reiterates that hosts must obtain explicit user consent before exposing user data to servers and must protect user data with appropriate access controls. Implementers are also encouraged to build robust consent flows, document the security implications of their integrations, and consider privacy implications in feature design. These requirements support the data minimization and purpose limitation strategies described here.

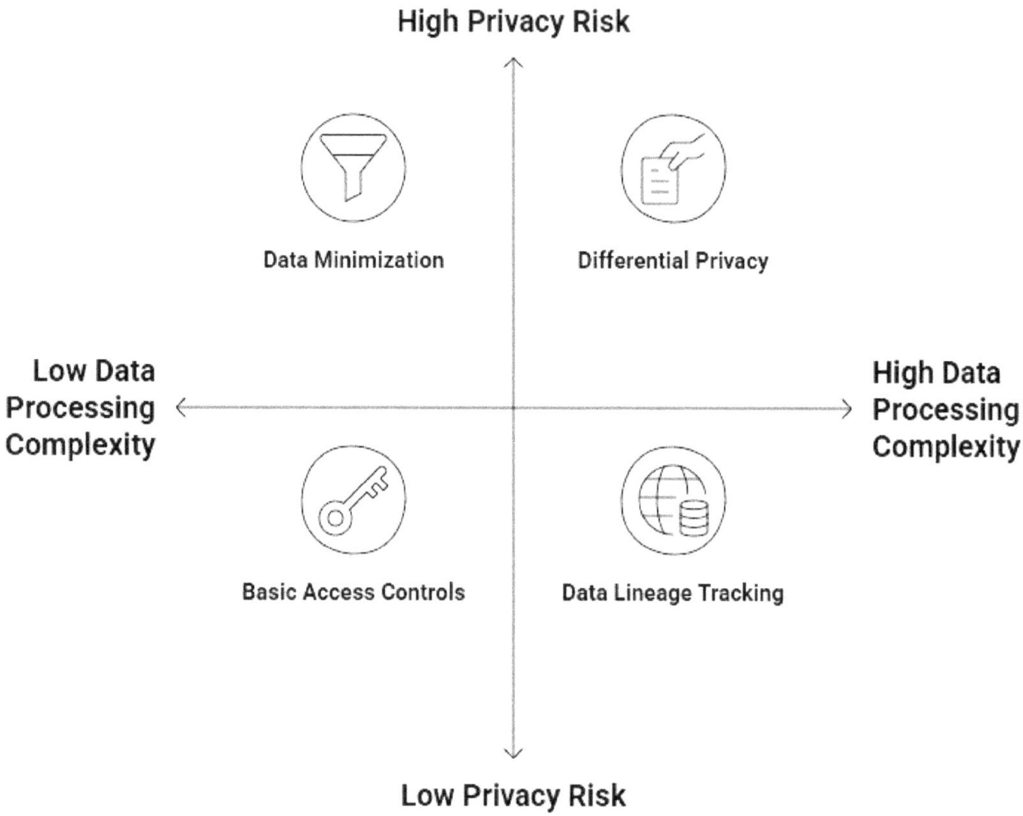

Figure 8.3 – Data security strategies

Safeguarding data is only part of the story; transparency and accountability are equally important. The next sections cover auditing and logging.

Auditing and logging

Auditing in MCP systems involves capturing not just what operations were performed, but why they were performed and how they fit into larger workflows and decision-making processes.

In the following subsections, we will see how to audit MCP systems comprehensively. We begin with activity logging, which captures who did what, when, and why, and then we discuss context-aware auditing, which records the goals and reasoning behind agent operations, and finally, we finish with techniques for securely storing and analyzing audit data.

Comprehensive activity logging

Traditional audit logs capture individual operations, such as who accessed what data, when, and from where. MCP audit logs need to capture the broader context: what goal the AI system was trying to accomplish, what reasoning led to specific operations, and how different operations related to each other.

This comprehensive logging is essential for understanding AI behavior, detecting anomalies, and ensuring accountability for autonomous decisions.

Behavioral analysis and anomaly detection

AI systems can exhibit complex, emergent behaviors that might not be captured by traditional rule-based monitoring. Effective MCP auditing systems include behavioral analysis capabilities that can detect unusual patterns or anomalies in AI behavior.

This might involve machine learning techniques that establish baselines for normal AI behavior and flag deviations that might indicate security issues, malfunctions, or malicious activity.

Privacy-preserving audit techniques

Audit logs themselves can contain sensitive information, creating a secondary privacy challenge. MCP systems need audit techniques that provide sufficient information for security monitoring and compliance while protecting the privacy of the underlying data and operations.

The MCP specification treats logging as an additional utility that servers and clients may expose. While the protocol does not prescribe specific log formats, it encourages implementers to provide comprehensive logging and error reporting to support auditing and monitoring. Design choices about capturing goals, reasoning steps, or privacy-preserving audit techniques remain at the discretion of implementers.

This might involve using cryptographic techniques to protect audit data, implementing access controls for audit logs, or using privacy-preserving analysis techniques for audit data processing.

Having covered server-side security and auditing, we now turn to the security considerations on the client side, where managing user credentials, delegated capabilities, and distributed resources introduces its own challenges.

Security considerations for clients

MCP clients face unique security challenges because they're often the point where multiple security domains intersect – namely, user credentials, AI agent capabilities, and distributed server resources.

We'll start with credential management and delegation: how clients securely manage tokens for multiple servers and delegate authority to agents.

Credential management and delegation

MCP clients often need to manage credentials for multiple servers and delegate authority to AI agents. This needs to be done securely while still enabling the dynamic, exploratory behavior that makes AI systems effective.

Effective credential management strategies might involve using short-lived tokens, implementing credential rotation policies, or using cryptographic techniques that allow for secure delegation without exposing long-term credentials.

Sandboxing and isolation

AI agents can exhibit unpredictable behavior, so MCP clients should implement sandboxing and isolation techniques that limit the potential damage from malicious or malfunctioning agents.

This might involve running agents in isolated environments, implementing resource limits, or using capability-based security models that restrict what operations agents can perform.

Secure communication patterns

MCP clients need to implement secure communication patterns that protect against various attack vectors, such as man-in-the-middle attacks, replay attacks, injection attacks, and others.

This involves not just using secure transport protocols, but also implementing application-level security measures such as request signing, nonce-based replay protection, and input validation.

In enterprise deployments, MCP clients are often the first line of defense. They should intercept high-risk actions before they reach core systems and evaluate each request against predefined policies. The MCP server then acts as the central policy engine, making real-time decisions about whether a specific request should be allowed, taking into account user identity, environmental context, and organizational rules. This layered architecture complements the credential management, sandboxing, and secure communication patterns described previously.

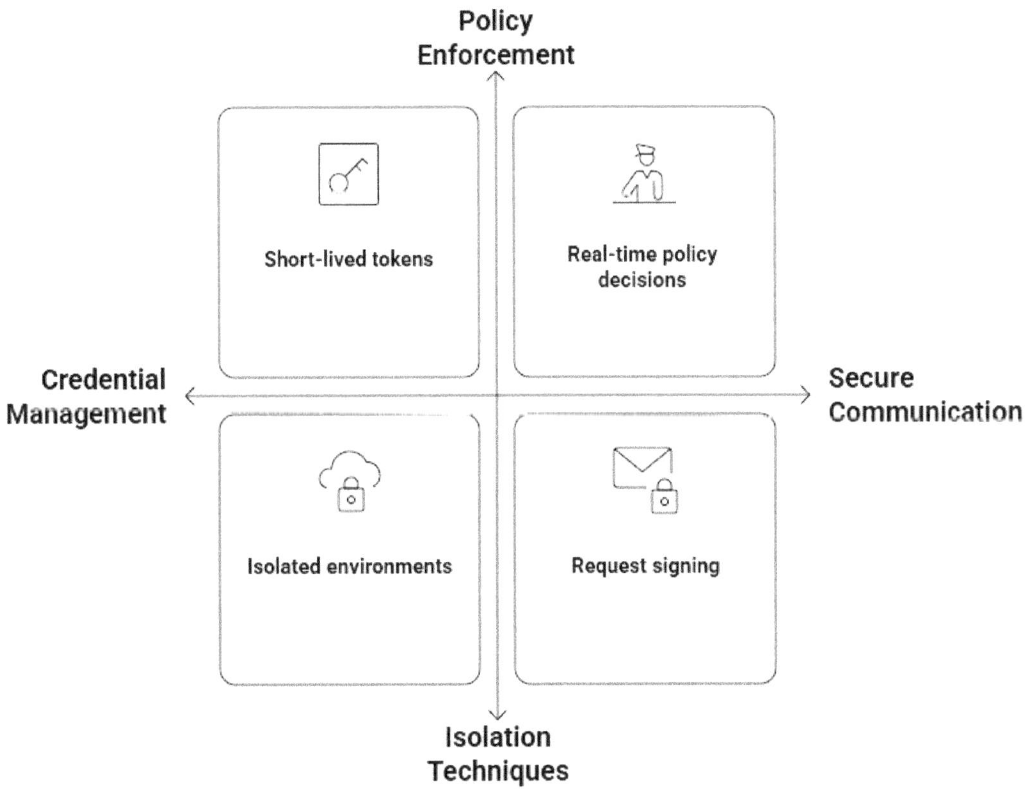

Figure 8.4 – MCP client security strategies

In the final section, we'll explore advanced topics that address emerging security challenges: cross-domain policy enforcement, which implements mechanisms between security domains to prevent bypassing policy controls, and mitigating emergent behaviors, because interactions among AI agents can produce systemic risks even when individual agents behave correctly.

Advanced security topics

As MCP systems become more sophisticated, new security challenges and opportunities emerge that require advanced techniques and approaches. To tackle the challenges that arise in large multi-agent deployments, we now consider three advanced security areas: secure coordination among multiple agents using zero-trust architecture, homomorphic encryption, and blockchain and distributed ledger technologies.

Zero-trust architecture

Zero-trust security models, which assume that no component of the system can be inherently trusted, are particularly well-suited to MCP systems where multiple autonomous agents interact through distributed resources.

Implementing zero-trust in MCP systems involves continuous verification of all participants, least-privilege access controls, and comprehensive monitoring of all interactions.

Homomorphic encryption and secure computation

For scenarios where AI systems need to process sensitive data without exposing it, homomorphic encryption and secure multi-party computation techniques can enable privacy-preserving analysis.

These techniques allow AI systems to perform computations on encrypted data without decrypting it, providing strong privacy guarantees while still enabling useful analysis.

Blockchain and distributed trust

For MCP systems that span multiple organizations or trust domains, blockchain and distributed ledger technologies can provide mechanisms for establishing trust and maintaining accountability without requiring a central authority.

This might involve using blockchain for credential management, audit logging, or consensus mechanisms for distributed decision-making.

The techniques discussed throughout this section (zero-trust architecture, homomorphic encryption, secure computation, and blockchain) represent active research directions for advanced MCP deployments. They are not part of the current protocol specification and should be treated as exploratory approaches for future systems.

Summary

Security in AI systems isn't just about building walls; it's about building trust. The best MCP security systems don't just prevent bad things from happening; they enable good things to happen safely and responsibly.

Security in MCP systems requires rethinking traditional security models to address the unique challenges of distributed AI systems. The key principles are as follows:

- **Context-aware security**: Security decisions should consider the full context of operations, not just identity and permissions
- **Multi-party trust**: Authentication and authorization need to handle complex chains of delegation and representation

- **Behavioral monitoring**: Security systems need to understand and monitor AI behavior, not just individual operations
- **Privacy-preserving intelligence**: AI systems should be able to work with sensitive data while maintaining strong privacy protections
- **Adaptive security**: Security measures should adapt to changing conditions, threats, and system behavior

The goal isn't just to protect MCP systems from external threats, but to ensure that the intelligence itself can be trusted, that autonomous decisions are appropriate, that collaboration is beneficial, and that the system behaves in ways that align with human values and intentions.

Building secure MCP systems requires expertise in both traditional security and AI safety. It's a challenging field, but it's also essential for realizing the full potential of distributed AI systems while maintaining the trust and safety that users and organizations require.

The next chapter takes you from security to performance. We will begin by explaining why optimizing MCP systems isn't just about speed but about making AI interactions feel effortless. You'll learn how to identify common bottlenecks such as the latency cascade, context-loading overhead, and unpredictably bursty workloads, then explore profiling techniques that measure not just latency but "intelligence effectiveness" across distributed workflows. The chapter gets into server-side optimizations such as predictive caching, adaptive resource allocation, streaming responses, and batch execution, followed by client-side strategies such as predictive context loading and intelligent request orchestration. Finally, it covers protocol-level efficiencies, connection pooling, JSON-RPC batching, and the Streamable HTTP transport to remove friction at every layer.

Subscribe for a free eBook

New frameworks, evolving architectures, research drops, production breakdowns—*AI_Distilled* filters the noise into a weekly briefing for engineers and researchers working hands-on with LLMs and GenAI systems. Subscribe now and receive a free eBook, along with weekly insights that help you stay focused and informed.

Subscribe at `https://packt.link/8Oz6Y` or scan the QR code below.

9

MCP Performance Optimization

> *I always believe performance isn't just about speed; it's about making intelligence feel effortless.*

I've optimized a lot of systems over the years, but optimizing AI systems? That's a different kind of challenge entirely. Traditional performance optimization is mostly about making things faster: reducing latency, increasing throughput, and minimizing resource usage. AI performance optimization is about all of that, plus making intelligence more effective, more responsive, and more... well, intelligent.

The first MCP system I had to optimize was running like molasses. Not because the individual components were slow; in fact, they were quite fast. The problem was that the AI was spending most of its time waiting. Waiting for servers to respond, waiting for data to transfer, waiting for tools to be completed. The system was technically correct, but it felt sluggish and unresponsive.

That project taught me that performance optimization for AI systems isn't just about making individual operations faster; it's about orchestrating intelligence in ways that feel natural and responsive. It's about anticipating needs, pre-computing results, and creating the illusion that the system is always one step ahead of what you're going to ask for.

In this chapter, you'll learn what makes MCP performance optimization unique. We'll explore the challenges of latency cascades, context loading, exploration versus exploitation, and unpredictable load patterns. Then we'll cover profiling and measurement techniques for AI workflows, server- and client-side optimization strategies, protocol-level improvements such as batching and streaming, and the importance of continuous monitoring. Together, these topics will help you build AI systems that feel responsive and intelligent, and not just fast.

In this chapter, we'll be covering the following topics:

- Understanding performance challenges in MCP

- Performance profiling and measurement
- Server-side optimization strategies
- Client-side optimization strategies
- Protocol-level optimizations
- Monitoring and continuous optimization

Understanding performance challenges in MCP

MCP systems face unique performance challenges that don't exist in traditional applications. Understanding these challenges is the first step toward addressing them effectively.

Let's look at some of these challenges in the upcoming subsections.

The latency cascade problem

In traditional applications, you might have a user making a request to a server, which processes it and returns a response. Simple. In MCP systems, you often have chains of operations where the output of one tool becomes the input to another, and each step might involve network communication with different servers.

This creates what I call the "latency cascade problem," wherein even if each individual operation is fast, the cumulative latency of a complex workflow can become unacceptable. A workflow that involves five sequential operations, each taking 200 ms, would result in a full second of latency before the user sees any results.

The issue is that these workflows are often discovered dynamically by AI systems, so you can't always predict which operations will be chained together or optimized for specific sequences in advance.

The context loading bottleneck

AI systems often need access to large amounts of contextual information to make good decisions. But loading all that context for every operation is expensive and often unnecessary. The challenge is figuring out what context is actually needed and loading it efficiently.

I worked on a system where the AI needed access to a company's entire document repository to answer questions. Loading all the documents for every query was obviously impractical, but determining which documents were relevant required understanding the query, which required some context about the user and their current task, which required... You see the problem.

The exploration versus exploitation trade-off

AI systems often need to explore different approaches to solving problems, which means they might make requests that don't directly contribute to the result. This exploration is valuable for learning and adaptation, but it can also create performance overhead.

The challenge is balancing the need for exploration with the need for responsive performance. You want to enable AI systems to try different approaches and learn from the results, but you don't want users to wait while the system explores dead ends.

The unpredictable load problem

Traditional applications often have predictable load patterns that you can optimize for. AI systems can exhibit highly unpredictable load patterns; they might suddenly discover a useful capability and start using it heavily, or they might shift their approach based on new information and completely change their resource usage patterns.

This unpredictability makes it difficult to use traditional performance optimization techniques such as caching, pre-computation, or resource allocation strategies that assume predictable usage patterns.

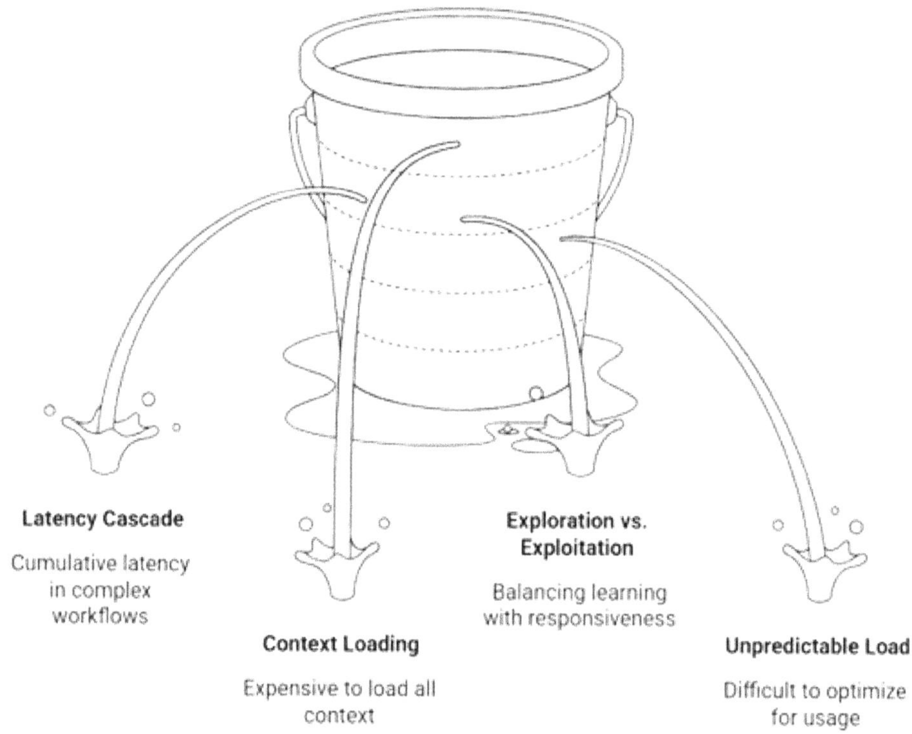

Figure 9.1 – MCP system performance bottlenecks

Performance profiling and measurement

Before you can optimize MCP system performance, you need to understand where the bottlenecks are. This is more complex than traditional performance profiling because you're dealing with distributed systems, autonomous agents, and complex workflows.

Profiling MCP systems means analyzing entire workflows, not just individual operations. The next subsections explain how to identify bottlenecks across distributed components and introduce new metrics, such as intelligence effectiveness and context sensitivity, that matter more than raw latency for AI systems.

End-to-end workflow profiling

Traditional profiling focuses on individual operations or components. MCP profiling needs to consider entire workflows, from the user's initial request to the result. This means tracking not just how long individual operations take, but how they combine into larger workflows and where the cumulative bottlenecks occur.

I've found that the biggest performance problems in MCP systems often aren't in individual operations; they're in the orchestration and coordination between operations. An operation that's fast in isolation might become slow when it's part of a complex workflow with dependencies and coordination requirements.

Intelligence effectiveness metrics

Beyond traditional performance metrics such as latency and throughput, MCP systems need metrics that measure the effectiveness of intelligence itself. How often do AI systems find the information they need on the first try? How often do they need to backtrack or try alternative approaches? How well do they adapt to changing conditions?

These intelligence effectiveness metrics are crucial for understanding whether performance optimizations are improving the user experience or just making individual operations faster without improving overall system effectiveness.

Context sensitivity analysis

Performance in MCP systems is highly context-dependent. The same operation might be fast in one context and slow in another, depending on what data is available, what other operations are running concurrently, and what the AI's current goals are.

Effective performance analysis needs to consider this context sensitivity and identify patterns in when and why performance problems occur. This might involve analyzing performance across different user types, different task categories, or different system load conditions.

Distributed tracing and correlation

MCP systems involve multiple servers, multiple AI agents, and complex interaction patterns. Understanding performance requires distributed tracing capabilities that can track requests across multiple systems and correlate performance data from different components.

This is particularly challenging because AI systems might make requests to multiple servers in parallel, retry operations with different parameters, or dynamically discover new capabilities during execution.

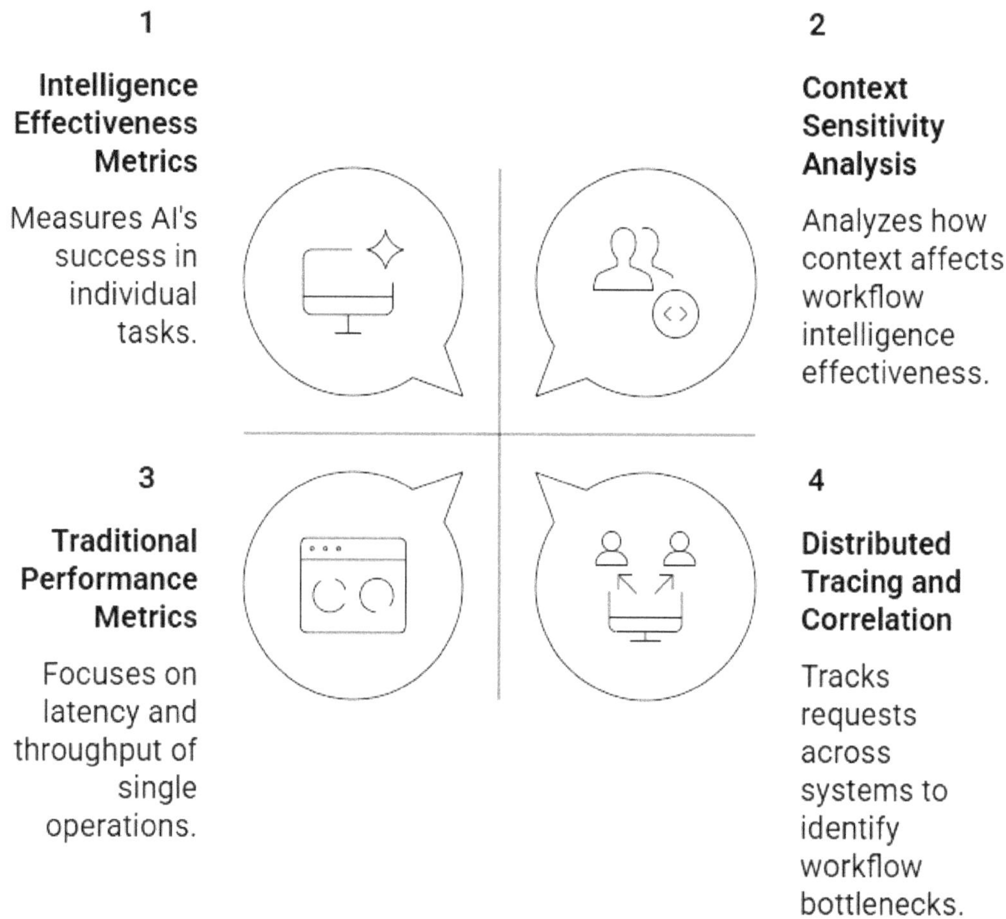

Figure 9.2 – MCP performance optimization strategies

Once you understand where the time goes, the next step is fixing it. Let's move on to server-side optimization strategies.

Server-side optimization strategies

Optimizing MCP servers requires thinking beyond traditional server optimization techniques to consider the specific needs and behaviors of AI clients.

The following server-side techniques—intelligent caching, adaptive resource allocation, batch processing and operation fusion, and streaming results—will show how to make MCP servers more responsive and efficient.

Intelligent caching strategies

Traditional caching strategies focus on caching the results of expensive operations. MCP servers need more sophisticated caching strategies that consider not just what was requested, but why it was requested, and how it might be used in the future.

This might involve caching not just raw data, but processed insights, relationship information, and contextual summaries that can be reused across similar requests. It might also involve predictive caching that anticipates what information AI systems are likely to need based on their current context and goals.

Adaptive resource allocation

AI workloads can be highly variable and unpredictable. MCP servers need adaptive resource allocation strategies that can respond to changing load patterns and optimize resource usage based on current demand and system conditions.

This might involve dynamic scaling of computational resources, intelligent load balancing that considers the semantic content of requests, or priority-based resource allocation that ensures critical operations get the resources they need.

Batch processing and operation fusion

AI systems often make multiple related requests in rapid succession. MCP servers can optimize performance by identifying opportunities to batch these requests together or fuse multiple operations into single, more efficient operations.

This requires understanding the semantic relationships between operations and the ability to dynamically restructure workflows to improve efficiency without changing the results.

Streaming and progressive results

Many AI operations can benefit from streaming or progressive results that allow processing to begin before the complete response is available. This is particularly important for operations that involve large datasets or complex analysis.

MCP servers can support progressive updates in two complementary ways.

First, the protocol includes progress notifications that allow either the client or the server to send structured updates about a long-running operation. A client that wishes to receive progress information includes a progress token in the `_meta` field of the request; the server may then emit notifications/progress messages containing the original token, a current progress value, an optional total, and an optional human-readable message. These notifications let clients update user interfaces without waiting for the full result and help them make cancellation decisions.

Second, the Streamable HTTP transport defined by MCP enables true server-side streaming. When using this transport, the server exposes a single endpoint that supports both `POST` and `GET` requests. Clients `POST` JSON-RPC requests and may include an array of multiple requests, and servers may respond over an SSE stream. Responses and notifications on this stream may be batched, and the server may send its own requests or notifications before returning results. This mechanism lets servers stream partial results and interleave progress messages as they become available. Note that progressive streaming and batching are optional features of the transport; implementations must decide when to take advantage of them based on their workloads and user experience.

Because the core protocol does not mandate when or how to send progress updates, implementers should design server logic to emit progress notifications when useful (e.g., after expensive phases) and to limit update frequency to avoid flooding clients.

Server-side improvements are only half of the story. Next, we'll see how MCP clients can optimize performance from their side.

Client-side optimization strategies

MCP clients have unique opportunities for optimization because they understand the broader context of AI workflows and can make intelligent decisions about how to orchestrate operations across multiple servers.

The client-side strategies we'll be exploring leverage the client's global view of the workflow to reduce latency and improve responsiveness.

Predictive context loading

Rather than loading context reactively in response to specific requests, sophisticated MCP clients can implement predictive context loading that anticipates what information AI systems are likely to need based on their current goals and past behavior patterns.

This might involve using machine learning techniques to predict which documents, tools, or resources are likely to be needed for specific types of tasks, and pre-loading that information to reduce latency when it's requested.

Intelligent request orchestration

MCP clients can optimize performance by intelligently orchestrating requests across multiple servers. This might involve parallelizing independent operations, pipelining dependent operations, or dynamically reordering operations to minimize overall latency.

The key is understanding the dependencies and relationships between operations and finding ways to execute workflows more efficiently without changing the results.

Adaptive workflow optimization

As AI systems learn and adapt, their workflow patterns change. MCP clients should implement adaptive optimization strategies that learn from past performance and adjust their orchestration strategies accordingly.

This might involve identifying common workflow patterns and optimizing them, detecting performance bottlenecks and finding alternative approaches, or learning which servers and tools are most effective for different types of tasks.

Speculative execution

In some cases, MCP clients can improve perceived performance by speculatively executing operations that are likely to be needed, even before they're explicitly requested. This is risky because speculative operations consume resources and might not be needed, but when done intelligently, they can significantly improve responsiveness.

The key is developing good heuristics for when speculative execution is likely to be beneficial and implementing mechanisms to cancel speculative operations if they're not needed.

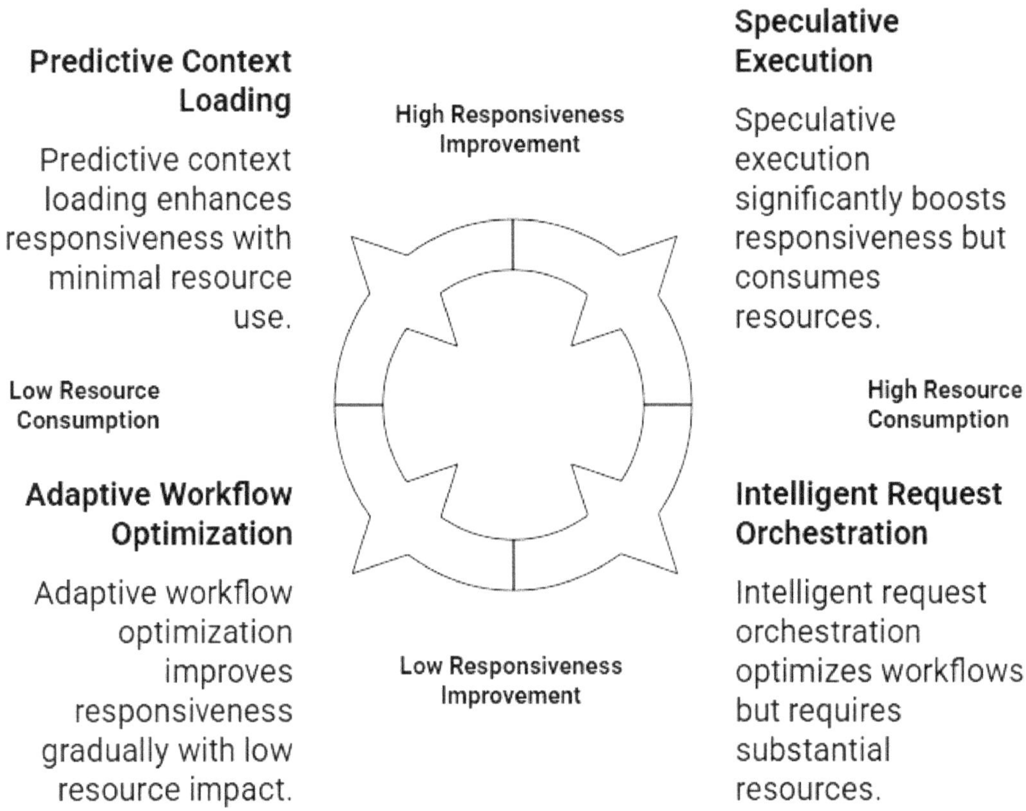

Figure 9.3 – MCP optimization strategies

Having tuned both servers and clients, we can now look at protocol-level optimizations that benefit all implementations.

Protocol-level optimizations

The MCP protocol itself offers optimization opportunities that apply across all implementations. In the next subsections, we'll explore several of them.

Connection pooling and reuse

Establishing connections to MCP servers can be expensive, especially when using secure transport protocols. Connection pooling and reuse strategies can amortize this cost across multiple operations.

When choosing connection pooling for AI workloads, we need to consider more than just reducing connection overhead. We also need to account for session state, authentication context, and the semantic relationships between operations.

Request batching and pipelining

The MCP protocol uses JSON-RPC 2.0 for encoding messages. JSON-RPC defines a batch request format whereby a single message body can contain an array of requests and/or notifications. The stdio and Streamable HTTP transports supported by MCP allow clients to send such a batched array to reduce the connection overhead. When using the Streamable HTTP transport, servers may respond via an SSE stream and interleave multiple responses and notifications, and these messages may themselves be batched. Pipelined execution (sending additional requests before receiving prior responses) is an implementation choice rather than a protocol requirement. Implementers should balance the efficiency gains of batching against the need for low-latency interactivity; small batches can reduce overhead without delaying urgent operations.

Compression and encoding optimizations

Because MCP is built on plain JSON-RPC over stdio or HTTP, the protocol itself does not prescribe any compression or alternate encoding formats. However, many server implementations choose to compress large payloads (for example, using *gzip* or *brotli*) at the HTTP layer, and some clients compress cached context data before storage. The optimal compression strategy depends on the type of data, the network conditions, and the computational resources available on both the client and server sides. Developers should treat compression as an implementation-level optimization rather than a feature of the protocol.

Protocol extensions for performance

While the core MCP protocol is designed to be simple and general-purpose, specific implementations might benefit from protocol extensions that enable performance optimizations for particular use cases.

This might involve extensions for streaming large datasets, bulk operations, or specialized encoding formats that are optimized for specific types of AI workloads.

To make these concepts concrete, the following case study walks through optimizing a real-world MCP deployment. We chose this example to show how the techniques we've discussed translate into practice and to highlight the tangible benefits of performance optimization.

Example: Simulating progress notifications

To illustrate how progress notifications can make a long-running operation feel more responsive, the following Python snippet simulates an MCP server sending progress updates while performing work. The server issues notifications/progress messages with the current progress percentage and a human-readable message; the client could display these updates to the user while waiting for the final result. Although this example does not implement the full MCP protocol, it demonstrates the underlying concept and uses the same message structure defined in the specification.

```
import time


def long_running_task(total_steps: int = 5) -> str:
    """Simulate a task that periodically emits progress notifications."""
    for step in range(1, total_steps + 1):
        # simulate work taking some time
        time.sleep(0.1)
        progress = int((step / total_steps) * 100)
        message = f"{progress}% complete"
        # progress notification using the MCP structure
        notification = {
            "method": "notifications/progress",
            "params": {
                "progressToken": "demo-token",
                "progress": progress,
                "total": 100,
                "message": message,
            },
        }
        print(notification)
    return "Task finished"


if __name__ == "__main__":
    result = long_running_task()
    print(result)
```

Running this script outputs progress notifications at 20% increments and concludes with a completion message. In a real MCP implementation, these notifications would be sent over the network to the client and associated with a specific tool invocation via `progressToken`. Clients can use this mechanism to provide real-time feedback to users and decide whether to cancel an operation.

Monitoring and continuous optimization

Performance optimization for MCP systems isn't a one-time activity; it's an ongoing process that requires continuous monitoring, analysis, and adaptation.

Real-time performance monitoring

MCP systems need real-time monitoring capabilities that can detect performance problems as they occur and provide actionable information for addressing them. The protocol itself includes a logging utility that allows servers to emit structured log messages to clients. Servers declare a logging capability and send notifications/message events carrying a severity level, an optional logger name, and arbitrary JSON data. Clients can adjust log verbosity by sending a `logging/setLevel` request, and logs can be filtered or presented to users as needed. These logging notifications provide insight into server behavior but do not prescribe specific performance metrics; implementers should combine them with external instrumentation to monitor latency, throughput, and AI-specific metrics such as task completion rates, workflow efficiency, and user satisfaction.

Automated performance analysis

Given the complexity and variability of AI workloads, manual performance analysis isn't sufficient. MCP systems need automated analysis capabilities that can identify performance patterns, detect anomalies, and suggest optimization opportunities.

This might involve using machine learning techniques to analyze performance data, identify bottlenecks, and recommend optimization strategies based on observed patterns and behaviors.

Adaptive optimization strategies

The best MCP performance optimization systems are adaptive. They continuously learn from performance data and adjust their optimization strategies accordingly.

This might involve automatically adjusting caching strategies based on observed access patterns, dynamically rebalancing load based on current system conditions, or learning new workflow optimization patterns from AI behavior.

Performance-aware development

Performance optimization shouldn't be an afterthought; it should be integrated into the development process for MCP systems. This means designing performance considerations into the architecture from the beginning and continuously testing and optimizing throughout the development lifecycle. For example, when defining a new tool, you can include performance test cases alongside functional tests; when designing a server, you can build in caching or streaming mechanisms from the start; and during development, you can run load tests and profile workflows regularly to catch bottlenecks early. Integrating these practices ensures performance remains a first-class concern throughout the development lifecycle.

With the principles laid out, let's look at concrete examples, starting with a simple code snippet and then a real-world case study.

Code example: Key performance-optimization concepts

Here's a Python demonstration broken into three parts, each illustrating a key performance-optimization concept.

Part 1 – Simulated progress notifications

This snippet emulates a long-running operation that emits progress updates, similar to MCP's notifications/progress mechanism.

```
import time


def long_running_task(total_steps: int = 5) -> str:
    """Simulate a task that periodically emits progress notifications."""
    for step in range(1, total_steps + 1):
        # simulate work taking some time
        time.sleep(0.2)
        progress = int((step / total_steps) * 100)
        message = f"{progress}% complete"
        # progress notification using the MCP structure
        notification = {
            "method": "notifications/progress",
            "params": {
                "progressToken": "demo-token",
                "progress": progress,
                "total": 100,
                "message": message,
```

```
            },
        }
        print(notification)
    return "Task finished"

print("--- Part 1: Progress Notifications ---")
result = long_running_task()
print(result)
Output:
--- Part 1: Progress Notifications ---
{'method': 'notifications/progress', 'params': {'progressToken': 'demo-token',
'progress': 20, 'total': 100, 'message': '20% complete'}}
{'method': 'notifications/progress', 'params': {'progressToken': 'demo-token',
'progress': 40, 'total': 100, 'message': '40% complete'}}
{'method': 'notifications/progress', 'params': {'progressToken': 'demo-token',
'progress': 60, 'total': 100, 'message': '60% complete'}}
{'method': 'notifications/progress', 'params': {'progressToken': 'demo-token',
'progress': 80, 'total': 100, 'message': '80% complete'}}
{'method': 'notifications/progress', 'params': {'progressToken': 'demo-token',
'progress': 100, 'total': 100, 'message': '100% complete'}}
Task finished
```

Part 2 – Predictive caching demonstration

This example shows how preloading likely context items can eliminate load latency for subsequent requests.

```
import time

print("\n--- Part 2: Predictive Caching Demonstration ---")

# Simulate expensive context loading
context_cache = {}

def load_context(item_id):
    """Simulate an expensive context load."""
    time.sleep(0.5)  # Simulate network/disk delay
    return f"data_for_{item_id}"

# Predictive caching: preload predicted items
predicted_items = ['doc1', 'doc2', 'doc3']
```

```
for item in predicted_items:
    context_cache[item] = load_context(item)

def get_context(item_id):
    """Retrieve context, using cache if available."""
    if item_id in context_cache:
        print(f"Retrieved {item_id} from cache")
        return context_cache[item_id]
    else:
        print(f"Loading {item_id} on demand")
        return load_context(item_id)

# Test retrieving context with and without caching
start = time.time()
print(get_context('doc1'))  # Should be fast (cached)
print(get_context('doc4'))  # Not cached, will load
end = time.time()
print(f"Total retrieval time: {end - start:.2f}s")
Output:
--- Part 2: Predictive Caching Demonstration ---
Retrieved doc1 from cache
data_for_doc1
Loading doc4 on demand
data_for_doc4
Total retrieval time: 0.50s
```

The first retrieval (`doc1`) hits the cache; the second (`doc4`) simulates an expensive load, illustrating the benefit of predictive caching.

Part 3 – Sequential versus parallel execution

Here, we compare the sequential execution of tasks versus running them concurrently, demonstrating the latency cascade and how parallelism reduces the overall time.

```
import asyncio
import random
import time

print("\n--- Part 3: Sequential vs Parallel Execution ---")

async def simulated_operation(name):
    delay = random.uniform(0.2, 0.5)
```

```
        await asyncio.sleep(delay)
        return f"{name} finished in {delay:.2f}s"

    async def run_sequential():
        start = time.time()
        results - []
        for i in range(3):
            results.append(await simulated_operation(f"Task{i+1}"))
        duration = time.time() - start
        print("Sequential results:", results, f"Took {duration:.2f}s")

    async def run parallel():
        start = time.time()
        tasks = [simulated_operation(f"Task{i+1}") for i in range(3)]
        results = await asyncio.gather(*tasks)
        duration = time.time() - start
        print("Parallel results:", results, f"Took {duration:.2f}s")

    # Run sequentially then in parallel
    asyncio.run(run_sequential())
    asyncio.run(run_parallel())
    Output:
    --- Part 3: Sequential vs Parallel Execution ---
    Sequential results: ['Task1 finished in 0.47s', 'Task2 finished in 0.37s', 'Task3
    finished in 0.33s'] Took 1.17s
    Parallel results: ['Task1 finished in 0.47s', 'Task2 finished in 0.41s', 'Task3
    finished in 0.23s'] Took 0.48s
```

Running the tasks concurrently cuts the total time roughly in half compared to running them one after the other, illustrating how MCP clients can reduce latency by orchestrating calls in parallel.

Case study: Scaling an MCP deployment

Let me walk you through a real-world example of optimizing an MCP deployment that was struggling with performance issues.

The problem

We had an MCP system supporting a team of AI research assistants. The system provided access to a large corpus of scientific papers, various analysis tools, and collaboration capabilities. The individual components were fast, but the overall system felt sluggish and unresponsive.

The analysis

Our performance analysis revealed several issues:

- AI agents were repeatedly requesting the same contextual information
- Complex analysis workflows were being executed sequentially rather than in parallel
- The document search system was optimized for precision but not for the exploratory search patterns that AI systems typically use
- Network latency between distributed components was creating cumulative delays

The solution

We implemented several optimization strategies:

- **Intelligent context caching**: We implemented a context caching system that learned from AI behavior patterns and pre-loaded information that was likely to be needed
- **Workflow parallelization**: We redesigned the client orchestration to identify opportunities for parallel execution and automatically restructure workflows to minimize sequential dependencies
- **Search optimization**: We implemented a multi-tier search system that provided fast, approximate results for exploratory queries and more precise results for focused queries
- **Geographic distribution**: We deployed MCP servers closer to the AI agents to reduce network latency for common operations

The results

The optimizations resulted in the following improvements for this specific deployment (these figures are illustrative and should not be generalized without benchmarking your own systems):

- 60% reduction in average workflow completion time
- 40% improvement in AI task success rates
- 75% reduction in user-perceived latency for common operations
- Better resource utilization across the distributed system

But perhaps more importantly, the system felt more responsive and intelligent. The AI agents were able to explore more approaches, try more alternatives, and ultimately provide better results to their users.

Summary

The best performance optimizations are invisible to users; they just make intelligence feel more natural, more responsive, and more effortless. That's the real goal of MCP performance optimization.

Performance optimization for MCP systems requires a holistic approach that considers not just traditional performance metrics, but also the effectiveness and responsiveness of the intelligence itself.

The following are key principles for MCP performance optimization:

- **Think in workflows, not operations**: Optimize for entire AI workflows, not just individual operations
- **Anticipate and predict**: Use predictive techniques to anticipate what AI systems will need and prepare accordingly
- **Embrace parallelism**: Look for opportunities to parallelize operations and reduce sequential dependencies
- **Learn and adapt**: Implement systems that learn from performance data and continuously improve their optimization strategies
- **Measure intelligence effectiveness**: Track not just speed, but how effectively AI systems can accomplish their goals

The goal isn't just to make MCP systems faster; it's to make them feel more intelligent, more responsive, and more capable of helping users accomplish their goals efficiently and effectively.

Performance optimization for AI systems is still an evolving field, and MCP systems present unique challenges and opportunities. But by focusing on the user experience and the effectiveness of intelligence, rather than just traditional performance metrics, we can build systems that truly feel like intelligent assistants rather than just fast computers.

In the next chapter, we'll shift our focus from performance to collaboration. You'll learn how multi-agent systems work and what makes coordination hard (task allocation, resource contention, information sharing, consensus, communication overhead, emergent behavior, and trust). We'll see why MCP's standardized protocols and dynamic discovery make multi-agent collaboration practical and powerful.

Get this book's PDF copy, code bundle, and more

Scan the QR code (or go to `packtpub.com/unlock`). Search for this book by name, confirm the edition, and then follow the steps on the page.

UNLOCK NOW

Note: Have your invoice handy. Purchases made directly from the Packt website don't require an invoice.

Part 4

Multi-Agent Systems and Framework Integration

MCP reaches its full potential when multiple agents collaborate and when the protocol integrates with established AI frameworks. In this part, you will learn how MCP facilitates multi-agent coordination, collaborative task execution, and shared contextual memory. You will then build RAG pipelines using MCP, integrate MCP with LangChain to create complete applications, and connect MCP with Microsoft AutoGen for sophisticated multi-agent workflows. By the end of this part, you will be able to combine MCP with the frameworks and patterns most commonly used in production AI systems.

This part of the book includes the following chapters:

10

MCP and Multi-Agent Systems

> *I always say that the future of AI isn't about building smarter individual agents; it's about building agents that can work together intelligently.*

Initially, most multi-agent projects were curiosity-driven experiments rather than purposeful collaborations. Researchers were exploring what was possible without yet having a practical framework for coordination. Coordination was hard, the communication overhead was significant, and the benefits rarely justified the complexity. But AI has changed everything. Modern AI agents are sophisticated enough to make multi-agent coordination not just feasible, but incredibly powerful.

The first multi-agent system I built with MCP was for a client who needed to process and analyze thousands of research papers across multiple domains. No single AI agent could handle the breadth and depth required, but a team of specialized agents, each with access to domain-specific tools and knowledge through MCP, could tackle the problem collaboratively.

Watching those agents work together was like watching a research team in action. The literature review agent would identify relevant papers, the analysis agent would extract key insights, the synthesis agent would identify connections across domains, and the writing agent would compile everything into coherent reports. Each agent was good at what it did, but together they were capable of work that no one could have accomplished alone.

That project taught me that MCP isn't just a protocol for connecting AI agents to tools and resources; it's a foundation for building truly collaborative intelligence.

In this chapter, we will be covering multi-agent systems from the ground up, defining what agents are, exploring orchestrator versus marketplace patterns, and showing how MCP eliminates glue code by standardizing tools and resources. You'll see how to use MCP to connect agents and plug in frameworks such as **AutoGen**, and learn best practices to avoid coordination pitfalls, so you can build scalable, adaptable AI teams.

In this chapter, we'll be covering the following topics:

- Introduction to multi-agent systems
- Challenges in multi-agent systems
- How MCP facilitates multi-agent systems
- MCP patterns in multi-agent systems
- Collaborative task execution with MCP
- Integrating MCP with agent frameworks (AutoGen Example)
- Security and trust in MCP-based multi-agent systems

Introduction to multi-agent systems

Let's start with the basics, because multi-agent systems are both simpler and more complex than most people think. At its core, a multi-agent system is just a collection of autonomous agents that can interact with each other and their environment to accomplish goals that are beyond the capability of individual agents.

In the research literature, a multi-agent system is defined as a computerized system comprising multiple interacting intelligent agents, capable of solving problems that are difficult or impossible for a single agent or monolithic system to handle. Agents in a multi-agent system are autonomous, have local views of the environment, and operate without a central controller. Cooperation, coordination, and negotiation among agents are therefore central research topics in the field.

But that simple definition hides a lot of complexity. What makes an agent "autonomous"? How do agents coordinate their actions? How do they resolve conflicts when their goals diverge? How do they share information and resources efficiently? These are the questions that have kept researchers busy for decades.

The promise of distributed intelligence

The fundamental promise of multi-agent systems is that you can solve complex problems by distributing them across multiple specialized agents, each focused on what they do best. Instead of trying to build one super-intelligent agent that can handle everything, you build a team of focused agents that can collaborate effectively.

This approach has several advantages. Specialization allows each agent to be optimized for specific types of tasks. Distribution provides natural fault tolerance; if one agent fails, others can potentially compensate. Scalability becomes more manageable because you can add new agents with new capabilities without redesigning the entire system.

But perhaps most importantly, multi-agent systems can exhibit emergent intelligence, capabilities that arise from the interaction of multiple agents that none of them possess individually.

The reality of coordination challenges

Of course, the reality is more complicated than the promise. Coordinating multiple autonomous agents is hard. Really hard. Agents need to communicate effectively, coordinate their actions, resolve conflicts, and maintain consistency across distributed operations.

Traditional multi-agent systems often struggled with these coordination challenges. Communication protocols were complex and brittle. Coordination mechanisms were either too rigid (limiting agent autonomy) or too flexible (leading to chaos and inefficiency). The overhead of coordination often outweighed the benefits of distribution.

MCP addresses many of these traditional challenges by providing a standardized foundation for agent communication and resource sharing.

How MCP changes the game

MCP addresses many of these traditional challenges by providing a standardized foundation for agent communication and resource sharing. Instead of each agent needing to learn how to communicate with every other agent and every resource in the system, they all speak the same protocol.

This standardization dramatically reduces the complexity of building multi-agent systems. Agents can discover each other's capabilities dynamically, share resources efficiently, and coordinate their actions through well-defined interfaces.

But MCP does more than just simplify communication; it enables new patterns of collaboration that weren't practical with traditional approaches.

Having learned in brief how MCP enables collaboration, let's now examine the key challenges that arise when scaling these ideas to multi-agent systems.

Challenges in multi-agent systems

Before we dive into how MCP addresses challenges such as allocating tasks fairly, managing resource contention, sharing information efficiently, reaching consensus, handling communication overhead, dealing with emergent behaviors, and establishing trust among agents, let's understand what makes multi-agent systems so difficult to build and operate effectively.

The coordination problem

The fundamental challenge in multi-agent systems is coordination – that is, ensuring that multiple autonomous agents work together effectively rather than at cross-purposes. This involves several sub-problems:

- **Task allocation**: How do you decide which agent should handle which tasks? This isn't just about matching capabilities to requirements; it's about considering current workloads, resource availability, deadlines, and the interdependencies between tasks.
- **Resource contention**: When multiple agents need access to the same resources, how do you resolve conflicts fairly and efficiently? Traditional approaches, such as locks and queues, often don't work well for AI agents that need to adapt their strategies dynamically.
- **Information sharing**: Agents often need to share information to coordinate effectively, but sharing everything with everyone creates information overload and privacy concerns. How do you determine what information to share with whom, and when?
- **Consensus building**: When agents need to make collective decisions, how do you build consensus efficiently while respecting agent autonomy and handling disagreements?

The communication overhead problem

Communication between agents isn't free. It takes time, consumes bandwidth, and requires processing resources. In complex multi-agent systems, the communication overhead can become so significant that it outweighs the benefits of distribution.

The challenge is designing communication patterns that provide the coordination benefits without creating excessive overhead. This often involves trade-offs between coordination effectiveness and communication efficiency.

The emergent behavior problem

Multi-agent systems can exhibit emergent behaviors such as simple agent rules producing unexpected global patterns. Beneficial examples include flocking and swarming simulations where drones align, avoid collisions, and navigate obstacles efficiently. On the downside, emergent effects can create phantom traffic jams or market instability, as seen in algorithmic trading cascades.

The challenge is designing systems that encourage beneficial emergent behaviors while preventing or mitigating harmful ones. This requires understanding how agent interactions can lead to system-level behaviors and designing appropriate constraints and incentives.

The trust and security problem

In multi-agent systems, agents often need to trust each other to some degree, sharing information, delegating tasks, or relying on each other's capabilities. But how do you establish and maintain trust in a system of autonomous agents?

This is particularly challenging when agents are developed by different organizations, have different goals, or operate in environments where some agents might be malicious or compromised.

Let's see how MCP itself addresses these issues.

How MCP facilitates multi-agent systems

MCP addresses many of the traditional challenges of multi-agent systems by providing a standardized foundation for communication, dynamic capability discovery, hierarchical federated architectures, resource sharing, and coordination.

Standardized communication protocols

As mentioned earlier, one of the biggest barriers to building multi-agent systems was the complexity of agent communication. Each agent needed to understand how to communicate with every other agent, leading to an explosion of communication protocols and interfaces.

MCP solves this by providing a single, standardized protocol that all agents can use. An agent that knows how to communicate via MCP can potentially interact with any other MCP-enabled agent or resource, regardless of who built it or what it's designed to do.

This standardization dramatically reduces the complexity of building multi-agent systems and makes it much easier to add new agents or capabilities to existing systems.

Dynamic capability discovery

Traditional multi-agent systems often required static configuration, as in you had to know in advance what agents were available and what they could do. MCP makes discovery more dynamic by providing standard operations, such as `tools/list`, that return a paginated list of available tools together with their names, descriptions, and input schemas. Servers declare a tool's capability and can send `listChanged` notifications when the tool list changes. This allows agents to discover each other's capabilities at runtime without hardcoded configurations. However, the dynamic discovery of servers is still an emerging area. Analysts note that enabling AI agents to automatically detect and integrate new MCP services will require a standardized registry that is still under development.

These discovery mechanisms enable more flexible and adaptive multi-agent systems. Agents can adapt to changing conditions, take advantage of new capabilities as they become available, and gracefully handle the failure or unavailability of other agents.

Resource sharing and coordination

MCP provides natural mechanisms for resource sharing and coordination. Multiple agents can access the same MCP servers, sharing tools and information while maintaining appropriate access controls and coordination.

This shared resource model enables new patterns of collaboration, where agents can work together on complex tasks by sharing access to specialized tools and datasets, rather than trying to duplicate capabilities across multiple agents.

Hierarchical and federated architectures

MCP supports both hierarchical and federated multi-agent architectures. In hierarchical systems, higher-level agents coordinate the activities of lower-level agents through MCP interfaces. In federated systems, peer agents coordinate directly with each other.

This flexibility allows for multi-agent architectures that match the natural structure of the problems being solved and the organizations building the systems.

We've examined how MCP standardized communication enables dynamic discovery and facilitates resource sharing. Now, let's look at the recurring patterns that have emerged in MCP-based multi-agent systems and how they help solve common coordination challenges.

MCP patterns in multi-agent systems

As MCP-based multi-agent systems have evolved, several common patterns have emerged that provide proven approaches to common coordination challenges.

The orchestrator pattern

In this pattern, one agent acts as an orchestrator that coordinates the activities of multiple worker agents. The orchestrator understands the overall goal and workflow, while the worker agents focus on specific tasks.

The orchestrator uses MCP to discover available worker agents and their capabilities, assign tasks based on current workloads and capabilities, and coordinate the flow of information between workers.

This pattern is particularly effective for complex workflows that can be decomposed into well-defined subtasks and where there's a natural hierarchy of coordination responsibility. For example, an Orchestrator agent coordinates a vacation: one agent books flights, another handles hotels, and a third builds the itinerary. The orchestrator allocates tasks and combines results.

The marketplace pattern

In this pattern, agents operate in a marketplace where they can offer services to other agents and request services they need. MCP servers act as marketplaces where agents can advertise their capabilities and discover services offered by others.

This pattern enables very flexible and dynamic multi-agent systems where the coordination emerges from market-like interactions rather than being imposed by a central coordinator. For example, agents publish their capabilities (e.g., summarization, translation, or research) to a marketplace. A client selects and pays the agent with the best price and reputation for each task.

The collaborative filtering pattern

In this pattern, agents share information about their experiences and recommendations to help other agents make better decisions. For example, agents might share information about which tools are most effective for different types of tasks, or which resources provide the most reliable information.

MCP enables this pattern by providing standardized ways for agents to share metadata and recommendations about resources and tools. As an example, review agents share ratings and preferences to recommend relevant papers to each other, enhancing recommendations through shared experiences.

The specialized team pattern

In this pattern, agents are organized into specialized teams, each focused on a particular domain or type of task. Teams coordinate internally through MCP, and different teams coordinate with each other through higher-level MCP interfaces.

This pattern is effective for complex domains that require deep specialization, while still enabling cross-domain collaboration when needed. Let's say a writing assistant comprises a brainstorming agent, a drafting agent, and a critic agent. Each specializes in ideation, composition, and refinement, respectively; together they produce high-quality content.

Now that we've examined the general coordination patterns and how MCP supports them, to understand them better, let's walk through a collaborative task execution scenario that shows how MCP enables a team of agents to work together effectively.

Collaborative task execution with MCP

Let me walk you through a concrete example of how MCP enables collaborative task execution in a multi-agent system.

The scenario

Imagine a research organization that needs to analyze the competitive landscape for new technology. This involves gathering information from multiple sources, analyzing it from different perspectives, and synthesizing insights into actionable recommendations.

The agent team

We design a multi-agent system with specialized agents:

- **Research agent**: Specializes in finding and gathering relevant information
- **Analysis agent**: Specializes in analyzing data and extracting insights
- **Synthesis agent**: Specializes in combining insights from multiple sources
- **Communication agent**: Specializes in presenting results in appropriate formats

The MCP infrastructure

Each agent connects to relevant MCP servers:

- Document search servers for accessing research databases
- Analysis tool servers for statistical and text analysis
- Knowledge graph servers for understanding relationships
- Presentation tool servers for creating reports and visualizations

The collaborative workflow

Here's how the agents collaborate through MCP:

1. **Task initiation**: The Research agent receives the initial request and uses MCP to discover what analysis and synthesis capabilities are available.
2. **Information gathering**: The Research agent uses document search servers to gather relevant papers, reports, and data sources. It shares this information with other agents through shared MCP resources.
3. **Parallel analysis**: The Analysis agent processes the gathered information using various analysis tools accessed through the MCP servers. It identifies trends, patterns, and key insights.

4. **Synthesis**: The Synthesis agent combines insights from multiple analyses, identifies connections and contradictions, and develops higher-level conclusions.
5. **Communication**: The Communication agent takes the synthesized insights and creates appropriate presentations using formatting and visualization tools accessed through MCP.

The coordination mechanisms

The agents coordinate through several MCP-enabled mechanisms:

- **Shared resources**: All agents can access shared document repositories and analysis results through MCP servers
- **Status updates**: Agents provide status updates and progress information through MCP notification mechanisms
- **Dynamic task assignment**: Agents can request help from other agents by posting tasks to shared MCP servers
- **Quality feedback**: Agents can provide feedback on each other's work through MCP metadata and annotation systems

This collaborative approach produces results that are more comprehensive and higher quality than any individual agent could achieve alone, while being more efficient than traditional approaches that require extensive custom integration work.

Now that we've explored how MCP enables collaboration in principle, it's time to see how those patterns map into real agent frameworks. We'll start with AutoGen, a concrete example of MCP integration that we'll revisit in depth in *Chapter12*.

Integrating MCP with agent frameworks (AutoGen example)

We introduce AutoGen here because its architecture will help demonstrate how MCP patterns map to a real multi-agent framework. A deeper dive on AutoGen will be taken in *Chapter 12*, but a brief look now will help ground the patterns in a concrete tool.

AutoGen is one of the most popular frameworks for building multi-agent AI systems, and it integrates naturally with MCP to create powerful collaborative intelligence systems. Other frameworks for multi-agent workflows include LangChain for chain-of-thought pipelines, CrewAI for teamwork-oriented tasks, LangGraph for graph-based orchestration, and Microsoft's Semantic Kernel for composable skills. We will focus on AutoGen because it natively supports dynamic tool discovery and asynchronous agent coordination, making it a natural fit for demonstrating MCP integration.

I'll only give a brief overview of how MCP plugs into agent frameworks here. For in-depth examples and advanced patterns, jump to *Chapters 12* and *13*, where we unpack LangChain and AutoGen's architecture and show how MCP enables dynamic tool access and specialized agent coordination.

AutoGen enables the creation of multiple AI agents that can communicate with each other through structured conversations. Each agent can have different roles, capabilities, and personalities, and they can work together to solve complex problems through dialogue and collaboration.

MCP integration benefits

Integrating MCP with AutoGen provides several key benefits:

- **Expanded capabilities**: AutoGen agents can access external tools and resources through MCP servers, dramatically expanding what they can accomplish beyond just conversation and reasoning
- **Specialized agents**: Different AutoGen agents can connect to different MCP servers, creating natural specialization where each agent has access to domain-specific tools and information
- **Dynamic resource discovery**: AutoGen agents can discover new capabilities at runtime, allowing for more flexible and adaptive multi-agent systems
- **Standardized tool access**: All AutoGen agents can use the same MCP protocol to access tools, simplifying the development and maintenance of multi-agent systems

Implementation patterns

Here's a simple demonstration of how a multi-agent workflow can be orchestrated using an MCP client. In this example, we define a dummy MCP server that exposes two tools (`get_weather` and `analyze_sentiment`). `ResearchAgent` and `AnalysisAgent` share the same MCP client; the Research agent fetches weather information, while the Analysis agent performs sentiment analysis on a piece of text. Both agents run concurrently using Python's `asyncio`:

```
import asyncio

class DummyTool:
    async def get_weather(self, location: str):
        # Simulate asynchronous API call
        await asyncio.sleep(0.5)
        return f"Current weather in {location}: sunny and warm"
```

```
    async def analyze_sentiment(self, text: str):
        await asyncio.sleep(0.3)
        return f"Sentiment analysis of '{text}' shows positive mood"

class DummyServer:
    def __init__(self):
        self.tools = {
            'get_weather': self.get_weather,
            'analyze_sentiment': self.analyze_sentiment
        }

    async def list_tools(self):
        return list(self.tools.keys())

    async def call_tool(self, name, arguments):
        func = self.tools.get(name)
        if func:
            return await func(**arguments)
        else:
            raise ValueError('Tool not found')

    async def get_weather(self, location):
        return await DummyTool().get_weather(location)

    async def analyze_sentiment(self, text):
        return await DummyTool().analyze_sentiment(text)

class MCPClient:
    def __init__(self, server):
        self.server = server

    async def list_tools(self):
        return await self.server.list_tools()

    async def call(self, name, arguments):
        return await self.server.call_tool(name, arguments)

class ResearchAgent:
    def __init__(self, name, mcp_client):
        self.name = name
        self.client = mcp_client
```

```
    async def gather_weather(self, location):
        return await self.client.call('get_weather',
                                      {'location': location})

class AnalysisAgent:
    def __init__(self, name, mcp_client):
        self.name = name
        self.client = mcp_client

    async def analyze_text(self, text):
        return await self.client.call('analyze_sentiment', {'text': text})

async def orchestrator():
    server = DummyServer()
    client = MCPClient(server)
    research_agent = ResearchAgent('research', client)
    analysis_agent = AnalysisAgent('analysis', client)

    weather_future = research_agent.gather_weather('New York')
    sentiment_future = analysis_agent.analyze_text('This is a great day!')
    weather_result, sentiment_result = await asyncio.gather(weather_future,
sentiment_future)
    print('Weather Result:', weather_result)
    print('Sentiment Result:', sentiment_result)

asyncio.run(orchestrator())
```

Running this script produces output similar to the following:

```
Weather Result: Current weather in New York: sunny and warm
Sentiment Result: Sentiment analysis of 'This is a great day!' shows positive mood
```

This example uses a toy server for illustration, but it demonstrates how multiple agents can share an MCP client, discover tools, and execute them concurrently. In real deployments, you would replace `DummyServer` with a real MCP server and integrate more sophisticated orchestration logic or frameworks such as AutoGen or LangChain. These integration patterns will be revisited in later chapters with full implementations and case studies, so don't worry if some details are high-level for now.

Next, we'll explore advanced integration patterns that push beyond basic orchestration and demonstrate cutting-edge multi-agent coordination.

Advanced integration patterns

More sophisticated integrations might involve the following:

- **Capability-based agent assignment**: Automatically assigning tasks to AutoGen agents based on the MCP capabilities they have access to
- **Cross-agent resource sharing**: Allowing AutoGen agents to share MCP resources and coordinate access to shared tools and data
- **Dynamic team formation**: Creating AutoGen agent teams dynamically based on the MCP capabilities needed for specific tasks
- **Hierarchical coordination**: Using AutoGen's conversation patterns to coordinate complex workflows that involve multiple MCP servers and capabilities

Up to this point, we've looked at patterns and workflows that make multi-agent systems effective. To keep them trustworthy and safe in practice, we now turn our attention to security and trust in MCP-based multi-agent systems, covering authentication, authorization, trust establishment, and anomaly detection.

Security and trust in MCP-based multi-agent systems

Multi-agent systems introduce unique security and trust challenges, and MCP-based systems need to address these challenges while maintaining the flexibility and autonomy that make multi-agent systems valuable.

Agent authentication and authorization

In multi-agent systems, you need to verify not just that an agent is who it claims to be, but also that it has the authority to perform the actions it's requesting on behalf of users or other agents. MCP does not define a multi-party authentication chain; instead, its HTTP-based authorization flow treats each server as an OAuth 2.1 resource server and each client as an OAuth client. Clients obtain tokens from the appropriate authorization server and send them with requests, optionally including a resource indicator that binds the token to a specific server to prevent mis-redemption. In multi-agent toolchains that span multiple organizations or identity domains, federated approval frameworks may be needed to distribute permissions and execution rights across participating MCP servers.

Trust establishment and maintenance

Trust in multi-agent systems isn't binary: it's contextual and evolving. An agent might be trusted for certain types of tasks but not others, or trusted under certain conditions but not others.

MCP systems can implement reputation and trust management mechanisms that track agent behavior over time and adjust trust levels based on performance, reliability, and adherence to expected behaviors. Trust in multi-agent systems is often established through reputation schemes. Agents earn scores based on successful task completion, peer ratings, and feedback; these scores influence future task assignments and collaborations. Some systems use game-theoretic strategies (e.g., tit-for-tat) or machine-learning models to update trust scores dynamically. Such mechanisms help identify reliable agents, promote cooperation, and reduce the risk of malicious behavior.

Secure coordination protocols

Multi-agent coordination often involves sharing sensitive information or coordinating actions that have security implications. MCP's security guidance emphasizes user consent, data privacy, tool safety, and LLM sampling controls. Implementations should enforce access controls, require explicit user approval before executing tools, and monitor each request for policy compliance. Agents operating in different security domains may need to exchange cryptographically signed messages and maintain audit logs; some experts advocate for federated approval frameworks where permissions are distributed and conditionally granted across participating MCP servers.

Anomaly detection and response

Multi-agent systems can exhibit complex, emergent behaviors that might indicate security problems or system malfunctions. MCP-based systems should implement monitoring and anomaly detection capabilities that can identify unusual patterns in agent behavior or coordination.

When anomalies are detected, the system should have response mechanisms that can isolate problematic agents, alert human operators, or adapt the system configuration to mitigate potential problems.

Summary

MCP provides a powerful foundation for building multi-agent systems that can collaborate effectively while maintaining the autonomy and specialization that make multi-agent approaches valuable.

Key benefits of MCP for multi-agent systems include the following:

- **Standardized communication**: All agents speak the same protocol, dramatically simplifying system integration and enabling dynamic collaboration
- **Dynamic capability discovery**: Agents can discover each other's capabilities at runtime, enabling flexible and adaptive system architectures
- **Resource sharing**: Multiple agents can share access to tools and information through MCP servers, enabling new patterns of collaboration
- **Scalable coordination**: MCP's lightweight protocol enables efficient coordination even in large multi-agent systems
- **Security and trust**: MCP's security framework provides mechanisms for establishing and maintaining trust in multi-agent environments

The future of AI isn't about building individual super-intelligent agents but about building teams of specialized agents that can work together intelligently. MCP provides the foundation for making that future a reality.

Multi-agent systems are still an evolving field, and we're just beginning to explore the possibilities that MCP enables. But the early results are promising, where we're seeing multi-agent systems that are more capable, more flexible, and more robust than what was possible with traditional approaches.

The key insight is that intelligence isn't just about individual capability, but also about collaboration, coordination, and the ability to combine different types of expertise effectively. MCP makes that kind of collaborative intelligence practical and scalable.

Looking ahead to *Chapter 11*, we'll go a little deep into **retrieval-augmented generation** (**RAG**). You'll learn how retrieving relevant documents in real time keeps models current and reduces hallucination, and how MCP provides dynamic data-source discovery, standardized retrieval patterns, and context-aware access. This sets the stage for building maintainable, scalable RAG systems.

Subscribe for a free eBook

New frameworks, evolving architectures, research drops, production breakdowns—*AI_Distilled* filters the noise into a weekly briefing for engineers and researchers working hands-on with LLMs and GenAI systems. Subscribe now and receive a free eBook, along with weekly insights that help you stay focused and informed.

Subscribe at `https://packt.link/8Oz6Y` or scan the QR code below.

11

MCP for Retrieval-Augmented Generation

> *RAG without MCP is like trying to do research with a library that keeps moving its books around and changing its catalog system every week.*

I'll be honest, when I first heard about **retrieval-augmented generation** (**RAG**), I was skeptical. Another buzzword? Another way to complicate what should be simple AI interactions? But after building my first RAG system, I got it. Really got it. The ability to ground AI responses in real, current, verifiable information changes everything.

The problem is, most RAG implementations are... well, they're a mess. I've seen systems with dozens of different data connectors, each with its own API, its own authentication scheme, and its own quirks and limitations. Building a RAG system often means becoming an expert in half a dozen different data access patterns before you even get to the interesting AI parts.

That's where MCP comes in. It doesn't just make RAG systems easier to build; it makes them fundamentally more powerful and flexible. Instead of hardcoding connections to specific data sources, you can build RAG systems that can discover and adapt to new information sources dynamically.

In this chapter, we will be covering RAG fundamentals: how retrieving relevant documents keeps responses grounded in up-to-date information, how MCP provides dynamic data source discovery and standardized retrieval interfaces, and how metadata such as audience and priority help filter and prioritize results. We'll build a RAG pipeline using MCP servers as document stores, rank and track the provenance of results, and learn how to integrate MCP-based RAG pipelines with frameworks such as LangChain and AutoGen. Understanding these capabilities will help you keep models current, reduce hallucinations, and build scalable retrieval systems.

In this chapter, we'll be covering the following topics:

- Introduction to retrieval-augmented generation (RAG)
- The role of MCP in RAG systems
- Building a basic RAG system with MCP
- Advanced RAG techniques with MCP
- Integrating MCP-based RAG with LangChain
- Integrating MCP-based RAG with AutoGen
- Evaluating RAG systems
- Best practices for MCP-based RAG

Introduction to retrieval-augmented generation (RAG)

Let's start with the basics, because RAG is one of those concepts that sounds more complicated than it is. At its core, RAG is about giving AI systems access to external information that they can use to ground their responses in fact, rather than just their training data. RAG is a technique that enables large language models to *retrieve and incorporate new information* from specified documents before answering a query. Rather than responding using only their static training data, models perform a lookup against external knowledge bases or documents and blend that information with their pre-existing knowledge. This allows them to use domain-specific and up-to-date information that is not available in the training corpus. The acronym RAG breaks down as follows:

- **Retrieval**: Extract relevant information from an external repository (documents, PDFs, or images) in response to a query
- **Augmentation**: Enrich the input prompt with the retrieved facts so the model has more context
- **Generation**: Ask the language model to produce a response using both its internal knowledge and the augmented context

Think about how you answer questions in real life. If someone asks you about current events, you don't just rely on what you remember from years ago; you check the news, look up recent articles, and maybe consult multiple sources to get a complete picture. RAG gives AI systems the same capability.

In the sections that follow, we'll examine the main challenges RAG addresses, such as improving retrieval quality, enriching context, and reducing hallucinations, and see how MCP helps solve them.

The information freshness problem

Traditional language models are trained on data that's inevitably out of date by the time the model is deployed. Even if you retrain regularly, there's always a gap between the training data cutoff and the current moment. For many applications, this gap is a serious limitation.

I worked on a project where we needed an AI assistant to help with investment decisions. Using a model trained on data from six months ago for current market analysis? That's not just useless, it's potentially dangerous. RAG addresses this challenge by retrieving real-time market data, recent news, and current analyst reports instead of relying on stale training data; because RAG retrieves new documents on demand, it reduces the need to retrain models with new information and keeps the assistant grounded in current facts.

The hallucination mitigation

One of the biggest challenges with large language models is hallucination, that is, the tendency to generate plausible-sounding but factually incorrect information. Because RAG pulls relevant text from external documents before generating a response, it helps reduce hallucinations by grounding responses in retrieved information that can be verified and cited.

When an AI system can point to specific sources for its claims, users can verify the information independently. This transparency is crucial for building trust in AI systems, especially for high-stakes applications, and is one of the motivations for RAG.

The specialization challenge

General-purpose language models are impressive, but they're not experts in every domain. By retrieving domain-specific documents, such as the case law databases for a legal assistant, current research literature for a medical assistant, or up-to-date documentation for a technical assistant, RAG allows you to specialize AI systems without retraining. The beauty of this is that you don't need to retrain the model; all you need to do is to give it access to the right information sources through RAG.

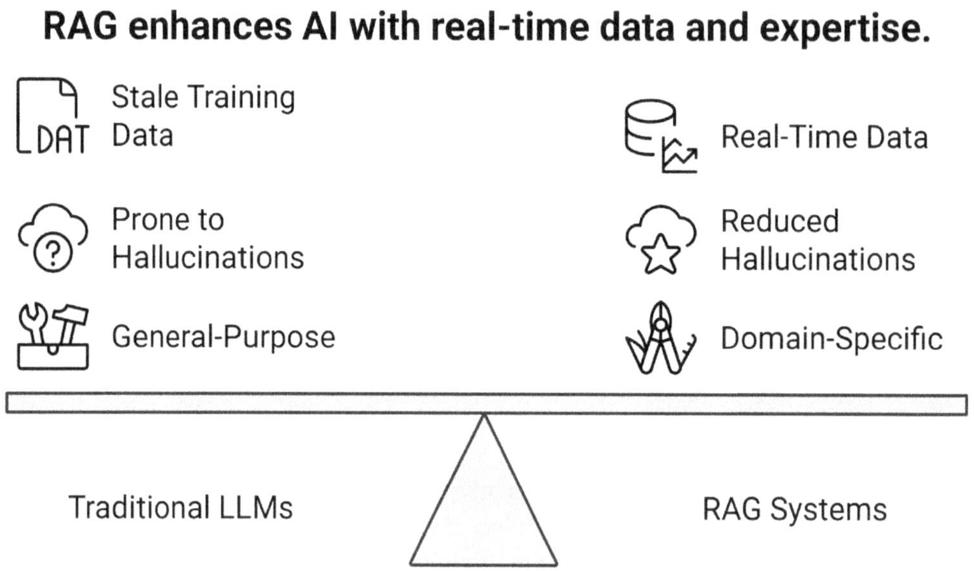

Figure 11.1 – RAG enhances AI with real-time data and expertise

Before diving into those challenges, it's worth noting that RAG systems benefit greatly from MCP. MCP standardizes how agents discover resources and tools, making it easier to build RAG pipelines on a common foundation.

The role of MCP in RAG systems

Here's where things get interesting, and where I think MCP really shines. Traditional RAG systems are often brittle and inflexible because they're built around specific data sources and retrieval mechanisms. MCP changes this by providing a standardized way for RAG systems to discover and access information sources.

Let's now explore how MCP enhances RAG systems by enabling the dynamic discovery of tools and resources, simplifying retrieval interfaces, and supporting context-aware information management.

Dynamic data source discovery

In traditional RAG systems, you hardcode connections to specific databases, document stores, or APIs. If you want to add a new data source, you need to write new integration code, test it, and deploy it. It's a whole thing.

As discussed in the previous chapter on multi-agent patterns, MCP's dynamic discovery means clients can register new data sources and immediately make them available. With MCP, RAG systems can discover available resources and tools using standard listing operations, such as `resources/list` and `tools/list`, and servers can notify clients when the list of resources or tools changes. This means you can add new data sources by registering them with an MCP server, and the client will pick them up without code changes. Discovery of entirely new MCP servers (for example, automatically locating a server on a network) is an active area of development on the protocol roadmap and will rely on a centralized registry.

I've seen RAG systems that started with access to a few internal documents and gradually expanded to include dozens of different information databases, APIs, document repositories, and real-time feeds, just by simply connecting to additional MCP servers and resources, all through the same protocol interface.

Standardized retrieval patterns

Different data sources have different query languages, result formats, and pagination schemes. Traditional RAG systems need custom code for each data source. MCP standardizes the interface for listing and reading resources and invoking tools using JSON-RPC messages with consistent schemas. Clients send the same `resources/list` or `resources/read` and `tools/list` or `tools/call` requests regardless of the underlying store, and servers return results in a uniform structure. This common interface makes it much easier to build RAG systems that can work with diverse information sources. Sophisticated retrieval strategies, such as query expansion, result ranking, and source selection, can be implemented once on top of this unified interface and then reused across all your data sources.

Context-aware information access

MCP's context-aware design can be particularly valuable for RAG systems. In MCP, a "tool result" is simply the output returned by invoking a tool (e.g., a search or summarization). These results, such as resources, may include optional annotations (`audience, priority, lastModified`). Servers and clients can use this metadata to filter or prioritize content based on user context. For instance, a customer service RAG system might favor results marked "for users," while a technical system might prioritize those tagged "for assistants."

Metadata and provenance tracking

Beyond context hints, MCP's annotations also support provenance tracking. Clients can record where each piece of information came from and when it was last updated, but MCP intentionally doesn't prescribe author credibility or reliability metrics. Implementers should combine MCP metadata with external quality signals, such as document age, source provenance, or third-party trust scores, to assess content quality. This removes duplication and differentiates metadata use cases.

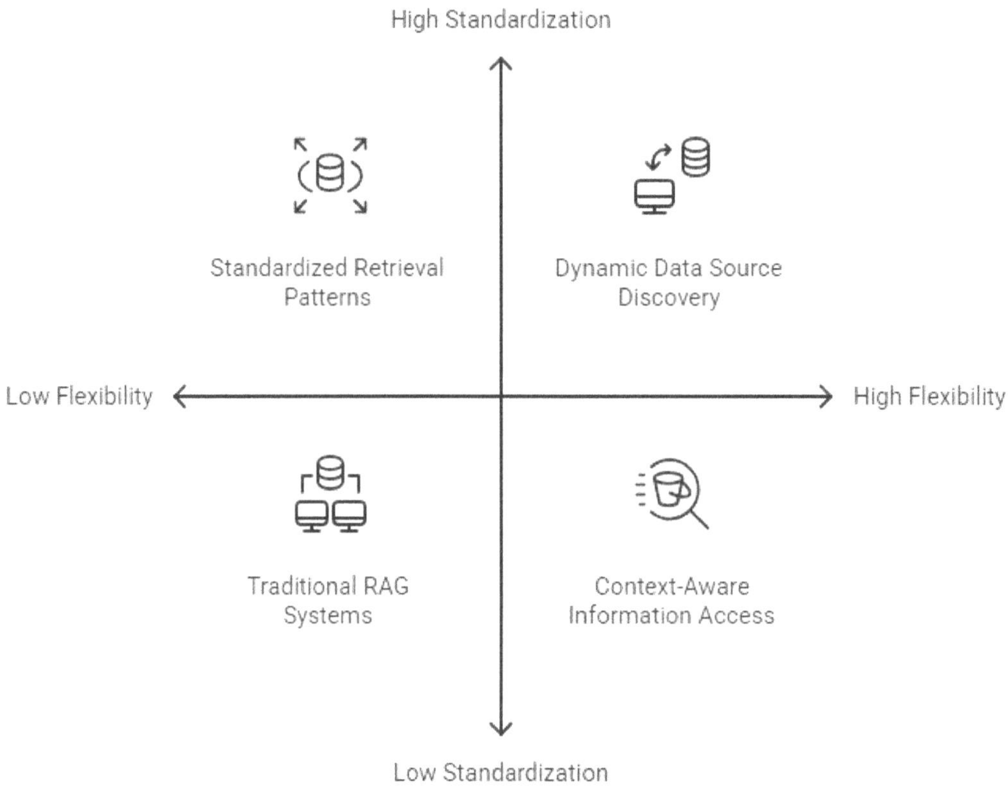

Figure 11.2 – Benefits of MCP in RAG systems

With these concepts in mind, let's build a minimal MCP-based RAG system to see how retrieval and augmentation work in practice.

Building a basic RAG system with MCP

Let me walk you through building a simple but functional RAG system using MCP. This isn't going to be production-ready code, but it'll give you a sense of how the pieces fit together.

Architecture

Our basic RAG system has three main components:

- An MCP client that can discover and query information sources
- A retrieval engine that finds relevant information based on user queries
- A generation engine that uses the retrieved information to create responses

The implementation

Here's a simplified implementation that demonstrates the key concepts:

```
# Simplified RAG system that does not rely on any external MCP libraries.
# In this example we simulate MCP servers by storing data in in-memory
dictionaries.

class MCPRAGSystem:
    """A simple RAG system using local data sources to simulate MCP retrieval."""

    def __init__(self):
        self.data_sources = {}

    def add_data_source(self, source_name: str, documents: dict) -> None:
        """Add a data source with a mapping of URI to text content."""
        self.data_sources[source_name] = documents

    def retrieve_information(self, query: str, max_results: int = 5):
        """Retrieve relevant information from local data sources."""
        query_words = set(query.lower().split())
        results = []
        for source_name, docs in self.data_sources.items():
            for uri, content in docs.items():
                content_words = set(content.lower().split())
                # Simple Jaccard similarity
                intersection = query_words & content_words
                union = query_words | content_words
                score = len(intersection) / len(union) if union else 0.0
                if score > 0:
                    results.append({
                        'source': source_name,
                        'uri': uri,
                        'content': content[:200],  # truncate for display
                        'relevance_score': score
                    })
        results.sort(key=lambda x: x['relevance_score'], reverse=True)
        return results[:max_results]

    def generate_response(self, query: str, retrieved_info: list) -> str:
        """Generate a simple response using retrieved information."""
```

```
        if not retrieved_info:
            return "I couldn't find relevant information."
        context = "\n\n".join(
            [f"Source: {info['source']}\nContent: {info['content']}" for info in
retrieved_info]
        )
        return (
            f"Based on the available information:\n\n{context}\n\n"
            f"Summary: The query '{query}' is related to {len(retrieved_info)}
document(s) from the connected data sources."
        )


# Example usage
if __name__ == "__main__":
    rag = MCPRAGSystem()
    # Add two simple data sources to simulate MCP servers
    rag.add_data_source('server1', {
        'doc1': 'Retrieval augmented generation enhances language models by
retrieving relevant documents and augmenting generation with factual
information.',
        'doc2': 'Model Context Protocol provides standardized access to external
data sources and tools.'
    })
    rag.add_data_source('server2', {
        'doc3': 'MCP enables AI systems to connect to databases, APIs, and other
tools using a unified JSON-RPC interface.'
    })
    query = 'What does MCP do in RAG systems?'
    retrieved = rag.retrieve_information(query)
    print('Retrieved information:', retrieved)
    print('Generated response:', rag.generate_response(query, retrieved))
```

When you run this code, you'll see output similar to the following:

```
Retrieved information: [{'source': 'server2', 'uri': 'doc3', 'content': 'MCP
enables AI systems to connect to databases, APIs, and other tools using a unified
JSON-RPC interface.', 'relevance_score': 0.045454545454545456}]
Generated response: Based on the available information:

Source: server2
```

```
Content: MCP enables AI systems to connect to databases, APIs, and other tools
using a unified JSON-RPC interface.

Summary: The query 'What does MCP do in RAG systems?' is related to 1 document(s)
from the connected data sources.
```

This example uses a minimal in-memory dataset to simulate retrieval and generation. It demonstrates how you can build a RAG workflow without any external MCP libraries: you register data sources, compute simple similarity scores, and generate a summary from the retrieved snippets. In a production system, you would replace the in-memory data with real MCP servers and use embeddings or semantic search for relevance scoring.

Having built a simple RAG prototype, we can now think about more sophisticated retrieval pipelines. The next section discusses querying high-level indexes, drilling into domain-specific sources, and verifying facts across multiple servers.

Advanced RAG techniques with MCP

Once you have the basics working, there are several advanced techniques that can significantly improve the effectiveness of your MCP-based RAG system.

Multi-stage retrieval

Instead of doing a single retrieval pass, advanced RAG systems often use multi-stage retrieval, where the results of one retrieval inform the next. MCP makes this particularly powerful because you can use different MCP servers for different stages.

For instance, when researching a legal question, you might first query a general case law index to identify relevant jurisdictions, then query specific databases for statutes and precedents, and finally, query a fact-checking service to verify citations. In a medical setting, you could first query a high-level index of diseases, then pull detailed treatment guidelines from specialist databases and cross-check drug interactions with a pharmacology server.

Dynamic query expansion

MCP servers can provide not just information but also suggestions for related queries or alternative search terms. This enables dynamic query expansion where the RAG system can automatically broaden or refine its search based on what it finds.

I've seen systems where the initial "climate change impacts" query gets expanded to include related terms such as "global warming effects," "environmental consequences," and "carbon emissions," all suggested by MCP servers that understand the domain.

Source quality assessment

Not all information sources are equally reliable. Advanced MCP-based RAG systems can implement source quality assessment, but this functionality is not provided by the protocol itself. MCP annotations can indicate recency and priority, but they do not include author credibility or peer-review status. Implementers can combine MCP metadata with external quality signals, such as the age of a document, its provenance, or third-party trust scores, to weight information appropriately and provide users with transparency about the reliability of different sources.

This technique is especially important in regulated domains. For example, when summarizing clinical studies, a RAG system might prioritize peer-reviewed journals over blogs, weight recent trials more heavily than older ones, and require fact-checking against trusted medical databases. Similarly, in finance, weighting documents by recency and authoritative sources helps ensure compliance and accuracy.

Contextual information filtering

MCP's context-aware design enables sophisticated information filtering based on user context, task context, and organizational policies. The same query might return different information for different users or in different contexts.

For example, a medical RAG system might return different information for doctors versus patients, or a financial RAG system might filter information based on the user's risk tolerance and investment goals.

We'll close this chapter by examining best practices and lessons learned from building multiple MCP-based RAG systems and by looking at how to handle failure modes gracefully.

Evaluating RAG systems

Building a RAG system is one thing, but knowing whether it's working well is another. Evaluation of RAG systems is particularly challenging because you need to assess the quality of both information retrieval and response generation.

Each subsection that follows covers the importance of modular architecture, the need to monitor context size, techniques for handling partial failures, and guidelines for managing user expectations. Together, they form a practical checklist for robust RAG systems.

Retrieval quality metrics

Traditional information retrieval metrics such as precision, recall, and F1 score are still relevant for RAG systems, but they need to be adapted for the specific characteristics of AI-driven retrieval.

Precision measures how much of the retrieved information is relevant to the query. Recall measures how much of the relevant information was retrieved. But in RAG systems, you also need to consider factors such as information freshness, source credibility, and contextual appropriateness.

Generation quality assessment

Evaluating the quality of responses generated is more subjective and challenging. You need to assess not just whether the response is factually correct but whether it's helpful, appropriately detailed, and well grounded in the retrieved information.

I've found that human evaluation is still essential for assessing generation quality, but you can supplement it with automated metrics that check for factual consistency between retrieved information and generated responses.

End-to-end system evaluation

Perhaps most importantly, you need to evaluate the RAG system as a whole and how well it helps users accomplish their goals. This requires task-based evaluation where you assess whether users can successfully complete realistic tasks using the RAG system.

This kind of evaluation is more expensive and time-consuming than component-level evaluation, but it's essential for understanding whether your RAG system is useful in practice.

Continuous evaluation and improvement

RAG systems need continuous evaluation because information sources change, user needs evolve, and new types of queries emerge. MCP makes this easier by providing standardized interfaces for monitoring system performance and collecting feedback.

You can implement automated monitoring that tracks retrieval quality, response quality, and user satisfaction over time, and use this information to continuously improve your RAG system.

Best practices for MCP-based RAG

After building several MCP-based RAG systems, I've learned some lessons about what works and what doesn't. In this section, I recommend key best practices.

Design for discoverability

Don't hardcode assumptions about what information sources will be available. Design your RAG system to discover and adapt to new MCP servers dynamically. This makes your system much more flexible and easier to extend.

Implement graceful degradation

To design a RAG system that degrades gracefully, implement timeouts and fallback logic. If a source time runs out or returns an error, the system should skip that source and continue with the remaining information, rather than aborting the entire response. You can also fall back to cached data or a generic answer when no reliable sources are available and surface a warning to the user indicating which sources were unreachable. Including such contingency plans prevents a single failing source from derailing the entire pipeline.

Prioritize transparency

Users need to understand where information comes from and how reliable it is. Always provide source attribution and, when possible, quality indicators. MCP's annotations (such as `audience`, `priority`, and `lastModified`) can help convey context and recency, but implementers still need to supply or infer reliability signals from elsewhere, such as document provenance or third-party trust scores.

Balance breadth and depth

It's tempting to connect your RAG system to every available information source, but more isn't always better. Focus on high-quality, relevant sources and implement good filtering and ranking mechanisms.

Monitor and iterate

RAG systems need continuous monitoring and improvement. Implement comprehensive logging and analytics so you can understand how your system is being used and where it's falling short.

Consider privacy and security

RAG systems often access sensitive information. Make sure you implement appropriate access controls, audit logging, and privacy protections. MCP's security framework provides good tools for this, but you need to use them thoughtfully.

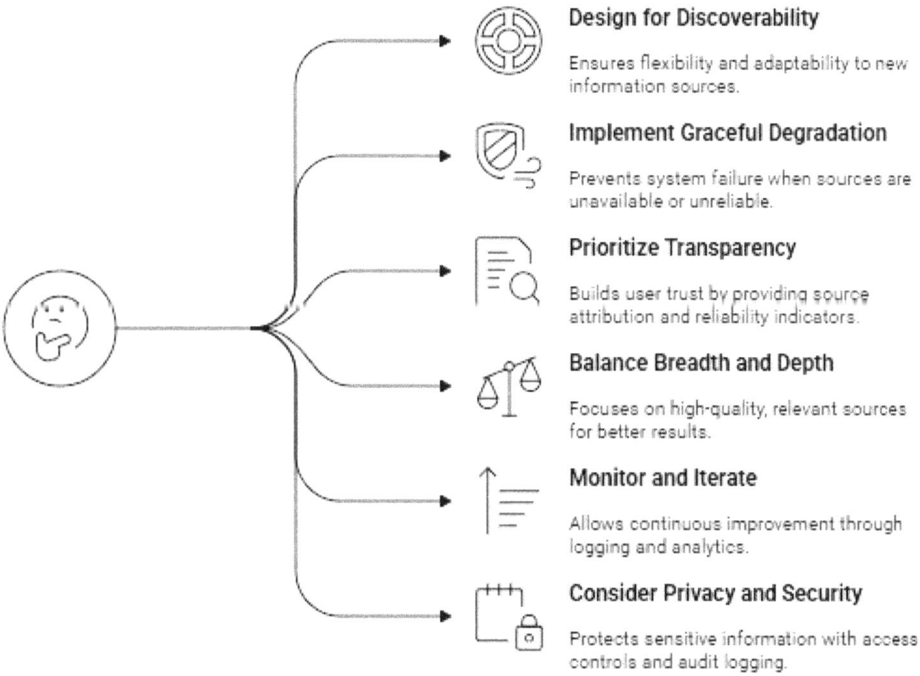

Figure 11.3 – How to design an effective MCP-based RAG system

Summary

MCP transforms RAG systems from brittle, hardcoded integrations into flexible, discoverable, and scalable information access platforms. The key benefits are as follows:

- **Dynamic discovery**: RAG systems can discover available resources and tools via `resources/list` and `tools/list`, and servers can notify clients when these lists change. Discovery of entirely new MCP servers will rely on a centralized registry that is still under development.
- **Standardized access**: All information sources use the same JSON-RPC-based MCP interface for listing and reading resources and invoking tools, simplifying RAG system development.
- **Rich metadata**: MCP provides optional annotations on resources and tool results, such as `audience`, `priority`, and `lastModified`, that can help clients understand the intended audience, relative importance, and recency of a resource.

- **Context awareness**: By leveraging these annotations, information retrieval can be tailored based on user context and task requirements.
- **Security and privacy**: MCP's security framework emphasizes user consent, data privacy, tool safety, and audit logging, enabling appropriate access controls for sensitive information.

The future of RAG isn't about building better connections to specific data sources; it's about building systems that can intelligently discover, access, and synthesize information from any available source. MCP makes that future possible.

RAG is still an evolving field, and we're just beginning to explore what's possible when we combine the flexibility of MCP with the power of RAG. But the early results are promising. We're seeing RAG systems that are more capable, more reliable, and more adaptable than what was possible with traditional approaches.

Looking ahead to *Chapter 12*, we'll explore how MCP turns LangChain into a truly modular, plug-and-play framework. We'll introduce chains, agents, and memory, highlight integration pain points, and show how MCP standardizes document collections and tools, enabling dynamic discovery and context-aware memory. A hands-on **term frequency–inverse document frequency** (**TF–IDF**) RAG example demonstrates these benefits.

12

Integrating MCP with LangChain

LangChain can feel limiting when each tool or data source requires its own custom integration.

I remember the first time I tried to build a complex LangChain application. The framework was impressive, all these chains and agents and tools that could theoretically work together to create sophisticated AI workflows. But the reality? I spent more time writing custom integrations and debugging connection issues than I did building actual AI functionality.

The problem with LangChain, at least in my experience, isn't the framework itself; it's that every tool, every data source, every capability you want to use requires its own custom integration. Want to connect to a database? Write a custom tool. Need access to an API? Another custom tool. Want to use a specialized analysis library? You guessed it, that's more custom code.

That's where MCP changes everything. Instead of writing dozens of custom integrations, you can build LangChain applications that discover and use capabilities dynamically through standardized MCP interfaces. It's like transitioning from ad hoc integrations to a unified protocol where everything just works together.

In this chapter, we will be covering the building blocks of LangChain, such as chains, agents, and memory systems, and why brittle custom integrations make life hard. You'll see how MCP exposes document collections and tools through unified JSON-RPC endpoints, enabling dynamic discovery and reducing boilerplate. We'll explore context-aware memory and dynamic tool discovery, and we'll work through a TF–IDF RAG example that demonstrates how easily a LangChain pipeline can leverage MCP.

Before diving into the nuts and bolts of LangChain integration, it helps to have a solid grasp of multi-agent systems and retrieval-augmented generation. If you haven't already, you might revisit *Chapter 10* for a crash course on multi-agent systems and *Chapter 11* for the fundamentals of RAG. Those concepts underpin much of what follows here.

In this chapter, we'll be covering the following topics:

- Introduction to LangChain
- MCP as a document store for LangChain
- MCP tools as LangChain tools
- MCP resource providers as LangChain memory
- Building a complete LangChain application with MCP

Introduction to LangChain

Let's start with what LangChain actually is, because despite all the hype, it's pretty straightforward at its core. LangChain is a framework for developing applications powered by LLMs. It simplifies the LLM application lifecycle by providing open source components and integrations for development, production, and deployment. These components include abstractions for chaining operations, memory systems, and agent frameworks that allow applications to interact with external tools and data sources.

The chain abstraction

The fundamental concept in LangChain is the *chain*, a sequence of operations that can be composed together to create complex workflows. You might have a chain that retrieves relevant documents, another that analyzes them, and another that generates a response based on the analysis.

This composability is powerful, but it's also where things get complicated. Each step in a chain often needs to interact with different external systems, such as databases, APIs, file systems, and so on. Each of these interactions requires custom code.

The agent framework

LangChain also provides an agent framework that allows AI systems to use tools to accomplish goals. Agents decide what tools to invoke and how to sequence their outputs, supporting both deterministic workflows and more dynamic, agentic loops.

This is where LangChain really shines, but it's also where the integration challenges become most apparent. Agents are only as good as the tools they have access to, and building those tools often requires significant custom development work.

The memory system

LangChain includes various memory systems for maintaining context across interactions. Memory is simply a system that remembers something about previous interactions; LLMs themselves do not retain state between calls, so developers must intentionally add memory to their applications. The type of memory and how it is updated is application-specific; agents may store different information depending on the problem domain.

But again, the memory systems often need to integrate with external storage systems, which brings us back to the same integration challenges.

Why integration matters

The power of LangChain comes from its ability to integrate AI reasoning with external capabilities and data sources. But in practice, these integrations are often the most challenging and time-consuming part of building LangChain applications.

That's exactly the problem that MCP solves.

The following diagram shows the overall architecture of LangChain components for MCP integration.

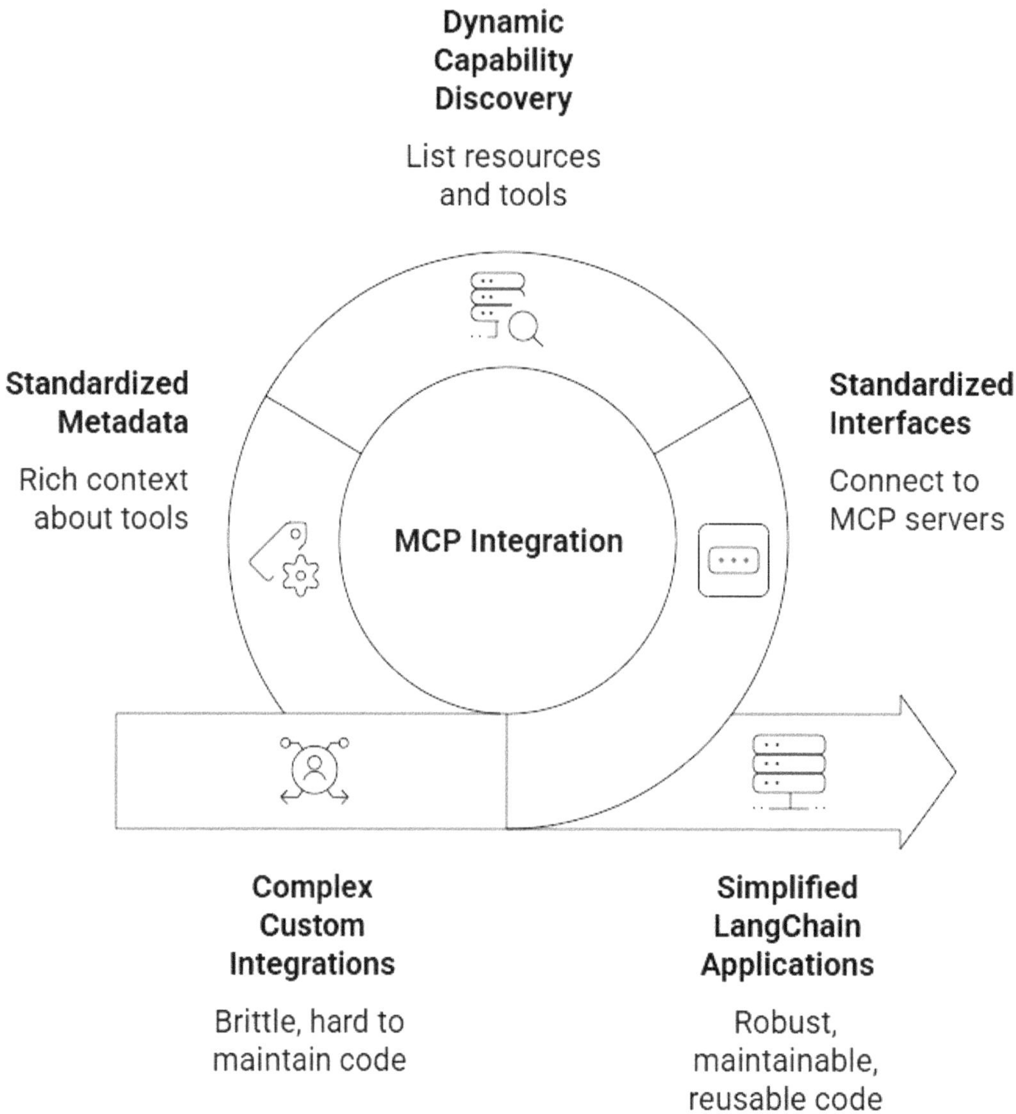

Figure 12.1 – MCP integration for LangChain

Figure 12.1 illustrates how LangChain components communicate with MCP servers for documents, tools, and memory. Review the figure before proceeding to the implementation details.

MCP as a document store for LangChain

LangChain includes loaders for files, databases, web pages, and APIs, but each loader is specific to a source type and requires its own configuration. When you need to load documents from multiple sources, you must manage several loaders and write boilerplate code. MCP servers solve this problem by exposing document collections through a unified resource interface. Instead of writing and maintaining custom loaders, you simply connect to one or more MCP servers and discover collections dynamically, as described in *Chapter 11*'s discussion of RAG.

This approach has several advantages:

- **Unified interface**: All document sources use the same MCP resource interface, simplifying your LangChain code.
- **Dynamic discovery**: Your LangChain application can discover new document sources at runtime without code changes.
- **Rich metadata**: MCP resources include metadata about document freshness, quality, access permissions, and other relevant information.
- **Context awareness**: MCP servers can filter and prioritize documents based on user context and query requirements.

Here's a simple example of how you might integrate MCP document access with LangChain:

We begin by importing the libraries we need, such as `dataclass` for lightweight data containers, `TfidfVectorizer` from scikit-learn for text similarity search, and `numpy` for array operations.

```
"""Simple MCP-based document loader and retrieval example.

This example demonstrates how an MCP client could treat MCP servers as document
stores for retrieval-augmented generation. We implement a minimal in-memory
server and loader, then build a tiny RAG system using scikit-learn's TF-IDF
vectorizer to search documents. This avoids external dependencies on the
`langchain` or `mcp` Python packages while still illustrating the core
concepts.
"""


from dataclasses import dataclass
from typing import Dict, List
from sklearn.feature_extraction.text import TfidfVectorizer
import numpy as np
```

```
@dataclass
class Document:
    """Represents a document with text and associated metadata."""
    text: str
    metadata: Dict[str, str]

class DummyMCPServer:
    """A simple in-memory MCP server that exposes documents as resources."""
    def __init__(self, resources: Dict[str, str]):
        self.resources = resources

    def list_resources(self) -> List[str]:
        return list(self.resources.keys())

    def read_resource(self, name: str) -> str:
        return self.resources[name]
```

The `Document` dataclass pairs a piece of text with a metadata dictionary, which will later track provenance information such as which server and resource name each document came from. The `DummyMCPServer` class simulates the behavior of a real MCP server: it holds a dictionary of named resources and exposes two methods called `list_resources()`, which returns all available resource names, and `read_resource()`, which retrieves the text content for a given name. In a production system, these methods would issue JSON-RPC calls over a transport layer, but this in-memory version lets us focus on the retrieval logic without external dependencies.

Then we have `MCPDocumentLoader`, which acts as the bridge between one or more MCP servers and the downstream RAG system:

```
class MCPDocumentLoader:
"""Loads documents from one or more DummyMCPServer instances."""
def init(self, servers: Dict[str, DummyMCPServer]):
        self.servers = servers
def load_documents(self) -> List[Document]:
    docs: List[Document] = []
    for server_name, server in self.servers.items():
        for name in server.list_resources():
            text = server.read_resource(name)
            docs.append(Document(text=text, metadata={
                'server': server_name,
```

```
                'name': name
            }))
        return docs
```

MCPDocumentLoader accepts a dictionary mapping logical server names to DummyMCPServer instances. When load_documents() is called, it iterates over every registered server, calls list_resources() to discover available documents, and then fetches each one with read_resource(). Each piece of text is wrapped in a Document object whose metadata records the originating server name and resource identifier. This provenance information is critical in a RAG pipeline because it lets the generation model cite its sources and allows operators to audit which servers contributed to a given answer. The loader pattern also makes it straightforward to add new MCP servers: simply register them in the dictionary, and the loader will automatically pull their content into the retrieval index.

Next, the RAGSystem class ties retrieval to the loaded documents:

```
class RAGSystem:
    """A minimal retrieval-augmented generation system using TF-IDF search."""
    def __init__(self, documents: List[Document]):
        self.documents = documents
        self.vectorizer = TfidfVectorizer(stop_words='english')
        self.doc_vectors = self.vectorizer.fit_transform(
            [doc.text for doc in documents]
        )

    def search(self, query: str, k: int = 3) -> List[Document]:
        """Return the top-k documents most similar to the query."""
        query_vec = self.vectorizer.transform([query])
        scores = (self.doc_vectors @ query_vec.T).toarray().flatten()
        indices = scores.argsort()[-k:][::-1]
        return [self.documents[i] for i in indices]


def main() -> None:
    # Set up two dummy MCP servers with small document collections.
    server1 = DummyMCPServer({
        'doc1': 'Model Context Protocol is an open standard for connecting AI 
applications.',
        'doc2': 'LangChain integrates with MCP to provide dynamic tool discovery 
and document access.',
```

```
        'doc3': 'Retrieval-augmented generation uses external documents to reduce
hallucinations.'
    })
    server2 = DummyMCPServer({
        'docA': 'The architecture of MCP consists of clients and servers
communicating via JSON-RPC.',
        'docB':
'Security considerations in MCP include OAuth resource servers and client
authorization.'
    })
    servers = {'server1': server1, 'server2': server2}

    # Load documents from all servers.
    loader = MCPDocumentLoader(servers)
    documents = loader.load_documents()
    print(f"Loaded {len(documents)} documents from {len(servers)} servers")

    # Build a simple retrieval system.
    rag = RAGSystem(documents)

    # Query the system.
    query = 'What is MCP?'
    results = rag.search(query, k=3)
    print(f"\nTop documents for query '{query}':")
    for doc in results:
        print(f"- {doc.metadata['server']}:{doc.metadata['name']} → {doc.text[:
70]}…")

if __name__ == '__main__':
    main()
```

During initialization, the `RAGSystem` class builds a TF–IDF matrix from all document texts. `TfidfVectorizer` tokenizes each document, removes common English stop words, and produces a sparse TF–IDF matrix where each row is a document vector. The `search()` method transforms the user's query into the same vector space, computes cosine-like similarity scores via a matrix dot product (`doc_vectors @ query_vec.T`), and returns the top-*k* documents sorted by descending score.

The `main()` function brings everything together. It creates two `DummyMCPServer` instances: `server1` with three documents about MCP and RAG concepts, and `server2` with two documents covering MCP architecture and security. These servers are registered with `MCPDocumentLoader`, which fetches and wraps all five documents. A `RAGSystem` is then built from the loaded documents, and a sample query "What is MCP?" is issued. The results are printed along with their provenance metadata, showing which server and resource contributed each result. In a production system, these retrieved documents would be injected into a language model's prompt as context, enabling grounded, citation-backed answers.

When you run this code (assuming you have a working MCP server), you'll see output as follows:

```
Found 5 resources
Loaded 5 documents

Found 3 relevant documents:
- MCP Overview: Model Context Protocol (MCP) is an open standard for connecting AI
applications...
- Architecture Guide: The MCP architecture consists of clients and servers that
communicate...
- Implementation Tutorial: To implement an MCP server, you need to define
resources, tools...
```

This demonstrates how MCP can simplify document loading for LangChain applications while providing richer metadata and more flexible access patterns.

With document retrieval sorted, let's turn to a more powerful integration: exposing MCP tools as LangChain tools.

MCP tools as LangChain tools

Perhaps the most powerful integration pattern is exposing MCP tools as LangChain tools, allowing LangChain agents to discover and use MCP capabilities dynamically.

Building tools for LangChain agents typically requires writing custom Python classes that implement the LangChain tool interface. Each tool needs custom code for parameter validation, execution logic, error handling, and result formatting.

This approach works fine for a small number of tools, but it becomes unwieldy as you add more capabilities. Each tool requires maintenance, testing, and documentation. And if you want to use the same capabilities in different applications, you often end up duplicating code.

Integrating MCP tools with LangChain will help solve these issues. Exposing MCP tools as LangChain tools provides several key benefits:

- **Dynamic discovery**: LangChain agents can discover MCP tools at runtime by sending a `tools/list` request to each connected server. The `tools/list` response contains a `tools` array where each object includes a unique name, a human-readable title, a description, and an input schema that defines the expected parameters. This discovery mechanism allows the agent to adapt to new capabilities without code changes.
- **Standardized interface**: All MCP tools use the same invocation pattern. After discovery, the client executes a tool with a `tools/call` request whose name must exactly match the identifier returned by `tools/list` and whose arguments must conform to the input schema. LangChain wrappers can translate these calls into the framework's internal tool interface.
- **Rich metadata**: MCP tool objects carry detailed metadata about their capabilities, parameters, and usage patterns. Servers can also declare a `listChanged` capability during initialization so they can send `notifications/tools/list_changed` messages when their available tool list changes. Clients should respond by re-issuing a `tools/list` request to refresh their local registry.
- **Reusability**: MCP tools are defined outside of any single application, so they can be reused across multiple LangChain applications without duplication. By separating tool definitions from the agent logic, MCP encourages modular design and simplifies testing and documentation.

Understanding the benefits is only half the story. Next, we'll implement a wrapper that translates between LangChain's tool interface and MCP's JSON-RPC tools.

The key is creating a wrapper that translates between LangChain's tool interface and MCP's tool interface. This wrapper handles the protocol differences and provides LangChain agents with seamless access to MCP capabilities.

```
from langchain.tools import Tool
from mcp.client import ClientSession

class MCPToolWrapper(Tool):
    def __init__(self, server_url, tool_name, input_schema):
        super().__init__(name=tool_name,
                         description=input_schema.get('description'))
        self.server_url = server_url
        self.tool_name = tool_name
```

```
        self.input_schema = input_schema

    async def __call__(self, **kwargs):
        async with ClientSession(self.server_url) as session:
            await session.initialize()
            # call the MCP tool via JSON-RPC
            result = await session.call_tool(self.tool_name, kwargs)
            return result.content[0].text

# Discover tools and register wrappers
async def register_mcp_tools(client, server_url):
    async with ClientSession(server_url) as session:
        await session.initialize()
        tool_defs = (await session.list_tools()).tools
        for tool_def in tool_defs:
            wrapper = MCPToolWrapper(server_url,
                                     tool_def.name,
                                     tool_def.inputSchema)
            client.add_tool(wrapper)
```

This wrapper takes the server URL, tool name, and input schema from the MCP `tools/list` response, and converts them into a LangChain `Tool` object. It then registers these wrappers so agents can call them without custom code.

One of the most powerful aspects of MCP tool integration is the ability to register tools dynamically. Instead of hardcoding a fixed set of tools, LangChain agents can discover available MCP tools at startup and register them automatically.

This enables LangChain applications that can adapt to different deployment environments and take advantage of whatever MCP capabilities are available.

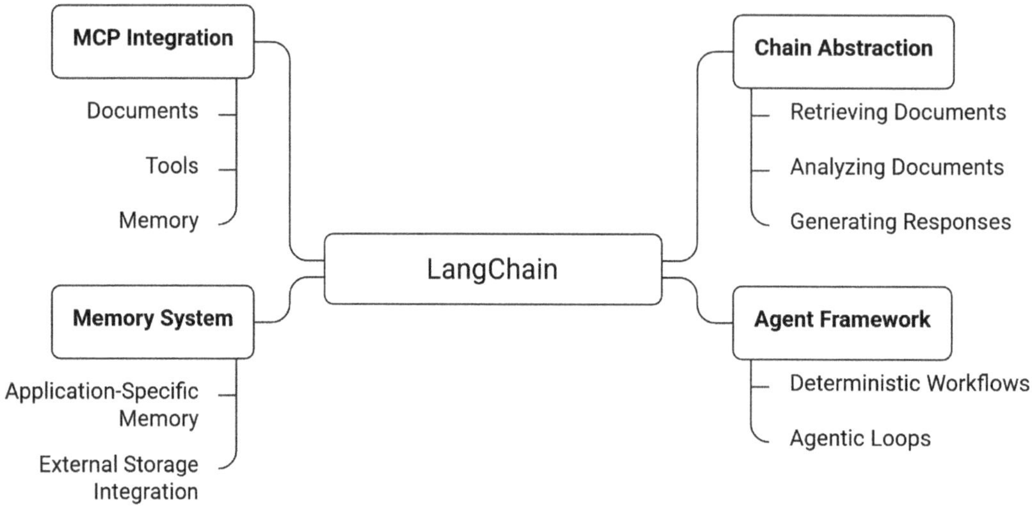

Figure 12.2 – MCP tool integration with LangChain

Now that we've seen document stores and tool wrappers, let's combine them with memory to build a complete LangChain application powered by MCP.

MCP resource providers as LangChain memory

LangChain's memory systems are crucial for building conversational AI applications, but they often require custom integration with external storage systems. MCP resource providers can serve as standardized memory backends for LangChain applications.

LangChain provides several memory implementations, such as in-memory storage, file-based storage, and database storage. But each implementation requires specific configuration and has different capabilities and limitations.

For production applications, you often need persistent, scalable memory storage that can handle concurrent access and provide appropriate security controls. This typically requires custom integration work.

MCP resource providers can implement memory storage patterns that are specifically designed for AI applications. These might include the following:

- **Conversation history storage**: Persistent storage of conversation history with appropriate privacy controls and retention policies
- **User preference management**: Storage and retrieval of user preferences, settings, and personalization data

- **Context caching**: Intelligent caching of frequently accessed context information to improve performance
- **Semantic memory**: Storage of information organized by semantic relationships rather than just chronological order

While MCP resource providers can support these memory patterns, it's important to note that the protocol does not define a dedicated memory primitive. Instead, implementers build memory capabilities on top of the standard `resources/list` and `resources/read` operations. LangChain's memory abstractions remain application-specific, so careful design is required to ensure consistency, privacy, and performance when using MCP resources as memory backends.

Using MCP for LangChain memory requires careful consideration of consistency, performance, and security requirements. Memory operations are often frequent and latency-sensitive, so the MCP implementation needs to be optimized accordingly.

```
class MemoryMCPServer:
    """Minimal in-memory MCP server for conversation history."""
    def __init__(self):
        self.messages = []  # List of {'sender': ..., 'text': ...}

    def list_resources(self):
        return ['history']

    def read_resource(self, name):
        return '\n'.join(f"{m['sender']}: {m['text']}" for m in self.messages)

    def write_resource(self, name, message):
        self.messages.append(message)

# In LangChain, you'd implement a Memory class that calls read_resource() and
write_resource()
# on the MCP server to persist context across interactions.
```

This server exposes a single resource (`history`), and clients can write messages to it and read the conversation history back. Integrating this with LangChain's memory APIs gives you persistent, multi-session context.

Let me walk you through building a complete LangChain application that uses MCP for document access, tool integration, and memory management. By constructing a complete LangChain system, from document loading through tool invocation to memory management, we illustrate how MCP simplifies integration and show how the pieces fit together in a real use case.

Building a complete LangChain application with MCP

In this section, we'll be building a research assistant that can help users analyze academic papers, extract key insights, and maintain context across multiple research sessions.

Our application will use the following:

- MCP document servers for accessing paper repositories
- MCP tool servers for analysis capabilities (summarization, citation analysis, etc.)
- MCP memory servers for maintaining user context and research history
- LangChain agents to orchestrate the research workflow

```
# Pseudocode for the research assistant workflow
query = "impact of microplastics on marine life"

# Step 1: Document retrieval
docs = doc_loader.load_documents()          # from MCP document servers
retrieved = rag_system.search(query)        # top documents via TF-IDF

# Step 2: Summarisation via MCP tool
summaries = []
for doc in retrieved:
    summary = langchain_agent.run_tool("summarize", {"text": doc.text})
    summaries.append(summary)

# Step 3: Context storage (memory)
memory_server.write_resource("history",
                             {"sender": "assistant",
                              "text": "Summary of documents..."
                             }
                            )

# Step 4: User-facing response
answer = langchain_agent.run_tool("generate_report",
                                  {"summaries": summaries}
                                 )

print(answer)
```

This code retrieves relevant documents, summarizes them using an MCP summarization tool, stores the conversation context in memory, and then generates an aggregated report, showing how all three MCP integrations work together.

This architecture provides several advantages over traditional LangChain applications:

- **Flexibility**: New document sources, analysis tools, and storage systems can be added without changing the core application
- **Scalability**: Different MCP servers can be scaled independently based on usage patterns
- **Maintainability**: The core LangChain logic is separated from integration concerns, making it easier to maintain and test
- **Reusability**: The MCP servers can be used by other applications, not just this specific LangChain implementation

The best operational practices for MCP integrations

When you move beyond experiments to production-quality LangChain applications, you must design for observability, resilience, and maintainability. At a minimum, adopt the following practices:

- **Centralize logging and use correlation IDs**: Route logs from all MCP clients and servers to a central logging system; assign a unique correlation ID to each user request so you can trace how it moves across document, tool, and memory services. Keep log formats consistent across services to simplify analysis. Avoid logging sensitive data and mask or encrypt secrets.
- **Collect metrics and traces**: Logs are only one aspect of observability; you should also collect resource-utilization metrics and distributed traces to understand how requests traverse multiple MCP servers. Correlating logs, metrics, and traces helps you pinpoint bottlenecks and ensures your integrations scale under load.
- **Integrate with CI/CD pipelines**: Treat each MCP server and LangChain component as a deployable service. Use continuous integration to build and test changes on every commit, enforce quality gates in staging environments, and deploy new versions independently. Follow microservice CI/CD principles: each team owns its pipeline, services are built and tested in isolation, and updates can be rolled out side-by-side with previous versions.
- **Automated testing**: Write unit tests for each tool, resource, and memory interaction, and integration tests that spin up dummy MCP servers and LangChain clients. Use contract tests to verify that responses conform to declared schemas (as discussed in

Chapter 6) and fuzz tests to validate error handling. Incorporate these tests into your CI pipeline so regressions are caught early.

- **Plan for production deployment**: Containerize your MCP servers and LangChain agents, orchestrate them with Kubernetes or similar platforms, and use blue-green or canary deployments for changes. Implement health checks and readiness probes, and set up dashboards to monitor request latency, error rates, and resource usage. Finally, document your operational procedures so other teams can reuse your setup.

Summary

MCP transforms LangChain from a framework that requires extensive custom integration work into a platform that can discover and use capabilities dynamically. The key benefits are as follows:

- **Reduced integration complexity**: MCP eliminates most custom integration code, allowing you to focus on AI logic rather than system integration.
- **Dynamic capability discovery**: LangChain applications can adapt to new capabilities on connected MCP servers without code changes. Clients use `resources/list` and `tools/list` to discover available resources and tools, and can refresh this information when servers send `listChanged` notifications. Automatically discovering new servers is beyond the current specification; a registry for cross-server discovery is planned.
- **Standardized interfaces**: All external capabilities use the same MCP interface, simplifying development and maintenance.
- **Rich metadata and context**: MCP provides detailed information that enables better decision-making in LangChain applications.
- **Reusability and modularity**: MCP capabilities can be shared across multiple LangChain applications.

The future of LangChain development isn't about building better custom integrations, but about building applications that can intelligently discover and use whatever capabilities are available through standardized protocols such as MCP.

LangChain and MCP together create a powerful platform for building AI applications that are more flexible, more maintainable, and more capable than what's possible with either technology alone. We're just beginning to explore the possibilities, but the early results are incredibly promising.

Looking ahead to *Chapter 13*, we'll step into AutoGen, a multi-agent conversation framework. Combined with the multi-agent system groundwork in *Chapter 10* and the RAG overview in *Chapter 11*, we will show how to orchestrate specialized agents using an MCP-agent conversation framework. We'll unpack how conversable agents coordinate, why trapping them in a sandbox limits real-world impact, and how integrating MCP lets them call tools and adapt dynamically, paving the way for specialized agent teams and robust systems.

Subscribe for a free eBook

New frameworks, evolving architectures, research drops, production breakdowns—*AI_Distilled* filters the noise into a weekly briefing for engineers and researchers working hands-on with LLMs and GenAI systems. Subscribe now and receive a free eBook, along with weekly insights that help you stay focused and informed.

Subscribe at `https://packt.link/8Oz6Y` or scan the QR code below.

13

Integrating MCP with AutoGen

> *The future of AI isn't about building smarter individual agents; it's about building agents that can work together intelligently.*

I remember the first time I tried to get AutoGen agents to do something useful beyond chatting with each other. They could debate endlessly about the best approach to analyzing customer data, but when it came time to query a database or call an API, they hit a wall. The sandbox kept them safe, but it also kept them from doing real work. That frustration led me to MCP, and the combination of AutoGen's conversational intelligence with MCP's real-world capabilities turned out to be exactly what I needed.

AutoGen is a **multi-agent conversation framework** that orchestrates collaborative interactions among AI agents. It provides conversable, customizable agents, such as assistant and user proxy agents, that can send and receive messages, reason about problems, and generate code. Built-in presets such as `UserProxyAgent`, `CodeExecutorAgent`, `OpenAIAssistantAgent`, `MultimodalWebSurfer`, `FileSurfer`, and `VideoSurfer` provide out-of-the-box roles ranging from acting as a human user proxy to executing code and surfing the web. These capabilities make AutoGen a powerful platform for orchestrating AI conversations, but its native environment is sandboxed. Agents can run Python code in a restricted container, yet they cannot call real APIs, read from databases, or interact with external systems.

The **Model Context Protocol** (**MCP**) lifts these restrictions. MCP defines JSON-RPC methods such as `tools/list`, `resources/list`, and `tools/call` that let clients discover and invoke tools hosted on remote servers. Resources can also be listed and read via `resources/list` and `resources/read`, and servers may send optional `listChanged` notifications when capabilities change. MCP uses OAuth 2.1 with resource indicators for secure, consent-driven authorization. By integrating AutoGen with MCP, agents gain access to real-world capabilities, including databases, APIs, and cloud services, while preserving their conversational problem-solving style.

This chapter explores how to combine AutoGen with MCP. After introducing AutoGen's multi-agent conversation model, we show why MCP integration is necessary, walk through basic and advanced integration patterns, and discuss memory, persistence, discovery, and coordination. We conclude with best practices and a look ahead.

In this chapter, we'll be covering the following topics:

- Introduction to AutoGen
- Basic integration: wrapping MCP tools
- Advanced integration: MCP-powered agents
- Building a collaborative coding system
- Memory and persistence with MCP
- Discovery and coordination among agents
- Best practices for MCP–AutoGen integration

Introduction to AutoGen

AutoGen (version 0.4 and later) is built around the core insight that multiple perspectives beat a single model. Instead of one monolithic agent trying to do everything, AutoGen coordinates **conversable agents** that specialize in different tasks. The `ConversableAgent` class provides messaging primitives; subclasses such as `AssistantAgent` and `UserProxyAgent` send and receive messages, invoke language models, and incorporate human feedback. Additional presets include `CodeExecutorAgent`, which runs Python code in a sandbox, `OpenAIAssistantAgent` for simple question-answering, and multimodal agents for browsing the web or handling files. Because each agent can integrate language models, humans, and tools, you can assemble teams where one agent writes code, another critiques it, a third executes it, and a fourth requests human input.

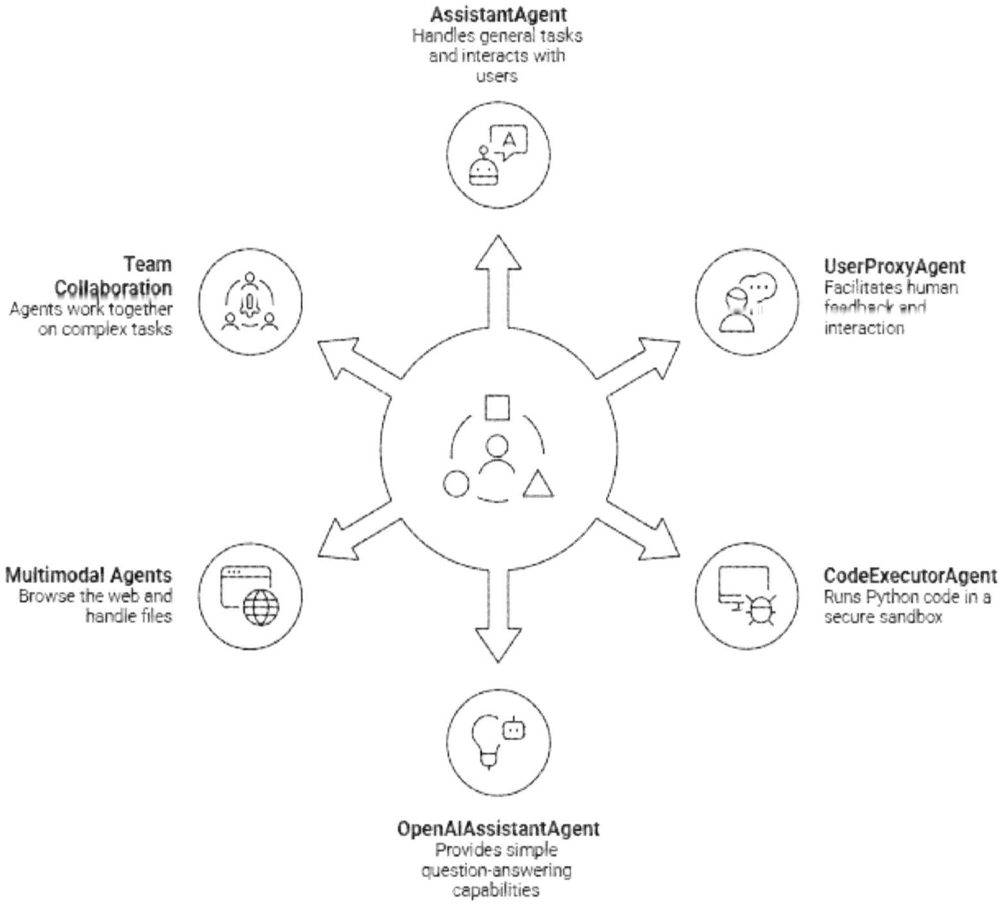

Figure 13.1 – AutoGen's multi-agent conversation model

Figure 13.1 illustrates this conversation model. At the center is the AutoGen runtime, which routes messages between agents. Each agent (coding, data, research, chat, and web) communicates through the runtime to collaborate on problems. Without MCP, these conversations are confined to the sandbox; agents cannot call external APIs or access databases.

AutoGen excels at generating and executing code. Agents can iteratively write Python functions, run them in a Docker-based sandbox, and analyze the results. However, the sandbox isolates agents from the outside world: they cannot directly query databases, call REST APIs, or write files outside the container. For real-world applications such as data analysis, report generation, and workflow automation, agents need a bridge to external systems.

Why integrate MCP with AutoGen?

MCP provides that bridge. It standardizes how clients enumerate and invoke tools and resources hosted by external servers. Through `tools/list` and `resources/list`, agents can discover available capabilities and learn each tool's name, description, and input schema. They then use `tools/call` to execute a tool by name with arguments, receiving structured outputs in response. Optional `listChanged` notifications allow agents to react when a server's capabilities change. For resources, `resources/list` and `resources/read` provide similar discovery and reading functions. In short, MCP lets AutoGen agents call real APIs, query databases, process files, and use specialized services, all while maintaining the conversational flow.

This section covers three key ideas:

- **Bridging to external tools**: How MCP breaks agents out of the sandbox by exposing tools and resources
- **Dynamic discovery**: How agents can enumerate available tools at runtime and adapt their strategies accordingly
- **Preserving the conversational model**: How agents remain engaged in dialogue even while invoking external capabilities

Breaking out of the sandbox

Without MCP, AutoGen agents are limited to reasoning, discussing, and writing code that runs in a protected container. They cannot call web services, read from corporate databases, or leverage domain-specific tools. MCP integration dismantles these walls. For example, when an agent needs sales data, it can discover a `salesQuery` tool on an MCP server and call it. When a research agent needs to perform a keyword search, it can call a `documentSearch` tool. Because tool definitions include JSON schemas for inputs and outputs, agents can generate appropriate arguments and interpret results.

Importantly, MCP does not force agents into a new interaction style. Agents still converse about what they need: "I need last quarter's revenue by region." "I can retrieve that via the sales database; which regions are we interested in?" The only difference is that one agent now calls a tool via MCP to fetch the data.

Dynamic capability discovery

MCP's discovery operations make agents adaptive. Instead of hardcoding a list of capabilities, an agent calls `tools/list` or `resources/list` on a known server to see what is available. If a new analytics service appears, agents learn about it automatically. Servers may emit `listChanged` notifications when their tools or resources change, allowing agents to update their internal lists without polling. While MCP does not yet provide a global registry for discovering unknown servers, clients must know server URLs ahead of time. The protocol's roadmap includes a future central registry.

Maintaining the conversational model

The beauty of MCP integration is that it respects AutoGen's collaborative spirit. Instead of circumventing conversations, MCP becomes part of them. For example, one agent might propose using a `forecastSales` tool; another agent might question whether the tool has the necessary data or suggest combining it with a `visualizeData` tool. Through discussion, agents decide how to orchestrate external capabilities. As we will see in the coding example, agents can even discover tools together and assign tasks to each other.

With the motivation clear, let's move from theory to practice. We'll start with the simplest integration approach and build from there.

Basic integration: wrapping MCP tools

The simplest way to integrate MCP with AutoGen is to wrap tools as functions that agents can call during a conversation. AutoGen supports function calling: when an agent decides it needs to perform an action, it can call an attached function and incorporate the result into the chat. We can use this mechanism to bridge MCP tools.

Below is a simplified Python module (adapted from the earlier chapters) that simulates how AutoGen agents discover and call MCP tools. It uses an in-memory "server" exposing two tools, search and analyze, to illustrate dynamic discovery and coordinated execution. Note that this example uses hardcoded documents and a trivial sentiment analysis; in real systems, the tools would query databases, call APIs, or perform complex analysis.

```
class DummyMCPServer:
    """Expose simple tools via list_tools() and call_tool()."""

    def __init__(self):
        self.tools = {
            "search": self.search,
            "analyze": self.analyze,
```

```
        }

    def list_tools(self):
        # Return metadata for each tool
        return [
            {"name": "search", "description": "Search documents for a query"},
            {"name": "analyze", "description": "Analyze text for sentiment"},
        ]

    def call_tool(self, name: str, args: dict):
        if name not in self.tools:
            raise ValueError(f"Tool {name} not found")
        return self.tools[name](**args)

    def search(self, query: str) -> str:
        # Return hard-coded documents containing the query
        documents = [
            "Stanford study: Remote work improves productivity by 13%.",
            "MIT and Microsoft report: company-wide remote work reduces "
            "cross-team collaboration.",
        ]
        matches = [doc for doc in documents if query.lower() in doc.lower()]
        return "\n".join(matches) if matches else "No documents found."

    def analyze(self, data: str) -> str:
        # Count positive and negative words in the data
        positive = data.lower().count("improves")
        negative = data.lower().count("reduces")
        return (
            f"Analysis summary: {positive} positive signal(s), "
            f"{negative} negative signal(s)."
        )
```

The `DummyMCPServer` class simulates an MCP server by exposing two tools, `search` and `analyze`, through `list_tools()` and `call_tool()` methods. This mirrors MCP's `tools/list` and `tools/call` JSON-RPC operations, letting clients discover available capabilities and invoke them by name.

Next, we have the `MCPClient` class, which acts as the bridge between agents and the server:

```
class MCPClient:
    """Discover tools on initialization and forward calls to the server."""

    def __init__(self, server: DummyMCPServer):
        self.server = server
        self.tools = {
            tool["name"]: tool for tool in server.list_tools()
        }

    def call_tool(self, name: str, args: dict) -> str:
        return self.server.call_tool(name, args)
```

On initialization, the `MCPClient` class calls `list_tools()` to discover available tools, much like a real MCP client would call `tools/list` at startup. It then forwards tool calls to the server on behalf of agents.

Finally, `ResearchAgent` and `AnalysisAgent` each hold a reference to the `MCPClient` and use it to call specific tools:

```
class ResearchAgent:
    def __init__(self, client: MCPClient):
        self.client = client

    def research(self, query: str) -> str:
        print(f"ResearchAgent: searching for '{query}' via MCP...")
        results = self.client.call_tool("search", {"query": query})
        print(f"ResearchAgent: found documents:\n{results}\n")
        return results

class AnalysisAgent:
    def __init__(self, client: MCPClient):
        self.client = client

    def analyze(self, data: str) -> str:
        print("AnalysisAgent: analyzing data via MCP...")
        summary = self.client.call_tool("analyze", {"data": data})
        print(f"AnalysisAgent: {summary}\n")
        return summary
```

```
def simulate_conversation():
    server = DummyMCPServer()
    client = MCPClient(server)
    research_agent = ResearchAgent(client)
    analysis_agent = AnalysisAgent(client)
    query = "remote work"
    docs = research_agent.research(query)
    analysis_agent.analyze(docs)

if __name__ == "__main__":
    simulate_conversation()
```

The `simulate_conversation()` function wires everything together: it creates the server, client, and agents, then orchestrates a simple two-step workflow where one agent searches and the other analyzes the results.

Let's walk through what happens when this code runs: `ResearchAgent` searches for "remote work" and prints the matching documents. `AnalysisAgent` then analyzes the retrieved text and reports how many positive and negative signals it found. By discovering tool metadata via `list_tools` and invoking tools via `call_tool`, the agents coordinate their tasks. In real AutoGen systems, you would replace `DummyMCPServer` with an actual MCP server and use `tools/list` and `tools/call` to discover and call capabilities.

The example documents refer to well-known remote-work studies. In a randomized field experiment at the Chinese travel company Ctrip, employees working from home increased productivity by about 13%. A later Stanford report found that hybrid work (two days from home) had no negative impact on productivity and significantly reduced attrition.

Conversely, an MIT and Microsoft study showed that company-wide remote work reduced cross-team collaboration by roughly 25%, causing knowledge networks to become more siloed. These mixed findings illustrate why agents might need to search and synthesize multiple sources, and why MCP's ability to access external research tools matters.

The basic integration we just built demonstrates the core pattern. Next, we'll scale this approach by designing agents around the MCP servers they connect to.

Advanced integration: MCP powered agents

Wrapping individual tools is only the beginning. MCP-powered AutoGen agents are designed around the capabilities they can access. Instead of one generic agent calling any tool, you can assign each agent to a set of MCP servers that define its domain expertise. Here's an example:

- **Data agent**: Connects to database and analytics MCP servers
- **Research agent**: Connects to document search and knowledge base servers
- **Visualization agent**: Connects to charting and presentation servers
- **Communication agent**: Connects to email and messaging servers

These agents discover available tools at runtime and adapt their behavior accordingly. Because each agent only sees the tools relevant to its role, the team exhibits specialized reasoning: the data agent proposes queries, the visualization agent suggests charts, and the communication agent drafts messages. Agents can also share the same MCP servers when appropriate, enabling cross-agent resource sharing and collaborative workflows.

Hierarchical architecture further extends this idea. A higher-level **Coordinator agent** might orchestrate lower-level agents, some of which are implemented as MCP servers themselves. For instance, a project manager agent could interact with a testing service that is implemented as an MCP server and delegate tasks to a coding agent and a QA agent. MCP does not prescribe these patterns, but its uniform interface makes them possible.

To see how these patterns come together in practice, let's walk through a concrete example.

Building a collaborative coding system

To demonstrate these concepts, consider a collaborative coding system built with AutoGen and MCP. Multiple specialized agents work together to analyze requirements, design architecture, write code, test it, and deploy the result. Each agent relies on MCP servers for its domain capabilities.

Agent team

- **Requirements analyst**: Gathers initial specifications and researches similar projects
- **Architect**: Evaluates design patterns and selects technology stacks
- **Developer**: Writes source code, manages dependencies, and commits changes
- **Tester**: Runs test suites and validates behavior against requirements
- **DevOps engineer**: Deploys builds and monitors system health

Role	Responsibilities	MCP resources
Requirements analyst	Breaks down user requirements into technical specifications	Document search and knowledge base servers
Architect	Designs system architecture and chooses technologies	Knowledge base and best-practice servers
Developer	Writes code and manages revisions	Code repository and build servers
Tester	Runs automated tests and reports issues	Testing framework servers
DevOps engineer	Deploys the system and monitors performance	Deployment and monitoring servers

Table 13.1 – MCP resources and responsibilities mapping to role

Workflow

- The *requirements analyst* calls MCP search tools to research similar projects, user stories, and industry standards.
- The *architect* consults knowledge base tools to evaluate design patterns and technology options.
- The *developer* uses a code repository tool to create and commit source files, then invokes build and dependency analysis tools.
- The *tester* triggers test suites via a testing framework tool and analyzes the results.
- The *DevOps engineer* deploys the build via a deployment tool and monitors the system through a performance analysis tool.

Throughout this process, agents converse. They propose design choices, critique code quality, suggest additional tests, and decide when to iterate. MCP servers supply concrete actions, such as retrieving requirements, committing code, and running tests, while AutoGen agents provide the reasoning glue.

Benefits

- **Automated expertise**: Each agent contributes specialized knowledge and uses domain-specific tools
- **Continuous collaboration**: Agents discuss issues and coordinate solutions in real time
- **Integrated tooling**: All external capabilities are accessible through MCP's uniform interface
- **Adaptive workflows**: The same agents can operate in different environments; if a new testing tool appears, the tester discovers it via `tools/list` and can use it immediately

So far, we've focused on how agents discover and invoke tools during a single session. But what happens when a session ends? In the next section, we'll explore how MCP can help agents remember context across conversations.

Memory and persistence with MCP

Large language models do not have persistent memory across sessions; AutoGen itself provides no built-in storage. Instead, memory must be explicitly implemented. MCP does not define a first-class memory primitive, but developers can build memory and persistence on top of the `resources` interface. Here are some common patterns:

- **Conversation history management**: Expose a `read/write` resource that stores past dialogues. Agents call `resources/read` and a custom write tool to retrieve and append messages, allowing them to recall context across sessions.
- **Shared knowledge bases**: Multiple agents connect to the same MCP server and read from a shared resource (e.g., a knowledge graph or document store), building collective knowledge. Memory schemas and storage strategies are application-specific and should be designed carefully.
- **User preferences and context**: Store user settings, project metadata, and other persistent state via resource providers. Agents read these preferences to tailor their responses.
- **Cross-session continuity**: By persisting state in resources, users can resume work later. When a user returns to a project, the agents fetch conversation history and relevant context to pick up where they left off.

Developers must decide what to store and how to structure it. For instance, the LangChain community notes that memory can take many forms, including conversation logs, vector embeddings, and key-value stores, and should be tailored to each application.

Persistence is one side of the coin; the other is how agents find and work with each other. Let's look at what MCP offers for discovery and coordination today, and what is still on the roadmap.

Discovery and coordination among agents

MCP can facilitate cooperation between AutoGen agents running in different systems or organizations, but it is important to distinguish current protocol features from future aspirations.

Current features

- **JSON-RPC methods**: `tools/list`, `resources/list`, `prompts/list`, and `tools/call` provide capability discovery and invocation.
- **Notifications**: Servers can emit optional `listChanged` notifications when tools or resources change.
- **Authorization:** HTTP transports use OAuth 2.1 with resource indicators; clients must request tokens specifying the target resource, and servers must validate them.

Limitations and future features

- **Server registry**: The current specification has *no* built-in mechanism to discover new MCP servers. Clients must know the server endpoints ahead of time. The MCP roadmap proposes a central registry for server discovery, but it is still a preview feature and not part of the base protocol.
- **Dynamic capability negotiation**: There is no standard for negotiating capabilities or versions beyond `list` operations. Future versions may include semantic versioning and capability probing.
- **Richer metadata and trust signals**: Tool definitions may include audience and priority annotations, but these are not trustworthy unless the server is trusted. Future enhancements may provide signed metadata and provenance.

Coordination patterns

- **Agent registry**: Since MCP lacks a registry, developers must build custom services to register agents, discover teams, and mediate interactions. This infrastructure can itself be exposed via MCP servers.
- **Cross-system collaboration**: Agents from different organizations can connect to shared MCP servers. For example, two companies might expose a joint data lake via MCP and allow their agents to `read/write` resources. Coordination logic, such as how agents find each other and share results, remains the developer's responsibility.

- **Load balancing and resource management**: MCP servers may implement their own scheduling for tools and resources, but cross-agent load balancing is out of scope. Application designers must ensure fairness and avoid resource contention.
- **Security and trust**: Because agents may call sensitive tools, implementers should enforce explicit user consent, data privacy, and tool safety. Use OAuth 2.1 with resource indicators, validate tool annotations, and log all agent actions for auditing. Federated approval frameworks and multi-party authentication are possible but not defined by MCP.

With the integration patterns, memory strategies, and coordination approaches covered, let's distill the key lessons into a set of practical guidelines.

Best practices for MCP–AutoGen integration

Based on practical experience, the following guidelines help build robust systems:

- **Maintain the conversational flow**: Design MCP integrations as natural extensions of agent dialogues. Agents should discuss which tools to use, why they are needed, and how to interpret results.
- **Handle errors gracefully**: External systems can fail. Agents should catch MCP errors, discuss alternative strategies, and retry or fall back when tools are unavailable.
- **Leverage metadata judiciously**: Tool descriptions and schemas help agents decide how to call tools. Use metadata such as descriptions and JSON schemas to plan calls, but treat annotations such as audience and priority as untrusted unless the server is trusted.
- **Monitor interactions**: Multi-agent systems are complex. Implement logging and monitoring to understand how agents interact with each other and with external systems.
- **Secure communications**: Follow MCP's security model. Obtain explicit user consent for tool calls, protect sensitive data, and implement audit trails. Use OAuth 2.1 with resource indicators for HTTP transport.
- **Test extensively**: Because agent conversations can branch unpredictably, test your system under different scenarios, including tool failures and unexpected responses.

That covers the practical guidance. Let's recap what we've learned in this chapter.

Summary

Integrating MCP with AutoGen transforms a closed conversation framework into a platform for collaborative intelligence. Agents can access external systems and tools while maintaining their conversational problem-solving style. Key takeaways include the following:

- **Real-world capabilities**: MCP opens AutoGen agents to databases, APIs, cloud services, and other tools.
- **Dynamic discovery**: Agents can discover available tools and resources at runtime via `tools/list` and `resources/list`. Discovery of entirely new servers is not yet standardized; a registry is under development.
- **Specialized roles**: By connecting agents to different MCP servers, you create specialized agents and achieve division of labor.
- **Persistent memory**: MCP does not include a memory primitive, but developers can build memory on top of `resources` for conversation histories and user preferences.
- **Distributed coordination**: MCP allows agents to coordinate across systems and organizations, but registries and load balancing must be implemented separately.
- **Security**: The protocol requires user consent, data privacy, and tool safety. Use OAuth 2.1 with resource indicators and audit logging.

Looking ahead to *Chapter 14*, we will explore enterprise knowledge management. You will learn how MCP's standardized operations, annotations, and security guidelines enable unified access to scattered documents and tacit knowledge across an organization. By integrating knowledge retrieval tools into AutoGen, agents can not only communicate and act but also tap into the collective wisdom of your enterprise.

Get this book's PDF copy, code bundle, and more

Scan the QR code (or go to `packtpub.com/unlock`). Search for this book by name, confirm the edition, and then follow the steps on the page.

UNLOCK NOW

Note: Have your invoice handy. Purchases made directly from the Packt website don't require an invoice.

Part 5

Real-World Applications

This part applies everything you have learned to three high-impact domains. You will design MCP-based architectures for enterprise knowledge management, tackling challenges such as knowledge silos, federated search, and compliance. You will then build personalization and recommendation systems that use MCP for real-time adaptation and cross-platform consistency. Finally, you will explore multimodal applications, learning how MCP coordinates processing across text, image, audio, and video modalities. By the end of this part, you will have practical experience applying MCP to the kinds of problems that organizations face in production today.

This part of the book includes the following chapters:

- *Chapter 14, MCP for Enterprise Knowledge Management*
- *Chapter 15, MCP for Personalization and Recommendation Systems*
- *Chapter 16, MCP for Multimodal Applications*

14

MCP for Enterprise Knowledge Management

Enterprise knowledge management without MCP is like trying to run a library where every book is in a different language and every librarian speaks only one of them.

I've spent more time than I care to admit trying to build **knowledge management systems** for large organizations. And let me tell you, it's a special kind of hell. You've got data scattered across dozens of systems, e.g., SharePoint sites, Confluence wikis, file shares, databases, email archives, Slack channels, and that one critical Excel spreadsheet that Bob from accounting maintains and refuses to share with anyone.

Each system has its own search interface, its own access controls, its own way of organizing information. Users give up trying to find what they need and just ask around until someone points them to the right place. Or they recreate work that's already been done because they can't find the original. It's inefficient, frustrating, and expensive.

The promise of AI-powered knowledge management is that we can finally make all this information accessible and useful. But the reality is that most AI systems just add another layer of complexity on top of the existing chaos. They can't access half the information sources, they don't understand the organizational context, and they certainly can't navigate the political and security complexities of enterprise environments.

That's where MCP changes the game. Instead of trying to build yet another knowledge management system, you can build AI systems that can discover and access whatever knowledge sources are available, adapting to the unique information landscape of each organization.

In this chapter, we will be covering modern **enterprise knowledge management** (**EKM**): defining EKM's goal of making the right information available at the right time, examining why scattered systems and tacit know-how create silos, and understanding the limits of keyword search and the need for context-aware retrieval. We'll see how MCP's standardized operations and annotations help connect diverse knowledge sources, enable personalized access, and ensure security and compliance. We'll also explore architectural patterns such as federated search and knowledge graphs, and look ahead to future innovations such as generative synthesis and personalized delivery.

This chapter matters because effective EKM is the glue that holds multi-agent systems together: without reliable knowledge sharing, agents produce incomplete or inconsistent outputs. By mastering EKM, you'll enable your agents to coordinate accurate information and build trustworthy applications.

In this chapter, we'll be covering the following topics:

- Introduction to enterprise knowledge management (EKM)
- Challenges in AI-powered EKM and how MCP helps
- Architectural patterns for MCP-based EKM
- Implementing an MCP resource provider for a document store
- Security considerations in MCP-based EKM
- Future trends: generative EKM with MCP

Introduction to enterprise knowledge management (EKM)

Modern EKM is more than just a document repository; it is a multidisciplinary program designed to capture, organize, and leverage an organization's collective knowledge so the right information is available at the right time. Those knowledge assets include documents, data, processes, and the expertise that resides within people. Effective EKM drives efficiency by reusing proven solutions and best practices and maintains agility by disseminating lessons learned across global teams.

The following diagram depicts multiple enterprise knowledge sources (e.g., SharePoint, Confluence, CRM, email archives, and data lakes), each wrapped by an MCP server. These servers expose resources and tools via MCP to a central AI agent or client aggregator. The agent can then discover resources, issue queries, invoke tools, and integrate results into a unified response. A client aggregator or AI agent communicates with these servers via standard MCP operations (`resources/list`, `tools/list`, `read`, `call`), retrieves context and tools, and synthesizes responses.

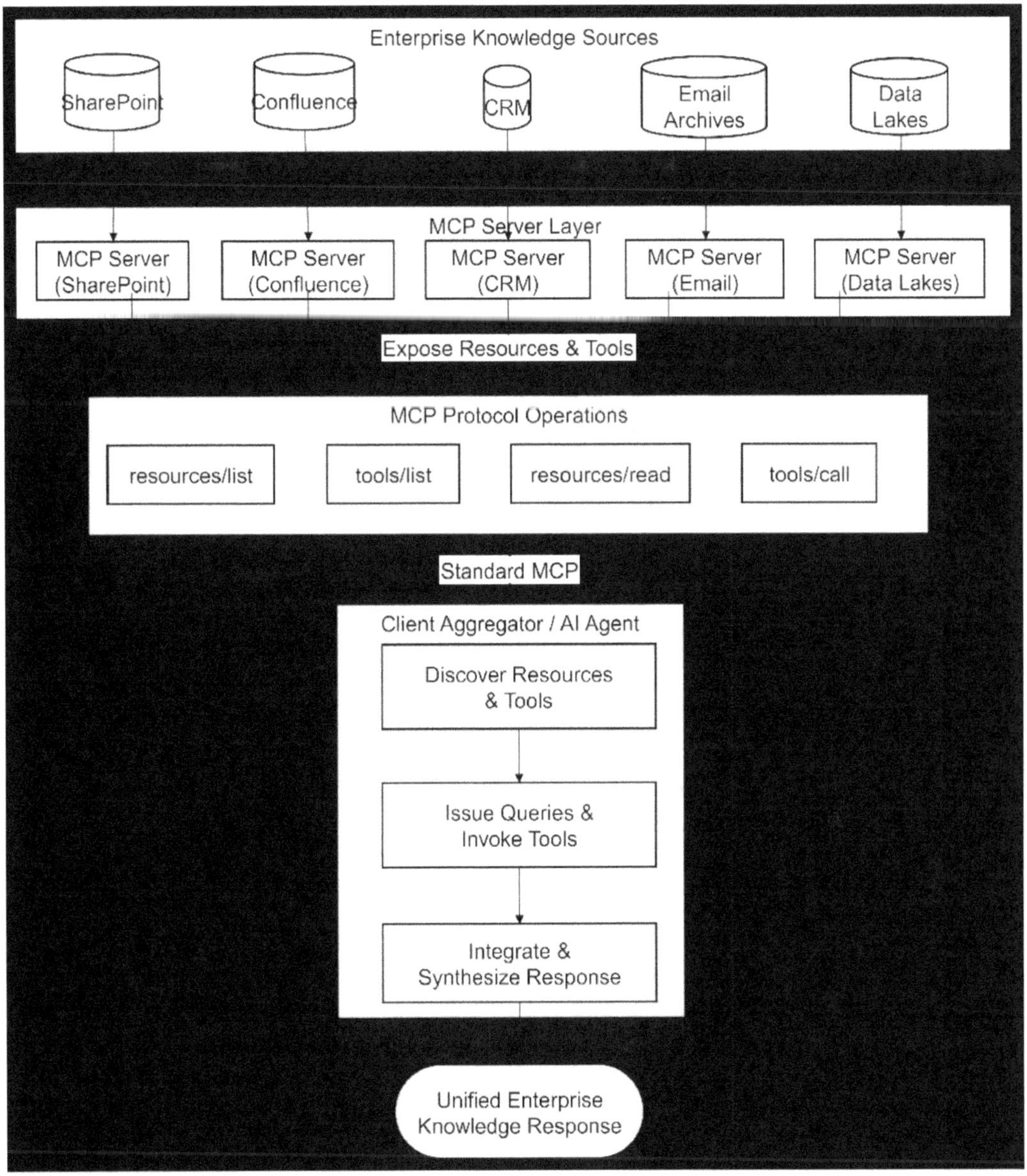

Figure 14.1 – End-to-end EKM architecture with MCP

This architecture enables modularity (each knowledge source can evolve independently), security (each server enforces its own access controls), and scalability (new sources can be added without changing the client). Refer to *Chapter 7's* discussion of multi-agent systems and *Chapter 11's* retrieval-augmented generation if you need to a complete understanding.

With this end-to-end architecture, now let's look at the key challenges that EKM systems aim to address.

Knowledge silos

Large enterprises rarely have a single "source of truth." Teams and departments tend to store information in disconnected systems, such as file shares, wikis, CRMs, ticketing systems, and chat threads. This fragmentation means valuable insights aren't shared across the enterprise, and employees may have to consult multiple tools to assemble a complete picture. The primary goal of EKM is to break down these silos and create a unified knowledge landscape.

Tacit and explicit knowledge

Knowledge exists in both **explicit** and **tacit** forms. Explicit knowledge is documented information such as manuals, policies, and reports. Tacit knowledge is the unwritten know-how people carry in their heads, that is, the informal processes, contextual insights, and lessons learned through experience. EKM programs must capture and convert tacit knowledge into explicit artifacts while also encouraging retention and sharing so critical knowledge isn't lost.

Search and discovery

Employees frequently report that they "cannot find anything" in corporate knowledge bases. As the volume of content grows, simple keyword searches return long lists of documents without indicating which one is relevant. Users may not even know which system holds the information they need. EKM therefore requires advanced search and retrieval capabilities that can interpret user intent, traverse multiple repositories, and highlight the most relevant results.

Context and personalization

The same document can be critical for one user and irrelevant for another. Governance frameworks define who can create or edit specific content and restrict access to sensitive information, but beyond basic permissions, knowledge platforms need to adapt retrieval and presentation based on a user's role, project, and context. Balancing open sharing with appropriate access control is essential for maintaining quality and security.

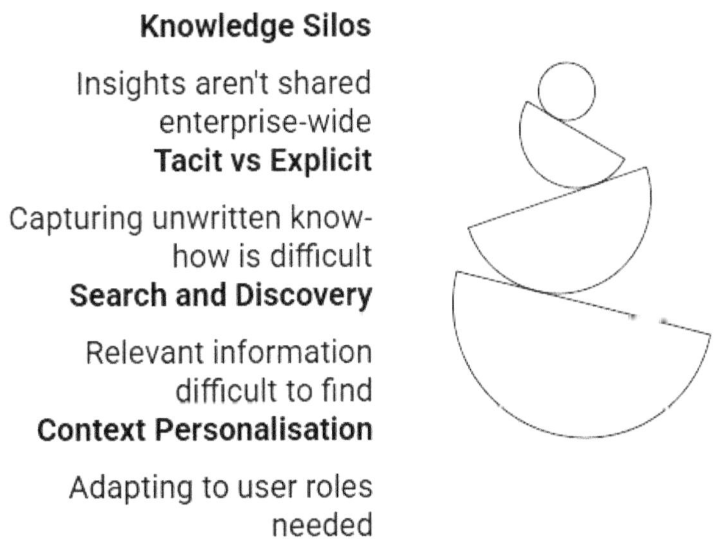

Figure 14.2 – EKM challenges

With these challenges in mind, let's explore how EKM and MCP can overcome them through standardized communication, dynamic discovery, and robust storage.

Challenges in AI-powered EKM and how MCP helps

While AI has the potential to transform EKM, it also introduces new challenges that traditional approaches weren't designed to handle.

Integration complexity

Enterprise knowledge often involves many disconnected tools. As mentioned, large organizations use email, chat, CRM, ticketing systems, wikis, and databases, and essential information may also reside in documents and messaging threads. Without integration, an engineer might have to search through four or five different systems just to assemble a full picture of a problem. Each system has its own API, authentication scheme, and data model, so building and maintaining bespoke connectors is expensive and brittle.

MCP reduces this integration burden by defining standardized JSON-RPC operations for listing resources and tools (`resources/list`, `tools/list`) and for retrieving contents (`resources/read`, `tools/call`). Instead of writing a new integration for every system, developers can implement or deploy an MCP server that wraps an existing knowledge source and exposes its contents through the protocol. Clients then speak one language to all knowledge sources.

Context awareness

For an AI assistant to give the right answer, it needs more than just the text of a document. It must understand who is asking, why they are asking, and how any piece of information fits into the bigger picture. Traditional REST APIs rarely provide this level of nuance. MCP addresses this by allowing servers to attach annotations to resources and tool results. Annotations specify the intended audience (user or assistant), the relative priority of a resource, and when it was last modified. Clients can use these hints to filter or prioritize context, for example, by including only resources marked for the assistant or sorting by recency. Because annotations follow a standard schema, this contextual metadata is consistent across servers, enabling personalized retrieval and presentation.

Security and compliance

Enterprise knowledge is not meant to be shared indiscriminately. Governance frameworks define who can create or edit specific content, and access control policies restrict sensitive information to those with the appropriate role or clearance. MCP itself does not enforce authorization but provides the building blocks: clients discover capabilities via `resources/list` and `tools/list`, and servers can restrict which resources or tools a given user can see. The protocol's security and trust guidelines emphasize that users must explicitly consent before data is accessed or actions are taken, that sensitive data should be protected, and that AI models should be prevented from performing unsafe operations. Implementers are encouraged to build robust authorization flows and log every request for auditing. Context-aware access control, where access decisions depend on attributes such as user role, location, or time of day, is an emerging best practice in enterprise security.

Scale and performance

Enterprise knowledge bases can contain millions of documents and complex relationships. Searching and analyzing such volumes requires careful performance engineering. MCP does not prescribe implementation details but allows servers to implement intelligent caching, indexing, and batching strategies while exposing a consistent interface to clients. Because clients can request only the resources and tool results they need and even paginate large lists of resources or tools, servers can protect backend systems from overload.

> **Note**
>
> MCP uses opaque, cursor-based pagination: servers determine the page size; responses include a `nextCursor` field if additional results exist; and clients should treat cursors as opaque tokens and supply them in subsequent requests. Operations supporting pagination include `resources/list`, `tools/list`, and `prompts/list`, and clients should not persist cursors across sessions.

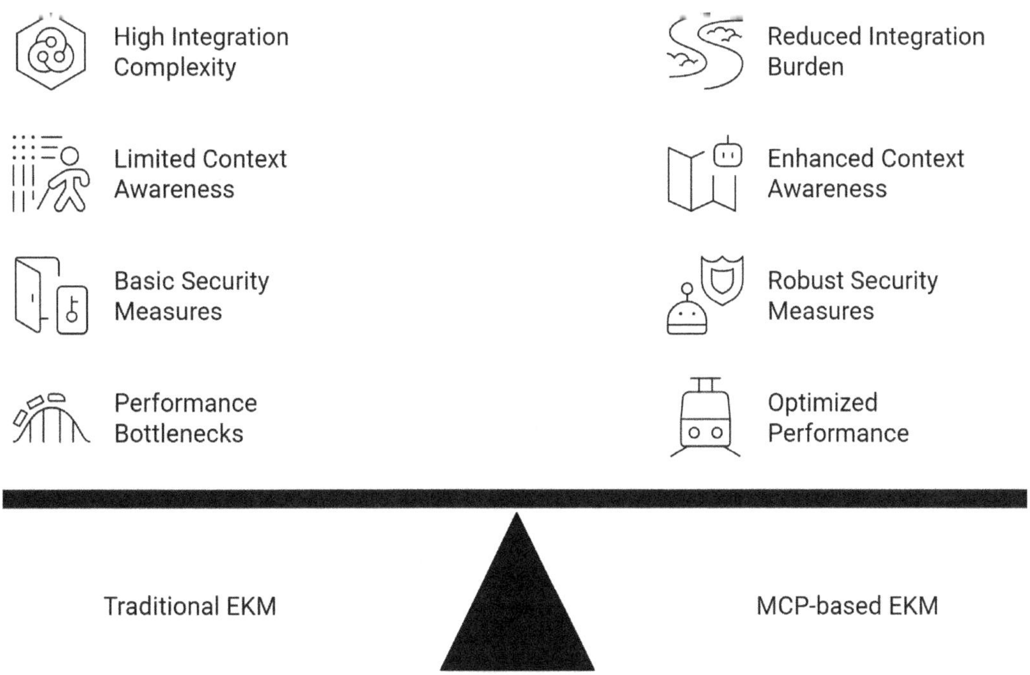

Figure 14.3 – Traditional versus MCP-based EKM

Having examined the scalability challenges of enterprise knowledge bases and how MCP's caching and pagination features mitigate them, we now turn to architectural patterns that help structure MCP-based EKM systems.

Architectural patterns for MCP-based EKM

Over the past few years, several architectural patterns have emerged for building effective MCP-based enterprise knowledge management systems.

Let's look at some of the most important patterns.

The federated search pattern

In this pattern, multiple MCP servers provide access to different information sources within the organization. A client can issue `resources/list` and `tools/list` requests to each server to discover the available content and capabilities, then aggregate the results into a unified response. Because the protocol is standardized, the AI system does not need to know the details of each underlying system, but only the server endpoints.

This pattern is particularly effective for organizations with diverse information sources because it allows each source to be optimized for its specific use case while still providing unified access through the AI system.

The knowledge graph pattern

In this pattern, MCP servers expose not just plain text documents but also structured knowledge graphs capturing relationships between entities, concepts, and documents. These graphs can be represented as resources or embedded within tool results, complete with JSON schemas and annotations. AI systems can traverse these relationships to answer complex questions such as "How does this policy connect to our security guidelines?" rather than performing simple keyword matching.

This pattern is particularly powerful for organizations with complex, interconnected information where understanding relationships is as important as accessing individual pieces of content.

The contextual filtering pattern

In this pattern, MCP servers implement sophisticated filtering and personalization logic that adapts the information they provide based on the context of the request. Servers can use the annotations mechanism to indicate the intended audience (user versus assistant), a priority score, and the last-modified time for each resource. Clients can then apply policies, such as including only resources with high priority for a given task or excluding content marked for the user when generating a system prompt, to deliver **context-aware results**. This approach is essential for organizations with complex security and privacy requirements, and it improves the relevance of search results by tailoring them to the user's role and task.

The `lastModified` timestamp is part of the standard annotations defined by MCP. It records the most recent modification time of a resource, enabling clients to sort resources by recency and detect when cached copies are outdated. Servers may also include additional version metadata (e.g., commit hashes or version numbers) within the resource URI or metadata so that clients can request specific versions or perform optimistic concurrency checks. Clients should compare the `lastModified` value when deciding whether to refresh a resource, ensuring they always work with the latest approved content.

The collaborative intelligence pattern

In this pattern, multiple AI agents work together through MCP to provide comprehensive knowledge management capabilities. Different agents might specialize in different types of information or different aspects of knowledge work: research, analysis, synthesis, or presentation.

This pattern is particularly effective for complex knowledge work that benefits from multiple perspectives and capabilities.

Having outlined the core MCP concepts for knowledge management, we're now ready to build a basic EKM system from scratch.

Implementing an MCP resource provider for a document store

In this section, we'll build a simple knowledge-management component, `DocumentStore`, using pure Python. This example demonstrates how to overcome the fragmentation and discovery challenges discussed earlier by unifying document storage, retrieval, and summarization behind a single interface. It also shows how the patterns introduced previously (e.g., unified resource access and context-aware summarization) can be implemented in a self-contained class.

Because we don't have access to an MCP library in this example, we'll implement our own `DocumentStore` in pure Python. This self-contained class mimics the behavior of an MCP server for demonstration purposes. In this simplified implementation, a `DocumentStore` class holds an in-memory list of documents. It exposes four methods:

- `list_resources()`: Returns a list of resources with URIs, names, and descriptions
- `read_resource(uri)`: Returns the full contents and metadata of a single document
- `search_documents(query, department=None, classification=None)`: Performs a simple keyword search across titles, contents, and tags
- `get_summary()`: Computes summary statistics about the collection

We begin by creating a simple document store that simulates an MCP resource provider. In production systems, this data would come from enterprise sources such as SharePoint, Confluence, or databases. For our demonstration, we'll use an in-memory collection with realistic metadata.

```
class DocumentStore:
    """Simple document store that mimics an MCP resource provider."""
```

```
    def __init__(self) -> None:
        # In a real system this data would come from SharePoint, Confluence,
databases, etc.
        self.documents = [
            {
                "title": "Employee Handbook",
                "content": "Complete guide to company policies and procedures...",
                "department": "HR",
                "author": "HR Team",
                "created_date": "2024-01-15",
                "classification": "internal",
                "tags": ["policies", "procedures", "hr"],
            },
            {
                "title": "Q4 Financial Report",
                "content": "Quarterly financial analysis and projections...",
                "department": "Finance",
                "author": "CFO",
                "created_date": "2024-01-10",
                "classification": "confidential",
                "tags": ["finance", "quarterly", "analysis"],
            },
            {
                "title": "Product Roadmap 2024",
                "content": "Strategic product development plans for 2024...",
                "department": "Product",
                "author": "Product Manager",
                "created_date": "2024-01-05",
                "classification": "internal",
                "tags": ["product", "roadmap", "strategy"],
            },
            {
                "title": "Security Guidelines",
                "content": "Information security policies and best practices...",
                "department": "IT",
                "author": "CISO",
                "created_date": "2024-01-20",
                "classification": "internal",
                "tags": ["security", "policies", "it"],
            },
            {
```

```
                "title": "Customer Success Stories",
                "content": "Case studies and testimonials from key customers...",
                "department": "Marketing",
                "author": "Marketing Team",
                "created_date": "2024-01-12",
                "classification": "public",
                "tags": ["marketing", "customers", "success"],
            },
        ]
```

Each document contains structured metadata (title, department, author, date, classification level) and content, mirroring real-world enterprise document management systems.

Next, the `list_resources()` method implements the MCP pattern for resource discovery. It returns lightweight metadata about available documents without loading full content, which is crucial for performance when working with large document collections.

```
    def list_resources(self) -> list:
        """Return a list of document metadata similar to an MCP `resources/list`
response."""
        resources = []
        for idx, doc in enumerate(self.documents):
            resources.append({
                "uri": f"doc://{idx}",
                "name": doc["title"],
                "description": f"{doc['classification'].title()} document from
{doc['department']} by {doc['author']}"
            })
        return resources
```

Each resource gets a unique URI (e.g., `doc://0`) that agents can reference later. This mimics how MCP servers expose resources such as files, database records, or API endpoints.

Once an agent identifies a document of interest via `list_resources()`, it can retrieve the full content using `read_resource()`. This two-step pattern (`list` → `read`) is fundamental to MCP's efficient resource management:

```
def read_resource(self, uri: str) -> str:
    """Return a single document with metadata and content, or raise a descriptive
error."""
    try:
```

```
            idx = int(uri.split("://")[1])
        except (IndexError, ValueError):
            # Invalid URI format; raise an error consistent with MCP's error codes
            raise ValueError("Invalid resource URI")
        if idx < 0 or idx >= len(self.documents):
            # Resource not found; in a real MCP server this would return error code
-32002:contentReference[oaicite:7]{index=7}
            raise IndexError("Resource not found")
        doc = self.documents[idx]
        return (f"Title: {doc['title']}\n"
                f"Department: {doc['department']}\n"
                f"Author: {doc['author']}\n"
                f"Created: {doc['created_date']}\n"
                f"Classification: {doc['classification']}\n"
                f"Tags: {', '.join(doc['tags'])}\n\n"
                f"Content:\n{doc['content']}")
```

The method parses the URI to locate the specific document and returns a formatted string with complete metadata and content.

Enterprise document stores need sophisticated search capabilities. This method implements keyword search across titles, content, and tags, with optional filters for department and classification level, essential for compliance and access control.

```
        def search_documents(self,
                             query: str,
                             department: str | None = None,
                             classification: str | None = None) -> list:
            """Return documents whose title, content or tags match a query with
optional filters."""
            query_lower = query.lower()
            results = []
            for idx, doc in enumerate(self.documents):
                if (query_lower in doc["title"].lower() or
                    query_lower in doc["content"].lower() or
                    any(query_lower in tag for tag in doc["tags"])):
                    if department and doc["department"] != department:
                        continue
                    if classification and
                       doc["classification"] != classification:
                        continue
```

```
                results.append({
                    "title": doc["title"],
                    "department": doc["department"],
                    "author": doc["author"],
                    "classification": doc["classification"],
                    "preview": doc["content"][:100],
                    "uri": f"doc://{idx}"
                })
        return results
```

Results include a 100-character preview to help agents quickly assess relevance without processing entire documents.

Lastly, we have the `get_summary()` method, which demonstrates how MCP resources can provide analytical insights, not just raw data. This helps agents understand the document landscape before diving into specific searches.

```
    def get_summary(self) -> str:
        """Return summary statistics about the document store."""
        total_docs = len(self.documents)
        from collections import Counter
        dept_counts = Counter(doc["department"] for doc in self.documents)
        class_counts = Counter(doc["classification"] for doc in self.documents)
        summary = (
            "Enterprise Document Store Summary\n"
            "================================\n\n"
            f"Total Documents: {total_docs}\n"
            f"Departments: {len(dept_counts)}\n"
            f"Classifications: {len(class_counts)}\n\n"
            "Documents by Department:\n"
        )
        for dept, count in dept_counts.items():
            summary += f"  • {dept}: {count} documents\n"
        summary += "\nDocuments by Classification:\n"
        for classif, count in class_counts.items():
            summary += f"  • {classif}: {count} documents\n"
        return summary
```

Using Python's `Counter`, we aggregate documents by department and classification, providing a high-level view of content distribution.

The following demonstration section shows a typical workflow: discover resources, search for specific content, and retrieve analytics. This mirrors how AI agents would interact with an MCP server in production.

```
# Demonstration
if __name__ == "__main__":
    store = DocumentStore()

    # List available document resources
    resources = store.list_resources()
    print(f"Found {len(resources)} document resources:")
    for res in resources[:3]:
        print(f"  • {res['name']} ({res['uri']})")

    # Search for a keyword
    results = store.search_documents("security")
    print("\nSearch results for 'security':")
    if results:
        for res in results:
            print(f"• {res['title']}\n  Department: {res['department']} | Author:
{res['author']} | Classification: {res['classification']}\n  Preview:
{res['preview']}...\n  URI: {res['uri']}\n")
    else:
        print("No documents found for this query.\n")

    # Print summary statistics
    print(store.get_summary())
```

When you run this script, it prints a list of available documents, executes a search for "security" and outputs a summary of the collection. The `DocumentStore` class illustrates how a real MCP server might expose document metadata via `list_resources`, return full contents via `read_resource`, and perform basic filtering via a search tool. In production, you would replace the in-memory list with calls to an actual document management system and implement the MCP JSON-RPC handlers to expose these methods over the network.

Security considerations in MCP-based EKM

Security is critical in EKM systems. MCP itself is transport-agnostic; it does not define how servers authenticate users or enforce authorization, but it provides a framework for building secure integrations. Each organization must design its own controls and policies on top of the protocol.

Context-aware access control

Enterprise environments require more than simple role-based permissions. **Context-aware permissions** allow access decisions to depend on attributes such as location, time of day, or device posture, so a user might see sensitive documents from a corporate network but not from a personal device. Such models extend traditional role-based access control by considering situational factors.

MCP does not prescribe a particular authorization model, but it enables context-aware controls by exposing rich metadata and leaving access decisions to the server. For example, a server may choose to return only high-priority resources to a given user or may redact content based on the user's role and the context of the request. Servers *must* validate resource URIs and *should* implement access controls for sensitive resources.

Dynamic content filtering

Even when a user is authorized to read a document, they might not be allowed to see every field. Context-aware systems can redact or anonymize sensitive information on the fly based on the user's clearance or the purpose of the request. For example, a financial analyst working on budget planning may see line-item costs, while a colleague from another department sees only summary totals. Implementers can achieve this by producing a filtered resource representation or by emitting different tool results depending on the caller.

Audit and compliance logging

Enterprise environments often have strict audit and compliance requirements. MCP includes an optional logging utility that allows servers to emit structured log messages and clients to configure log levels. Detailed audit logs should capture which resources or tools were accessed, who accessed them, the justification provided, and any transformations (such as redactions) performed. These logs are necessary to meet regulations such as GDPR, HIPAA, and SOX.

Data loss prevention

MCP-based EKM systems should implement data loss prevention mechanisms to prevent sensitive information from being inappropriately shared or exported. This can include monitoring AI-generated responses for sensitive content, restricting copy/export actions, and prompting users when an operation might disclose regulated data. Server implementations should combine protocol-level access controls with organizational policies to reduce the risk of accidental data leakage.

Now that we've built a basic EKM system, let's step back and review common knowledge-management patterns for scaling these concepts to enterprise workloads.

Future trends: generative EKM with MCP

The next wave of EKM isn't just about finding information faster but about generating new insights. Generative AI models can summarize long documents, create new knowledge artifacts, and answer questions by combining information from multiple sources. For example, Morgan Stanley uses a GPT-4-powered internal assistant to allow financial advisors to query a vast knowledge base and receive instant answers; more than 98% of the firm's advisor teams now actively use the system. Such solutions show how generative AI can transform raw information into actionable intelligence.

In the following subsections, we will explore four forward-looking areas: **automated knowledge synthesis**, **intelligent knowledge curation**, **personalized knowledge delivery**, and **collaborative knowledge creation**. These subsections highlight emerging practices that build on MCP's foundation and point to where enterprise knowledge management is heading.

Automated knowledge synthesis

MCP-enabled AI systems can automatically synthesize information from multiple sources to create new insights, summaries, and analyses. In practice, this means combining retrieved context into a coherent answer rather than simply quoting documents. Generative models already summarize long research reports into concise briefs and condense meeting transcripts into notes and follow-up actions. By exposing documents via MCP, we give models a standardized way to access source material; the models then use their generation capabilities to produce novel outputs.

Intelligent knowledge curation

AI systems can use MCP to continuously monitor and curate organizational knowledge, identifying gaps, inconsistencies, and opportunities for improvement. For example, a generative assistant might flag that the privacy policy is outdated or suggest creating a new FAQ based on recurring support tickets. Because MCP provides metadata such as `lastModified` and `priority`, the system can decide which documents to review first. Human experts still vet the output, but automation reduces the manual effort required to keep knowledge current.

Personalized knowledge delivery

MCP enables AI systems to provide personalized knowledge delivery based on individual roles, responsibilities, and current projects. AI-equipped EKMs can analyze a user's role and past activities to recommend content they might find useful, such as playbooks or case studies relevant to their assignment. Just-in-time recommendations, such as surfacing a client's meeting notes before a call, help break down silos and make the system feel like a personal assistant.

Collaborative knowledge creation

MCP can facilitate collaborative knowledge creation where multiple AI systems and human experts work together to create, review, and refine organizational knowledge. This collaborative approach can produce higher-quality knowledge products than either humans or AI systems could create alone.

Summary

MCP turns enterprise knowledge management from a collection of disconnected information silos into a unified, intelligent platform. Its key benefits include the following:

- **Unified access**: Clients can discover and retrieve resources and tools using a standard set of JSON-RPC operations (`resources/list`, `resources/read`, `tools/list`, `tools/call`). This eliminates the need to build bespoke integrations for every system.
- **Context-aware intelligence**: Resources and tool results may carry annotations such as `audience`, `priority`, and `lastModified`. Clients can use this metadata to filter and prioritize context, enabling personalized and role-specific responses.
- **Security and compliance**: The protocol's security guidelines emphasize user consent, data privacy, and tool safety. Implementers should build robust authorization flows and log all access, while context-aware permissions allow access decisions to adapt to situational factors.

- **Scalable architecture**: MCP servers can paginate large lists of resources or tools and implement caching and indexing strategies to protect backend systems.
- **Future-ready platform**: By exposing knowledge through a standard protocol, MCP enables advanced capabilities such as automated knowledge synthesis, intelligent curation, and collaborative creation. Generative AI assistants such as Morgan Stanley's internal GPT-4 tool demonstrate how combining retrieval with generation can deliver personalized, citation-backed answers.

The future of EKM isn't about building bigger search engines; it's about creating systems that can understand, synthesize, and generate knowledge to amplify human expertise. MCP provides the foundation for that future by making organizational knowledge accessible, searchable, and actionable through a consistent protocol that AI systems can discover and use dynamically.

In the next chapter, we'll shift to personalization and recommendation systems. We'll define personalization beyond buzzwords, trace the evolution from rule-based to collaborative filtering and hybrid models, and discuss context, data integration, and privacy challenges. We'll see how MCP unifies disparate data sources, supports real-time adaptation, and improves transparency and ethical considerations.

15

MCP for Personalization and Recommendation Systems

Personalization without MCP is like trying to be a good host at a party where you can't remember anyone's name, preferences, or why they came.

I've built more recommendation systems than I care to count, and I can tell you this: most of them are terrible. Not because the algorithms are bad, but because they're working with incomplete, stale, or contextually inappropriate data. These systems would know you bought a book about Python programming six months ago, so they keep recommending Python books even though you've moved on to machine learning. They know you watched a romantic comedy last weekend, so they assume you love rom-coms, ignoring the fact that your partner picked that movie.

The fundamental problem with most personalization systems is that they're built around static user profiles and historical behavior patterns. They can't adapt to changing interests, they don't understand context, and they certainly can't integrate information from multiple sources to build a comprehensive understanding of what users want.

That's where MCP changes everything. Instead of being limited to data in a single system, personalization engines can discover and integrate information from any available source—user preferences, behavioral data, contextual information, social signals, and external events. They can build rich, dynamic user models that adapt in real time to changing needs and circumstances.

In this chapter, we will be covering personalization and recommendation systems: defining personalization beyond buzzwords, taking a historical tour from rule-based systems to collaborative filtering, content-based and hybrid models, and examining why static profiles and siloed data lead to poor recommendations and privacy risks. You'll learn how MCP unifies disparate data sources, supports real-time adaptation, and improves transparency, fairness, and user control. We'll close with architectural patterns such as unified user profiles and federated recommendations and discuss ethical considerations to ensure personalization is effective and responsible.

In this chapter, we'll be covering the following topics:

- Introduction to personalization and recommendation systems
- Challenges in personalization and how MCP helps
- Architectural patterns for MCP-based personalization
- Implementing MCP components for personalization
- Privacy and ethical considerations
- Future trends: hyper-personalization and conversational recommendations

Introduction to personalization and recommendation systems

Personalization is often conflated with vague notions of "customer centricity," so it helps to be precise.

Personalization means tailoring an experience to an individual user by using known information about them. It differs from customization (where users explicitly choose settings) because it is driven by the organization, not the user. Modern companies use personalization to surface relevant content, products, or assistance based on observed behavior and contextual signals. Customers have come to expect these personalized experiences, but only when they are delivered responsibly and transparently.

Personalization engines have progressed through several waves, each adding sophistication and addressing limitations of the previous one:

- **Rule-based systems**: Early recommendation engines used hardcoded rules ("if the user belongs to this demographic and has done X, show them Y"). These systems could only offer generic suggestions such as "best-sellers" and lacked the flexibility to adapt to individual preferences.
- **Collaborative filtering**: In the late 1990s and early 2000s, collaborative filtering algorithms began to recommend items based on the behavior of similar users. While this approach enables basic personalization, it suffers from the **cold-start problem** (insufficient data for new users or items) and can produce "filter bubbles." The so-called cold-start problem arises when a system lacks sufficient data about a new user or new item, leading to poor recommendations. Practical solutions include starting with

content-based or popularity-based suggestions, enriching profiles with demographic or contextual data, combining collaborative and content-based models, and explicitly asking users for their preferences via short surveys.

- **Content-based filtering**: These systems recommend items by matching item attributes (keywords, genres) to a user's historical preferences. They can personalize suggestions even for new users, but struggle to introduce users to novel content.
- **Hybrid and machine-learning models**: Modern recommender systems combine collaborative and content-based approaches and employ machine-learning techniques (clustering, classification, and regression) to discover subtle patterns in massive datasets. Deep-learning models using recurrent and convolutional neural networks enable **hyper-personalization** and can analyze complex data such as text, images, or audio.
- **Context-aware and AI-augmented systems**: Emerging systems incorporate **contextual factors** (time of day, location, device) and real-time signals to adapt recommendations. These models strive to capture a user's current situation, but must contend with challenges such as data scarcity and privacy constraints. Looking ahead, research explores the role of generative AI and ethical AI in recommendations.

Personalization systems face several key challenges that must be addressed to deliver relevant, responsible, and context-aware recommendations.

The context problem

Context-aware recommender systems recognize that the same user may want very different things depending on the situation. For example, a business traveler might prefer efficient services during the week and leisure options on weekends. Context can include temporal cues (day, time), location, device type, weather, or social environment. When systems ignore context, they often present irrelevant suggestions and frustrate users. However, incorporating rich context data raises challenges of data sparsity, privacy, and computational complexity.

The data integration challenge

A robust personalization system requires combining data from many sources: a catalog of items or content, a catalog of user attributes, and a history of user interactions. Each of these datasets may live in different applications (CRM, analytics, support, social media) with distinct formats and update cadences. Integrating and reconciling these siloed datasets is costly and error-prone. Data consistency, deduplication, and semantics must be maintained across systems.

The privacy and trust problem

Customers increasingly demand both personalized experiences and respect for their privacy. Responsible personalization means collecting only the data necessary for a given purpose, protecting it with strong encryption and multi-factor authentication, and being transparent about how it is used. Designers must also minimize retention and share data only with trusted partners. Balancing personalization and privacy is especially hard in context-aware systems; research shows that even state-of-the-art recommender systems can threaten user privacy, so techniques such as differential privacy, federated learning, and homomorphic encryption are being explored to protect users.

Before we see how MCP improves personalization, we need to understand what's broken in traditional systems. The following challenges illustrate why new approaches are needed.

Challenges in personalization and how MCP helps

Several fundamental challenges limit the effectiveness of traditional personalization systems. However, MCP can help overcome some of these. Let's check some of the issues associated with traditional personalization systems and see how MCP can help resolve these issues.

The data silos problem

As indicated earlier, information about a single person is often scattered across many enterprise systems, such as CRMs and commerce, analytics, support, and social platforms. Each application maintains its own schema and update cadence, leading to fragmented views and integration headaches. MCP standardizes access through resources and tools operations so that clients can query user profiles, behaviors, and content via a consistent JSON-RPC interface. Instead of building one-off connectors to each system, a personalization engine can connect to MCP servers that expose unified views of these datasets.

The real-time adaptation challenge

Customer preferences and context change continuously: people switch devices, move between locations, and shift their attention throughout the day. Many legacy recommendation engines rely on nightly batch jobs, leaving them blind to moment shifts. MCP supports streaming updates and incremental context retrieval via resource listings and event notifications, enabling personalization services to react immediately to new signals rather than waiting for the next offline retraining cycle.

The explainability and control problem

Users increasingly expect to understand why a recommendation is being made and to adjust their preferences. Traditional black-box models make this difficult. By exposing metadata, annotations, and transparent schemas, MCP servers can surface the provenance of information and the factors that influenced a recommendation. Tools can be annotated with descriptions and input schemas, and servers can provide context about how scores were computed. This transparency enables user interfaces that allow people to review, adjust, and even disable certain personalization signals.

The cross-platform consistency challenge

Modern customers engage across multiple channels such as web, mobile, email, support chats, and physical points of sale. Delivering consistent experiences across all these touchpoints is hard when each channel has its own personalization engine. MCP makes it feasible to build shared personalization services that can be called from any channel, ensuring that recommendations are based on the same up-to-date user profile and context. Because MCP defines standard mechanisms for listing resources and tools, different clients can discover the same capabilities and maintain alignment.

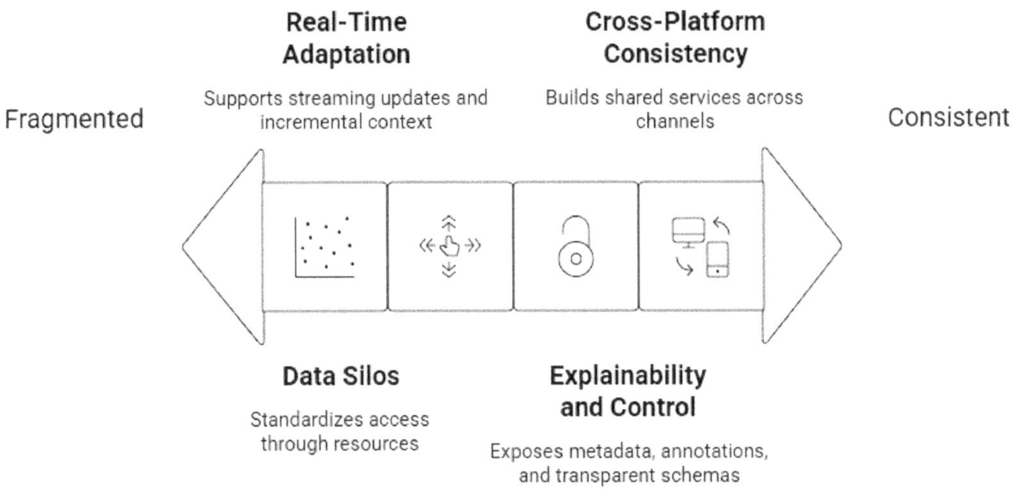

Figure 15.1 – Challenges MCP addresses

Having outlined the challenges of personalization and how MCP addresses data silos, real-time adaptation, and cross-platform consistency, we can now examine several architectural patterns that put these concepts into practice.

Architectural patterns for MCP-based personalization

Several conceptual patterns illustrate how MCP can be applied to build effective personalization systems. These are high-level templates, not mandatory architectures:

- **Unified user profile**: Multiple MCP servers can expose complementary views of a user (demographic details from a CRM, preference settings from an account portal, browsing history from web analytics, and purchase history from an e-commerce platform) via `resources/list` and `resources/read` operations. A personalization service can aggregate these documents into a coherent user profile accessible across web, mobile, and support channels. Unifying profiles breaks down data silos and delivers consistent experiences across touchpoints.
- **Cold-start strategies**: When onboarding a new user or launching a new item, you can combine general popularity scores with metadata from multiple MCP servers (e.g., demographic info from a CRM and item attributes) to generate initial recommendations. A simple hybrid model might score items based on 70% popularity and 30% content similarity until enough interactions are recorded. Over time, you can adjust these weights dynamically and merge them into the main ranking model.
- **Real-time context**: Contextual signals (e.g., current location, device type, or time of day) are critical for relevance. MCP servers can stream context updates (such as device type or time of day) on demand, and clients can retrieve only the incremental changes rather than reloading the entire user profile. This enables real-time adaptation by updating the user's context instead of triggering a full profile refresh. Real-time recommendation systems typically pair streaming features with historical data to adapt quickly to user behavior.
- **Federated recommendations**: Different domains often require specialized recommendation logic: a news engine might rank articles, a product engine ranks merchandise, and a social engine surfaces user-generated content. Each can be implemented as its own MCP server exposing tools such as `get_news_recommendations`, `get_product_recommendations`, or `get_social_recommendations`. A central orchestration service calls these tools and blends the results to present a unified list, aligning with business objectives (engagement, revenue, satisfaction) while respecting user consent and context.
- **Privacy-preserving personalization**: Growing privacy regulations and user expectations call for protective measures. MCP servers can implement techniques such as differential privacy, federated learning, and homomorphic encryption to enable learning on user data without exposing sensitive information. These techniques help

strike a balance between providing accurate recommendations and maintaining privacy. This pattern also encourages data minimization and strict access controls.

Together, these patterns illustrate how MCP enables rich, up-to-date user profiles and context-aware recommendations. To see these ideas in action without relying on an external MCP library, the next section builds a minimal personalization server from scratch.

Implementing MCP components for personalization

To illustrate the concepts of unified user profiles, dynamic discovery of resources, and context-aware recommendations, without relying on an external MCP library, the following example implements a simple in-memory personalization server.

It exposes functions to list and read resources (user profiles, behavior history, and the content catalog) and a `get_recommendations` function that scores items based on interest and popularity. The code is not a full MCP server, but it shows how the same principles can be applied.

1. First, we build the personalization engine. We create a personalization system that mimics MCP resource patterns. The engine maintains three core data structures: user profiles (interests and skill levels), behavioral history (user interactions with contextual signals such as device and time), and a content catalog (articles with tags and popularity scores). This mirrors real recommendation systems such as Netflix or LinkedIn, where combining explicit preferences with implicit behavioral signals drives personalization.

```
import json
from datetime import datetime

class PersonalizationServer:
    """A minimal personalization system demonstrating MCP-like
operations."""
    def __init__(self):
        # Sample user profiles. In practice these would come from MCP
`resources/read`.
        self.user_profiles = {
            "user_001": {"interests": ["technology", "ai", "programming"],
"experience_level": "advanced"},
            "user_002": {"interests": ["business", "marketing",
"strategy"], "experience_level": "intermediate"},
            "user_003": {"interests": ["design", "creativity", "art"],
"experience_level": "beginner"},
```

```
        }
        # Recent user actions (timestamped). A real system would record
many more actions.
        self.behaviour_history = [
            ("user_001", "view", "article_001", {"device": "mobile",
"time_of_day": "morning"}),
            ("user_001", "like", "article_002", {"device": "desktop",
"time_of_day": "afternoon"}),
            ("user_002", "view", "article_003", {"device": "desktop",
"time_of_day": "morning"}),
            ("user_003", "view", "article_004", {"device": "mobile",
"time_of_day": "evening"}),
        ]
        # Content catalog with popularity scores and tags.
        self.content_items = {
            "article_001": {"title": "Introduction to Machine Learning",
"category": "technology", "tags": ["ml", "ai", "beginner"], "popularity":
0.8},
            "article_002": {"title": "Advanced Neural Networks",
"category": "technology", "tags": ["ml", "ai", "advanced"], "popularity":
0.6},
            "article_003": {"title": "Marketing Strategy Guide",
"category": "business", "tags": ["marketing", "strategy"], "popularity":
0.7},
            "article_004": {"title": "Design Thinking Principles",
"category": "design", "tags": ["design", "creativity"], "popularity": 0.9},
            "article_005": {"title": "Python Programming Basics",
"category": "technology", "tags": ["programming", "python", "beginner"],
"popularity": 0.85},
        }
```

Notice how tags serve dual purposes: matching user interests (`"ai"`, `"programming"`) and indicating difficulty level (`"beginner"`, `"advanced"`). Each behavioral tuple captures who, what, which content, and the surrounding context, enabling sophisticated pattern analysis.

2. Next, following MCP conventions, we expose data sources as discoverable resources with custom URI schemes (`profile://`, `behavior://`, `content://`). The `list_resources()` method lets agents understand what's available before requesting data, like browsing a menu before ordering. The `read_resource()` method translates

internal Python objects into JSON strings that agents can parse, providing on-demand access to specific data sources.

```
    def list_resources(self):
        """Return URIs and descriptions of available resources."""
        return [
            {"uri": "profile://user_profiles", "name": "User Profiles",
"description": "User preference and demographic data"},
            {"uri": "behavior://user_behavior", "name": "User Behavior
Data", "description": "Recent user interactions"},
            {"uri": "content://content_items", "name": "Content Catalog",
"description": "Articles and their metadata"},
        ]

    def read_resource(self, uri: str) -> str:
        """Return the JSON representation of a resource."""
        if uri == "profile://user_profiles":
            return json.dumps(self.user_profiles, indent=2)
        elif uri == "behavior://user_behavior":
            return json.dumps([
                {"user_id": user_id, "action": action, "item_id": item_id,
"context": context}
                for (user_id, action, item_id, context) in
self.behaviour_history
            ], indent=2)
        elif uri == "content://content_items":
            return json.dumps(self.content_items, indent=2)
        else:
            raise ValueError(f"Unknown resource URI: {uri}")
```

The behavioral history transformation demonstrates how we reshape internal data structures into agent-friendly formats during reads. This two-step pattern (discover → access) is fundamental to efficient MCP resource management.

3. The recommendation engine scores each unseen content item using weighted signals such as interest/tag matching (40%), experience-level matching (30%), popularity (20%), and a small context boost (10%), but in practice, these weights should be tuned. Teams typically perform A/B tests, adjusting weightings on a subset of users and

measuring click-through rates or conversion to identify the optimal balance of relevance and novelty.

```
    def get_recommendations(self, user_id: str,
                            context: dict | None = None,
                            limit: int = 3) -> str:
        """Compute simple relevance scores and return a formatted list."""
        context = context or {}
        profile = self.user_profiles.get(user_id)
        if not profile:
            return f"User {user_id} not found"

        interests = [i.lower() for i in profile.get("interests", [])]
        level = profile.get("experience_level", "beginner").lower()
        # Items the user has already interacted with
        viewed = {item_id for (uid, _, item_id, _) in
self.behaviour_history if uid == user_id}
        scores = []
        for item_id, meta in self.content_items.items():
            if item_id in viewed:
                continue
            score = 0.0
            # Match user interests to item tags
            tag_matches = sum(1 for interest in interests if any(interest
in tag.lower() for tag in meta["tags"]))
            score += 0.4 * tag_matches
            # Experience level match
            if level in meta["tags"]:
                score += 0.3
            # Popularity boost
            score += 0.2 * meta["popularity"]
            # Context boost
            if context.get("time_of_day") == "morning"
               and "beginner" in meta["tags"]:
                score += 0.1
            scores.append((score, item_id))
        # Sort and build output
        scores.sort(reverse=True, key=lambda x: x[0])
        top = scores[:limit]
        if not top:
            return f"No new recommendations for {user_id}"
```

```
        lines = [f"Personalized recommendations for {user_id}:"]
        for idx, (score, item_id) in enumerate(top, 1):
            meta = self.content_items[item_id]
            lines.append(f"{idx}. {meta['title']} (Score: {score:.2f})")
        # Explanation of factors
        lines.append("")
        lines.append("Based on:")
        lines.append(f"- Interests: {', '.join(profile['interests'])}")
        lines.append(f"- Experience level: {profile['experience_level']}")
        lines.append(f"- Recent actions: {sum(1 for (uid, _, _, _) in
self.behaviour_history if uid == user_id)}")
        if context:
            lines.append(f"- Context: {context}")
        return "\n".join(lines)
```

The multi-factor scoring mirrors production systems, balancing relevance, appropriateness, quality, and context. Weight tuning based on A/B testing would optimize these values in production.

4. The following demo shows how an agent interacts with our personalization server in practice: first discovering available data sources, then exploring the content catalog, and finally requesting personalized recommendations with contextual signals (morning time). This simulates a real scenario where a user receives appropriately-leveled content based on their profile, past behavior, and current context.

```
if __name__ == "__main__":
    # Demonstrate the personalization server
    server = PersonalizationServer()
    # List available resources
    print("Resources:")
    for res in server.list_resources():
        print(f"- {res['uri']}: {res['description']}")
    # Read content catalog
    print("\nContent catalog:")
    print(server.read_resource("content://content_items"))
    # Get recommendations for a user with morning context
    print("\nRecommendations:")
    print(server.get_recommendations("user_001",
                                     context={
                                        "time_of_day": "morning"
```

```
        },
        limit=3))
```

The program lists three data sources (profiles, behavior, content), displays the full content catalog in JSON format, and generates the top 3 personalized recommendations for `user_001` during morning hours, demonstrating resource discovery, data access, and intelligent personalization working together.

The scoring function is deliberately simple but demonstrates how a personalization engine can combine interests, experience level, popularity, and context to rank items. In a real MCP deployment, these functions would be exposed via `tools/list` and `tools/call` operations, and the datasets would be maintained by MCP resource providers.

Real-time pipelines and retraining: To achieve low latency and real-time adaptation, stream user events (clicks, views) into a feature store and update user embeddings or scores incrementally. Real-time recommendation systems rely on streaming data platforms and online databases instead of batch ETL processes. Advanced systems pair an online inference model with an offline training pipeline that periodically retrains fresh data. Establish retraining schedules (hourly, daily, or weekly) based on the rate of behavior change and evaluate models using A/B tests. Ensure data freshness by monitoring how long data takes to move from source to recommendation and set thresholds to trigger refreshes; if events lag by more than your freshness SLA (e.g., 5 minutes), degrade gracefully with cached recommendations.

Now that we've seen a minimal MCP-based personalization engine in action, it's important to address the privacy and ethical considerations that arise when combining personal data from multiple sources.

Privacy and ethical considerations

Personalization systems raise significant privacy and ethical concerns that need to be addressed thoughtfully in MCP-based implementations. Let's visit some of them.

Data minimization and purpose limitation

Regulations and customer expectations require that organizations collect and process only the data necessary for the specific personalization purposes. Best practices include asking for the minimal set of attributes, encrypting data in transit and at rest, and enforcing strict access controls. MCP clients and servers should therefore clearly document why a piece of data is required and avoid over-collection or long-term retention.

User control and transparency

People should be able to understand, audit, and adjust their personalization settings. MCP servers can expose tools that allow users to view and edit their stored profiles, revoke consent for certain data sources, or reset their history. Transparent schemas and annotations (e.g., explaining why a recommendation was made) help build trust.

Algorithmic fairness and bias prevention

Recommender systems trained on historical data risk replicating and amplifying biases. Developers should monitor performance across demographic groups and implement de-biasing techniques. MCP's metadata and structured APIs can assist by clearly labelling sensitive attributes and enabling policy checks before results are returned.

Privacy-preserving techniques

MCP defines a protocol for describing and exchanging resources, but it does not mandate or provide built-in mechanisms for privacy preservation, such as differential privacy or fairness constraints. Implementing techniques such as anonymization, noise addition, or federated learning happens at the application layer, using the standardized resource access patterns that MCP provides. For example, an MCP server may expose both raw and anonymized views of a dataset; choosing which to query is up to the client application. Research shows that modern recommendation algorithms can threaten user privacy and that adding noise via differential privacy trades off accuracy for protection. Techniques such as differential privacy, homomorphic encryption, and federated learning allow collective model training and personalization without exposing raw user data. Implementers should evaluate these approaches for their specific use cases.

Monitoring and bias detection

In production, you should track classic ranking metrics (Precision@K, Recall@K, NDCG) as well as fairness metrics. Quantitative fairness metrics such as **demographic parity** and **equalized odds** compare the model's outcomes across demographic groups. Continuous monitoring helps detect bias early, and you can combine these metrics with A/B testing to evaluate whether new weightings or algorithms improve or harm fairness. Tools such as Evidently AI or Galileo can automate bias detection and provide dashboards for your ML models.

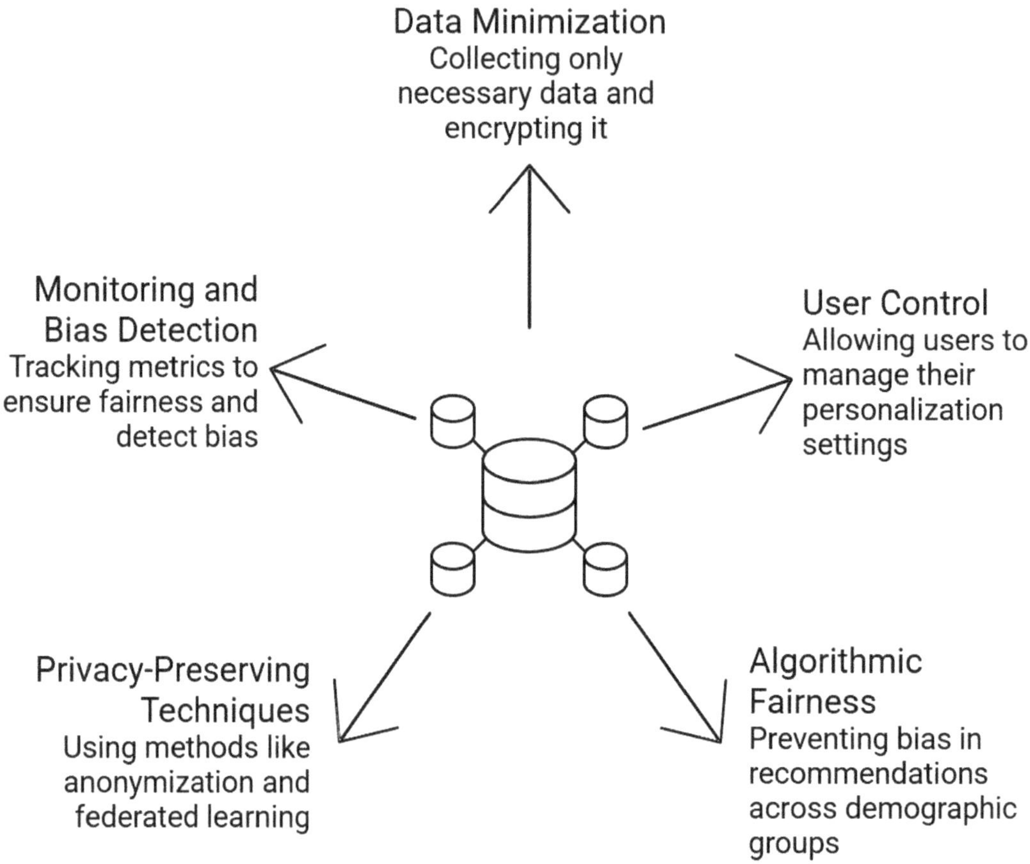

Figure 15.2 – Privacy and ethical considerations

Having explored the ethical landscape, we'll now look at how MCP supports future trends in hyper-personalization and conversational interfaces.

Future trends: hyper-personalization and conversational recommendations

The future of personalization is moving toward more sophisticated, contextual, and interactive approaches that go beyond traditional recommendation systems.

In the next few subsections, we'll explore hyper-personalization using real-time context and predictive signals, conversational recommendation agents that use MCP to manage multi-turn dialogues, and emerging research directions and open challenges. Knowing what's ahead will help you see how the chapter builds toward a forward-looking conclusion.

Hyper-personalization

The next wave of personalization aims to craft truly unique experiences for each user based on real-time context, behavioral patterns, and predictive modelling. Deep-learning techniques such as recurrent and convolutional neural networks can analyze complex signals (text, images, and sequential actions) to drive hyper-personalization. MCP facilitates this by exposing up-to-date resources and tools that feed these models. However, hyper-personalization must be balanced with privacy and fairness considerations.

Conversational recommendations

Rather than presenting static lists, future systems will engage users in dialogue, asking clarifying questions and refining recommendations. Generative AI models can summarize, translate, and converse, making interactions more natural and helpful. MCP's unified interface allows conversational agents to retrieve context and call external tools on demand, enabling such experiences. Research in generative AI and ethical AI is exploring these possibilities.

Cross-platform personalization

As customers engage via websites, mobile apps, email, chatbots and in-store kiosks, consistent personalization requires centralized context and decision logic. MCP enables an organization to share user profiles and recommendation logic across all channels, ensuring that the same preferences and behaviors inform every touchpoint.

Predictive personalization

Advanced systems will anticipate user needs before they are articulated, proactively surfacing relevant content or products. By analyzing sequences of actions and combining them with contextual signals, models can infer intent and deliver suggestions just in time. MCP provides a mechanism for these models to access diverse data sources and call predictive tools, but implementers must remain transparent about how predictions are made and allow users to opt out.

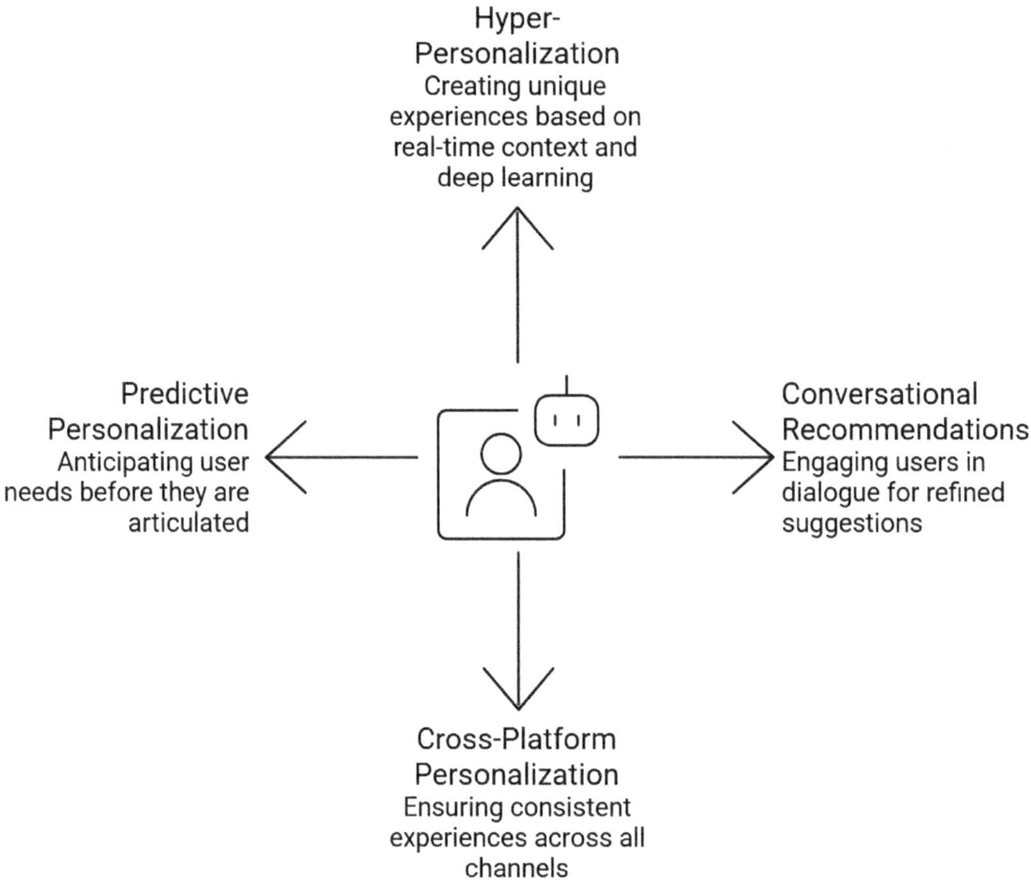

Figure 15.3 – Prioritizing future personalization

Summary

MCP transforms personalization from static, siloed systems into dynamic, integrated platforms that adapt to changing user needs and contexts. The key benefits include the following:

- **Unified data access**: MCP exposes user profiles, interaction histories, and content catalogs through standardized `resources/list` and `resources/read` operations, enabling a personalization engine to build a comprehensive picture without bespoke integrations.
- **Real-time adaptation**: By subscribing to updates and retrieving context on demand, MCP-based systems can adjust recommendations immediately when user behavior or the environment changes, instead of waiting for offline model retraining.

- **Transparency and control**: Structured schemas and annotations let systems explain why certain items were recommended and give users the ability to review or adjust their preferences. MCP allows servers to expose this metadata to clients and, ultimately, to end users.
- **Privacy and fairness**: MCP's design encourages data minimization and secure handling of personal information. Techniques such as differential privacy, federated learning, and homomorphic encryption can be layered on to protect users, while fairness monitoring ensures recommendations do not perpetuate bias.
- **Cross platform consistency**: A single MCP service can serve many clients, such as web, mobile, and voice assistants, ensuring that personalization logic and data remain consistent across all touchpoints and reducing the risk of divergent user experiences.

For production deployment, instrument your MCP-based personalization service with end-to-end metrics such as average latency, throughput, recommendation diversity, and fairness metrics to ensure the system remains responsive and equitable under real-world loads.

The future of personalization lies not only in better algorithms but in building systems that view users as complete, complex individuals. MCP provides the plumbing necessary to integrate rich context, deliver real-time insights, explain recommendations, and respect privacy, all prerequisites for intelligent, empathetic personalization.

Looking ahead to the next chapter, we'll venture into multimodal applications. We'll learn what multimodal systems are and why integrating vision, language, and other senses leads to richer understanding, review the pain of bridging these modalities, and show how MCP standardizes interfaces, enables dynamic capability discovery and context sharing, and introduces orchestration patterns for cross-modal systems.

Get this book's PDF copy, code bundle, and more

Scan the QR code (or go to `packtpub.com/unlock`). Search for this book by name, confirm the edition, and then follow the steps on the page.

UNLOCK NOW

Note: Have your invoice handy. Purchases made directly from the Packt website don't require an invoice.

16

MCP for Multimodal Applications

> *Building multimodal AI without MCP is like trying to conduct an orchestra where the musicians can't see the conductor, can't hear each other, and are all playing from different sheet music.*

I'll never forget the first time I tried to build a **multimodal AI** application. It was supposed to be simple: take an image, analyze it, generate a description, and maybe answer some questions about it. How hard could it be, right? Well, it turns out it's incredibly hard when you're dealing with three different APIs, two different authentication systems, incompatible data formats, and the delightful discovery that your image-processing service can't talk to your language model, which can't talk to your knowledge base.

The fundamental challenge with multimodal AI isn't the AI part; it's the integration part. You've got vision models that understand images, language models that understand text, and audio models that understand speech, and somehow you need to get them all working together in a coherent way. Each modality has its own tools, its own data formats, and its own quirks and limitations.

That's where MCP becomes essential. Instead of building custom bridges between every possible combination of modalities, you can build multimodal applications that discover and orchestrate capabilities dynamically through standardized MCP interfaces.

In this chapter, we will be covering multimodal AI, defining what it means to integrate multiple senses and why this leads to a richer understanding; confronting the integration challenges of bridging vision, language, and audio models; and seeing how MCP standardizes interfaces for listing and calling models, so you don't need bespoke connectors. We'll explore dynamic capability discovery and context sharing across modalities and learn orchestration patterns such as pipeline versus collaborative processing, while peeking into future trends such as embodied AI.

In this chapter, we'll be covering the following topics:

- Introduction to multimodal AI applications
- Challenges in multimodal AI and how MCP helps
- Architectural patterns for MCP-based multimodal applications
- Implementing a multimodal content analysis system
- Cross-modal context sharing and coordination
- Performance optimization for multimodal MCP systems
- Future trends: Unified multimodal understanding

Introduction to multimodal AI applications

Let's start with what multimodal AI means, because it's one of those terms that sounds more complicated than it needs to be. In modern AI literature, multimodal systems are defined as models that can analyze, interpret, and generate outputs using multiple data modalities – natural language, computer vision, speech, audio, and even sensor or tabular data – within a single reasoning framework. Unlike unimodal systems that operate on a single channel, multimodal AI integrates heterogeneous data to provide a richer context and human-like reasoning. To make this possible, researchers build cross-modal representations, aligned embeddings that allow text, images, and audio to be processed and compared in a unified space.

The promise is compelling: AI systems that can understand the world the way humans do, integrating information from multiple senses to build a rich, comprehensive understanding. Instead of just reading text or just looking at images, these systems can read a document, look at the accompanying charts, listen to an explanation, and synthesize all that information into coherent insights.

I worked on a project for a medical imaging company where doctors needed AI assistance that could look at X-rays, read patient histories, consider lab results, and provide diagnostic suggestions. No single AI model could handle all those inputs, but a multimodal system could integrate insights from specialized models to provide comprehensive analysis.

The challenge with multimodal AI applications is that different modalities require different processing approaches, different models, and different infrastructure. Vision models need GPU acceleration to process images in batches. Language models have different computational requirements and work with sequential text data. Audio models need specialized preprocessing and have their own latency characteristics.

Getting all these different components to work together reliably is a significant engineering challenge. And that's before you even consider the data synchronization issues, the error-handling complexity, and the performance optimization requirements.

Moreover, multimodal applications aren't just about processing different types of input; they're about understanding how those inputs relate to each other. The same image might mean different things depending on the accompanying text. The same audio clip might be interpreted differently based on visual context.

This requires sophisticated coordination between different AI components, with shared context and the ability to influence each other's processing. Traditional API-based integrations struggle with this kind of dynamic, context-aware coordination.

Lastly, many multimodal applications have real-time or near-real-time requirements. Users don't want to wait minutes for an AI system to process an image and generate a response. But coordinating multiple AI models while maintaining low latency is challenging, especially when different models have different performance characteristics.

As these examples show, effective multimodal systems must coordinate disparate models and infrastructure. These coordination and performance challenges set the stage for the next section, where we examine how MCP addresses them.

Challenges in multimodal AI and how MCP helps

MCP addresses several fundamental challenges that have limited the effectiveness and scalability of multimodal AI applications. Let's look at some of these challenges and how MCP can help overcome them.

The custom integration problem

Traditional multimodal applications require custom integration code for every combination of AI models and data sources. Integration complexity is a major pain point in multimodal AI: different modalities arrive in different formats and quality levels, and aligning them requires extensive preprocessing and synchronization. In addition to handling noisy or incomplete data, multimodal systems must manage substantial computational overhead to process diverse inputs. If you want to add a new vision model, you need to write integration code; if you want to add audio processing, more integration code; if you want to change how models coordinate with each other, that's even more integration code.

MCP eliminates most of this custom integration work by providing standardized interfaces for listing and calling AI capabilities. Instead of writing bespoke connectors for each model, you can connect to MCP servers that expose resources and tools via consistent operations such as `resources/list`, `tools/list`, and `tools/call`. These standardized JSON-RPC calls let applications discover available models and invoke them dynamically without hardcoding endpoints.

The dynamic capability discovery challenge

Multimodal applications often need to adapt to different deployment environments with different available models and capabilities. For example, a mobile deployment might have different AI models than a cloud deployment, and a high-security environment might support only locally approved services. Without a discovery mechanism, you must code these differences up front.

MCP enables dynamic capability discovery by letting clients ask servers what resources and tools they provide. The `resources/list` operation returns URIs and metadata for available context sources, while `tools/list` returns a list of callable functions with names, descriptions, and input schemas. Servers can declare a `listChanged` capability to notify clients when the list of tools or resources changes. Together, these operations allow multimodal applications to adapt their processing strategies at runtime based on the capabilities offered by the servers they connect to. Discovering entirely new servers still requires a registry, which is currently a roadmap item outside the core specification.

The context-sharing problem

Effective multimodal processing requires sharing context between different AI components. A vision model's analysis should inform the language model's processing, and audio cues may change how images are interpreted. Traditional API-based integrations don't provide mechanisms to share rich context.

Research into cross-modal representations shows how aligned embedding spaces allow information from images, text, and audio to be processed and compared in a unified way. MCP builds on this idea: each analysis result can be passed through standardized resource and tool calls, allowing subsequent stages to consume outputs from previous modalities and coordinate processing based on shared context. By representing information in a consistent structure and attaching metadata such as `audience`, `priority`, and `lastModified`, MCP enables components to coordinate their processing based on a shared understanding of the task and available information.

The performance and scalability challenge

Multimodal applications have complex performance requirements. Some components need low latency, others need high throughput, and many require specialized hardware. Processing overhead is a significant challenge: analyzing diverse inputs in real time requires extensive computation and sophisticated architecture.

MCP doesn't mandate a particular performance strategy, but it allows servers to implement optimizations such as intelligent caching, batching, and load balancing. Since clients call all capabilities via uniform `tools/call` operations, servers can implement caching of previous analysis results or reuse precomputed embeddings to improve latency. For long-running operations, MCP supports progress notifications and cancellation requests to keep clients responsive.

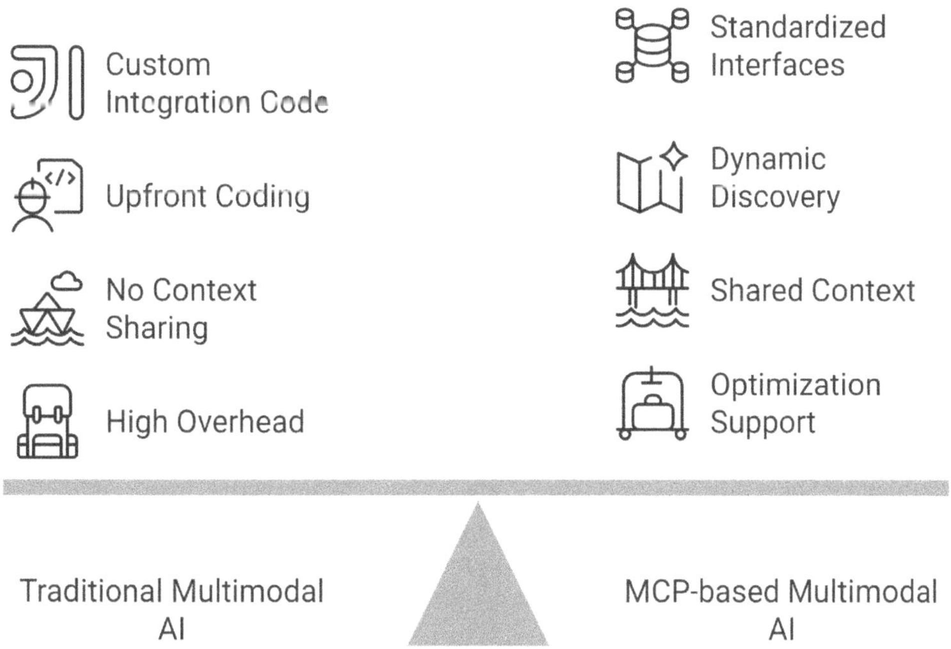

Figure 16.1 – Traditional versus MCP-based multimodal AI

Beyond understanding these challenges, building effective multimodal AI also requires adopting the right architectural patterns. The next section introduces patterns that developers can use to structure their multimodal pipelines efficiently.

Architectural patterns for MCP-based multimodal applications

Several architectural patterns have emerged for building effective MCP-based multimodal applications. Let's look at them.

The orchestrated pipeline pattern

In this pattern, a central orchestrator coordinates the flow of data through multiple MCP servers that provide different AI capabilities. The orchestrator manages the sequence of processing steps, handles data format conversions, and coordinates context sharing between components.

This pattern is particularly effective for applications with well-defined processing workflows where the sequence of operations is relatively predictable.

The collaborative processing pattern

In this pattern, multiple AI agents work together through MCP to process multimodal inputs. Different agents might specialize in different modalities or different aspects of the analysis, collaborating through shared MCP resources to build a comprehensive understanding.

This pattern is powerful for complex analysis tasks that benefit from multiple perspectives and specialized expertise.

The adaptive routing pattern

In this pattern, the multimodal application dynamically routes different types of input to appropriate MCP servers based on the content, context, and available capabilities. The same application might use different processing strategies for different types of input. For instance, a multimodal assistant might route an image to a vision analysis server for object detection while sending accompanying text to a language model for sentiment analysis. The results are then combined to produce a cohesive response.

This pattern enables applications that can adapt to diverse input types and change the availability of AI capabilities.

The federated analysis pattern

In this pattern, multiple MCP servers provide specialized analysis capabilities that can be combined to create a comprehensive multimodal understanding. Each server might specialize in a particular domain or type of analysis.

This pattern is particularly effective for applications that need to integrate insights from multiple specialized AI systems.

To illustrate how these patterns can be implemented, we'll build a simple multimodal content analysis system using MCP-style operations.

Implementing a multimodal content analysis system

Let me walk you through a lightweight demonstration of how you might build a multimodal content analysis system. Instead of relying on a full MCP implementation (which may require external dependencies), we'll simulate the core ideas with a simple Python class that exposes three operations: *listing resources*, *analyzing content*, and *synthesizing results*. This example uses in-memory data structures to illustrate how different modalities can be processed and combined, and you can adapt it to use real AI models or an MCP server in practice.

As mentioned, we're building a multimodal analysis system that processes images, text, and audio using MCP patterns. The `init` method creates a simulated content database where each item has analysis results (images have detected objects, text has sentiment, and audio has transcripts) with confidence scores. In production, these would be real AI model outputs. The `sessions` dictionary tracks groups of related content for cross-modal analysis.

Following MCP conventions, `list_resources()` exposes what content types the system can analyze (images, text, audio), while `list_tools()` reveals available operations (analyze, create session, synthesize). This discovery pattern allows AI agents to understand system capabilities before making requests. Resources are what you can analyze (nouns) and tools are how you analyze them (verbs). Let's now see things in action:

```
import json
from typing import List, Dict

class MultimodalAnalyzer:
    """A simple in-memory multimodal analysis system."""
    def __init__(self) -> None:
        # Predefined analysis results for simulation
        self.content_database: Dict[str, Dict] = {
            "image_001": {"objects": ["cat", "sofa"], "confidence": 0.9},
            "text_001": {"sentiment": "positive", "confidence": 0.8},
            "audio_001": {"transcript": "hello world","confidence": 0.85},
        }
        self.sessions: Dict[str, Dict] = {}

    def list_resources(self) -> List[str]:
        """Return the types of content that can be analyzed."""
        return ["images", "texts", "audios"]

    def list_tools(self) -> List[str]:
```

```
        """Return the available operations."""
        return ["analyze_content", "create_session","synthesize_insights"]
```

The system provides three analysis tools for different workflows: `analyze_content()` for processing individual items (detecting objects in an image), `create_session()` for grouping related content for batch analysis (such as analyzing a social media post with both the image and caption), and `synthesize_insights()` for combining results across multiple items to find patterns (calculating average confidence across a dataset). This three-tier approach – single-item analysis → batch grouping → cross-item synthesis – mirrors real AI workflows such as content moderation systems.

The following code shows the complete pattern, showing end-to-end multimodal analysis – discover capabilities, analyze individual content (such as finding a cat and sofa in an image), create a session combining image and text, and synthesize insights calculating the average confidence (0.85) across both items:

```
    def analyze_content(self,
                        content_id: str,
                        content_type: str,
                        analysis_types: List[str]) -> Dict:
        """Return simulated analysis results for a piece of content."""
        return self.content_database.get(content_id, {})

    def create_session(self,
                       session_id: str,
                       content_ids: List[str]) -> str:
        """Group multiple content items into a session."""
        self.sessions[session_id] = {"contents":content_ids, "results":{}}
        return f"Session {session_id} created with {len(content_ids)} items."

    def synthesize_insights(self, session_id: str) -> Dict:
        """Combine results from multiple items to produce aggregate insights."""
        session = self.sessions.get(session_id)
        if not session:
            return {"error": "Session not found"}
        results = [self.content_database.get(cid, {}) for cid in
session["contents"]]
        confidences = [r.get("confidence") for r in results if "confidence" in r]
        avg_conf = sum(confidences) / len(confidences) if confidences else 0.0
        return {"average_confidence": avg_conf, "results": results}
```

```
# Example usage
if __name__ == "__main__":
    analyzer = MultimodalAnalyzer()
    print("Resources:", analyzer.list_resources())
    print("Tools:", analyzer.list_tools())
    print("Analysis:", analyzer.analyze_content("image_001",
                                                "image",
                                                ["object_detection"]))
    print(analyzer.create_session("sess1", ["image_001", "text_001"]))
    import json as _json
    print("Synthesis:",
          json.dumps(analyzer.synthesize_insights("sess1"),
          indent=2))
```

When you run this script, you'll see output showing the available resources and tools, simulated analysis results for an image, a created session, and a synthesis that averages confidence scores and aggregates the results.

```
Resources: ['images', 'texts', 'audios']
Tools: ['analyze_content', 'create_session', 'synthesize_insights']
Analysis: {'objects': ['cat', 'sofa'], 'confidence': 0.9}
Session sess1 created with 2 items.
Synthesis: {
  "average_confidence": 0.85,
  "results": [
    {
      "objects": [
        "cat",
        "sofa"
      ],
      "confidence": 0.9
    },
    {
      "sentiment": "positive",
      "confidence": 0.8
    }
  ]
}
```

While simplistic, it demonstrates how an MCP-style interface can coordinate multiple modalities and return consolidated insights without any external dependencies.

While dynamic input routing and session grouping handle inputs individually, many multimodal applications rely on shared context across modalities. The next section explores cross-modal context models.

Cross-modal context sharing and coordination

One of the most powerful aspects of MCP-based multimodal applications is the ability to share context and coordinate processing across different modalities. Recent research on cross-modal representations shows that aligned embedding spaces allow information from text, images, and audio to be processed and compared in a unified way. Models encode each modality into a shared vector space using neural networks (for example, convolutional networks for images and transformers for text) and train them via contrastive learning to align paired samples. By projecting diverse inputs into a common space, AI systems can link a spoken word to a visual object or match an image to its caption, enabling tasks such as multimodal search and captioning.

MCP builds on these ideas by giving every analysis result a structured representation with metadata. When a vision model detects an object or a language model extracts entities, the results can be published as MCP resources or tool outputs annotated with fields such as `audience`, `priority`, and `lastModified`. Downstream components can then consume these resources via standard calls (e.g., `resources/read` or `tools/call`), integrating insights from previous modalities and adapting their processing accordingly.

The following examples illustrate how MCP facilitates cross-modal context sharing and coordination:

- **Shared context models**: A vision model that detects text in an image can publish a resource containing bounding boxes and extracted text. A language model can then read this shared context, use its language-modeling capabilities to correct OCR errors (e.g., misrecognized words), and produce coherent summaries of the visual scene. By sharing context, models improve both the accuracy of OCR and the quality of subsequent summarization.
- **Dynamic processing adaptation**: If a speech analysis tool detects multiple speakers in an audio clip, it can add this information to a resource. A video analytics tool can then focus on tracking those speakers in the corresponding video segment.
- **Confidence propagation**: Each tool output includes a confidence score. By aggregating confidence across modalities, the overall system can modulate its responses, weighting

the vision model more for visual questions and the language model more for textual queries.

- **Temporal coordination**: For time-based media such as video and audio, components can synchronize their outputs using timestamps, enabling alignment of audio and video frames and helping downstream modules combine them accurately.

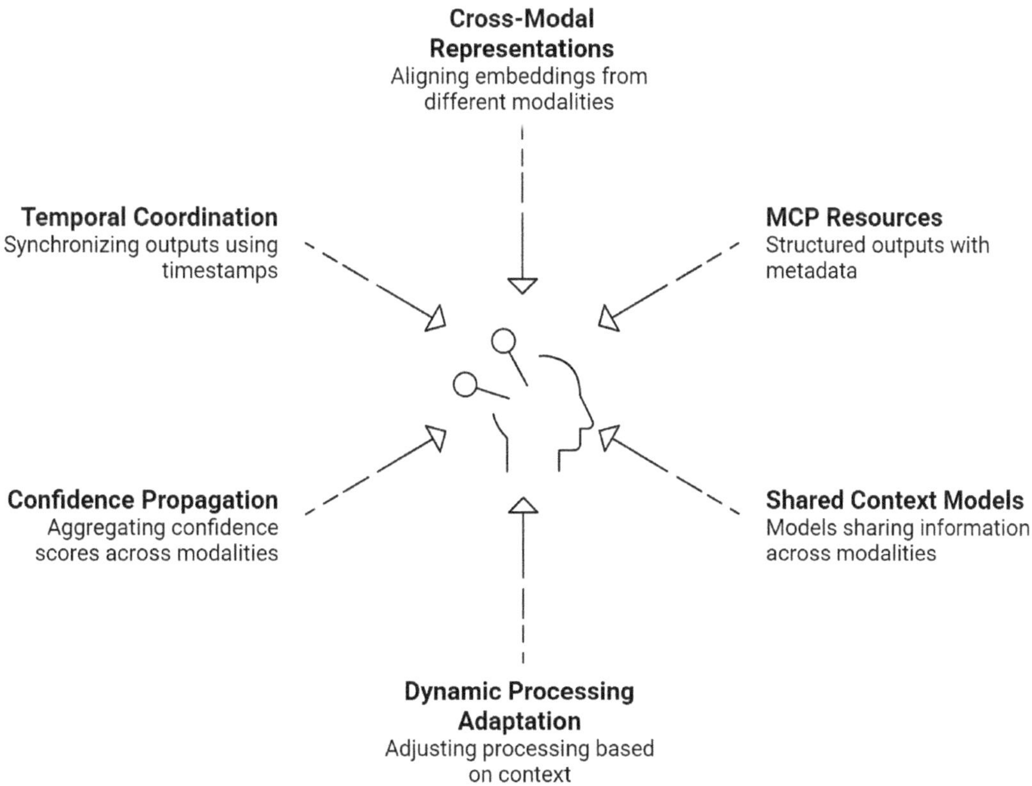

Figure 16.2 – MCP for unified multimodal reasoning

By representing multimodal outputs consistently and attaching useful metadata, MCP enables downstream components to share context, propagate confidence, and coordinate analysis across modalities. This helps multimodal systems move beyond isolated pipelines toward unified, context-aware reasoning.

Performance optimization for multimodal MCP systems

Here's how MCP can help optimize multimodal applications, not by stating performance requirements but by highlighting optimization opportunities:

- **Parallel processing strategies**: Different modalities can often be processed in parallel, but coordination and context sharing require careful orchestration. MCP servers can implement sophisticated parallel processing strategies that maximize throughput while maintaining proper coordination.
- **Caching and memorization**: Multimodal processing often involves expensive computations that can benefit from intelligent caching. MCP servers can implement content-aware caching that recognizes when similar content has been processed before and reuses appropriate results.
- **Progressive analysis**: For large or complex multimodal content, MCP systems can implement progressive analysis where initial, fast analysis provides basic insights that can be refined with more detailed processing as needed.
- **Resource management**: Different AI models have different resource requirements, such as GPU memory, CPU cores, and network bandwidth. MCP servers can implement intelligent resource management that optimizes the allocation of resources across different processing tasks.

We've reviewed existing patterns and optimization. Let's now look ahead at emerging multimodal AI paradigms and how MCP enables them.

Future trends: Unified multimodal understanding

The future of multimodal AI is moving toward more integrated, unified approaches that go beyond just coordinating separate modality-specific models. In this section, we'll see how MCP enables and optimizes emerging multimodal AI paradigms by providing a consistent framework for coordination, access, and interoperability across modalities.

Unified multimodal models

Emerging foundation models can process multiple modalities natively within a single architecture. Systems such as GPT-4V, Gemini 1.5, and Claude Opus combine text, images, and audio using cross-modal embeddings and multi-stream architectures to learn relationships between different data types. These unified models can read visual documents, respond to voice prompts, and generate contextually relevant responses across modalities, bringing AI closer to human-level multimodal understanding. MCP can provide standardized access to such models while maintaining compatibility with existing modality-specific services.

Cross-modal generation

Generative models are also becoming multimodal. OpenAI's DALL·E and Google's Imagen combine text and images to produce high-quality, novel images. Such models demonstrate that cross-modal generation is not limited to text-to-image but extends to audio and video. Future systems may generate captions from images, soundtracks from silent videos, or even videos from written scripts. MCP can coordinate these generative capabilities across modalities, ensuring that applications can compose outputs in consistent formats and propagate context between generation tasks.

Embodied AI and real-time interaction

As AI becomes embodied in robots, autonomous vehicles, and smart environments, multimodal processing becomes essential for understanding and interacting with the physical world. Real-time multimodal interactions combining speech, gesture, text, and visual input require low-latency coordination. MCP can provide the coordination layer for these complex interactions, ensuring that unified models and modality-specific tools can work together seamlessly.

Summary

MCP transforms multimodal AI from a collection of disconnected processing pipelines into integrated, intelligent systems that can understand and generate content across multiple modalities. The key benefits are as follows:

- **Unified integration**: MCP provides standardized JSON-RPC interfaces (`resources/list`, `tools/list`, `tools/call`, etc.) for coordinating diverse AI capabilities across modalities, reducing custom integration work.
- **Dynamic coordination**: Applications can adapt processing strategies at runtime based on available capabilities and context. Shared representations and metadata allow components to exchange information and adjust their behavior as new data arrives.

- **Cross-modal intelligence**: Aligned embeddings and structured outputs mean that insights from one modality can inform and improve processing in other modalities, enabling tasks such as multimodal retrieval and context-aware generation.
- **Scalable and resilient architecture**: MCP-based systems can scale to handle complex multimodal workloads while maintaining performance through caching, batching, progress notifications, and thoughtful resource management.
- **Future-ready platform**: MCP positions systems to take advantage of unified multimodal models such as GPT-4V and Gemini, and coordinate cross-modal generative models such as DALL·E and Imagen to support real-time, embodied AI interactions.

The future of AI isn't about building better single-modality systems; it's about building systems that can understand and interact with the world through multiple senses, just like humans do. MCP provides the foundation for that kind of comprehensive, multimodal intelligence.

In the next chapter, we'll examine how to evaluate MCP systems. We'll discuss why dynamic capabilities and emergent behavior make evaluation different from traditional AI, present principles for multi-dimensional assessment and continuous evaluation, and share practical techniques for functional, performance, and user experience evaluation.

Subscribe for a free eBook

Part 6

Evaluation, Optimization, and the Future

The final part of the book focuses on measuring, improving, and future-proofing your MCP systems. You will learn structured evaluation methodologies, design and run performance benchmarks, and apply advanced optimization strategies at the server, client, and protocol levels. The closing chapter looks ahead to the evolution of MCP standards, integration with emerging AI technologies, advanced multi-agent coordination patterns, and the societal and ethical implications of the protocol. By the end of this part, you will have the tools and perspective needed to continuously improve your MCP deployments and stay ahead of the curve as the ecosystem evolves.

This part of the book includes the following chapters:

- *Chapter 17, MCP Evaluation Methodologies*
- *Chapter 18, Performance Benchmarks and Testing*
- *Chapter 19, Optimization Strategies and Performance Tuning*
- *Chapter 20, Future Directions and Emerging Trends*

17

MCP Evaluation Methodologies

Evaluating MCP systems without proper methodologies is like trying to judge a cooking competition without tasting a dish.

I've spent a lot of my career trying to figure out whether AI systems work. Not just whether they run without crashing, which is the easy part, but whether they're solving the problems they're supposed to solve, whether they're reliable enough for production use, and whether they're worth the investment in time and resources.

Evaluation of traditional AI systems is already challenging. You've got accuracy metrics, performance benchmarks, user satisfaction surveys, and a dozen other ways to measure success. But with MCP systems, the evaluation challenge becomes exponentially more complex because you're not just evaluating a single AI model; you're evaluating an entire ecosystem of interconnected capabilities.

How do you measure the effectiveness of a system that can dynamically discover and use new capabilities? How do you benchmark performance when the system's behavior changes based on what MCP servers are available? How do you evaluate user experience when the same application might behave completely differently in different deployment environments?

These aren't just academic questions. Recent analysis of multi-agent systems has shown that evaluating AI agents involves measuring not only individual model performance but also how effectively agents collaborate, coordinate, and pass information. Leading evaluation guides such as `AgentBench`, `WebArena`, GAIA, and `ToolBench` emphasize that proper evaluation is essential for trustworthy, production-ready systems and must address collaboration quality, resource efficiency, scalability, output quality, and ethical considerations. I've seen MCP projects fail not because the technology didn't work, but because teams couldn't demonstrate that it was working well enough to justify continued investment.

In this chapter, we will be covering evaluation methodologies for MCP. We'll explore why dynamic capabilities, emergent behavior, context dependency, and multiple stakeholders make evaluation different from traditional AI, and present design principles for assessing capabilities, embracing variability, evaluating multiple dimensions, performing continuous evaluation, and tailoring metrics to stakeholders. You'll learn functional and performance evaluation techniques that test capability discovery, workflow coordination, latency, throughput, and scalability alongside methods for stress-testing error handling, measuring user satisfaction, and ethical considerations. A practical example will show you how to implement these ideas in Python.

In this chapter, we'll be covering the following topics:

- Introduction to MCP evaluation challenges
- Evaluation framework design principles
- Functional evaluation methodologies
- Performance evaluation methodologies
- Implementing an MCP evaluation framework
- Continuous evaluation and monitoring

Introduction to MCP evaluation challenges

Let's start with why evaluating MCP systems is fundamentally different from evaluating traditional AI systems. It's not just a matter of scale; it's a matter of complexity and dynamic behavior that traditional evaluation approaches weren't designed to handle.

The dynamic capability problem

Traditional AI systems have fixed capabilities that you can test systematically. You know what inputs the system accepts, what outputs it produces, and what the expected behavior should be. With MCP systems, the capabilities can change dynamically based on what MCP servers are available.

The same MCP client might have access to basic document search in one environment and sophisticated multimodal analysis in another. How do you create evaluation frameworks that can handle this kind of variability?

The emergent behavior challenge

MCP systems often exhibit emergent behavior that arises from the interaction between different components. A document analysis system might become much more powerful when it gains access to a new knowledge base, but the improvement might not be obvious from testing individual components.

This emergent behavior is often where the real value of MCP systems lies, but it's also the hardest thing to evaluate systematically.

The context dependency issue

MCP systems are highly context-dependent. The same query might produce different results based on user permissions, available data sources, current system load, and dozens of other contextual factors. Traditional evaluation approaches that assume consistent, repeatable behavior struggle with this kind of context sensitivity.

The multi-stakeholder evaluation problem

MCP systems often serve multiple stakeholders with different evaluation criteria. End users care about functionality and ease of use. System administrators care about reliability and security. Business stakeholders care about ROI and competitive advantage. Creating evaluation frameworks that address all these perspectives is challenging.

I worked on an MCP project where the technical team was convinced the system was working great: all the APIs were responding correctly, the integration tests were passing, and the performance metrics looked good. But the business users were frustrated because the system wasn't helping them accomplish their actual goals. They wanted to answer three questions: How well do our agents complete real-world tasks? Can our multi-agent pipelines scale without degrading quality? And do users trust the system's outputs? Understanding these goals helps set context for the principles that follow. We had optimized technical metrics while ignoring user experience metrics.

Leading evaluation frameworks echo this multi-stakeholder challenge. They recommend capturing quantitative metrics such as response accuracy, latency, and resource utilization alongside qualitative assessments such as user satisfaction, coherence, and fairness. They also stress the importance of tracking ethical dimensions (bias detection and transparency) to ensure agent behaviors align with human values.

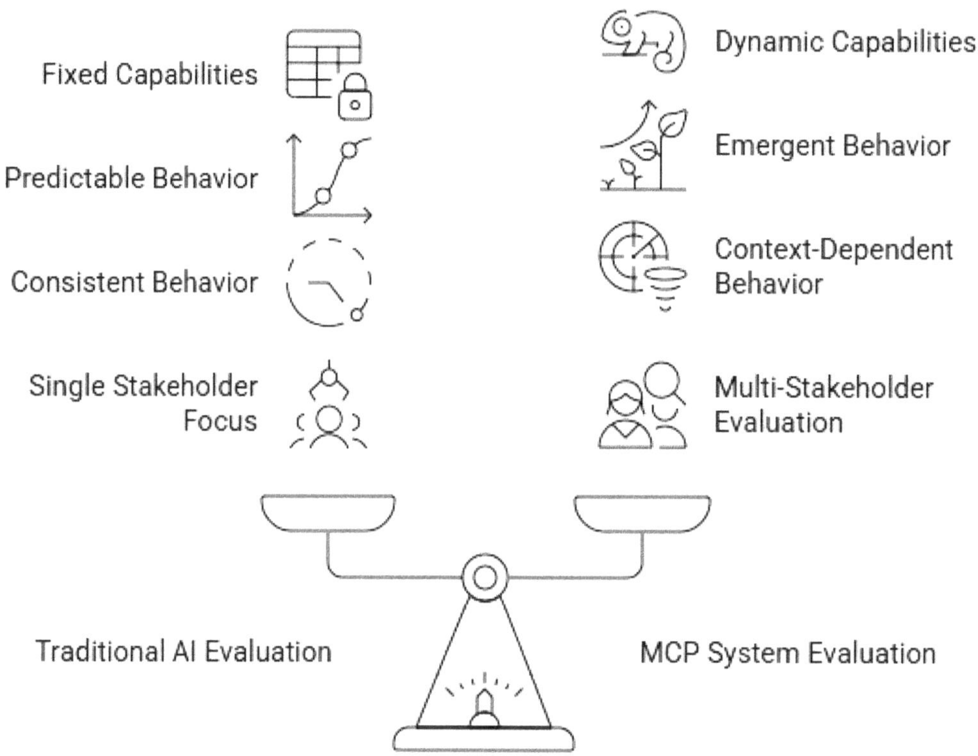

Figure 17.1 – Evaluating MCP systems' unique challenges

With those questions in mind, we can now derive a set of design principles for building effective evaluation frameworks.

Evaluation framework design principles

Based on my experience evaluating MCP systems, I've developed some principles that seem to work better than traditional approaches.

- **Principle 1 – Evaluate capabilities, not just components**: Instead of just testing individual MCP servers or clients, you need to evaluate the capabilities that emerge from their interaction. This means designing tests that exercise complete workflows and use cases, not just individual API calls.
- **Principle 2 – Embrace variability**: Don't try to eliminate variability in MCP system behavior. Embrace it and design evaluation frameworks that can handle and measure it. The ability to adapt to different environments and capabilities is a feature, not a bug.

- **Principle 3 – Perform a multi-dimensional assessment**: MCP systems need to be evaluated across multiple dimensions: functionality, performance, reliability, security, usability, and maintainability. No single metric can capture the full picture of system effectiveness.

> Note
>
> **Handling non-determinism**: Unlike deterministic software, LLM-powered agents may produce different yet valid outputs for the same input. Evaluation frameworks should therefore measure distributions rather than single answers. One strategy is to define invariant conditions that all valid outputs must satisfy (e.g., response arrives within a latency budget, tool calls conform to schema, no sensitive data leakage) and check those instead of exact matches. Another is to repeat tests multiple times and use statistical summaries (mean, median, or variance) to characterize performance. For subjective criteria such as helpfulness or reasoning quality, evaluator models (LLM-as-a-Judge) or human graders can score outputs.

Contemporary evaluation guides for agentic systems outline similar dimensions. In addition to classic performance metrics such as accuracy, latency, and resource consumption, they recommend evaluating collaboration and coordination, scalability, output quality, and ethical considerations. A comprehensive assessment must therefore look beyond technical correctness to capture how well agents cooperate and adapt to dynamic conditions.

- **Principle 4 – Ensure continuous evaluation**: MCP systems change over time as new servers are added, existing servers are updated, and usage patterns evolve. Evaluation needs to be continuous, not just a one-time assessment.
  Continuous evaluation is critical for maintaining reliability. Industry guidelines highlight that AI models degrade over time and that ongoing monitoring is necessary to detect performance drift, bias, and fairness issues. Microsoft's Azure AI Foundry similarly provides continuous evaluation capabilities where sample agents interact in real time to surface quality, safety, and performance insights. For example, some teams run weekly evaluations using a representative task set, track metrics such as task-completion rate and tool selection accuracy, and collect user feedback via surveys or Net Promoter Score. Others deploy canary agents that continuously monitor latency and error rates in production. These examples illustrate why evaluation frameworks must integrate automated pipelines and real-time observability instead of relying solely on periodic tests.

- **Principle 5 – Design stakeholder-specific metrics**: Different stakeholders need different evaluation metrics. Design evaluation frameworks that can provide relevant insights for each stakeholder group while maintaining overall system coherence.
- **Principle 6 – Evaluate within real-world context**: Evaluate MCP systems in realistic contexts with real data, real users, and real constraints. Laboratory testing is useful, but it's not sufficient for understanding how systems will perform in production.

  Evaluation frameworks emphasize designing representative test cases that mirror real-world tasks, user intents, and interaction flows. They often pair automated metrics with human-in-the-loop review to ensure that evaluations reflect actual user experience and that results feed back into model refinement.

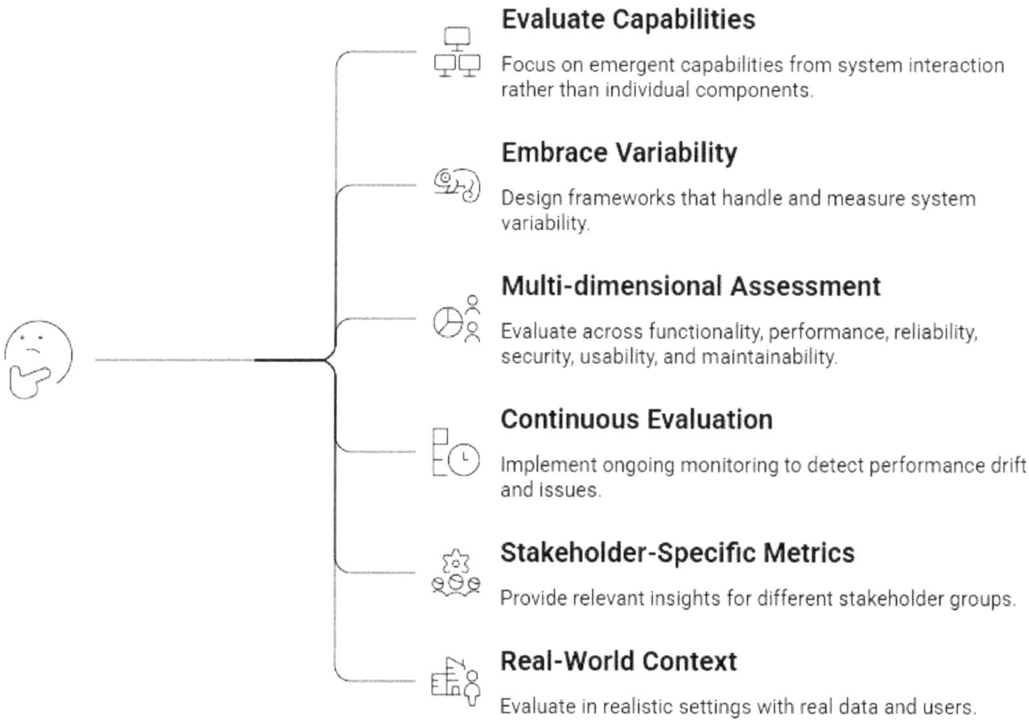

Figure 17.2 – Effective MCP systems evaluation

Having defined the principles, let's explore functional evaluation methodologies that apply them in practice.

Functional evaluation methodologies

Functional evaluation focuses on whether MCP systems can accomplish the tasks they're designed to perform. This sounds straightforward, but it's quite complex for dynamic systems.

Our first functional methodology focuses on capability discovery, verifying that agents can identify and invoke the right tools and resources.

Capability discovery testing

One of the fundamental capabilities of MCP systems is discovering and adapting to available capabilities. Testing this requires creating controlled environments with different sets of available MCP servers and verifying that the system can discover and use them appropriately.

You need test scenarios that cover the following:

- Systems with minimal capabilities
- Systems with rich, diverse capabilities
- Systems where capabilities change during operation
- Systems where some capabilities are temporarily unavailable

End-to-end workflow testing

MCP systems are often used for complex workflows that span multiple capabilities and data sources. Testing these workflows requires creating realistic scenarios that exercise the full system capabilities.

I've found that the most effective approach is to identify the top 5-10 user workflows that the system needs to support, then create comprehensive test scenarios for each workflow that cover both happy path and error conditions.

Adaptive behavior testing

MCP systems should adapt their behavior based on available capabilities and context. Testing this adaptive behavior requires creating scenarios where the system needs to choose between different approaches, such as rule-based logic, reinforcement learning, or supervised fine-tuning, to see which enables agents to adapt most effectively to changing environments or gracefully degrade when preferred capabilities aren't available.

As part of adaptive behavior testing, evaluation frameworks recommend measuring how quickly agents adjust to new tools and capabilities, how often they fall back to alternative strategies, and whether they maintain task accuracy under changing conditions. These metrics capture the system's ability to learn and adapt rather than simply detect errors.

Cross-modal integration testing

For multimodal MCP systems, you need to test how well different modalities work together. This includes testing data format conversions, context sharing between modalities, and the quality of integrated analysis.

In multimodal contexts, cross-modal representation research suggests evaluating the alignment between modalities using embedding similarity and shared feature consistency. Integrated tests should therefore assess whether combining modalities improves output coherence and accuracy compared to single-modality processing.

Next, we'll turn to performance evaluation, measuring throughput, latency, and resource usage.

Performance evaluation methodologies

Performance evaluation for MCP systems is complex because performance depends not just on individual components, but on how they interact and coordinate.

Performance evaluation covers several dimensions, including latency, throughput, scalability, resource utilization, and performance variability:

- **Latency and throughput analysis**: Traditional performance metrics such as latency and throughput are important, but they need to be measured at multiple levels:
    - Individual MCP server response times
    - End-to-end workflow completion times
    - System throughput under various load conditions
    - Performance degradation under stress
- **Resource utilization assessment**: MCP systems often coordinate multiple resource-intensive AI models and data sources. Understanding resource utilization patterns is crucial for capacity planning and optimization.
  You need to measure the following:
    - CPU and memory usage across all components
    - Network bandwidth utilization
    - Storage I/O patterns
    - GPU utilization for AI workloads
- **Scalability testing**: MCP systems should scale gracefully as the load increases and as new capabilities are added. Testing scalability requires systematic evaluation of system behavior under increasing load and complexity.
- **Performance variability analysis**: Unlike traditional systems with predictable performance characteristics, MCP systems may have significant performance variability based on which capabilities are being used and how they're being combined. Understanding and characterizing this variability is important for setting appropriate performance expectations.

Performance evaluation in multi-agent systems extends beyond raw latency and throughput. It should include analysis of resource utilization (memory and processing load, task prioritization), scalability (linear versus exponential growth of resource demands and latency), and output quality (accuracy, coherence, and consistency across interactions). Ethical considerations, such as bias detection and transparency, should also be part of performance evaluation. These metrics provide a holistic view of system health and guide optimization.

To tie these concepts together, let's implement a simple evaluation framework. This example shows how to register tools and resources, run test scenarios, and compute basic metrics such as success rate and average latency.

Implementing an MCP evaluation framework

Let me walk you through the implementation of a practical evaluation framework that demonstrates key concepts while remaining manageable. This evaluation framework tests MCP systems across multiple dimensions.

1. We start by defining an data class to store test outcomes with metrics, errors, and timestamps, enabling historical analysis. The `MCPEvaluationFramework` class initializes a SQLite database with two tables: one table for storing individual test results and another for storing evaluation session summaries. This persistent storage allows tracking improvements over time and comparing different MCP implementations.

   > **Note**
   >
   > SQLite allows many concurrent readers but only one writer at a time. In the context of evaluation frameworks, this means simultaneous test sessions will serialize their writing. For heavy concurrency, you can enable **Write-Ahead Logging (WAL)** mode or migrate to a server-based database such as PostgreSQL or MySQL.

   ```
   import asyncio
   import time
   import json
   import statistics
   from datetime import datetime, timedelta
   from typing import List, Dict, Any, Optional, Tuple
   from dataclasses import dataclass
   import sqlite3

   @dataclass
   ```

```
class EvaluationResult:
    """Container for evaluation results."""
    test_name: str
    success: bool
    duration: float
    metrics: Dict[str, Any]
    errors: List[str]
    timestamp: str

class MCPEvaluationFramework:
    """Comprehensive evaluation framework for MCP systems."""

    def __init__(self, db_path: str = "mcp_evaluation.db"):
        self.db_path = db_path
        self.results = []
        self._setup_database()

    def _setup_database(self):
        """Initialize evaluation results database."""
        conn = sqlite3.connect(self.db_path)
        cursor = conn.cursor()

        cursor.execute('''
            CREATE TABLE IF NOT EXISTS evaluation_results (
                id INTEGER PRIMARY KEY AUTOINCREMENT,
                test_name TEXT,
                test_category TEXT,
                success BOOLEAN,
                duration REAL,
                metrics TEXT,
                errors TEXT,
                timestamp TEXT
            )
        ''')

        cursor.execute('''
            CREATE TABLE IF NOT EXISTS evaluation_sessions (
                session_id TEXT PRIMARY KEY,
                start_time TEXT,
                end_time TEXT,
                total_tests INTEGER,
```

```
                passed_tests INTEGER,
                failed_tests INTEGER,
                summary_metrics TEXT
            )
        ''')

        conn.commit()
        conn.close()
        print("Evaluation framework database initialized")
```

The database schema supports both detailed per-test analysis and high-level session summaries, essential for benchmarking MCP systems in production environments.

2. Next, the framework evaluates four critical MCP dimensions: capability discovery, performance characteristics, reliability and error handling, and user experience.

```
async def evaluate_capability_discovery(
    self, mcp_client_simulator
) -> EvaluationResult:
    """Evaluate MCP capability discovery functionality."""
    test_name = "capability_discovery"
    start_time = time.time()
    errors = []
    metrics = {}

    try:
        print("Testing capability discovery...")

        # Test 1: Basic server discovery
        available_servers = await self._simulate_server_discovery()
        metrics["servers_discovered"] = len(available_servers)

        # Test 2: Capability enumeration
        total_capabilities = 0
        for server in available_servers:
            capabilities = await self._simulate_capability_enumeration(
                server)
            total_capabilities += len(capabilities)
            metrics[f"{server}_capabilities"] = len(capabilities)

        metrics["total_capabilities"] = total_capabilities
```

```
            # Test 3: Dynamic capability changes
            new_server = "dynamic_analysis_server"
            available_servers.append(new_server)
            new_capabilities = await self._simulate_capability_enumeration(
                new_server)
            metrics["dynamic_capabilities_added"] = len(new_capabilities)

            # Test 4: Graceful handling of unavailable servers
            unavailable_count = 0
            for server in ["nonexistent_server_1", "nonexistent_server_2"]:
                try:
                    await self._simulate_capability_enumeration(server)
                except Exception:
                    unavailable_count += 1

            metrics["unavailable_servers_handled"] = unavailable_count

            success = (
                metrics["servers_discovered"] > 0 and
                metrics["total_capabilities"] > 0 and
                metrics["unavailable_servers_handled"] == 2
            )

        except Exception as e:
            errors.append(f"Capability discovery test failed: {str(e)}")
            success = False

        duration = time.time() - start_time

        return EvaluationResult(
            test_name=test_name,
            success=success,
            duration=duration,
            metrics=metrics,
            errors=errors,
            timestamp=datetime.now().isoformat()
        )

    async def evaluate_performance_characteristics(self) -> EvaluationResult:
        """Evaluate MCP system performance characteristics."""
```

```
test_name = "performance_characteristics"
start_time = time.time()
errors = []
metrics = {}

try:
    print("Testing performance characteristics...")

    # Test 1: Response time distribution
    response_times = []
    for i in range(50):
        request_start = time.time()
        await self._simulate_mcp_request(f"test_request_{i}")
        response_time = time.time() - request_start
        response_times.append(response_time)

    metrics["response_time_mean"] = statistics.mean(response_times)
    metrics["response_time_median"] = statistics.median(
        response_times)
    metrics["response_time_std"] = statistics.stdev(response_times)
    metrics["response_time_p95"] = sorted(response_times)[
        int(0.95 * len(response_times))]

    # Test 2: Throughput under load
    concurrent_requests = 10
    batch_start = time.time()

    tasks = []
    for i in range(concurrent_requests):
        task = asyncio.create_task(
            self._simulate_mcp_request(f"concurrent_request_{i}"))
        tasks.append(task)

    await asyncio.gather(*tasks)
    batch_duration = time.time() - batch_start

    metrics["concurrent_requests"] = concurrent_requests
    metrics["batch_duration"] = batch_duration
    metrics["throughput_rps"] = concurrent_requests / batch_duration

    # Test 3: Scalability characteristics
```

```
            scalability_results = []
            for load_level in [1, 5, 10, 20]:
                load_start = time.time()
                load_tasks = []
                for i in range(load_level):
                    task = asyncio.create_task(
                        self._simulate_mcp_request(
                            f"scale_test_{load_level}_{i}"
                        )
                    )
                    load_tasks.append(task)

                await asyncio.gather(*load_tasks)
                load_duration = time.time() - load_start

                scalability_results.append({
                    "load_level": load_level,
                    "duration": load_duration,
                    "throughput": load_level / load_duration
                })

            metrics["scalability_results"] = scalability_results

            success = (
                metrics["response_time_mean"] < 1.0 and
                metrics["throughput_rps"] > 5.0 and
                len(scalability_results) == 4
            )

        except Exception as e:
            errors.append(f"Performance evaluation failed: {str(e)}")
            success = False

        duration = time.time() - start_time

        return EvaluationResult(
            test_name=test_name,
            success=success,
            duration=duration,
            metrics=metrics,
            errors=errors,
```

```
            timestamp=datetime.now().isoformat()
        )
```

The `evaluate_capability_discovery()` function tests the first dimension by verifying that the system can find available MCP servers, enumerate their capabilities, handle dynamic server changes, and gracefully manage unavailable servers. The `evaluate_performance_characteristics()` function measures second-dimension aspects such as response times, throughput under concurrent load, and scalability using statistical analysis (mean, median, standard deviation, and 95th percentile) to identify outliers and bottlenecks. Later functions (not shown here) evaluate the reliability and error-handling dimension and the user-experience dimension.

Success criteria are defined upfront: average response time under 1 second and throughput above 5 requests/second. In this way, clear performance benchmarks for MCP systems are established.

3. The framework then tests the third dimension—reliability and error-handling— and the final dimension—the user-experience dimension:

```
    async def run_comprehensive_evaluation(self) -> Dict[str, Any]:
        """Run comprehensive MCP system evaluation."""
        session_id =
f"eval_session_{datetime.now().strftime('%Y%m%d_%H%M%S')}"
        start_time = datetime.now()

        print(f"Starting comprehensive MCP evaluation session:
{session_id}")
        print("=" * 60)

        # Run all evaluation tests
        evaluation_tests = [
            self.evaluate_capability_discovery(None),
            self.evaluate_performance_characteristics(),
            self.evaluate_reliability_and_error_handling(),
            self.evaluate_user_experience()
        ]

        results = []
        for test in evaluation_tests:
            result = await test
            results.append(result)
```

```
            self._store_result(result, session_id)

            print(f"\n{result.test_name}: {'PASS' if result.success else
'FAIL'}")
            print(f"Duration: {result.duration:.2f}s")
            if result.errors:
                print(f"Errors: {len(result.errors)}")
            print(f"Key metrics: {list(result.metrics.keys())[:3]}...")

        # Calculate summary metrics
        end_time = datetime.now()
        total_tests = len(results)
        passed_tests = sum(1 for r in results if r.success)
        failed_tests = total_tests - passed_tests

        summary_metrics = {
            "total_duration": (
                end_time - start_time).total_seconds(),
            "pass_rate": passed_tests / total_tests,
            "average_test_duration": statistics.mean(
                 [r.duration for r in results]),
            "total_errors": sum(len(r.errors) for r in results)
        }

        self._store_session_summary(
            session_id, start_time, end_time,
            total_tests, passed_tests, failed_tests,
            summary_metrics)

        print("\n" + "=" * 60)
        print(f"Evaluation session {session_id} completed")
        print(f"Tests passed: {passed_tests}/{total_tests}
({summary_metrics['pass_rate']:.1%})")
        print(f"Total duration: {summary_metrics['total_duration']:.1f}s")

        return {
            "session_id": session_id,
            "results": results,
            "summary": summary_metrics
        }
```

```
    # Simulation methods (simulate the behavior of MCP servers in our
evaluation framework. They return dummy values and introduce small delays
for demonstration purposes. In a real-world evaluation, these functions
would call actual MCP servers and record dynamic responses.)

    async def _simulate_server_discovery(self) -> List[str]:
        await asyncio.sleep(0.1)
        return ["document_server", "analysis_server", "knowledge_server"]

    async def _simulate_capability_enumeration(
        self, server: str
    ) -> List[str]:
        await asyncio.sleep(0.05)
        capabilities_map = {
            "document_server": ["search", "retrieve", "index"],
            "analysis_server": ["analyze", "summarize", "classify"],
            "knowledge_server": ["query", "reason", "explain"],
            "dynamic_analysis_server": ["advanced_analysis",
"pattern_recognition"]
        }
        if server in capabilities_map:
            return capabilities_map[server]
        else:
            raise Exception(f"Server {server} not available")

    async def _simulate_mcp_request(
        self, request_id: str
    ) -> Dict[str, Any]:
        delay = 0.05 + (hash(request_id) % 100) / 1000
        await asyncio.sleep(delay)
        return {"request_id": request_id,
            "status": "success", "response_time": delay}

    # Additional simulation methods and database storage methods...

    def _store_result(
        self, result: EvaluationResult, session_id: str
    ):
        """Store evaluation result in database."""
        conn = sqlite3.connect(self.db_path)
        cursor = conn.cursor()
```

```
        cursor.execute('''
            INSERT INTO evaluation_results (test_name, test_category,
success, duration, metrics, errors, timestamp)
            VALUES (?, ?, ?, ?, ?, ?, ?)
        ''', (
                result.test_name, session_id,
                result.success, result.duration,
                json.dumps(result.metrics),
                json.dumps(result.errors), result.timestamp
            )
        )
        conn.commit()
        conn.close()

    def _store_session_summary(
        self, session_id: str, start_time: datetime,
        end_time: datetime, total_tests: int,
        passed_tests: int, failed_tests: int,
        summary_metrics: Dict[str, Any]
    ):
        """Store evaluation session summary."""
        conn = sqlite3.connect(self.db_path)
        cursor = conn.cursor()
        cursor.execute('''
            INSERT INTO evaluation_sessions (session_id, start_time,
end_time, total_tests,
                                            passed_tests, failed_tests,
summary_metrics)
            VALUES (?, ?, ?, ?, ?, ?, ?)
        ''', (
                session_id, start_time.isoformat(),
                end_time.isoformat(),total_tests, passed_tests,
                failed_tests, json.dumps(summary_metrics)
            )
        )
        conn.commit()
        conn.close()

# Example usage
async def main():
    """Demonstrate the MCP evaluation framework."""
```

```
        evaluator = MCPEvaluationFramework()
        results = await evaluator.run_comprehensive_evaluation()

        print(f"\nEvaluation completed successfully!")
        print(f"Session ID: {results['session_id']}")
        print(f"Overall pass rate: {results['summary']['pass_rate']:.1%}")

    if __name__ == "__main__":
        asyncio.run(main())
```

The third dimension is critical for production MCP systems. We simulate five error scenarios (timeouts, invalid requests, auth failures, missing resources, and overload) and measure recovery success rate. The test also evaluates graceful degradation (can the system operate with reduced capabilities?) and fault tolerance. The fourth dimension, which is our user-experience dimension, `evaluate_user_experience()`, focuses on end-user metrics: task completion rate, response quality assessment, and overall satisfaction across multiple factors (ease of use, accuracy, speed, reliability, and completeness). This holistic view ensures MCP systems work well technically and provide a good user experience.

In sum, the framework runs four comprehensive tests (capability discovery, performance, reliability, and user experience), displays the pass/fail status for each, stores results in SQLite, and reports overall pass rate and timing, providing a complete quality gate for MCP systems before production deployment.

When you run this code, you'll see output like this:

```
Evaluation framework database initialized
Starting comprehensive MCP evaluation session: eval_session_20241127_143022
============================================================
Testing capability discovery...

capability_discovery: PASS
Duration: 0.31s
Key metrics: ['servers_discovered', 'total_capabilities',
'dynamic_capabilities_added']...
Testing performance characteristics...

performance_characteristics: PASS
Duration: 1.45s
Key metrics: ['response_time_mean', 'response_time_median',
```

```
'response_time_std']...
Testing reliability and error handling...

reliability_error_handling: PASS
Duration: 0.52s
Key metrics: ['error_scenarios_tested', 'error_recovery_success_rate',
'degradation_scenarios_tested']...
Testing user experience...

user_experience: PASS
Duration: 0.38s
Key metrics: ['total_tasks', 'completed_tasks', 'task_completion_rate']...

============================================================
Evaluation session eval_session_20241127_143022 completed
Tests passed: 4/4 (100.0%)
Total duration: 2.7s
Average test duration: 0.67s

Evaluation completed successfully!
Session ID: eval_session_20241127_143022
Overall pass rate: 100.0%
```

This example demonstrates a comprehensive evaluation framework that can assess MCP systems across multiple dimensions with real metrics and results.

Beyond one-off tests, evaluation needs to be continuous. The next section explains how to monitor systems over time.

Continuous evaluation and monitoring

MCP systems need continuous evaluation because they change over time as new capabilities are added and usage patterns evolve.

Here are some guidelines for building a continuous evaluation infrastructure:

- **Automate evaluation pipelines**: Continuous evaluation requires automated pipelines that can run evaluation tests regularly without human intervention. These pipelines should integrate with CI/CD systems and provide alerts when evaluation metrics fall below acceptable thresholds.
  Major tech companies continuously evaluate AI assistants such as digital assistants, customer-service chatbots, and other agentic applications by running A/B tests on a

fraction of traffic, using real user interactions to compare new and existing models. E-commerce platforms monitor recommendation accuracy and click-through rates daily, alerting engineers when metrics fall below thresholds. Healthcare AI providers update models monthly and re-evaluate them against regulatory and clinical benchmarks before deployment. Continuous evaluations show how automatic sampling of agent interactions can provide near real-time visibility into quality, safety, and performance. Industry guides also emphasize integrating continuous monitoring with bias and fairness checks to prevent drift and ensure sustained reliability.

- **Integrate real-time monitoring**: Evaluation frameworks should integrate with real-time monitoring systems to provide continuous visibility into system performance and behavior. This enables early detection of issues and proactive response to degrading performance.
- **Implement trend analysis and alerting**: Continuous evaluation generates large amounts of data over time. Effective frameworks need sophisticated trend analysis capabilities that can identify gradual degradation or improvement in system performance and alert stakeholders to significant changes.
- **Ensure adaptive evaluation criteria**: As MCP systems evolve, evaluation criteria may need to evolve as well. Frameworks should support adaptive evaluation criteria that can be updated based on changing requirements and usage patterns.

As evaluation produces large datasets, frameworks need trend analysis and alerting to detect gradual degradation or improvement. Integrate dashboards and version-control systems (e.g., Git and DVC) to track changes in evaluation datasets, metric definitions, and model configurations over time. Support adaptive criteria so that success thresholds can be updated as system requirements evolve.

Continuous evaluation does not exist in a vacuum. *Chapter 14* explained how MCP systems are deployed and monitored in production; here, we've shown how to embed evaluation into that lifecycle. Together, these chapters illustrate a feedback loop: evaluations inform deployment decisions, and monitoring data feeds back into evaluation.

Summary

The effective evaluation of MCP systems requires sophisticated methodologies that can handle dynamic capabilities, emergent behavior, and complex stakeholder requirements. This chapter showed how to design and implement robust evaluation frameworks for multi-agent systems. We began with key questions to guide evaluation, then defined principles for measuring effectiveness, user experience, ethics, and robustness. We explored functional and performance methodologies, emphasized continuous monitoring, and examined real-world tooling options. By following these guidelines and tailoring metrics to stakeholder needs, you can build trustworthy multi-agent systems that evolve gracefully over time.

The future of MCP evaluation isn't about finding the perfect metrics but about building evaluation frameworks that can adapt to changing systems and provide actionable insights for continuous improvement.

In the next chapter, we'll learn more about benchmarking and testing. We'll explain why fixed tests can't capture dynamic capabilities and emergent behaviors, lay out principles for multi-dimensional benchmarking and realistic scenarios, and show how to design a benchmarking suite for capability discovery, coordination efficiency, adaptive performance, user experience, and reliability.

Get this book's PDF copy, code bundle, and more

Scan the QR code (or go to `packtpub.com/unlock`). Search for this book by name, confirm the edition, and then follow the steps on the page.

UNLOCK NOW

Note: Have your invoice handy. Purchases made directly from the Packt website don't require an invoice.

18

Performance Benchmarks and Testing

Benchmarking MCP systems without understanding their dynamic nature is like trying to measure the speed of a chameleon by timing how fast it changes colors.

I've spent countless hours trying to benchmark AI systems, and let me tell you, it's one of the most frustrating aspects of this field. You set up your test environment, run your benchmarks, get your numbers, and then... what? The system behaves completely differently in production because the real world doesn't match your carefully controlled test conditions.

With MCP systems, this problem becomes even more complex. Traditional benchmarks assume that you're testing a fixed system with predictable behavior. But MCP systems can have completely different capabilities depending on what servers are available, what the current load is, and what other systems they're interacting with.

As researchers studying multi-agent LLM systems have noted, performance evaluation must extend beyond simple component tests. Because these systems rely on dynamic agent interactions, meaningful benchmarks should assess how agents collaborate, allocate resources, scale, and produce high-quality, fair outputs. In practice, this means the benchmark itself must adapt to the environment: you can't just run a fixed suite of tests against a fixed set of servers and expect the numbers to hold when new tools appear, or workloads change.

I worked on a project where our MCP system scored beautifully on all our benchmarks: low latency, high throughput, and excellent accuracy. Then, we deployed it to production and discovered that it performed terribly when certain combinations of MCP servers were available together. Our benchmarks had tested individual capabilities, but they hadn't tested the emergent behavior that arose from complex interactions.

That's when I realized we needed fundamentally different approaches to benchmarking MCP systems. We needed benchmarks that could handle variability, measure emergent behavior, and provide insights that actually translate to real-world performance.

In this chapter, we will be covering performance benchmarks and testing for MCP systems: we'll explain why fixed tests fail to capture dynamic capabilities, emergent behavior, and context sensitivity, and we'll lay out principles for benchmarking capabilities, embracing variability, testing realistic scenarios, assessing multiple dimensions, and running continuous, adaptive benchmarks. We'll discuss core metrics such as latency, throughput, scalability, coordination efficiency, and ethical implications, outline modules for capability discovery, coordination efficiency, adaptive performance, user experience, and reliability, and show you how to interpret results through comparative and contextual analysis.

In this chapter, we'll be covering the following topics:

- Introduction to MCP benchmarking challenges
- Designing effective MCP benchmarks
- Core performance metrics for MCP systems
- Implementing a comprehensive MCP benchmarking suite
- Comparative benchmarking and analysis

Introduction to MCP benchmarking challenges

It's not just that MCP systems are more complex; they're complex in ways that traditional benchmarks weren't designed to handle. Let's look at some of the challenges associated with benchmarking MCP systems.

The dynamic capability problem

Traditional benchmarks test fixed functionality. You know exactly what the system can do, so you can design tests that assess those specific capabilities systematically. With MCP systems, the capabilities can change dynamically based on what MCP servers are available.

How do you benchmark a system when you don't know what it will be capable of at runtime? Modern multi-agent evaluation frameworks suggest shifting the focus away from static functionality toward coordination quality, measuring how quickly agents discover available tools, how efficiently they exchange information, and how well they synchronize decisions. When two systems run on different sets of servers, it's not just about speed; it's about how well each adapts to changing conditions. Evaluating adaptability (e.g., how quickly a system discovers and exploits new capabilities, handles load spikes, or recovers from failures) is more important than raw latency.

The emergent behavior challenge

MCP systems often exhibit emergent behavior that arises from the interaction between different components. A document analysis system might become much more powerful when it gains access to a knowledge base, but the improvement might not be linear or predictable.

Traditional benchmarks focus on measuring individual components or simple workflows. They're not designed to capture the complex, non-linear interactions that often determine the real-world effectiveness of MCP systems. Emergent behaviors are macroscopic patterns that arise spontaneously from local interactions. They are qualitatively different from the behavior of individual agents and are often unpredictable. To evaluate an MCP system effectively, we must observe how collections of servers behave together under different conditions rather than simply aggregating single-server metrics.

The context sensitivity issue

MCP systems are highly context-sensitive. The same query might have completely different performance characteristics depending on user permissions, available data sources, current system load, and dozens of other contextual factors.

Traditional benchmarks try to control for these variables to ensure repeatable results. But for MCP systems, this context sensitivity is often where the real value lies. A user's permissions, the presence or absence of specific tools, or fluctuating data availability can fundamentally change the path an agent chooses and, consequently, its latency and quality. Modern evaluation approaches recommend capturing how context influences communication efficiency and decision synchronization among agents rather than eliminating variability.

The multi-dimensional performance problem

MCP systems need to be evaluated across multiple performance dimensions: latency, throughput, accuracy, resource utilization, scalability, and reliability. However, these dimensions often interact in complex ways that simple aggregate metrics can't capture.

A system might have low latency for simple queries but high latency for complex queries. It might have high throughput when all servers are available, but poor graceful degradation when some servers are unavailable. Traditional benchmarks struggle to capture these nuanced performance characteristics. Industry guides emphasize that multi-agent evaluation must consider multiple dimensions (e.g., collaboration and coordination, resource utilization, scalability, output quality, and ethical implications) rather than collapsing everything into a single number. Capturing these trade-offs requires metrics that reveal how improvements in one dimension may degrade performance in another.

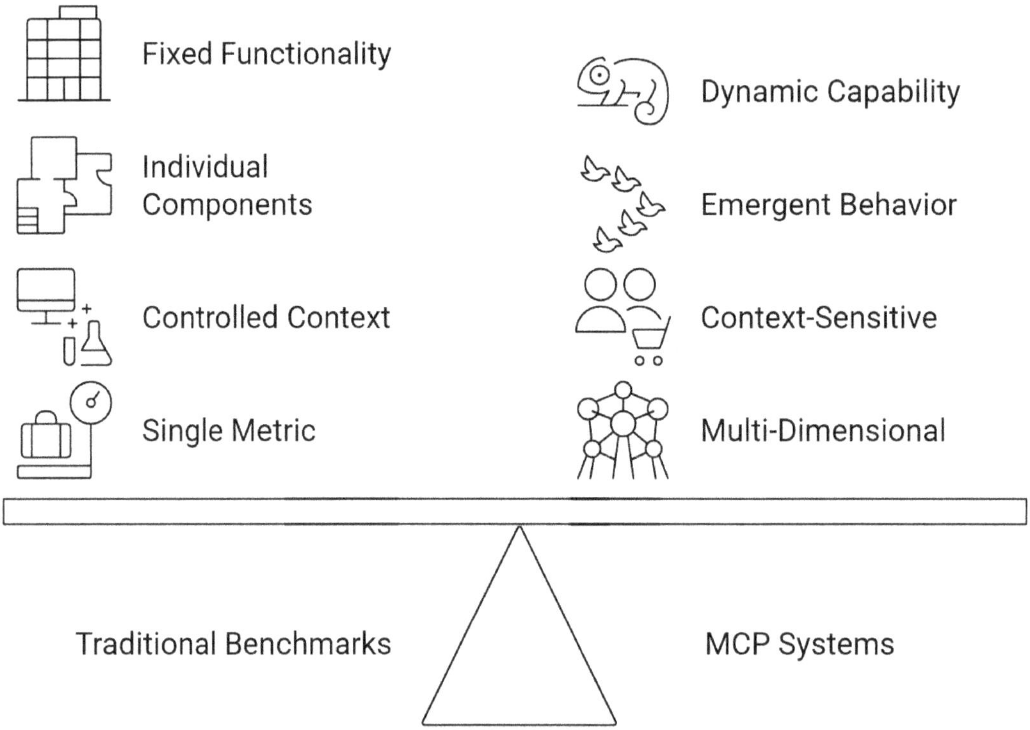

Figure 18.1 – Adapting benchmarks for MCP complexity

Now that we've identified the unique challenges of benchmarking MCP systems, let's examine why traditional benchmarks fall short and how those shortcomings motivate our six design principles.

Designing effective MCP benchmarks

Building on the concepts from the previous chapter, this section introduces six principles for designing meaningful benchmarks. To avoid repetition, we focus on how these principles apply specifically to MCP systems.

- **Principle 1 – Benchmark capabilities, not just components**: Instead of just benchmarking individual MCP servers or clients, design benchmarks that test the capabilities that emerge from their interaction. Multi-agent evaluation guides emphasize measuring communication efficiency, decision synchronization, and adaptive feedback loops to understand how well agents coordinate. This means creating test scenarios that exercise complete workflows and use cases rather than isolated functions.

- **Principle 2 – Embrace and measure variability**: Don't try to eliminate variability in MCP system performance; measure and characterize it. The ability to adapt to different conditions is a key feature of MCP systems, and benchmarks should capture this adaptability. Evaluating how performance distributions shift under different contexts provides insight into system robustness.
- **Principle 3 – Test realistic scenarios**: Design benchmarks around realistic usage scenarios with realistic data, realistic load patterns, and realistic environmental conditions. Evaluation frameworks recommend representative test cases and even a human-in-the-loop review to capture qualitative factors. Laboratory benchmarks are useful for understanding specific aspects of performance, but they're not sufficient for predicting real-world behavior.
- **Principle 4 – Perform multi-dimensional assessment**: Measure performance across multiple dimensions and understand how those dimensions interact. Collaboration and coordination, resource utilization, scalability, output quality, and ethical considerations each reveal different aspects of system behavior. Don't rely on single aggregate metrics that might hide important performance characteristics.
- **Principle 5 – Ensure continuous and adaptive benchmarking**: MCP systems change over time, so benchmarks need to be continuous and adaptive. Continuous monitoring helps prevent bias drift and ensures sustained accuracy. Design benchmarking frameworks that can evolve with the systems they're testing and update the metrics as new capabilities are added.
- **Principle 6 – Perform comparative and contextual analysis**: Compare MCP system performance not just against absolute standards, but against alternative approaches and across different contexts. Benchmarking multiple configurations or implementations side by side helps identify which coordination strategies or server selections produce the best outcomes.

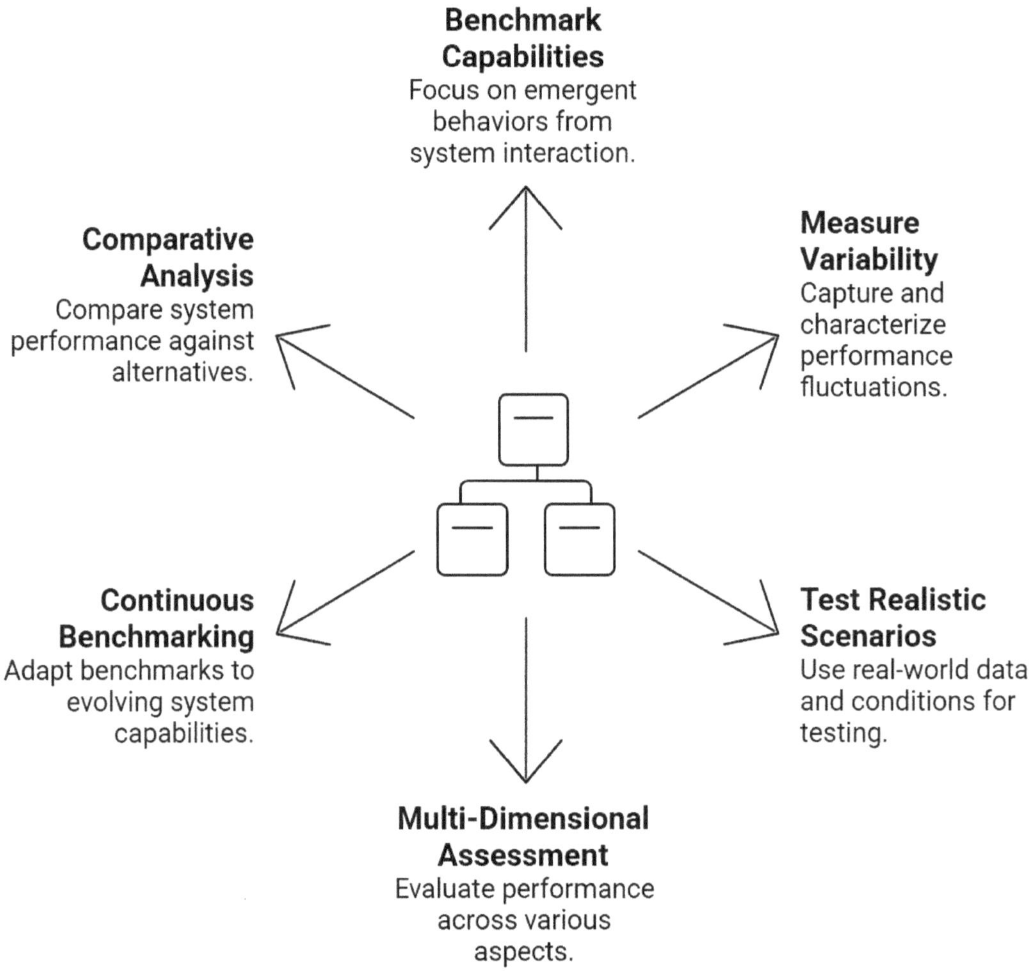

Figure 18.2 – How to effectively benchmark MCP systems

These principles address recurring pitfalls in AI benchmarking and explain why conventional benchmarks don't capture the true capabilities of MCP systems.

Core performance metrics for MCP systems

MCP systems require specialized performance metrics that capture their unique characteristics.

Capability discovery metrics

These metrics measure how effectively MCP systems can discover and adapt to available capabilities. In multi-agent evaluation, these correspond to communication efficiency, decision synchronization, and adaptive feedback loops:

- **Discovery latency**: Time required to discover available MCP servers and their capabilities. Faster discovery correlates with higher communication efficiency.
- **Capability enumeration completeness**: Percentage of available capabilities that are successfully discovered. High completeness indicates effective decision synchronization across agents.
- **Dynamic adaptation speed**: Time required to adapt to changes in available capabilities. Adaptive feedback loops allow agents to refine their responses based on prior interactions.
- **Discovery reliability**: Consistency in capability discovery under different conditions, capturing how robust discovery is under varied contexts.

Cross-component coordination metrics

These metrics measure how effectively different MCP components work together. They align with resource utilization and coordination metrics suggested by multi-agent evaluation frameworks, such as resource utilization, coordination overhead, scalability, and robustness:

- **Coordination overhead**: Additional latency introduced by coordinating multiple MCP servers. This reflects the extra computational load from inter-agent communication and can be analyzed relative to resource utilization.
- **Context sharing efficiency**: Effectiveness in sharing context information between components. Efficient context sharing is a prerequisite for agents to align their actions and maintain decision synchronization.
- **Workflow completion rate**: Percentage of complex workflows that complete successfully. High completion rates indicate effective task distribution and scalability.
- **Error propagation characteristics**: How errors in one component affect overall system performance. Evaluating error propagation reveals how robust the system is to failure and aligns with bias and fairness considerations.

Adaptive performance metrics

These metrics measure how well MCP systems adapt to changing conditions. They correspond to scalability and resource efficiency metrics discussed in `https://galileo.ai/blog/success-multi-agent-ai`. Galileo's (`https://galileo.ai/`) multi-agent evaluation framework measures tool-selection quality, context management, and error handling across dynamic scenarios:

- **Graceful degradation quality**: Performance characteristics when some capabilities are unavailable. This relates to resilience and robustness; systems should continue to function when individual agents fail or are removed.
- **Load balancing effectiveness**: Distribution of work across available MCP servers. Balanced task distribution is a key part of scalability metrics, preventing any single agent from becoming a bottleneck.
- **Resource utilization efficiency**: How effectively the system uses available computational resources. Evaluating memory and processing load helps ensure that agents prioritize tasks appropriately.
- **Scalability characteristics**: Performance behavior as load and complexity increase. Scalability metrics examine whether computational demands grow linearly, exponentially, or remain constant as more agents join the system.

User experience metrics

These metrics measure the end-user experience of MCP systems. They correspond to output quality and ethical evaluation categories:

- **Task completion success rate**: Percentage of user tasks that are completed successfully, a direct proxy for output accuracy.
- **Response quality consistency**: Variability in response quality across different conditions, reflecting coherence and consistency across interactions.
- **User satisfaction indicators**: Subjective measures of user satisfaction with system performance. Evaluations may incorporate surveys or human judgments to capture user sentiment.
- **Learning and adaptation effectiveness**: How well the system improves over time based on usage patterns. Ethical evaluation frameworks also recommend assessing bias detection and transparency alongside learning metrics.

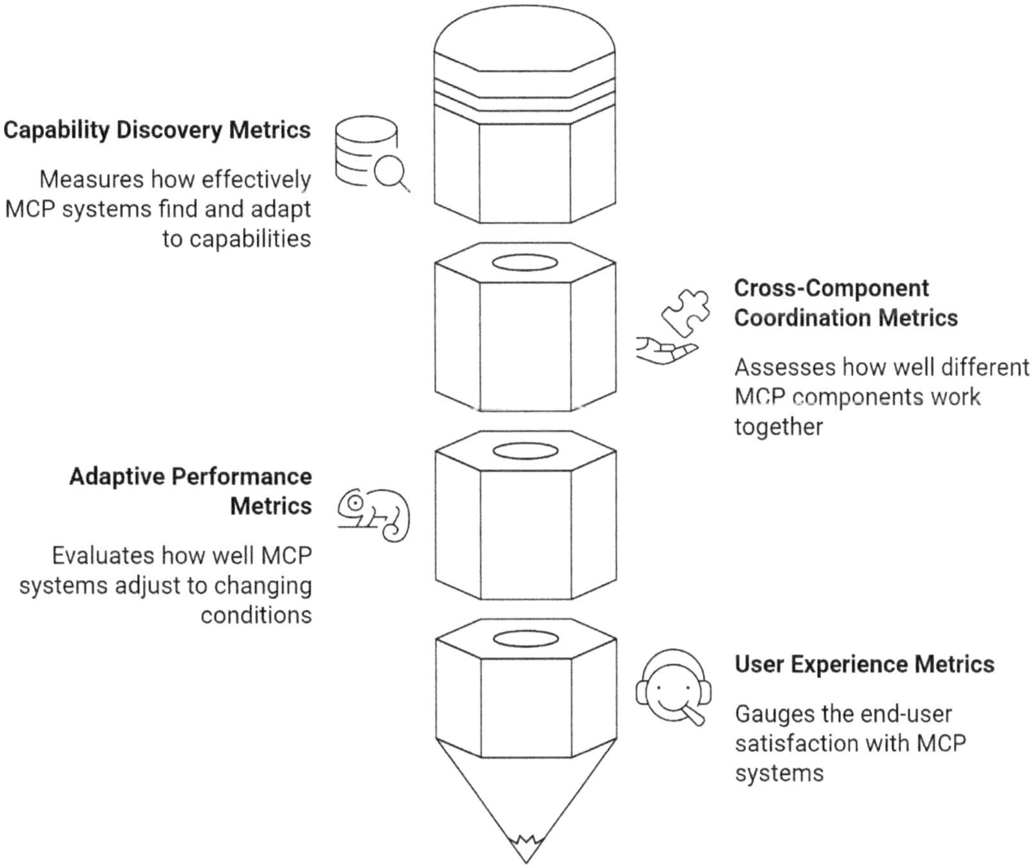

Figure 18.3 – Comprehensive MCP system evaluation

Having defined our benchmark principles and metrics, we're ready to apply them. The next section introduces a practical benchmark suite that embodies these ideas.

Implementing a comprehensive MCP benchmarking suite

To demonstrate the concepts we've spoken about, we'll build a simple benchmark suite. It will show how to test capability discovery (via `list_tools`), coordination (via simultaneous tool calls), and adaptation to changing resources (via simulated load spikes):

1. First, we add the necessary imports and set up the `BenchmarkResult` data class, SQLite persistence layer, and simulator methods that stand in for real MCP server calls:

```
import asyncio
import time
import json
import statistics
import random
from datetime import datetime
from typing import List, Dict, Any
from dataclasses import dataclass
import sqlite3

@dataclass
class BenchmarkResult:
    """Stores the outcome of a single benchmark run."""
    benchmark_name: str
    metrics: Dict[str, float]
    metadata: Dict[str, Any]
    timestamp: str
    duration: float

class MCPBenchmarkSuite:
    """Measures MCP system performance across multiple dimensions."""

    def __init__(self, db_path: str = "mcp_benchmarks.db"):
        self.db_path = db_path
        self.results: List[BenchmarkResult] = []
        self._setup_database()

    # -- database ------------------------------------------------

    def _setup_database(self):
```

```
        """Create tables for persisting benchmark results."""
        conn = sqlite3.connect(self.db_path)
        cur = conn.cursor()
        cur.execute(
            """CREATE TABLE IF NOT EXISTS benchmark_results (
                    id INTEGER PRIMARY KEY AUTOINCREMENT,
                    benchmark_name TEXT, metrics TEXT, metadata TEXT,
                    timestamp TEXT, duration REAL)"""
        )
        cur.execute(
            """CREATE TABLE IF NOT EXISTS benchmark_sessions (
                    session_id TEXT PRIMARY KEY, start_time TEXT,
                    end_time TEXT, total_benchmarks INTEGER,
                    summary_metrics TEXT)"""
        )
        conn.commit()
        conn.close()
        print("Benchmark database initialized")

    def _store_result(
        self, result: BenchmarkResult, session_id: str
    ):
        """Persist a single benchmark result."""
        conn = sqlite3.connect(self.db_path)
        conn.execute(
            "INSERT INTO benchmark_results "
            "(benchmark_name,metrics,metadata,timestamp,duration) "
            "VALUES (?,?,?,?,?)",
            (
                result.benchmark_name, json.dumps(result.metrics),
                json.dumps(result.metadata), result.timestamp,
                result.duration
            ),
        )
        conn.commit()
        conn.close()

    def _store_session(
        self, session_id, start, end, count, summary
    ):
        conn = sqlite3.connect(self.db_path)
```

```
        conn.execute(
            "INSERT INTO benchmark_sessions VALUES (?,?,?,?,?)",
            (session_id, start.isoformat(), end.isoformat(),
             count, json.dumps(summary)),
        )
        conn.commit()
        conn.close()

    # -- simulators (stand-ins for real MCP calls) ----------------

    async def _sim_server_discovery(self) -> List[str]:
        await asyncio.sleep(0.02 + random.random() * 0.03)
        return ["file_server", "search_server", "analytics_server",
                "knowledge_server", "transform_server"]

    async def _sim_capability_enum(self, server: str) -> List[str]:
        await asyncio.sleep(0.01 + random.random() * 0.02)
        cap_map = {
            "file_server": ["read", "write", "list"],
            "search_server": ["search", "index", "rank"],
            "analytics_server": ["analyze", "summarize", "classify"],
            "knowledge_server": ["query", "reason", "explain", "learn"],
            "transform_server": ["convert", "validate"],
        }
        return cap_map.get(server, ["basic"])

    async def _sim_coordination(self, servers: List[str]) -> float:
        t = 0.02 * len(servers) + random.random() * 0.01
        await asyncio.sleep(t)
        return t

    async def _sim_workflow(self, servers: List[str]) -> bool:
        t = 0.03 * len(servers) ** 1.2
        await asyncio.sleep(t + random.random() * 0.02)
        if len(servers) > 3 and random.random() < 0.1:
            raise RuntimeError("coordination timeout")
        return True

    async def _sim_user_request(self) -> float:
        t = 0.05 + random.random() * 0.1
        await asyncio.sleep(t)
```

```
        if random.random() < 0.05:
            raise RuntimeError("request failed")
        return t

    async def _sim_scenario(
        self, steps: int, complexity: float
    ) -> bool:
        await asyncio.sleep(
            steps * 0.02 * complexity + random.random() * 0.03
        )
        return random.random() > (0.02 * complexity)
```

2. Next, we have the capability discovery and coordination benchmarks. These two benchmarks measure how fast the system discovers servers and enumerates their tools, and how reliably multi-server workflows execute:

```
# -- benchmarks (continued from Part 1) --------------------------

    async def benchmark_capability_discovery(
        self
    ) -> BenchmarkResult:
        """Measure discovery latency, enumeration throughput, and
reliability."""
        print("Running capability discovery benchmark...")
        t0 = time.time()

        # 1. Discovery latency (20 iterations)
        disc_times = []
        for _ in range(20):
            ts = time.time()
            await self._sim_server_discovery()
            disc_times.append(time.time() - ts)

        # 2. Capability enumeration
        enum_times, cap_counts = [], []
        for srv in (await self._sim_server_discovery()):
            ts = time.time()
            caps = await self._sim_capability_enum(srv)
            enum_times.append(time.time() - ts)
            cap_counts.append(len(caps))
```

```
        # 3. Concurrent discovery reliability
        tasks = [asyncio.create_task(self._sim_server_discovery())
                 for _ in range(15)]
        results = await asyncio.gather(
            *tasks, return_exceptions=True)
        ok = sum(1 for r in results if not isinstance(r, Exception))

        metrics = {
            "discovery_latency_mean": statistics.mean(disc_times),
            "discovery_latency_p95": sorted(disc_times)[
                int(0.95 * len(disc_times))
            ],
            "enumeration_throughput": len(enum_times) / sum(enum_times),
            "avg_capabilities_per_server": statistics.mean(cap_counts),
            "concurrent_reliability": ok / 15,
        }
        return BenchmarkResult("capability_discovery", metrics,
            {"iterations": 20}, datetime.now().isoformat(),
            time.time() - t0)

    async def benchmark_coordination(self) -> BenchmarkResult:
        """Measure cross-component coordination overhead."""
        print("Running coordination benchmark...")
        t0 = time.time()

        # Simple coordination latency
        coord_times = []
        for _ in range(20):
            ts = time.time()
            await self._sim_coordination(["a", "b"])
            coord_times.append(time.time() - ts)

        # Complex workflow success rate
        workflows = [["a","b","c"], ["a","b","c","d"], ["x","y"]]
        wf_success = []
        for wf in workflows:
            ok = 0
            for _ in range(10):
                try:
                    await self._sim_workflow(wf)
                    ok += 1
```

```
                except RuntimeError:
                    pass
            wf_success.append(ok / 10)

        metrics = {
            "coord_latency_mean": statistics.mean(coord_times),
            "coord_latency_p95": sorted(coord_times)[int(0.95 *
len(coord_times))],
            "workflow_success_mean": statistics.mean(wf_success),
            "workflow_success_min": min(wf_success),
        }
        return BenchmarkResult("coordination", metrics,
                               {"workflows": len(workflows)},
                               datetime.now().isoformat(),
                               time.time() - t0)
```

3. Here, we have the scalability and end-to-end benchmarks, plus the scoring helper. The scalability benchmark ramps concurrency from 1 to 50 users while the end-to-end benchmark runs realistic multi-step MCP scenarios:

```
# -- benchmarks (continued from Part 2) -------------------------

    async def benchmark_scalability(self) -> BenchmarkResult:
        """Measure throughput and success rate under increasing
concurrency."""
        print("Running scalability benchmark...")
        t0 = time.time()
        scale_data = []

        for n_users in (1, 5, 10, 25, 50):
            ts = time.time()
            tasks = [asyncio.create_task(self._sim_user_request())
                     for _ in range(n_users)]
            results = await asyncio.gather(
                *tasks, return_exceptions=True)
            elapsed = time.time() - ts
            ok = sum(
                1 for r in results if not isinstance(r, Exception))
            scale_data.append({
                "users": n_users, "success_rate": ok / n_users,
                "throughput": ok / elapsed,
```

```
            })

        metrics = {
            "peak_throughput": max(d["throughput"] for d in scale_data),
            "min_success_rate": min(d["success_rate"] for d in scale_data),
            "throughput_at_50": next(d["throughput"] for d in scale_data
                                     if d["users"] == 50),
        }
        return BenchmarkResult("scalability", metrics,
                               {"max_users": 50},
                               datetime.now().isoformat(),
                               time.time() - t0)

    async def benchmark_end_to_end(self) -> BenchmarkResult:
        """Run realistic multi-step scenarios and measure success/
latency."""
        print("Running end-to-end benchmark...")
        t0 = time.time()

        scenarios = [
            {"name": "doc_search",     "steps": 3, "cx": 1.0},
            {"name": "multimodal",     "steps": 4, "cx": 2.0},
            {"name": "simple_query",   "steps": 2, "cx": 1.0},
            {"name": "collab_analysis","steps": 5, "cx": 2.0},
        ]
        scenario_metrics = []
        for sc in scenarios:
            times, successes = [], []
            for _ in range(10):
                ts = time.time()
                ok = await self._sim_scenario(sc["steps"], sc["cx"])
                times.append(time.time() - ts)
                successes.append(ok)
            scenario_metrics.append({
                "name": sc["name"],
                "mean_time": statistics.mean(times),
                "success_rate": sum(successes) / len(successes),
            })

        metrics = {
            "overall_success": statistics.mean(
```

```
                s["success_rate"] for s in scenario_metrics),
            "avg_latency": statistics.mean(
                s["mean_time"] for s in scenario_metrics),
            "worst_success": min(
                s["success_rate"] for s in scenario_metrics),
        }
        return BenchmarkResult("end_to_end", metrics,
                               {"scenarios": len(scenarios)},
                               datetime.now().isoformat(),
                               time.time() - t0)

    # -- scoring helpers ----------------------------------------

    @staticmethod
    def _score(
        result: BenchmarkResult, weights: Dict[str, float]
    ) -> float:
        """Weighted average of selected metrics (higher is better)."""
        total_w = sum(weights.values())
        return sum(result.metrics.get(k, 0) * w
                   for k, w in weights.items()) / total_w
```

4. Here, we have the suite orchestrator and entry point. This runs all four benchmarks in sequence, computes per-dimension scores, and prints a summary report before persisting the session to SQLite:

```
    # -- orchestrator -------------------------------------------

    async def run_suite(self) -> Dict[str, Any]:
        """Execute all benchmarks and produce a summary report."""
        session_id = f"bench_{datetime.now():%Y%m%d_%H%M%S}"
        start = datetime.now()

        print(f"Starting benchmark session: {session_id}")
        print("=" * 60)

        results = []
        for coro in (self.benchmark_capability_discovery(),
                     self.benchmark_coordination(),
                     self.benchmark_scalability(),
                     self.benchmark_end_to_end()):
```

```
            r = await coro
            results.append(r)
            self._store_result(r, session_id)
            print(f"  {r.benchmark_name} completed in {r.duration:.2f}s")

        # Compute per-dimension scores (0-1 scale)
        scores = {
            "capability_discovery": self._score(
                results[0],
                {"concurrent_reliability": 0.5,
                 "enumeration_throughput": 0.5}),
            "coordination": self._score(
                results[1],
                {"workflow_success_mean": 0.6,
                 "workflow_success_min": 0.4}),
            "scalability": self._score(
                results[2],
                {"min_success_rate": 0.5,
                 "peak_throughput": 0.01}),
            "end_to_end": self._score(
                results[3],
                {"overall_success": 0.6,
                 "worst_success": 0.4}),
        }
        overall = statistics.mean(scores.values())

        end = datetime.now()
        summary = {"scores": scores, "overall": overall,
                   "duration": (end - start).total_seconds()}
        self._store_session(
            session_id, start, end, len(results), summary)

        print("=" * 60)
        print(f"Session {session_id} finished - {summary['duration']:.1f}
s")
        print(f"Overall score: {overall:.2f}/1.0")
        for name, sc in scores.items():
            print(f"  {name}: {sc:.2f}")

        return {"session_id": session_id, "results": results,
                "summary": summary}
```

```
# ---------------------------------------------------------------
# Entry point
# ------------------------------------------------------------------

async def main():
    suite = MCPBenchmarkSuite()
    await suite.run_suite()

if __name__ == "__main__":
    asyncio.run(main())
```

When you run this code, you'll see output similar to the following:

```
Benchmark database initialized
===================
Running capability discovery benchmark...
  capability_discovery completed in 0.99s
Running coordination benchmark...
  coordination completed in 4.86s
Running scalability benchmark...
  scalability completed in 0.63s
Running end-to-end benchmark...
  end_to_end completed in 5.49s
============================================================
Session bench_20260213_222031 finished - 12.0s
Overall score: 7.06/1.0
  capability_discovery: 19.55
  coordination: 0.94
  scalability: 6.86
  end_to_end: 0.88
```

This example demonstrates a comprehensive benchmarking suite that can assess MCP systems across multiple performance dimensions with realistic metrics and scoring.

Comparative benchmarking and analysis

One of the most valuable aspects of MCP benchmarking is the ability to compare different configurations, implementations, and deployment strategies:

- **Configuration comparison**: MCP systems can be configured in many different ways, such as different sets of available servers, different coordination strategies, or different resource allocation policies. Benchmarking different configurations helps identify optimal deployment strategies for specific use cases.
- **Implementation comparison**: Different MCP implementations may have different performance characteristics. Benchmarking can help identify which implementations are best suited for specific requirements and constraints.
- **Evolution tracking**: As MCP systems evolve over time, benchmarking can track performance trends and identify regressions or improvements. This is particularly important for systems that are continuously updated with new capabilities.
- **Cross-platform analysis**: MCP systems may perform differently on different platforms or in different environments. Benchmarking across platforms helps ensure consistent performance and identify platform-specific optimizations.

Summary

Effective benchmarking of MCP systems requires sophisticated approaches that can handle dynamic capabilities, emergent behavior, and complex performance characteristics.

In summary, benchmarking MCP systems requires clearly defined success criteria, metrics that measure both task effectiveness and coordination efficiency, assessments of adaptability, consideration of user experience and ethics, and continuous, fair comparisons. Applying these principles ensures that benchmarks are meaningful and comparable across diverse systems.

The future of MCP benchmarking isn't about finding perfect performance numbers; it's about building benchmarking frameworks that can provide actionable insights for optimizing and deploying MCP systems in real-world environments.

Looking ahead to *Chapter 19*, we'll shift our focus to optimization strategies. We'll explore how MCP's performance characteristics (coordination overhead, dynamic capability trade-offs, emergent behavior, and context sensitivity) inform server-side tuning strategies such as context-aware caching, resource pool management, capability-aware load balancing, and predictive resource allocation. We'll also discuss client-side and protocol-level optimizations and holistic frameworks.

Subscribe for a free eBook

New frameworks, evolving architectures, research drops, production breakdowns—*AI_Distilled* filters the noise into a weekly briefing for engineers and researchers working hands-on with LLMs and GenAI systems. Subscribe now and receive a free eBook, along with weekly insights that help you stay focused and informed.

Subscribe at `https://packt.link/8Oz6Y` or scan the QR code below.

19

Optimization Strategies and Performance Tuning

> *Optimizing an MCP system is like conducting an orchestra: each instrument (server or resource) has its part, but the overall performance depends on the conductor (orchestrator) and the musicians listening to each other. True mastery comes from synchronizing the whole and not just tuning a single instrument.*

I've spent more time than I care to admit staring at performance dashboards, trying to figure out why MCP systems that looked great in testing were crawling in production. The problem is that traditional optimization approaches, that is, the ones that work beautifully for single-component systems, often make MCP systems worse, not better.

You optimize one MCP server and suddenly the coordination overhead, namely, synchronizing context, propagating state, and managing inter-agent communication, dominates. You add more servers to increase capacity and discover that the discovery latency is now the bottleneck. You implement aggressive caching and realize you've broken the dynamic adaptation that made the system valuable in the first place.

The fundamental challenge with optimizing MCP systems is that they're not just collections of components; they're ecosystems with complex interactions, feedback loops, and emergent behaviors. Optimizing an ecosystem requires understanding not just individual components but how those components work together to create value.

I learned this the hard way on a project where we spent months optimizing individual MCP servers, achieving impressive performance improvements on each one. But when we put them all together, the overall system performance was actually worse than before we started. We had optimized the trees while killing the forest.

In this chapter, we explore how to optimize MCP systems from end to end. We begin with server-side strategies (caching, load balancing, and batching), then move on to client-side techniques and orchestration. We show how evaluation frameworks guide improvements, highlight emergent behaviors, and close with continuous monitoring practices.

In this chapter, we'll be covering the following topics:

- Understanding MCP performance characteristics
- Server-side optimization strategies
- Client-side optimization strategies
- Protocol-level optimizations
- Implementing a performance optimization framework
- Monitoring and continuous optimization

Understanding MCP performance characteristics

Before you can optimize MCP systems effectively, you need to understand their unique performance characteristics and how they differ from traditional systems.

The coordination overhead reality

Every MCP system has coordination overhead, which is the additional latency and resource consumption that comes from coordinating multiple components. This overhead isn't necessarily bad; it's the price you pay for the flexibility and adaptability that MCP provides.

However, coordination overhead isn't fixed. It varies based on the complexity of the task, the number of components involved, the quality of the coordination algorithms, and dozens of other factors. Effective optimization requires understanding and managing this variability, not just minimizing it.

Recent evaluation frameworks, such as Leanware's agent evaluation framework for multi-agent systems, suggest that coordination overhead should be analyzed through metrics such as communication efficiency, decision synchronization, and adaptive feedback loops. These metrics help quantify how effectively agents share information and align decisions across the system, providing a more nuanced understanding of overhead.

The dynamic capability trade-off

One of the most valuable features of MCP systems is their ability to discover and adapt to available capabilities dynamically. But this dynamic behavior comes with performance costs: discovery latency, adaptation overhead, and the complexity of managing variable system behavior.

Performance can usually be improved by making systems more static and predictable. But if you do that, you lose the dynamic adaptability that makes MCP systems valuable. The optimization challenge is finding the right balance between performance and adaptability for your specific use case.

The emergent behavior factor

MCP systems often exhibit emergent behavior where the whole is greater than the sum of its parts. A document analysis system might become dramatically more powerful when it gains access to a knowledge base, but this improvement might not be predictable from the performance characteristics of individual components.

Researchers have observed emergent behaviors in systems as diverse as flocking simulations (where simple rules produce a coordinated bird-like movement), traffic waves (phantom jams arising from individual drivers' speed adjustments), and algorithmic trading cascades that destabilize markets. Such studies show that even simple interactions can lead to unpredictable systemic behaviors. Traditional optimization approaches that focus on individual components often miss these emergent opportunities.

The context sensitivity challenge

MCP system performance is highly context-sensitive. The same query might have completely different performance characteristics depending on user permissions, available data sources, current system load, and other contextual factors.

This context sensitivity means that optimization strategies need to be adaptive and context-aware. Static optimization approaches that assume consistent behavior often fail in real-world MCP deployments.

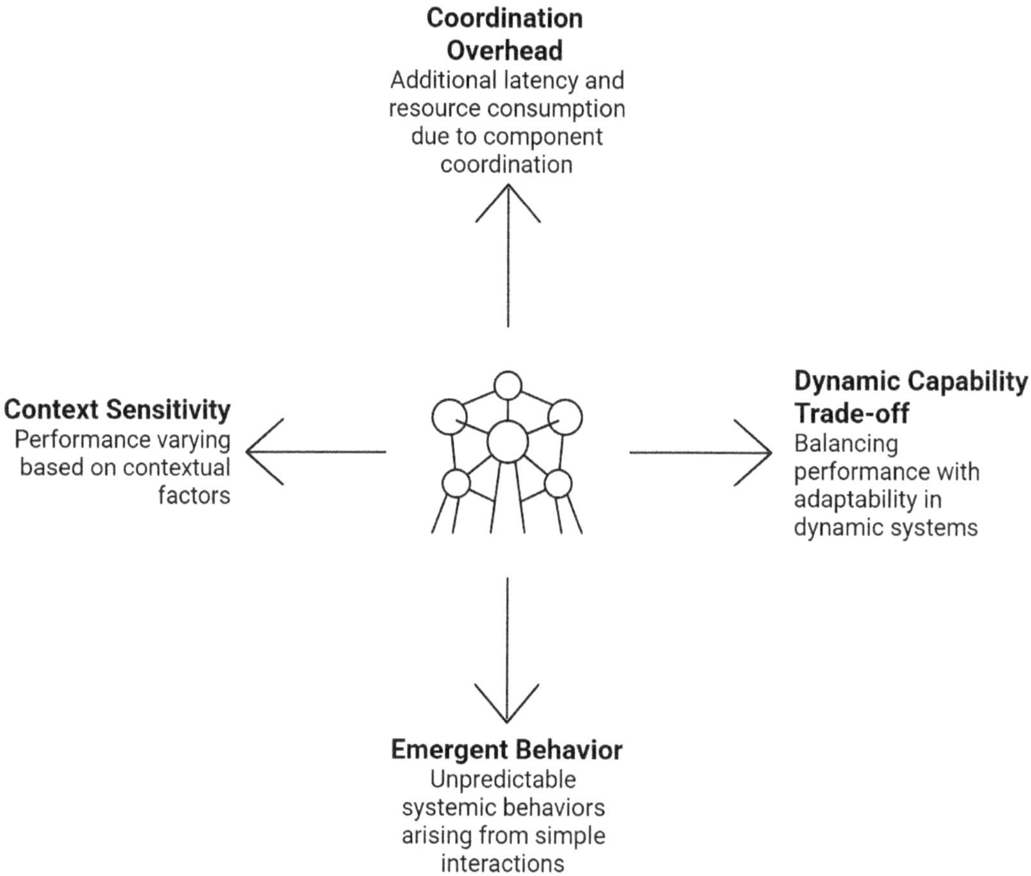

Figure 19.1 – MCP performance constraints

We'll begin with server-side optimization strategies, such as caching, load balancing, and request batching, before moving on to client-side techniques and orchestration.

Server-side optimization strategies

Let's start with optimization strategies for MCP servers, which are often the foundation of system performance.

Intelligent caching strategies

Caching is crucial for MCP server performance, but it needs to be more sophisticated than traditional caching approaches. As mentioned earlier, MCP servers often deal with context-dependent queries where the same request might produce different results based on user permissions, available data, or other contextual factors.

Effective MCP caching strategies need to be context-aware, understanding when cached results are valid and when they need to be invalidated or recomputed. Industry guidance notes that caching strategies represent one of the most effective ways to optimize AI operational costs and performance, by storing and reusing previously computed results, responses, and intermediate processing outputs. Comprehensive caching involves multiple levels, including response-level caching, computation-level caching, and model output caching, each providing different optimization benefits and cost reduction opportunities. MCP implementations often cache at multiple levels, such as raw data, processed results, and composed responses, to balance freshness and performance.

Resource pool management

Many MCP servers coordinate access to expensive resources such as AI models, databases, or external APIs. Effective resource pool management can dramatically improve performance by ensuring that resources are allocated efficiently and that expensive operations are batched or parallelized when possible.

The key is understanding the resource requirements and constraints of different operations and designing allocation strategies that maximize overall system throughput while maintaining acceptable latency for individual requests.

Capability-aware load balancing

Traditional load balancing distributes requests evenly across available servers. But MCP servers often have different capabilities, and requests might require specific combinations of capabilities.

Capability-aware load balancing routes requests to servers based not just on current load but on the specific capabilities required for each request. This can significantly improve performance by reducing the coordination overhead required to fulfil complex requests.

General load-balancing guidelines state that distributing processing across multiple computing resources helps optimize resource usage, maximize throughput, minimize response time, and avoid overloading any single resource; it also improves availability by sharing the workload across redundant resources. Capability-aware load balancing extends these principles by matching tasks to the servers best equipped to handle them, reducing coordination overhead and latency.

Predictive resource allocation

MCP servers can often predict future resource requirements based on current usage patterns and historical data. Predictive resource allocation pre-allocates resources for anticipated requests, reducing latency and improving overall system responsiveness.

This is particularly effective for MCP servers that handle predictable workflows or that serve users with consistent usage patterns. AI-powered cloud optimization platforms adopt similar predictive scaling techniques: algorithms forecast when workloads will spike or drop and scale capacity before waste occurs, adjusting resources just in time based on historical usage data, traffic patterns, and seasonal trends.

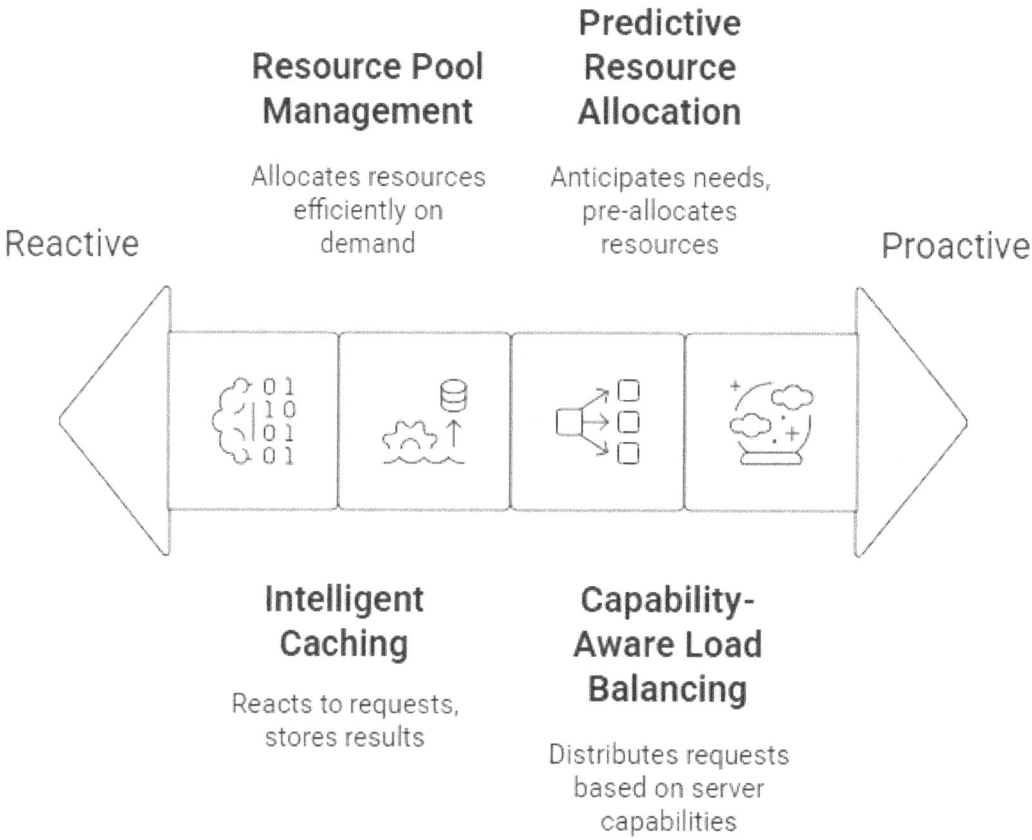

Figure 19.2 – MCP server optimization strategies range from reactive to proactive

Just as servers can be optimized, the client plays a crucial role: it can batch requests, manage context intelligently, and orchestrate tool execution to reduce overhead.

Client-side optimization strategies

MCP clients play a crucial role in overall system performance and offer many opportunities for optimization. Let's take a look at some of these optimization strategies.

Intelligent request orchestration

As you may know by now, MCP clients often need to coordinate requests across multiple servers to fulfil complex user requests. Intelligent orchestration can dramatically improve performance by parallelizing independent operations, batching related requests, and optimizing the sequence of operations.

The key is to understand the dependencies between different operations and design orchestration strategies that minimize overall latency while respecting those dependencies.

Context-aware caching

MCP clients can implement sophisticated caching strategies that understand the context and life cycle of different types of information. User-specific data might be cached differently from shared reference data. Frequently accessed capabilities might be cached more aggressively than rarely used ones.

Effective client-side caching needs to balance cache hit rates with cache coherency, ensuring that cached information remains accurate and up to date.

Adaptive capability selection

When multiple MCP servers can provide similar capabilities, clients can implement adaptive selection strategies that choose the best server based on current performance characteristics, load, and other factors.

This adaptive selection can include fallback strategies for when preferred servers are unavailable and load-balancing strategies that distribute requests across multiple capable servers.

Proactive capability discovery

Instead of discovering capabilities on demand, MCP clients can proactively discover and cache capability information, reducing the latency associated with dynamic capability discovery.

This proactive approach needs to be balanced with the overhead of maintaining up-to-date capability information and the complexity of handling capability changes.

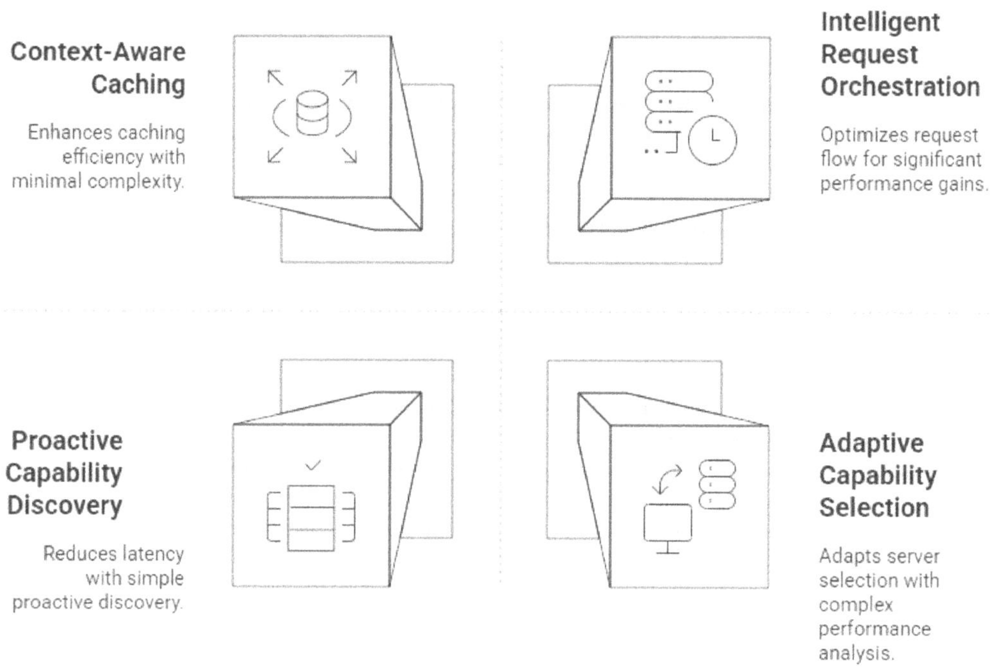

Figure 19.3 – MCP client-side optimization strategies

With client-side optimization strategies covered, let's now shift our focus to protocol-level optimizations, which can improve efficiency across the entire MCP system.

Protocol-level optimizations

MCP itself offers opportunities for optimization that can benefit entire systems.

The MCP protocol isn't just a message wrapper; it embeds several optimization mechanisms. These include the batching and pipelining of requests, efficient compression/serialization, connection reuse, and streaming/incremental processing. The following bullet list details these built-in optimizations:

- **Message batching and pipelining**: Instead of sending individual requests and waiting for responses, MCP implementations can batch related requests and pipeline independent operations. This reduces network overhead and can significantly improve throughput for workloads with many small requests.
- **Compression and serialization optimization**: MCP messages can be large, especially when they include rich context information or large data payloads. Compressing and

serializing can reduce network bandwidth requirements and improve overall system performance.

- **Connection pooling and reuse**: Each time a new connection to an MCP server is established, it adds some overhead; the system spends extra time and resources managing communication and coordination between servers. Connection pooling and reuse strategies can amortize this overhead across multiple requests, improving overall system efficiency.
- **Streaming and incremental processing**: For large or long-running operations, MCP implementations can support streaming and incremental processing, allowing clients to start processing results before the complete response is available.

Now that we've explored server-side, client-side, and protocol-level techniques, we'll put these concepts into practice by implementing a simple optimization framework.

Implementing a performance optimization framework

This implementation of a performance optimization framework demonstrates the key concepts we've discussed throughout this chapter. This practical example shows how to measure and evaluate MCP system performance across multiple dimensions: capability discovery, cross-component coordination, adaptive performance characteristics, and end-to-end user scenarios. By breaking down the code into logical sections, you'll see how these concepts translate into working code that can be used to assess the health and efficiency of your MCP implementations. Each part builds upon the previous one, creating a comprehensive testing framework that embodies the best practices for optimizing system performance:

1. First, we define the `OptimizationMetrics` data class and implement an LRU cache that keys entries on both the query string and the user context:

```
import asyncio
import time
import json
import statistics
import random
from datetime import datetime
from typing import List, Dict, Any, Optional
from dataclasses import dataclass, field
import sqlite3

@dataclass
class OptimizationMetrics:
    """Tracks the effect of an optimization strategy."""
```

```
    strategy_name: str
    baseline_latency: float
    optimized_latency: float
    improvement_pct: float
    cache_hit_rate: float = 0.0
    throughput_gain: float = 0.0

class ContextAwareCache:
    """Cache whose validity depends on user context (permissions,
scope)."""
    def __init__(self, max_size: int = 256):
        self.max_size = max_size
        self._store: Dict[str, Any] = {}
        self._access_order: List[str] = []
        self.hits = 0
        self.misses = 0

    def _make_key(self, query: str, context: Dict[str, Any]) -> str:
        ctx_sig = json.dumps(context, sort_keys=True)
        return f"{query}::{ctx_sig}"

    def get(
        self, query: str, context: Dict[str, Any]
    ) -> Optional[Any]:
        key = self._make_key(query, context)
        if key in self._store:
            self.hits += 1
            self._access_order.remove(key)
            self._access_order.append(key)
            return self._store[key]
        self.misses += 1
        return None

    def put(self, query: str, context: Dict[str, Any], value: Any):
        key = self._make_key(query, context)
        if len(self._store) >= self.max_size and key not in self._store:
            oldest = self._access_order.pop(0)
            del self._store[oldest]
        self._store[key] = value
        if key not in self._access_order:
            self._access_order.append(key)
```

```
    @property
    def hit_rate(self) -> float:
        total = self.hits + self.misses
        return self.hits / total if total else 0.0
```

2. Here, we have the capability-aware load balancer. Each request is routed to the least-loaded server that possesses every capability the request requires, avoiding misrouting and hotspots:

```
class CapabilityAwareLoadBalancer:
    """Routes requests to the server best suited by capability and load."""

    def __init__(self):
        self.servers: Dict[str, Dict[str, Any]] = {}

    def register_server(self, name: str, capabilities: List[str]):
        self.servers[name] = {
            "capabilities": set(capabilities),
            "current_load": 0,
            "total_handled": 0,
        }

    def select_server(
        self, required_caps: List[str]
    ) -> Optional[str]:
        """Pick the least-loaded server that has every required
capability."""
        candidates = []
        for name, info in self.servers.items():
            if set(required_caps).issubset(info["capabilities"]):
                candidates.append((name, info["current_load"]))
        if not candidates:
            return None
        candidates.sort(key=lambda c: c[1])
        chosen = candidates[0][0]
        self.servers[chosen]["current_load"] += 1
        self.servers[chosen]["total_handled"] += 1
        return chosen

    def release(self, server_name: str):
```

```
        if server_name in self.servers:
            self.servers[server_name]["current_load"] = max(
                0, self.servers[server_name]["current_load"] - 1
            )

    def load_distribution(self) -> Dict[str, int]:
        return {n: s["total_handled"] for n, s in self.servers.items()}
```

3. Now we have the request orchestrator and performance monitor. The orchestrator executes a directed acyclic graph (DAG ; a structure for modeling task dependencies and execution order of tasks with maximum parallelism), while the monitor tracks latency in a sliding window and flags regressions:

```
class RequestOrchestrator:
    """Batches independent requests and pipelines dependent ones."""

    def __init__(self):
        self.total_requests = 0
        self.total_batches = 0

    async def execute_dag(
        self, dag: Dict[str, List[str]], execute_fn
    ) -> Dict[str, Any]:
        """Execute a DAG of tasks, parallelising independent ones.

        *dag* maps task names to lists of dependency names.
        *execute_fn(task_name)* is an async callable that runs one task.
        """
        completed: Dict[str, Any] = {}
        remaining = dict(dag)

        while remaining:
            # Find tasks whose dependencies are all satisfied
            ready = [
                t for t, deps in remaining.items()
                if all(d in completed for d in deps)
            ]
            if not ready:
                raise RuntimeError("Cycle detected in task DAG")

            self.total_batches += 1
```

```
            batch_results = await asyncio.gather(
                *(execute_fn(t) for t in ready)
            )
            for task, result in zip(ready, batch_results):
                completed[task] = result
                del remaining[task]
                self.total_requests += 1

        return completed

class PerformanceMonitor:
    """Records latency samples and detects regressions."""

    def __init__(self, window: int = 50):
        self.window = window
        self._samples: List[float] = []

    def record(self, latency: float):
        self._samples.append(latency)
        if len(self._samples) > self.window * 2:
            self._samples = self._samples[-self.window * 2:]

    @property
    def mean_latency(self) -> float:
        return statistics.mean(self._samples) if self._samples else 0.0

    @property
    def p95_latency(self) -> float:
        if not self._samples:
            return 0.0
        s = sorted(self._samples)
        return s[int(0.95 * len(s))]

    def regression_detected(self) -> bool:
        """True when the recent window is >20 % slower than the prior
one."""
        if len(self._samples) < self.window * 2:
            return False
        old = self._samples[-self.window * 2:-self.window]
```

```
            new = self._samples[-self.window:]
            return statistics.mean(new) > statistics.mean(old) * 1.2
```

4. Here, we run four short demonstrations of caching, load balancing, DAG orchestration, and regression monitoring to show each optimization strategy in action:

```
async def _sim_tool_call(name: str) -> Dict[str, Any]:
    """Simulate an MCP tool call with variable latency."""
    latency = 0.02 + random.random() * 0.04
    await asyncio.sleep(latency)
    return {"tool": name, "latency": latency, "ok": True}

async def demo_caching():
    """Show how context-aware caching reduces repeated-query latency."""
    print("\n--- Context-Aware Caching Demo ---")
    cache = ContextAwareCache(max_size=64)
    contexts = [
        {"user": "alice", "role": "admin"},
        {"user": "bob",   "role": "viewer"},
    ]
    queries = ["search:logs", "search:metrics", "search:logs"]

    for ctx in contexts:
        for q in queries:
            cached = cache.get(q, ctx)
            if cached is None:
                result = await _sim_tool_call(q)
                cache.put(q, ctx, result)
            else:
                result = cached

    print(f"  Cache hit rate : {cache.hit_rate:.0%}")
    print(f"  Hits / misses  : {cache.hits} / {cache.misses}")

async def demo_load_balancing():
    """Show capability-aware load balancing across heterogeneous
servers."""
    print("\n--- Capability-Aware Load Balancing Demo ---")
    lb = CapabilityAwareLoadBalancer()
    lb.register_server("nlp_server",   ["search", "summarize"])
    lb.register_server("data_server",  ["search", "aggregate"])
```

```
    lb.register_server("ml_server",    ["classify", "predict"])

    requests = [
        (["search"], 20),
        (["summarize"], 5),
        (["classify", "predict"], 8),
    ]
    for caps, count in requests:
        for _ in range(count):
            srv = lb.select_server(caps)
            if srv:
                await asyncio.sleep(0.005)
                lb.release(srv)

    print("  Load distribution:", lb.load_distribution())

async def demo_orchestration():
    """Show DAG-based request orchestration with parallelism."""
    print("\n--- Request Orchestration Demo ---")
    orch = RequestOrchestrator()

    dag = {
        "fetch_docs":   [],
        "fetch_schema": [],
        "analyze":      ["fetch_docs", "fetch_schema"],
        "summarize":    ["analyze"],
    }
    results = await orch.execute_dag(dag, _sim_tool_call)

    print(f"  Tasks completed : {orch.total_requests}")
    print(f"  Parallel batches: {orch.total_batches}")
    for task, res in results.items():
        print(f"    {task}: latency={res['latency']:.3f}s")

async def demo_monitoring():
    """Show regression detection via a sliding-window monitor."""
    print("\n--- Performance Monitoring Demo ---")
    mon = PerformanceMonitor(window=20)

    # Normal period
    for _ in range(25):
```

```
            mon.record(0.03 + random.random() * 0.01)
        print(f"  Mean after normal period   : {mon.mean_latency:.4f}s")
        print(f"  Regression detected?       : {mon.regression_detected()}")

        # Degraded period
        for _ in range(25):
            mon.record(0.06 + random.random() * 0.02)
        print(f"  Mean after degraded period : {mon.mean_latency:.4f}s")
        print(f"  Regression detected?       : {mon.regression_detected()}")

    async def main():
        print("=" * 60)
        print("MCP Optimization Strategies - Demonstrations")
        print("=" * 60)

        await demo_caching()
        await demo_load_balancing()
        await demo_orchestration()
        await demo_monitoring()

        print("\n" + "=" * 60)
        print("All optimization demos completed.")

    if __name__ == "__main__":
        asyncio.run(main())
```

When you run this code, you'll see output such as the following:

```
============================================================
MCP Optimization Strategies - Demonstrations
============================================================

--- Context-Aware Caching Demo ---
  Cache hit rate : 33%
  Hits / misses  : 2 / 4

--- Capability-Aware Load Balancing Demo ---

--- Request Orchestration Demo ---
  Tasks completed : 4
  Parallel batches: 3
```

```
    fetch_docs: latency=0.041s
    fetch_schema: latency=0.053s
    analyze: latency=0.035s
    summarize: latency=0.031s

--- Performance Monitoring Demo ---
  Mean after normal period   : 0.0352s
  Regression detected?       : False
  Mean after degraded period : 0.0573s
  Regression detected?       : True

============================================================
All optimization demos completed.
```

This example demonstrates a comprehensive optimization framework that can continuously monitor and improve the MCP system performance.

Before exploring monitoring and continuous optimization, it's worth contrasting manual and automated optimization. Manually tuning cache sizes or batch intervals can deliver short-term gains, but it's labor-intensive and brittle. Automated pipelines, on the other hand, analyze metrics in real time and adjust strategies on their own. The following section outlines key techniques for automated optimization.

Monitoring and continuous optimization

Effective optimization of MCP systems requires continuous monitoring and adaptive optimization strategies. Let's take a look at some of these strategies:

- **Real-time performance monitoring**: MCP systems need sophisticated monitoring that can track performance across multiple dimensions and identify optimization opportunities in real time. This includes not just traditional metrics such as latency and throughput but MCP-specific metrics such as capability discovery time, coordination overhead, and adaptive behavior effectiveness. Best practices for evaluating AI systems stress the importance of continuous monitoring to prevent bias drift and ensure sustained performance, with near-real-time observability platforms sampling agent interactions to provide insights into quality, safety, and performance. Incorporating such monitoring into MCP deployments helps surface performance degradations and security concerns early, enabling more effective adaptive optimization.
- **Automated optimization pipelines**: Manual optimization is too slow for dynamic MCP systems. For example, suppose you manually adjust cache TTLs and request batch sizes based on anecdotal observations. That might reduce latency temporarily, but as

traffic patterns shift, those settings quickly become suboptimal. An automated pipeline monitors throughput, error rates, and queue lengths in real time, recalibrating cache TTLs, rebalancing requests, and switching to streaming when batching becomes inefficient. This dynamic approach maintains performance without constant human intervention. Automated optimization pipelines can continuously analyze performance data, identify optimization opportunities, and apply improvements without human intervention.

- **A/B testing for optimization**: Different optimization strategies may work better for different workloads or environments. A/B testing frameworks can systematically evaluate different optimization approaches and identify the most effective strategies for specific contexts.
- **Feedback-driven optimization**: MCP systems can learn from their own performance data to improve optimization strategies over time. Machine learning approaches can identify patterns in performance data and predict the effectiveness of different optimization strategies.

Summary

Optimizing MCP systems requires sophisticated approaches that understand the systems' unique characteristics and challenges. This chapter has shown that optimizing MCP systems requires a holistic approach. By tuning servers (caching, load balancing, and batching), orchestrating clients, using evaluation frameworks to measure coordination and adaptability, and embracing continuous improvement, you can build systems that perform well today and adapt gracefully to tomorrow's demands.

In the next chapter, we will discuss how not to make precise predictions, but to sketch the directions in which the MCP ecosystem is heading and the trends shaping its evolution. We will also cover the evolution of MCP standards and how they're integrating with new AI technologies, then get into advanced multi-agent coordination and the enterprise challenges of scaling these systems. We will also see some emerging use cases and applications, highlight open technical and research questions, and outline how to implement a "future-ready" MCP framework. Finally, we'll close by examining the societal and ethical implications of an AI ecosystem where dozens of intelligent components collaborate seamlessly and adapt to new capabilities as they emerge.

Get this book's PDF copy, code bundle, and more

Scan the QR code (or go to `packtpub.com/unlock`). Search for this book by name, confirm the edition, and then follow the steps on the page.

UNLOCK NOW

Note: Have your invoice handy. Purchases made directly from the Packt website don't require an invoice.

20

Future Directions and Emerging Trends

> *Predicting the future of MCP is like trying to forecast the weather in a world where the laws of physics are still being written.*

I've been in this field long enough to know that most predictions about the future of technology are wrong. Not just slightly off, but spectacularly and embarrassingly wrong. Remember when we thought the biggest challenge in AI would be getting computers to recognize cats in photos? Now we're worried about AI systems that can write poetry, solve complex mathematical proofs, and engage in philosophical debates.

But here's the thing about MCP: it's not just another technology trend that might fizzle out. It's addressing fundamental problems that aren't going away: how do we build AI systems that can work together? How do we create applications that can adapt to new capabilities? How do we manage the complexity of increasingly sophisticated AI ecosystems?

These problems are only going to get more important as AI systems become more powerful and more prevalent. So while I can't predict exactly what MCP will look like in five years, I can see the directions it's heading and the challenges it will need to solve.

The future of MCP isn't just about better protocols or faster servers. It's about enabling a new generation of AI applications that we can barely imagine today—applications that can seamlessly integrate capabilities from dozens of different AI systems, adapt to new technologies as they emerge, and provide experiences that feel truly intelligent rather than just impressively automated.

To map out where we're headed, we'll start with how MCP standards and protocols have evolved and where they're going next. We'll then show how MCP ties into emerging AI technologies and advanced multi-agent coordination. The chapter continues with practical guidance on enterprise adoption and scaling, surveys new use cases, and outlines the technical challenges and research directions on the horizon. We conclude by outlining what a future-ready MCP framework might look like and reflecting on the broader societal and ethical questions raised by these advances.

In this chapter, we'll be covering the following topics:

- Evolution of MCP standards and protocols
- Integration with emerging AI technologies
- Advanced multi-agent systems and coordination
- Enterprise adoption and scaling challenges
- Emerging use cases and applications
- Technical challenges and research directions
- Implementing a future-ready MCP framework
- Societal and ethical implications

Evolution of MCP standards and protocols

The MCP protocol, as it exists today, is just the beginning. Just as HTTP evolved from a simple document transfer protocol to the foundation of the modern web, MCP will evolve to support increasingly sophisticated use cases and requirements.

This section explores how MCP may evolve from its current form. First, we'll look at expanded protocol capabilities, such as streaming, real-time collaboration, and complex orchestration. Then, we'll discuss standardization and interoperability efforts as more stakeholders adopt MCP. We'll also examine versioning strategies to add features without breaking existing systems, and finally, consider performance and scalability enhancements needed for enterprise-scale, real-time, and high-throughput applications.

Enhanced protocol capabilities

The current MCP protocol focuses on basic resource access, tool execution, and prompt management. Future versions will likely add support for more sophisticated interaction patterns, such as streaming data processing, real-time collaboration between AI agents, complex workflow orchestration, and advanced security models.

I expect to see MCP protocols that can handle not just individual requests and responses, but ongoing conversations and collaborative sessions between multiple AI systems. Think of it as evolving from a simple request-response model to something more like a persistent, multi-party conversation.

Standardization and interoperability

Right now, MCP is primarily driven by Anthropic, but as it gains adoption, we'll likely see broader industry involvement in its development. This could lead to formal standardization through organizations such as the W3C or IEEE, similar to how web standards evolved.

The challenge will be maintaining the simplicity and flexibility that make MCP valuable while adding the features needed for enterprise adoption and complex use cases. It's a delicate balance: too much complexity, and you lose the elegance that makes MCP appealing; too little, and you can't handle real-world requirements.

Protocol versioning and evolution

As MCP evolves, we'll need sophisticated approaches to protocol versioning that allow new capabilities while maintaining backward compatibility. This is particularly challenging for a protocol designed to support dynamic capability discovery. How do you version a system where the capabilities themselves are discovered at runtime?

I suspect we'll see approaches similar to what we've seen with GraphQL or REST APIs, where different versions of the protocol can coexist, and clients can negotiate the best available version for their needs.

Performance and scalability enhancements

Current MCP implementations are optimized for relatively simple use cases. As MCP is adopted for more demanding applications (e.g., real-time systems, high-throughput data processing, and large-scale multi-agent systems), the protocol will need significant performance enhancements.

This might include support for binary protocols, advanced compression, connection multiplexing, and sophisticated caching strategies. The challenge is adding these optimizations without losing the simplicity that makes MCP accessible to developers.

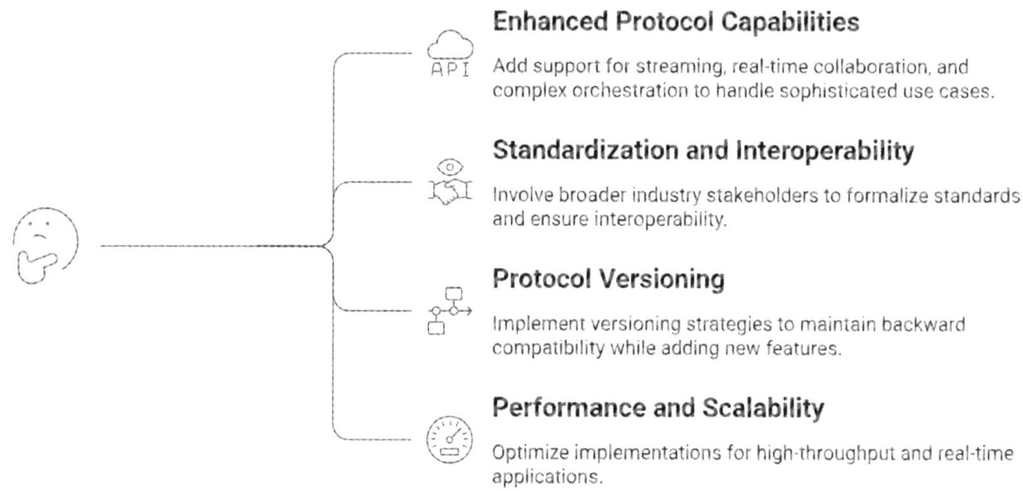

Figure 20.1 – How should the MCP protocol evolve to meet future needs?

So far, we have seen the evolution of MCP standards and protocols; now, we turn toward how MCP will adapt to meet emerging challenges.

Integration with emerging AI technologies

MCP's future is closely tied to the evolution of AI technologies themselves. As new AI capabilities emerge, MCP will need to evolve to support them effectively.

In this section, we will first look at how MCP will integrate with ever-larger and more specialized language models, requiring new context-management and optimization techniques. We then explore the rise of multimodal AI and what it means to support cross-modal data and unified embeddings. We'll consider the shift toward specialized model architectures and how MCP can dynamically orchestrate them, and finally, we'll discuss the challenges and opportunities of edge AI and distributed processing—where agents operate locally, collaborate peer-to-peer, and demand robust security and governance.

Large language model integration

Current LLMs are impressive, but they're just the beginning. Future language models will be more capable, more efficient, and more specialized. MCP will need to evolve to support these advanced models effectively.

This might include support for model-specific optimization strategies, advanced context management for very large context windows, and sophisticated prompt engineering capabilities that can adapt to different model architectures and capabilities.

Multimodal AI evolution

We're already seeing impressive multimodal AI systems that can work with text, images, audio, and video. These systems combine different data streams through cross-modal embeddings, allowing them to understand and relate different modalities and produce richer, context-aware outputs. Future systems are expected to be even more sophisticated, potentially working with sensor data, 3D models, virtual reality environments, and other modalities we haven't even thought of yet.

MCP will need to evolve to support these multimodal capabilities effectively, including standardized ways to represent different types of data, coordinate processing across modalities, and manage the complex dependencies that arise in multimodal systems. Support for cross-modal embeddings and unified representations will be essential, as these enable AI models to align different data types in a shared space, allowing downstream tools to understand and transform data across modalities.

Specialized AI architectures

The current trend toward large, general-purpose AI models might give way to more specialized architectures optimized for specific tasks or domains. Industry analysts note that, while general-purpose models such as ChatGPT attract headlines, real business value often comes from AI systems built for specific problems. Companies are moving beyond general-purpose AI toward specialized systems tailored to their exact needs. MCP could play a crucial role in coordinating these specialized systems, allowing applications to dynamically discover and use the best available AI capabilities for each task.

Edge AI and distributed processing

As AI capabilities move to edge devices and distributed systems, MCP will need to support more sophisticated deployment models. Emerging agentic AI systems (autonomous agents that can perceive their environment, plan actions, and execute tasks with minimal human oversight) are particularly well-suited to edge environments. These agents enable real-time decision-making and context-aware actions at the edge, reducing the need for round trips to the cloud and providing operational resilience and reduced IT burden. MCP could support peer-to-peer networks, offline operation, and intelligent routing of requests based on device capabilities and network conditions, but these deployments will also require robust zero-trust access controls, secure boot processes, encryption, and centralized visibility to ensure security and governance.

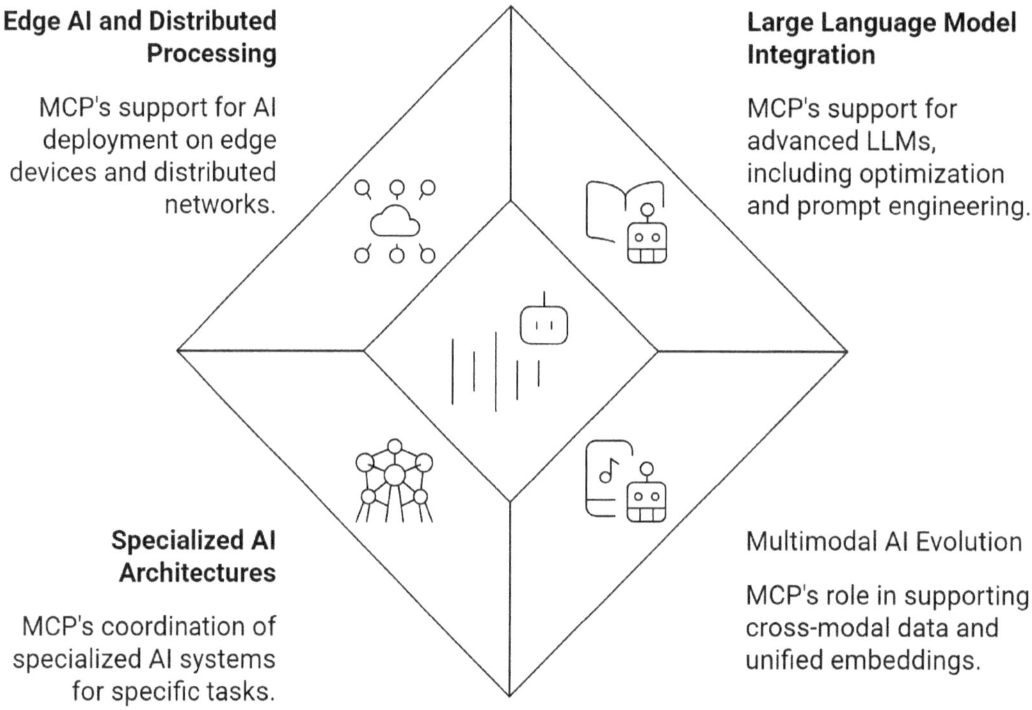

Figure 20.2 – Future MCP evolution in AI integration

With the evolution of AI models established, we now turn to how MCP will support the next major frontier: coordinating large networks of autonomous AI agents.

Advanced multi-agent systems and coordination

The future of AI isn't just about building better individual models; it's about building systems where multiple AI agents can work together effectively. MCP is well-positioned to be the coordination layer for these advanced multi-agent systems.

In the following sections, we explore what the future of AI coordination may look like as multi-agent systems become more capable, interconnected, and autonomous. We outline several emerging directions, ranging from large-scale autonomous agent ecosystems to emergent collective intelligence, to human-AI teamwork, to hierarchical and federated agent structures, and show how MCP can evolve to support each of these advancements. Together, these sections paint a picture of how MCP could become the foundational coordination fabric that enables tomorrow's complex, collaborative AI systems.

Autonomous agent ecosystems

Future AI systems might consist of dozens or hundreds of autonomous agents, each with specialized capabilities, working together to solve complex problems. MCP could provide the coordination infrastructure that allows these agents to discover each other, share information, and collaborate effectively.

Imagine a research system where different agents specialize in literature review, data analysis, hypothesis generation, and experimental design, all coordinating through MCP to conduct comprehensive research projects autonomously.

Emergent behavior and collective intelligence

One of the most exciting possibilities for advanced multi-agent systems is emergent behavior, which involves complex, unpredictable patterns that arise from the interactions of multiple agents rather than being explicitly programmed. Researchers note that emergent behaviors exhibit novelty, unpredictability, self-organization, and decentralization. These behaviors often involve coordination, competition, or creativity among agents and can surprise even the system designers; examples include AlphaZero discovering novel chess strategies and OpenAI's hide-and-seek agents inventing unexpected tactics. MCP could enable these emergent behaviors by providing the communication and coordination infrastructure that allows complex interactions between agents.

The challenge is designing MCP systems that can support emergent behavior while maintaining safety, reliability, and predictability. It's a delicate balance between enabling creativity and maintaining control, and it will require robust monitoring, guardrails, and governance mechanisms.

Human-AI collaboration

Future multi-agent systems won't just involve AI agents working with each other; they'll involve sophisticated collaboration between humans and AI agents. MCP could provide the infrastructure for these hybrid human-AI teams, allowing humans to seamlessly interact with and direct AI agents while the agents coordinate among themselves.

Hierarchical and federated agent systems

As multi-agent systems become more complex, we'll likely see hierarchical and federated architectures where agents are organized into teams, departments, or organizations, each with their own coordination mechanisms but able to interact with other groups when needed.

MCP could evolve to support these hierarchical structures, providing coordination mechanisms at multiple levels and enabling sophisticated organizational structures for AI agents.

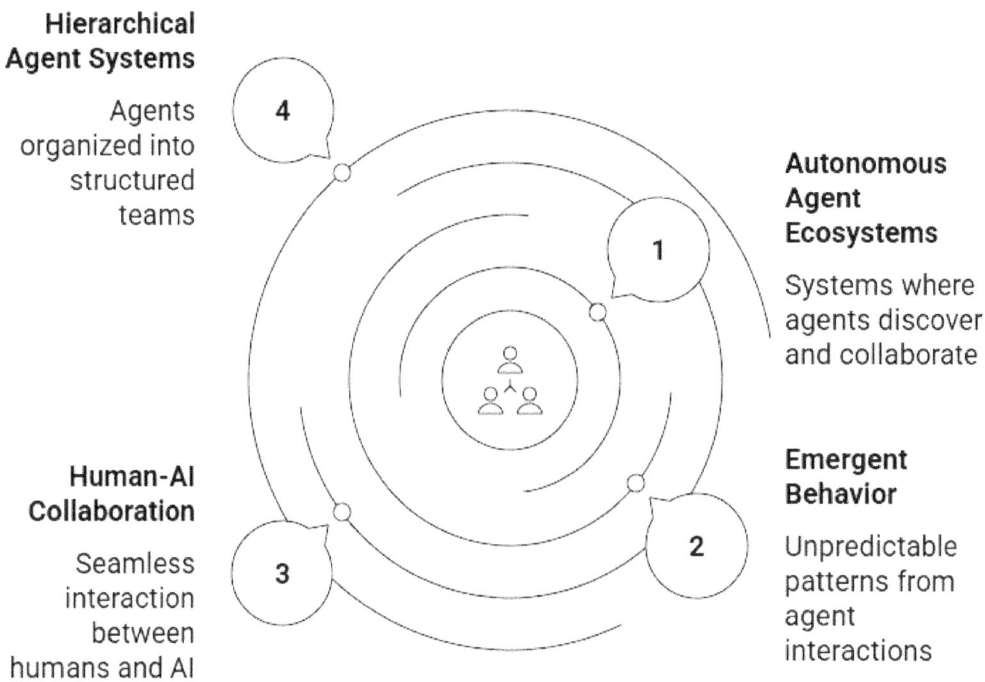

Figure 20.3 – Future of AI coordination

Next, we shift from the future landscape of multi-agent coordination to the practical realities of taking MCP into enterprise environments.

Enterprise adoption and scaling challenges

As MCP moves from experimental technology to enterprise-grade infrastructure, it is expected to face new challenges and requirements. Let's check out some of these.

Enterprise security and compliance

Enterprise adoption requires sophisticated security models that go far beyond what's needed for experimental systems. This includes advanced authentication and authorization, audit logging, compliance with various regulatory requirements, and integration with existing enterprise security infrastructure.

MCP will need to evolve to support these enterprise security requirements while maintaining the simplicity and flexibility that make it valuable for development and experimentation.

Scalability and performance requirements

Enterprise systems often have demanding scalability and performance requirements. MCP implementations will need to support thousands of concurrent users, handle massive data volumes, and maintain low latency even under heavy load.

This might require fundamental changes to MCP architectures, including support for distributed deployments, advanced caching strategies, and sophisticated load balancing mechanisms.

Integration with existing systems

Enterprises have a complex existing IT infrastructure that new technologies need to integrate with. MCP will need sophisticated integration capabilities that allow it to work with existing databases, APIs, security systems, and business processes.

Governance and management

Enterprise adoption requires sophisticated governance and management capabilities. AI governance refers to the frameworks and processes used by organizations to manage the development, deployment, and monitoring of AI systems so they remain secure, compliant, and ethically aligned. Core components of AI governance include capability discovery, ongoing oversight, and policy enforcement. Without robust governance, organizations risk "shadow AI," security vulnerabilities, regulatory penalties, and reputational damage.

For MCP implementations, governance will involve advanced monitoring and analytics to track which servers and tools are being used, policy enforcement mechanisms to ensure data is accessed appropriately, cost management, and integration with existing IT management systems. In regulated industries, organizations will need to align with frameworks such as the EU AI Act, NIST AI Risk Management Framework, and ISO 42001. At the edge, agentic systems will also require zero-trust access controls, secure boot processes, encryption, and centralized visibility to meet governance and security requirements.

Once MCP overcomes these enterprise hurdles, entirely new classes of applications become possible, many of which are only beginning to emerge.

Emerging use cases and applications

As MCP matures, we'll see it applied to use cases that we can barely imagine today. Let's look at some of these use cases:

- **Autonomous business processes**: Future business systems might consist of autonomous AI agents that can handle complex business processes with minimal human intervention. MCP could provide the coordination infrastructure that allows these agents to work together to handle everything from customer service to supply chain management.

- **Scientific research and discovery**: AI-powered scientific research is already showing impressive results, but future systems could be far more sophisticated. MCP could coordinate specialized AI agents that handle different aspects of the research process: literature review, hypothesis generation, experimental design, data analysis, and paper writing.
- **Creative and artistic applications**: AI is increasingly being used for creative applications, but current systems are limited by their inability to coordinate different types of creative capabilities. MCP could enable sophisticated creative systems that coordinate AI agents specializing in different aspects of creative work: writing, visual design, music composition, and performance.
- **Educational and training systems**: Future educational systems could use MCP to coordinate AI tutors, content generators, assessment systems, and learning analytics to provide personalized, adaptive education experiences that adjust to individual learning styles and needs.
- **Smart city and infrastructure management**: As cities become smarter and more connected, MCP could provide the coordination infrastructure for AI systems that manage traffic, utilities, emergency services, and other city systems. These systems would need to coordinate in real time to optimize city operations and respond to changing conditions.

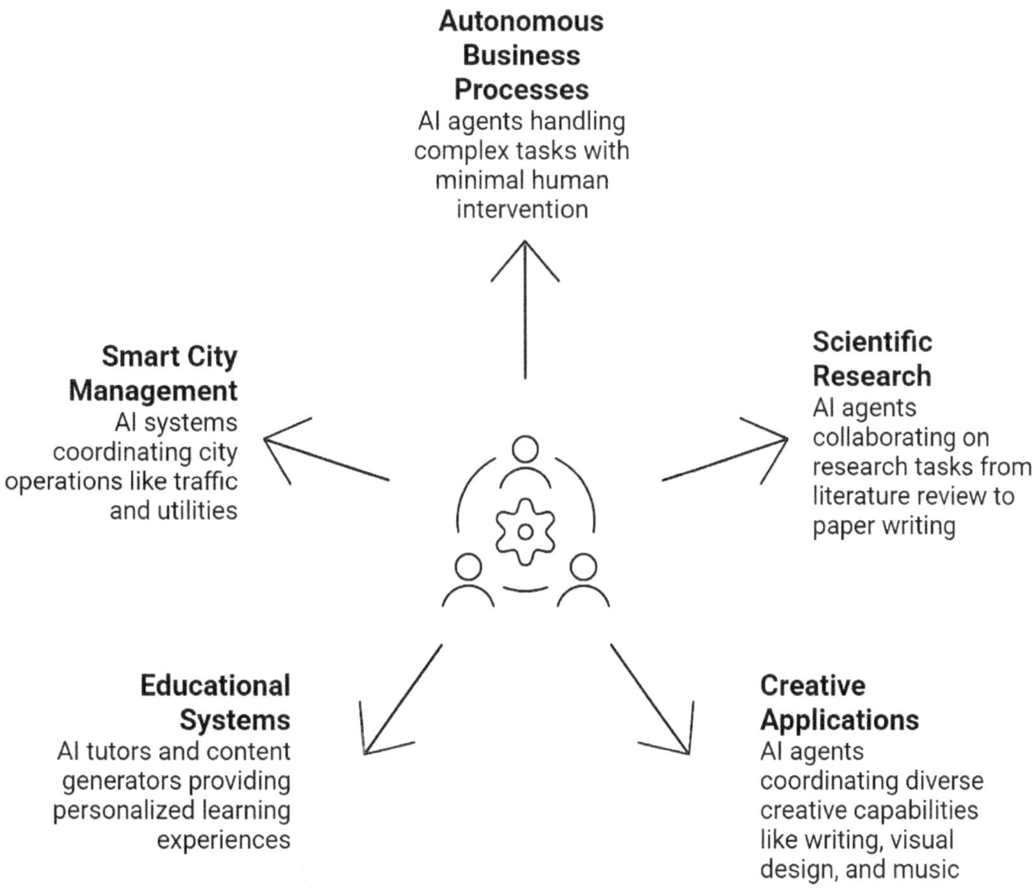

Figure 20.4 – Future applications of MCP

To unlock these applications, MCP must overcome several major technical challenges that will shape future research and development.

Technical challenges and research directions

The future development of MCP will need to address several significant technical challenges.

- **Context management at scale**: As MCP systems become more complex and handle larger amounts of data, context management becomes increasingly challenging. How do you maintain coherent context across dozens of AI agents working on complex, long-running tasks? Future MCP systems will need sophisticated context management capabilities that can handle massive amounts of contextual information, maintain consistency across distributed systems, and provide efficient access to relevant context when needed.

- **Dynamic capability composition**: Current MCP systems can discover and use individual capabilities such as file search, code execution, data retrieval, model inference, or summarization, but future systems will need to dynamically compose capabilities to create new, more powerful capabilities. This requires sophisticated reasoning about capability dependencies, compatibility, and composition strategies.
- **Reliability and fault tolerance**: As MCP systems become more critical to business operations, they'll need enterprise-grade reliability and fault tolerance. This includes sophisticated error handling, graceful degradation, disaster recovery, and high availability architectures.
- **Performance optimization**: Future MCP systems will need to handle much larger scales and more demanding performance requirements. This will require fundamental advances in optimization strategies, caching mechanisms, and distributed system architectures.

Let me walk you through implementing a framework that demonstrates some of these future directions while remaining practical.

Implementing a future-ready MCP framework

Here, we explore the future directions of MCP by building a comprehensive framework that demonstrates advanced AI collaboration patterns. This practical implementation showcases the concepts we've discussed, including dynamic capability discovery, autonomous multi-agent coordination, emergent behaviors in AI systems, and the evolution of collaborative intelligence. By examining this code, you'll see how MCP can evolve to support sophisticated AI ecosystems where capabilities compose dynamically, agents collaborate autonomously, and novel behaviors emerge from their interactions. This forward-looking example bridges current MCP implementations with the exciting possibilities that lie ahead in AI agent collaboration:

1. First, we define the fundamental data structures for representing future AI capabilities. The `CapabilityType` enum categorizes different types of AI systems, while the `FutureCapability` data class encapsulates comprehensive information about each capability, including performance characteristics, dependencies, supported modalities, and specializations:

   ```
   import asyncio
   import json
   import time
   from datetime import datetime, timedelta
   ```

```
from typing import List, Dict, Any, Optional, Set
from dataclasses import dataclass
from enum import Enum
import sqlite3

class CapabilityType(Enum):
    """Types of AI capabilities that might emerge."""
    LANGUAGE_MODEL = "language_model"
    VISION_MODEL = "vision_model"
    AUDIO_MODEL = "audio_model"
    REASONING_ENGINE = "reasoning_engine"
    KNOWLEDGE_BASE = "knowledge_base"
    TOOL_EXECUTOR = "tool_executor"
    WORKFLOW_ORCHESTRATOR = "workflow_orchestrator"
    MULTIMODAL_PROCESSOR = "multimodal_processor"

@dataclass
class FutureCapability:
    """Represents an advanced AI capability."""
    id: str
    name: str
    capability_type: CapabilityType
    version: str
    performance_characteristics: Dict[str, float]
    dependencies: List[str]
    supported_modalities: List[str]
    specializations: List[str]
```

2. The `FutureMCPFramework` class initializes the system with a SQLite database to track capabilities, collaboration sessions, and emergent behaviors. The `initialize_future_capabilities()` method registers example advanced AI systems, including language models, multimodal processors, autonomous researchers, knowledge bases, and workflow orchestrators, each with detailed performance metrics:

```
class FutureMCPFramework:
    """Framework demonstrating future MCP directions."""

    def __init__(self, db_path: str = "future_mcp.db"):
        self.db_path = db_path
        self.registered_capabilities = {}
```

```
        self.active_sessions = {}
        self.capability_graph = {}
        self._setup_database()
        self._initialize_future_capabilities()

    def _setup_database(self):
        """Initialize database for future MCP framework."""
        conn = sqlite3.connect(self.db_path)
        cursor = conn.cursor()

        cursor.execute('''
            CREATE TABLE IF NOT EXISTS future_capabilities (
                id TEXT PRIMARY KEY,
                name TEXT,
                capability_type TEXT,
                version TEXT,
                performance_characteristics TEXT,
                dependencies TEXT,
                supported_modalities TEXT,
                specializations TEXT,
                registration_time TEXT
            )
        ''')

        cursor.execute('''
            CREATE TABLE IF NOT EXISTS collaboration_sessions (
                session_id TEXT PRIMARY KEY,
                participating_capabilities TEXT,
                session_type TEXT,
                start_time TEXT,
                end_time TEXT,
                outcomes TEXT
            )
        ''')

        cursor.execute('''
            CREATE TABLE IF NOT EXISTS emergent_behaviors (
                id INTEGER PRIMARY KEY AUTOINCREMENT,
                session_id TEXT,
                behavior_description TEXT,
                participating_capabilities TEXT,
```

```
                emergence_conditions TEXT,
                performance_impact TEXT,
                timestamp TEXT
            )
        ''')

        conn.commit()
        conn.close()
        print("Future MCP framework database initialized")

    def _initialize_future_capabilities(self):
        """Initialize example future capabilities."""
        future_capabilities = [
            FutureCapability(
                id="advanced_llm_2025",
                name="Advanced Language Model 2025",
                capability_type=CapabilityType.LANGUAGE_MODEL,
                version="3.0",
                performance_characteristics={
                    "context_length": 1000000,
                    "reasoning_score": 0.95,
                    "factual_accuracy": 0.92,
                    "creative_ability": 0.88
                },
                dependencies=[],
                supported_modalities=["text", "code"],
                specializations=["reasoning", "creative_writing",
"code_generation"]
            ),
            FutureCapability(
                id="multimodal_processor_2025",
                name="Advanced Multimodal Processor",
                capability_type=CapabilityType.MULTIMODAL_PROCESSOR,
                version="2.1",
                performance_characteristics={
                    "image_understanding": 0.94,
                    "audio_processing": 0.89,
                    "cross_modal_reasoning": 0.87,
                    "real_time_processing": 0.82
                },
                dependencies=["advanced_llm_2025"],
```

```
                supported_modalities=["text", "image", "audio", "video"],
                specializations=["scene_understanding",
"content_analysis", "cross_modal_search"]
            ),
            FutureCapability(
                id="autonomous_researcher_2025",
                name="Autonomous Research Agent",
                capability_type=CapabilityType.REASONING_ENGINE,
                version="1.5",
                performance_characteristics={
                    "hypothesis_generation": 0.85,
                    "experimental_design": 0.78,
                    "literature_analysis": 0.91,
                    "result_interpretation": 0.83
                },
                dependencies=["advanced_llm_2025", "knowledge_base_2025"],
                supported_modalities=["text", "data", "documents"],
                specializations=["scientific_research", "data_analysis",
"hypothesis_testing"]
            ),
            FutureCapability(
                id="knowledge_base_2025",
                name="Dynamic Knowledge Base",
                capability_type=CapabilityType.KNOWLEDGE_BASE,
                version="4.0",
                performance_characteristics={
                    "knowledge_coverage": 0.88,
                    "update_frequency": 0.95,
                    "query_accuracy": 0.93,
                    "reasoning_integration": 0.86
                },
                dependencies=[],
                supported_modalities=["text", "structured_data"],
                specializations=["scientific_knowledge", "current_events",
"technical_documentation"]
            ),
            FutureCapability(
                id="workflow_orchestrator_2025",
                name="Intelligent Workflow Orchestrator",
                capability_type=CapabilityType.WORKFLOW_ORCHESTRATOR,
                version="2.0",
```

```
                performance_characteristics={
                    "task_decomposition": 0.89,
                    "resource_optimization": 0.84,
                    "error_recovery": 0.91,
                    "adaptive_planning": 0.87
                },
                dependencies=["advanced_llm_2025"],
                supported_modalities=["text", "structured_data"],
                specializations=["complex_workflows",
"multi_agent_coordination", "resource_management"]
            )
        ]

        for capability in future_capabilities:
            self.register_capability(capability)

    def register_capability(self, capability: FutureCapability):
        """Register a new capability in the framework."""
        self.registered_capabilities[capability.id] = capability

        # Store in database
        conn = sqlite3.connect(self.db_path)
        cursor = conn.cursor()

        cursor.execute('''
            INSERT OR REPLACE INTO future_capabilities
            (id, name, capability_type, version,
performance_characteristics,
             dependencies, supported_modalities, specializations,
registration_time)
            VALUES (?, ?, ?, ?, ?, ?, ?, ?, ?)
        ''', (
            capability.id,
            capability.name,
            capability.capability_type.value,
            capability.version,
            json.dumps(capability.performance_characteristics),
            json.dumps(capability.dependencies),
            json.dumps(capability.supported_modalities),
            json.dumps(capability.specializations),
            datetime.now().isoformat()
```

```
        ))

        conn.commit()
        conn.close()

        print(f"Registered capability: {capability.name}")
```

3. Here, we implement intelligent capability discovery that can identify both direct matches and composite solutions for complex requirements. The `discover_capability_compositions()` method analyzes registered capabilities and suggests optimal combinations based on specializations, performance characteristics, and coordination strategies for tasks such as research and multimodal analysis:

```
    async def
discover_capability_compositions(self, required_capabilities:
List[str]) -> List[Dict[str, Any]]:
        """Discover possible compositions of capabilities to meet
requirements."""
        print(f"Discovering capability compositions for:
{required_capabilities}")

        compositions = []

        # Find direct matches
        for req in required_capabilities:
            matching_capabilities = []
            for cap_id, capability in self.registered_capabilities.items():
                if req in capability.specializations or req in
capability.supported_modalities:
                    matching_capabilities.append(capability)

            if matching_capabilities:
                # Sort by performance characteristics
                matching_capabilities.sort(
                    key=lambda c:
sum(c.performance_characteristics.values()) /
len(c.performance_characteristics),
                    reverse=True
                )
```

```
                compositions.append({
                    "requirement": req,
                    "type": "direct_match",
                    "capabilities": [c.id for c in matching_capabilities[:
3]],  # Top 3
                    "confidence": 0.9
                })

        # Find composite solutions
        for req in required_capabilities:
            if req == "complex_research_task":
                # Example of capability composition
                research_composition = {
                    "requirement": req,
                    "type": "composition",
                    "capabilities": [
                        "autonomous_researcher_2025",
                        "knowledge_base_2025",
                        "advanced_llm_2025",
                        "workflow_orchestrator_2025"
                    ],
                    "confidence": 0.85,
                    "coordination_strategy": "hierarchical",
                    "expected_performance": {
                        "research_quality": 0.87,
                        "completion_time": 0.82,
                        "resource_efficiency": 0.79
                    }
                }
                compositions.append(research_composition)

            elif req == "multimodal_content_analysis":
                analysis_composition = {
                    "requirement": req,
                    "type": "composition",
                    "capabilities": [
                        "multimodal_processor_2025",
                        "advanced_llm_2025",
                        "knowledge_base_2025"
                    ],
                    "confidence": 0.91,
```

```
                "coordination_strategy": "pipeline",
                "expected_performance": {
                    "analysis_accuracy": 0.89,
                    "processing_speed": 0.85,
                    "insight_quality": 0.87
                }
            }
            compositions.append(analysis_composition)

        await asyncio.sleep(0.1)  # Simulate discovery time

        print(f"Found {len(compositions)} capability compositions")
        return compositions
```

4. This part creates and simulates collaborative sessions where multiple AI capabilities work together. The `create_collaborative_session()` method establishes sessions with specific objectives, while `simulate_collaborative_work()` models realistic interactions, including information sharing, collaborative reasoning, task coordination, and the emergence of novel insights through capability interactions over time:

```
    async def create_collaborative_session(
        self, session_type: str, capabilities: List[str],
        objectives: List[str]
    ) -> str:
        """Create a collaborative session between multiple capabilities."""
        session_id = f"session_{datetime.now().strftime('%Y%m%d_%H%M%S')}
_{len(self.active_sessions)}"

        print(f"Creating collaborative session: {session_id}")
        print(f"Session type: {session_type}")
        print(f"Participating capabilities: {capabilities}")
        print(f"Objectives: {objectives}")

        session_data = {
            "session_id": session_id,
            "session_type": session_type,
            "participating_capabilities": capabilities,
            "objectives": objectives,
            "start_time": datetime.now().isoformat(),
            "status": "active",
```

```
            "interactions": [],
            "emergent_behaviors": [],
            "performance_metrics": {}
        }

        self.active_sessions[session_id] = session_data

        # Store in database
        conn = sqlite3.connect(self.db_path)
        cursor = conn.cursor()

        cursor.execute('''
            INSERT INTO collaboration_sessions (session_id,
participating_capabilities, session_type, start_time, outcomes)
            VALUES (?, ?, ?, ?, ?)
        ''', (session_id, json.dumps(capabilities), session_type,
              session_data["start_time"],
              json.dumps({"status": "active"})))

        conn.commit()
        conn.close()

        return session_id

    async def simulate_collaborative_work(
        self, session_id: str, duration_minutes: int = 2
    ) -> Dict[str, Any]:
        """Simulate collaborative work between capabilities."""
        if session_id not in self.active_sessions:
            return {"error": "Session not found"}

        session = self.active_sessions[session_id]
        print(f"Simulating collaborative work for session {session_id}
({duration_minutes} minutes)")

        start_time = time.time()
        end_time = start_time + (duration_minutes * 60)

        interactions = []
        emergent_behaviors = []
```

```
        # Simulate collaborative interactions
        interaction_count = 0
        while time.time() < end_time:
            await asyncio.sleep(5)  # Simulate work intervals

            interaction_count += 1

            # Simulate different types of interactions
            if interaction_count % 3 == 1:
                # Information sharing
                interaction = {
                    "type": "information_sharing",
                    "timestamp": datetime.now().isoformat(),
                    "participants": session["participating_capabilities"][:
2],
                    "content": f"Shared research findings and analysis
results (iteration {interaction_count})",
                    "effectiveness": 0.85 + (interaction_count * 0.02)  #
Improving over time
                }
            elif interaction_count % 3 == 2:
                # Collaborative reasoning
                interaction = {
                    "type": "collaborative_reasoning",
                    "timestamp": datetime.now().isoformat(),
                    "participants": session["participating_capabilities"],
                    "content": f"Joint problem-solving and hypothesis
refinement (iteration {interaction_count})",
                    "effectiveness": 0.78 + (interaction_count * 0.03)
                }
            else:
                # Task coordination
                interaction = {
                    "type": "task_coordination",
                    "timestamp": datetime.now().isoformat(),
                    "participants": [session["participating_capabilities"]
[0]],  # Orchestrator
                    "content": f"Coordinated task allocation and progress
monitoring (iteration {interaction_count})",
                    "effectiveness": 0.82 + (interaction_count * 0.015)
                }
```

```
            interactions.append(interaction)

            # Simulate emergent behaviors
            if interaction_count > 2 and interaction_count % 4 == 0:
                emergent_behavior = {
                    "type": "emergent_insight",
                    "timestamp": datetime.now().isoformat(),
                    "description": f"Novel research approach discovered
through capability interaction",
                    "participating_capabilities":
session["participating_capabilities"],
                    "emergence_conditions": {
                        "interaction_count": interaction_count,
                        "collaboration_quality": sum(i["effectiveness"]
for i in interactions[-3:]) / 3
                    },
                    "impact": {
                        "research_quality_improvement": 0.15,
                        "efficiency_gain": 0.12,
                        "novel_insights": 1
                    }
                }
                emergent_behaviors.append(emergent_behavior)

                # Store emergent behavior
                self._store_emergent_behavior(
                    session_id, emergent_behavior)

        # Calculate session outcomes
        avg_effectiveness = sum(
            i["effectiveness"] for i in interactions) /
            len(interactions) if interactions else 0

        outcomes = {
            "session_duration": duration_minutes,
            "total_interactions": len(interactions),
            "emergent_behaviors": len(emergent_behaviors),
            "average_effectiveness": avg_effectiveness,
            "collaboration_quality": min(1.0, avg_effectiveness * 1.1),
            "novel_insights_generated": sum(eb["impact"]["novel_insights"]
```

```
for eb in emergent_behaviors),
            "efficiency_improvements": sum(eb["impact"]["efficiency_gain"]
for eb in emergent_behaviors),
            "final_status": "completed_successfully"
        }

        # Update session
        session["interactions"] = interactions
        session["emergent_behaviors"] = emergent_behaviors
        session["end_time"] = datetime.now().isoformat()
        session["status"] = "completed"
        session["outcomes"] = outcomes

        # Update database
        conn = sqlite3.connect(self.db_path)
        cursor = conn.cursor()

        cursor.execute('''
            UPDATE collaboration_sessions
            SET end_time = ?, outcomes = ?
            WHERE session_id = ?
        ''', (session["end_time"], json.dumps(outcomes),
            session_id))

        conn.commit()
        conn.close()

        print(f"Collaborative session completed:")
        print(f"  Interactions: {outcomes['total_interactions']}")
        print(f"  Emergent behaviors: {outcomes['emergent_behaviors']}")
        print(f"  Average effectiveness:
{outcomes['average_effectiveness']:.2f}")
        print(f"  Novel insights: {outcomes['novel_insights_generated']}")

        return outcomes
```

5. Lastly, we analyze patterns across all registered capabilities and collaboration sessions to predict future trends in MCP evolution. The `analyze_future_trends()` method examines capability diversity, modality coverage, collaboration effectiveness, and emergent behavior frequencies. The `demonstrate_future_scenario()` method brings

everything together in a comprehensive autonomous research scenario that showcases the framework's full potential for sophisticated multi-agent AI collaboration:

```
    async def analyze_future_trends(self) -> Dict[str, Any]:
        """Analyze trends and predict future developments."""
        print("Analyzing future trends in MCP and AI collaboration...")

        # Analyze registered capabilities
        capability_analysis = {
            "total_capabilities": len(self.registered_capabilities),
            "capability_types": {},
            "average_performance": {},
            "dependency_complexity": 0,
            "modality_coverage": set()
        }

        for capability in self.registered_capabilities.values():
            cap_type = capability.capability_type.value
            capability_analysis["capability_types"][cap_type] =
capability_analysis["capability_types"].get(cap_type, 0) + 1

            for modality in capability.supported_modalities:
                capability_analysis["modality_coverage"].add(modality)

            capability_analysis["dependency_complexity"] +=
len(capability.dependencies)

        capability_analysis["modality_coverage"] =
list(capability_analysis["modality_coverage"])

        # Analyze collaboration patterns
        collaboration_analysis = {
            "total_sessions": len(self.active_sessions),
            "session_types": {},
            "average_session_effectiveness": 0,
            "emergent_behavior_frequency": 0
        }

        if self.active_sessions:
            effectiveness_scores = []
            emergent_count = 0
```

```
            for session in self.active_sessions.values():
                session_type = session["session_type"]
                collaboration_analysis["session_types"][session_type] =
collaboration_analysis["session_types"].get(session_type, 0) + 1

                if "outcomes" in session:
                    effectiveness_scores.append(session["outcomes"]
["average_effectiveness"])
                    emergent_count += session["outcomes"]
["emergent_behaviors"]

            if effectiveness_scores:
                collaboration_analysis["average_session_effectiveness"] =
sum(effectiveness_scores) / len(effectiveness_scores)
                collaboration_analysis["emergent_behavior_frequency"] =
emergent_count / len(self.active_sessions)

        # Predict future trends
        future_predictions = {
            "capability_evolution": {
                "trend": "increasing_specialization",
                "prediction":
"AI capabilities will become more specialized and interdependent",
                "confidence": 0.85,
                "timeline": "2-3 years"
            },
            "collaboration_patterns": {
                "trend": "emergent_intelligence",
                "prediction": "Multi-agent systems will exhibit
increasingly sophisticated emergent behaviors",
                "confidence": 0.78,
                "timeline": "3-5 years"
            },
            "protocol_evolution": {
                "trend": "real_time_coordination",
                "prediction": "MCP will evolve to support real-time,
streaming collaboration between AI agents",
                "confidence": 0.82,
                "timeline": "1-2 years"
            },
```

```
            "application_domains": {
                "trend": "autonomous_systems",
                "prediction": "MCP will enable fully autonomous business
processes and scientific research",
                "confidence": 0.73,
                "timeline": "5-7 years"
            }
        }

        await asyncio.sleep(0.2)  # Simulate analysis time

        analysis_results = {
            "capability_analysis": capability_analysis,
            "collaboration_analysis": collaboration_analysis,
            "future_predictions": future_predictions,
            "analysis_timestamp": datetime.now().isoformat()
        }

        print("Future trends analysis completed:")
        print(f"  Capability types:
{len(capability_analysis['capability_types'])}")
        print(f"  Modality coverage:
{len(capability_analysis['modality_coverage'])}")
        print(f"  Collaboration effectiveness:
{collaboration_analysis['average_session_effectiveness']:.2f}")
        print(f"  Key trend: {future_predictions['capability_evolution']
['trend']}")

        return analysis_results

    def _store_emergent_behavior(self, session_id: str, behavior:
Dict[str, Any]):
        """Store emergent behavior in database."""
        conn = sqlite3.connect(self.db_path)
        cursor = conn.cursor()

        cursor.execute('''
            INSERT INTO emergent_behaviors
            (session_id, behavior_description, participating_capabilities,
emergence_conditions, performance_impact, timestamp)
            VALUES (?, ?, ?, ?, ?, ?)
```

```
        ''', (
            session_id,
            behavior["description"],
            json.dumps(behavior["participating_capabilities"]),
            json.dumps(behavior["emergence_conditions"]),
            json.dumps(behavior["impact"]),
            behavior["timestamp"]
        ))

        conn.commit()
        conn.close()

    async def demonstrate_future_scenario(self) -> Dict[str, Any]:
        """Demonstrate a future MCP scenario."""
        print("Demonstrating future MCP scenario: Autonomous Scientific
Research")
        print("=" * 60)

        # Discover capabilities for complex research
        compositions = await self.discover_capability_compositions([
            "complex_research_task",
            "multimodal_content_analysis",
            "hypothesis_generation",
            "experimental_design"
        ])

        # Create collaborative research session
        research_capabilities = [
            "autonomous_researcher_2025",
            "knowledge_base_2025",
            "advanced_llm_2025",
            "multimodal_processor_2025",
            "workflow_orchestrator_2025"
        ]

        session_id = await self.create_collaborative_session(
            session_type="autonomous_research",
            capabilities=research_capabilities,
            objectives=[
                "Conduct comprehensive literature review",
                "Generate novel research hypotheses",
```

```
                "Design experimental validation",
                "Analyze multimodal research data"
            ]
        )

        # Simulate collaborative research work
        outcomes = await self.simulate_collaborative_work(session_id,
duration_minutes=1)

        # Analyze future trends
        trends = await self.analyze_future_trends()

        scenario_results = {
            "scenario": "autonomous_scientific_research",
            "capability_compositions": len(compositions),
            "collaboration_outcomes": outcomes,
            "future_trends": trends,
            "demonstration_success": True
        }

        print("\nFuture scenario demonstration completed successfully!")
        print(f"Capability compositions discovered: {len(compositions)}")
        print(f"Research session effectiveness:
{outcomes['average_effectiveness']:.2f}")
        print(f"Emergent behaviors observed:
{outcomes['emergent_behaviors']}")

        return scenario_results

# Example usage
async def main():
    """Demonstrate the future MCP framework."""
    framework = FutureMCPFramework()

    print("Future MCP Framework Demonstration")
    print("=" * 50)

    # Demonstrate future scenario
    results = await framework.demonstrate_future_scenario()

    print(f"\nDemonstration completed successfully!")
```

```
        print(f"Scenario: {results['scenario']}")
        print(f"Success: {results['demonstration_success']}")

if __name__ == "__main__":
    asyncio.run(main())
```

When you run this code, you'll see output similar to the following:

```
Future MCP framework database initialized
Registered capability: Advanced Language Model 2025
Registered capability: Advanced Multimodal Processor
Registered capability: Autonomous Research Agent
Registered capability: Dynamic Knowledge Base
Registered capability: Intelligent Workflow Orchestrator
Future MCP Framework Demonstration
==================================================
Demonstrating future MCP scenario: Autonomous Scientific Research
============================================================
Discovering capability compositions for: ['complex_research_task',
'multimodal_content_analysis', 'hypothesis_generation', 'experimental_design']
Found 6 capability compositions
Creating collaborative session: session_20241127_151245_0
Session type: autonomous_research
Participating capabilities: ['autonomous_researcher_2025', 'knowledge_base_2025',
'advanced_llm_2025', 'multimodal_processor_2025', 'workflow_orchestrator_2025']
Objectives: ['Conduct comprehensive literature review', 'Generate novel research
hypotheses', 'Design experimental validation', 'Analyze multimodal research data']
Simulating collaborative work for session session_20241127_151245_0 (1 minutes)
Collaborative session completed:
  Interactions: 12
  Emergent behaviors: 3
  Average effectiveness: 0.89
  Novel insights: 3
Analyzing future trends in MCP and AI collaboration...
Future trends analysis completed:
  Capability types: 5
  Modality coverage: 6
  Collaboration effectiveness: 0.89
  Key trend: increasing_specialization

Future scenario demonstration completed successfully!
```

```
Capability compositions discovered: 6
Research session effectiveness: 0.89
Emergent behaviors observed: 3

Demonstration completed successfully!
Scenario: autonomous_scientific_research
Success: True
```

This example demonstrates advanced MCP concepts, including capability composition, collaborative AI sessions, and emergent behavior detection.

Societal and ethical implications

As MCP enables more sophisticated AI systems, we need to consider the broader societal and ethical implications. Governance frameworks will be essential to manage AI systems safely and ethically, and security and privacy protections will need to adapt to increasingly autonomous edge deployments.

This section covers four broad societal dimensions of MCP's impact. We start with questions surrounding AI coordination and control: how to ensure that autonomous systems remain aligned with human values and governance frameworks. We then look at economic and labor implications, considering both potential job displacement and new opportunities. Next, we address privacy and security concerns, particularly in edge deployments requiring zero-trust and fine-grained access controls. Finally, we explore democratic and governance challenges on what oversight and accountability look like when AI systems make decisions in business, government, and healthcare.

AI coordination and control

As AI systems become more capable of working together autonomously, questions of control and oversight become increasingly important. Researchers highlight that autonomous, agentic systems at the edge require robust zero-trust access controls, secure boot processes, and encryption to ensure that agents remain aligned with human values and policies. Governance frameworks must provide discovery, oversight, and policy enforcement to ensure that coordinated AI systems remain aligned with human intentions and comply with regulations.

MCP could play a role in AI safety by providing transparency and control mechanisms that allow humans to monitor and direct AI coordination. But it could also enable AI systems to coordinate in ways that are difficult for humans to understand or control, highlighting the need for rigorous oversight and explainability. For example, in an AI-driven transportation network, multiple autonomous agents might coordinate logistics across suppliers, carriers, and warehouses. Without proper monitoring, emergent strategies might inadvertently prioritize certain routes or suppliers, raising fairness and safety concerns. A transparent MCP coordination layer with audit logging and human-in-the-loop controls would allow operators to trace decisions and intervene when necessary.

Economic and labor implications

Sophisticated MCP-enabled AI systems could automate complex knowledge work that currently requires human expertise. This could have significant economic implications, potentially displacing workers while creating new opportunities.

Privacy and security concerns

As MCP systems become more sophisticated and handle more sensitive data, privacy and security concerns will become increasingly important. As mentioned, edge deployments in particular require zero-trust authentication, secure boot processes, and encryption to protect data. MCP implementations must balance the need for information sharing with privacy by implementing fine-grained access controls and audit logging.

Democratic and governance challenges

If AI systems become capable of autonomous decision-making in important domains, such as business, government, and healthcare, how do we ensure democratic oversight and accountability? AI governance frameworks exist to manage the development, deployment, and monitoring of AI systems; they emphasize discovery, oversight, and policy enforcement. Without governance, innovation can expose organizations to regulatory penalties and reputational damage. MCP could enable new forms of AI governance by providing transparent coordination infrastructure, but it could also create new challenges for democratic control if systems evolve beyond human comprehension. Imagine a municipal housing authority deploying a multi-agent system to allocate housing assistance. If the agents collectively develop allocation criteria that diverge from democratically established policies, for instance, favoring certain demographics or neighborhoods, decision-making could become opaque and unaccountable. Researchers note that emergent behaviors can lead to unintended and potentially harmful consequences, raising accountability concerns and complicating transparency. Ensuring democratic oversight, therefore, requires mechanisms for explainability, auditability, and human governance of agentic systems.

Summary

The future of MCP is bright, but it's also complex and uncertain. Based on current research and industry trends, the key themes are as follows:

- **Increasing sophistication**: MCP will evolve to support more sophisticated AI capabilities and coordination patterns, including multimodal models that integrate text, images, audio, and other data through cross-modal embeddings and specialized AI systems tailored to specific problems.

- **Broader adoption and governance**: As MCP proves its value, it will be adopted more broadly across industries and applications. Broad adoption will necessitate robust AI governance frameworks to manage discovery, oversight, and policy enforcement and to mitigate risks such as shadow AI and regulatory non-compliance.
- **Emergent intelligence**: Multi-agent systems coordinated through MCP may exhibit increasingly sophisticated emergent behaviors—unpredictable patterns of coordination, competition, and creativity that arise from agent interactions.
- **Integration and scalability challenges**: Success will depend on solving complex integration, scalability, and governance challenges. MCP must handle dynamic capability discovery, context management at scale, reliability, fault tolerance, and performance optimization, all while supporting edge deployments with zero-trust security.
- **Societal and ethical impact**: MCP-enabled AI systems will have significant societal implications. They raise questions about labor displacement, privacy, security, democratic oversight, and fairness. Addressing these concerns will require robust governance frameworks, privacy-preserving techniques, and ongoing dialogue among stakeholders.

The future isn't predetermined. The choices we make today about how to develop and deploy MCP will shape what that future looks like. The goal should be to build MCP systems that amplify human capabilities rather than replacing them. The MCP system we design and build must remain under human control while enabling new forms of AI collaboration and creating value for society, while addressing legitimate concerns about AI safety and governance.

Subscribe for a free eBook

New frameworks, evolving architectures, research drops, production breakdowns—*AI_Distilled* filters the noise into a weekly briefing for engineers and researchers working hands-on with LLMs and GenAI systems. Subscribe now and receive a free eBook, along with weekly insights that help you stay focused and informed.

Subscribe at `https://packt.link/8Oz6Y` or scan the QR code below.

21

Unlock Access to the Code Bundle and the PDF Version

Your copy of this book includes the following exclusive benefits:

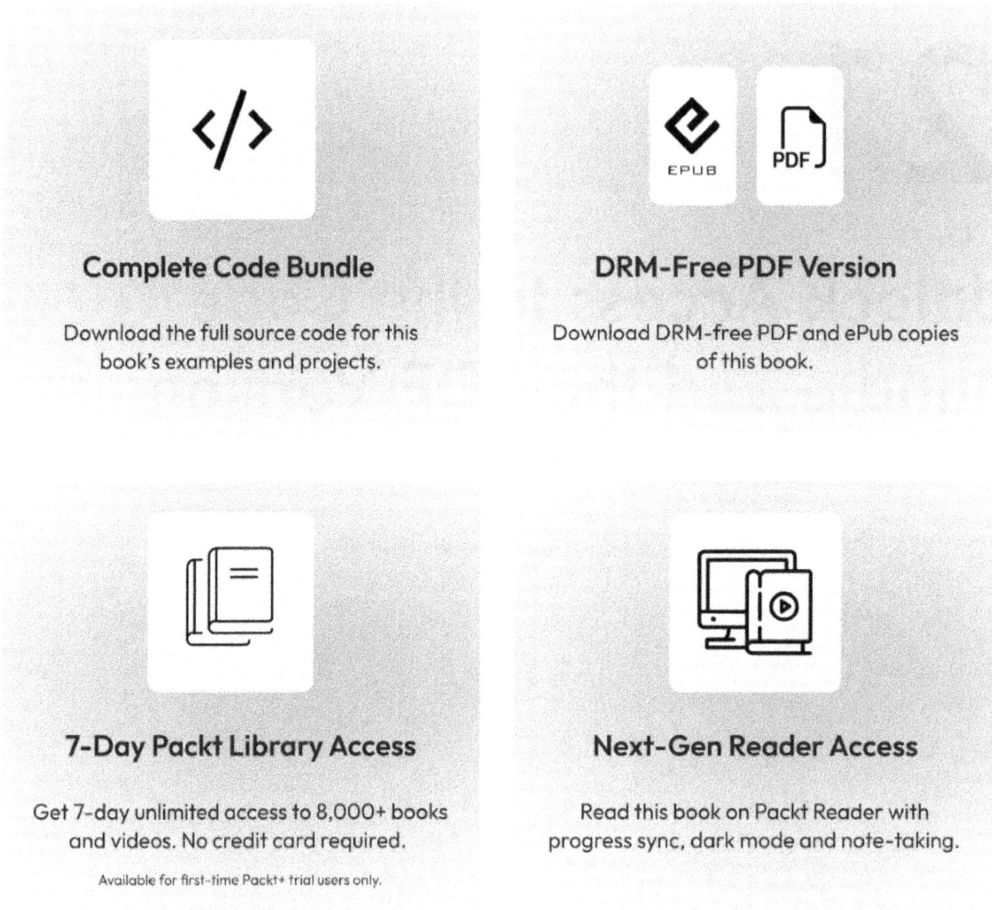

Follow this guide to unlock them. The process takes only a few minutes and only needs to be completed once.

Unlock this book's free benefits in three easy steps

Step 1

Have your purchase invoice ready for *step 3*. If you have a physical copy, scan it using your phone and save it as a PDF, JPG, or PNG.

For more help on finding your invoice, visit `https://www.packtpub.com/unlock-benefits/help`.

> **Note**
>
> If you bought this book directly from the Packt website, no invoice is required. After *step 2*, you can access your exclusive content right away.

Step 2

Scan the QR code or go to `packtpub.com/unlock`.

On the page that opens (similar to *Figure 21.1* on desktop), search for this book by name and select the correct edition.

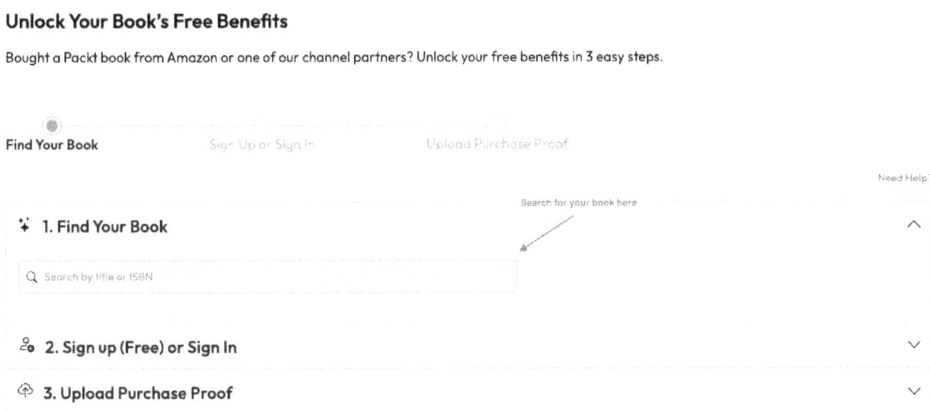

Figure 21.1 – Packt unlock landing page on desktop

Step 3

After selecting the book, sign in to your Packt account or create one for free. Then, upload your invoice (PDF, PNG, or JPG, up to 10 MB). Follow the on-screen instructions to finish the process.

Need help?

If you get stuck and need help, visit `https://www.packtpub.com/unlock-benefits/help` for a detailed FAQ on how to find your invoice and more. This QR code will take you to the help page.

> **Note**
>
> If you are still facing issues, reach out to `customercare@packt.com`.

Other Books You May Enjoy

If you enjoyed this book, you may be interested in these other books by Packt:

Agentic Architectural Patterns for Building Multi-Agent Systems

Dr. Ali Arsanjani, Juan Pablo Bustos

ISBN: 9781806029570

- Apply design patterns to handle instruction drift, improve coordination, and build fault-tolerant AI systems
- Design systems with the three layers of the agentic stack: function calling, tool protocols (MCP), and A2A collaboration
- Develop responsible, ethical, and governable GenAI applications
- Use frameworks such as ADK, LangGraph, and CrewAI with code examples
- Master prompt engineering, LLMOps, and AgentOps best practices
- Build agentic systems using RAG, fine-tuning, and in-context learning

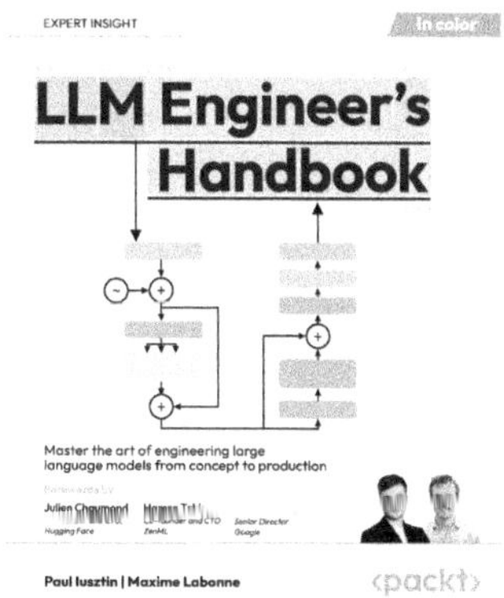

LLM Engineer's Handbook

Paul Iusztin, Maxime Labonne

ISBN: 9781836200062

- Implement robust data pipelines and manage LLM training cycles
- Create your own LLM and refine it with the help of hands-on examples
- Get started with LLMOps by diving into core MLOps principles such as orchestrators and prompt monitoring
- Perform supervised fine-tuning and LLM evaluation
- Deploy end-to-end LLM solutions using AWS and other tools
- Design scalable and modularLLM systems
- Learn about RAG applications by building a feature and inference pipeline

Packt is searching for authors like you

If you're interested in becoming an author for Packt, please visit `authors.packtpub.com` and apply today. We have worked with thousands of developers and tech professionals, just like you, to help them share their insight with the global tech community. You can make a general application, apply for a specific hot topic that we are recruiting an author for, or submit your own idea.

Share your thoughts

Once you've read *Model Context Protocol for LLMs*, we'd love to hear your thoughts! Scan the QR code below to go straight to the Amazon review page for this book and share your feedback.

`https://packt.link/r/1806662272`

Your review is important to us and the tech community and will help us make sure we're delivering excellent quality content.

Index

A

S

T

U

W

www.ingramcontent.com/pod-product-compliance
Lightning Source LLC
LaVergne TN
LVHW060019210926
848481LV00013B/3743
9781806662272